EARLY CHILDHOOD EDUCATION
93/94

Fourteenth Edition

A Library of Information from the Public Press

Editor

Karen Menke Paciorek
Eastern Michigan University

Karen Menke Paciorek is an assistant professor of Early Childhood Education at Eastern Michigan University. All of her education has been in the field of early childhood with a B.S. from the University of Pittsburgh, an M.A. from George Washington University, and a Ph.D. from Peabody College of Vanderbilt University. She is very active in the Michigan Association for the Education of Young Children. Her presentations at local and national conferences focus on teacher preparation, quality programming, and establishment of the learning environment.

Editor

Joyce Huth Munro
Centenary College

Joyce Huth Munro is chair of the Education Division at Centenary College. She received her Ph.D. from Peabody College of Vanderbilt University. In addition to administration and teaching, she directs the Children's Center at Centenary College. Regionally and nationally, she presents seminars on curriculum design and teacher education. Currently, she is coordinator of a research project on case studies in teacher education for the National Association for Early Childhood Teacher Educators.

Cover illustration by Mike Eagle

The Dushkin Publishing Group, Inc.
Sluice Dock, Guilford, Connecticut 06437

The Annual Editions Series

Annual Editions is a series of over 55 volumes designed to provide the reader with convenient, low-cost access to a wide range of current, carefully selected articles from some of the most important magazines, newspapers, and journals published today. Annual Editions are updated on an annual basis through a continuous monitoring of over 300 periodical sources. All Annual Editions have a number of features designed to make them particularly useful, including topic guides, annotated tables of contents, unit overviews, and indexes. For the teacher using Annual Editions in the classroom, an Instructor's Resource Guide with test questions is available for each volume.

VOLUMES AVAILABLE

Africa
Aging
American Government
American History, Pre-Civil War
American History, Post-Civil War
Anthropology
Biology
Business Ethics
Canadian Politics
China
Commonwealth of Independent States
Comparative Politics
Computers in Education
Computers in Business
Computers in Society
Criminal Justice
Drugs, Society, and Behavior
Dying, Death, and Bereavement
Early Childhood Education
Economics
Educating Exceptional Children
Education
Educational Psychology
Environment
Geography
Global Issues
Health
Human Development
Human Resources
Human Sexuality
India and South Asia

International Business
Japan and the Pacific Rim
Latin America
Life Management
Macroeconomics
Management
Marketing
Marriage and Family
Microeconomics
Middle East and the Islamic World
Money and Banking
Nutrition
Personal Growth and Behavior
Physical Anthropology
Psychology
Public Administration
Race and Ethnic Relations
Social Problems
Sociology
State and Local Government
Third World
Urban Society
Violence and Terrorism
Western Civilization, Pre-Reformation
Western Civilization, Post-Reformation
Western Europe
World History, Pre-Modern
World History, Modern
World Politics

Library of Congress Cataloging in Publication Data
Main entry under title: Annual Editions: Early Childhood Education. 1993/94.
    1. Education, Preschool—Periodicals. 2. Child development—Periodicals. 3. Child rearing—United States—Periodicals. I. Paciorek, Karen Menke, comp.; Munro, Joyce Huth, comp. II. Title: Early Childhood Education.
ISBN 1–56134–195–9   372.21′05   77–640114
HQ777.A7A

© 1993 by The Dushkin Publishing Group, Inc., Guilford, CT 06437

Copyright law prohibits the reproduction, storage, or transmission in any form by any means of any portion of this publication without the expressed written permission of The Dushkin Publishing Group, Inc., and of the copyright holder (if different) of the part of the publication to be reproduced. The Guidelines for Classroom Copying endorsed by Congress explicitly state that unauthorized copying may not be used to create, to replace, or to substitute for anthologies, compilations, or collective works.

Annual Editions® is a Registered Trademark of The Dushkin Publishing Group, Inc.

Fourteenth Edition

Printed in the United States of America

Printed on Recycled Paper

Editors/ Advisory Board

EDITORS

Karen Menke Paciorek
Eastern Michigan University

Joyce Huth Munro
Centenary College

ADVISORY BOARD

Anna Lou Blevins
University of Pittsburgh

Robert L. Doan
University of South Alabama

Linda C. Edwards
College of Charleston

Richard Fabes
Arizona State University

Kathy Fite
Southwest Texas State University

Samuel Harris
Wright State University

John R. Hranitz
Bloomsburg University

Richard T. Johnson
University of Hawaii

Katharine C. Kersey
Old Dominion University

Dene G. Klinzing
University of Delaware

Charles May
University of Northern Iowa

Judy Spitler McKee
Eastern Michigan University

Joan S. McMath
Ohio University

George S. Morrison
Florida International University

Linda S. Nelson
Indiana University of Pennsylvania

R. Robert Orr
University of Windsor

Jack V. Powell
University of Georgia

Liz Rothlein
University of Miami

William Strader
Fitchburg State College

Jeanene Varner
University of South Carolina
Aiken

Lewis Walker
Shorter College

John Worobey
Rutgers University

Members of the Advisory Board are instrumental in the final selection of articles for each edition of Annual Editions. Their review of articles for content, level, currentness, and appropriateness provides critical direction to the editor and staff. We think you'll find their careful consideration well reflected in this volume.

STAFF

Ian A. Nielsen, Publisher
Brenda S. Filley, Production Manager
Roberta Monaco, Editor
Addie Raucci, Administrative Editor
Cheryl Greenleaf, Permissions Editor
Diane Barker, Editorial Assistant
Lisa Holmes-Doebrick, Administrative Coordinator
Charles Vitelli, Designer
Shawn Callahan, Graphics
Meredith Scheld, Graphics
Steve Shumaker, Graphics
Lara M. Johnson, Graphics
Libra A. Cusack, Typesetting Supervisor
Juliana Arbo, Typesetter

To the Reader

In publishing ANNUAL EDITIONS we recognize the enormous role played by the magazines, newspapers, and journals of the *public press* in providing current, first-rate educational information in a broad spectrum of interest areas. Within the articles, the best scientists, practitioners, researchers, and commentators draw issues into new perspective as accepted theories and viewpoints are called into account by new events, recent discoveries change old facts, and fresh debate breaks out over important controversies.

Many of the articles resulting from this enormous editorial effort are appropriate for students, researchers, and professionals seeking accurate, current material to help bridge the gap between principles and theories and the real world. These articles, however, become more useful for study when those of lasting value are carefully *collected, organized, indexed,* and *reproduced* in a *low-cost format,* which provides easy and permanent access when the material is needed. That is the role played by *Annual Editions.* Under the direction of each volume's *Editor,* who is an expert in the subject area, and with the guidance of an *Advisory Board,* we seek each year to provide in each *ANNUAL EDITION* a current, well-balanced, carefully selected collection of the best of the public press for your study and enjoyment. We think you'll find this volume useful, and we hope you'll take a moment to let us know what you think.

The United States has decided it is time for a change and has elected a new president. In the first year of the Clinton administration, Americans will watch for signs indicating a renewed interest and commitment to young children and their families. Shrinking federal dollars pit the needs of senior citizens against America's youngest citizens. Children do not vote, contribute to political action campaigns, or lobby Congress. They, and their families, depend on us to speak for them and to describe their struggle to develop and learn in a healthy and safe environment.

A major purpose of the fourteenth edition of *Annual Editions: Early Childhood Education 93/94* is to highlight the progress made on issues facing young children and their families and to plan the hard work that lies ahead. The new administration is faced with depressed economic conditions, tensions related to diversity, and lack of available health care for all Americans. Many groups have drafted position papers or documents outlining proposals to improve the lives of children and families. The issues of family leave, national health insurance, revised tax laws for dependent deductions, the availability and quality of child care, and divorce laws focusing first on the children are discussed in many of these proposals. As citizens concerned with the care and education of children and the quality of life for their families, the most important step we can take is to educate others on what is needed and to work diligently to make life better for all our children. Become involved and make your voice heard.

Three central themes are evident in the 54 articles chosen for this *Annual Editions*. The first theme is *collaboration*. No one group can do all the work or provide all the necessary skills for change to be implemented. Families, school personnel and community groups are vital to the success of children. The second theme is *diversity*. We need teachers who are committed to providing educational environments that are antibias and relevant to the lives of all children. *Readiness* is the final theme evident in many of the articles. All children should enter school ready to learn physically, emotionally, socially, and cognitively. Schools must be prepared to meet the children at their individual developmental level of readiness.

The role of professionals in the field of early childhood education, as well as others concerned with the education and welfare of young children, is to capitalize on the renewed societal interest in the field, while bringing to light the contradictory tapestry of attitudes and actions regarding young children and their families. Another purpose is to stimulate awareness, interest, and inquiry into the historical trends, issues, controversies, and realities of early childhood education.

Given the range of topics included in the volume, it may be used with several audiences: with parents as an available resource in an early childhood center, with undergraduate or graduate students studying early childhood education, or with professionals pursuing further development. It is also useful in many ways as an anthology of primary and secondary sources; as supplementary readings correlated with textbooks in developmental or child psychology, human development, special education, family life, pediatrics, or child care; as a source book for individual term papers, oral presentations, or projects; or for class discussions, group work, panel discussions, or debates.

The selection of articles for the fourteenth edition has been a cooperative venture between the two editors and members of the advisory board. We would especially like to thank the advisory board who share with us in the selection process. Your comments on this edition are welcomed and will serve to modify future anthologies. Please fill out and return the article rating form on the last page. Continue to work diligently for young children, their families, and teachers. Our future depends on it now.

Karen Menke Paciorek

Joyce Huth Munro
Editors

Contents

Unit 1

Perspectives

Thirteen selections consider both the national and international development of early childhood education.

A look at the **history of programs serving young children** shows the variety in program offerings that are available. Early programs provided either **child care** or education. As the profession developed and family needs changed, the two tracks began to merge. By examining our roots, we can begin to plot strategies necessary to meet the needs of young children and their families in the twenty-first century.

Being a child in America today is a difficult task. Children under five suffer from **poverty** more than any other age group. **Children are at risk** of facing the effects of abuse, **homelessness, drugs,** and **poverty.** The **federal government** has set goals to assist children and families, but it may be too little, too late. We need strong **advocates** to be the voice for children.

The passage of the McKinney Act made funds available for states to provide **free education to homeless children.** The authors address the characteristics and needs of homeless families who are living in poverty. Recommendations for collaborative efforts are provided.

Media attention to **babies born addicted to drugs** has raised public concern about the health and education of these children. Researchers are looking at all the factors that affect education, health, and behavior of prenatally drug-exposed children. Strategies for helping families and teachers are included in this article.

The interest in **early childhood education** has never been stronger than it is today. Recent innovations have made the early childhood education classroom bright, inviting, and a true learning area.

The world's largest **child-care** centers were organized during World War II. Their exceptional **quality** was a function of a highly trained early childhood staff (teachers, nurses, family consultants, and nutritionists) well-equipped indoor and outdoor areas, and special services to accommodate working mothers.

At a time when most **child-care centers** are struggling to make ends meet, the educational level of the teaching staff determines the quality of the program. We cannot afford to offer minimal care without regard for the future of children.

According to Dr. Edward Zigler of Yale University, "At least one-third of the children in America are having **child-care** experiences that will compromise their development." The fact that so many children are receiving poor care is compounded by the acceptance of this inadequate care by their **parents.** Professionals need to work diligently to educate parents and to lobby for **health and safety** standards and **quality programming** for all children.

The concepts in bold italics are developed in the article. For further expansion please refer to the Topic Guide and the Index.

Unit 2

Child Development and Families

Ten selections consider the effects of family life on the
growing child and the importance of parent education.

Unit 3

Appropriate Educational Practices

Fourteen selections examine various educational programs, assess the effectiveness of some teaching methods, and consider some of the problems faced by students with special needs.

The concepts in bold italics are developed in the article. For further expansion please refer to the Topic Guide and the Index.

The concepts in bold italics are developed in the article. For further expansion please refer to the Topic Guide and the Index.

Unit 4

Guiding Behavior

Seven selections examine the importance of establishing self-esteem in the child and consider the effects of stressors and stress reduction on behavior.

The concepts in bold italics are developed in the article. For further expansion please refer to the Topic Guide and the Index.

Unit
5

Curricular
Applications

Six selections consider various curricular choices. The
areas covered include creating, inventing, emergent
literacy, motor development, and conceptualizing
curriculum.

Unit 6

Reflections

Four selections consider the present and future of early childhood education.

The concepts in bold italics are developed in the article. For further expansion please refer to the Topic Guide and the Index.

Topic Guide

This topic guide suggests how the selections in this book relate to topics of traditional concern to students and professionals involved with early childhood education. It is useful for locating articles that relate to each other for reading and research. The guide is arranged alphabetically according to topic. Articles may, of course, treat topics that do not appear in the topic guide. In turn, entries in the topic guide do not necessarily constitute a comprehensive listing of all the contents of each selection.

TOPIC AREA	TREATED IN:	TOPIC AREA	TREATED IN:
Advocacy	2. Children in Peril 8. When Parents Accept the Unacceptable 51. Ten Lessons to Help Us Through the 1990s 52. Sixty Years of Save the Children 53. You Can Make a Difference for America's Children	Discipline	38. Managing the Early Childhood Classroom 39. Positive Approach to Discipline 41. Solving Problems Together
Affective Development	43. Tasks of Early Childhood	Diversity	9. Meeting the Challenge of Diversity 27. What Good Prekindergarten Programs Look Like 36. Implementing Individualized Family Service Planning
Antibias	9. Meeting the Challenge of Diversity	Divorce	22. Children of Divorce 23. Single-Parent Families
Assessment	30. Assessment Portfolio as an Attitude 31. Tests, Independence, and Whole Language 32. Tracking Progress Toward the School Readiness Goal 34. Collaborative Training in the Education of Early Childhood Educators	Drugs	2. Children in Peril 4. Prenatal Exposure to Cocaine and Other Drugs
		Dual-Income Families	8. When Parents Accept the Unacceptable
Child Care: Full Day/Half Day	1. Where Did Our Diversity Come From? 6. Best Day Care There Ever Was 7. Who's Taking Care of the Children? 8. When Parents Accept the Unacceptable 12. Public Preschool From the Age of Two 29. School-Age Child Care	Emergent Literacy	21. How Schools Perpetuate Illiteracy 31. Tests, Independence, and Whole Language 35. Preschool Classroom Environments That Promote Communication 49. Writing in Kindergarten
Child Development	14. Why Kids Are the Way They Are 17. Feeding Preschoolers 18. Child's Cognitive Perception of Death 30. Assessment Portfolio as an Attitude	Equipment/Materials	27. What Good Prekindergarten Programs Look Like 28. Structure Time and Space to Promote Pursuit of Learning 35. Preschool Classroom Environments That Promote Communication 38. Managing the Early Childhood Classroom 47. Learning Through Block Play
Collaboration	3. Homeless Children 19. Beyond Parents 30. Assessment Portfolio as an Attitude 34. Collaborative Training in the Education of Early Childhood Educators 36. Implementing Individualized Family Service Planning 37. Parental Feelings	Families	19. Beyond Parents 20. Easing Separation 22. Children of Divorce 23. Single-Parent Families 36. Implementing Individualized Family Service Planning 51. Ten Lessons to Help Us Through the 1990s 52. Sixty Years of Save the Children 54. Children
Creativity	11. Reggio Emilia		
Curriculum	9. Meeting the Challenge of Diversity 29. School-Age Child Care 34. Collaborative Training in the Education of Early Childhood Educators 46. Serious Play in the Classroom	Federal Government	2. Children in Peril 54. Children
Death	18. Child's Cognitive Perception of Death	Guiding Behavior	38. Managing the Early Childhood Classroom 39. Positive Approach to Discipline 41. Solving Problems Together
Developmentally Appropriate Practice	16. Holding Back to Get Ahead 24. Readiness: Children and Their Schools 25. Myths Associated With Developmentally Appropriate Programs 27. What Good Prekindergarten Programs Look Like 30. Assessment Portfolio as an Attitude	Health	4. Prenatal Exposure to Cocaine and Other Drugs 54. Children
		History	1. Where Did Our Diversity Come From?

Perspectives

- National Perspectives (Articles 1–9)
- International Perspectives (Articles 10–13)

The vast numbers of young children being born into and raised in environments where poverty, drugs, abuse, homelessness, and lack of medical care are prevalent pose special challenges for early childhood educators. The 26 percent of American children under the age of six living in poverty are denied medical care, proper nutrition, shelter, and educational opportunities necessary for survival in America today. Families living in poverty are faced with a multitude of concerns, but few resources. They must find a safe place to sleep for the night or a church offering a meal and a box of used clothing. The children receive so little of quality. Often their lives are affected by the constant turmoil of moving from one temporary housing setting to the next.

The President's National Drug Control Strategy Report estimates that 100,000 cocaine-exposed children are born each year. After their birth, these children live in environments where drugs are an everyday part of their lives.

Within a few years, they enter preschool and public school settings, and very few professionals are ready to meet the special needs these children and their families bring to the schools. Children born exposed to crack are challenging for even the most experienced and seasoned professionals, yet they leave the hospital and enter homes often headed by poor, drug-addicted young mothers who are not able to cope with the demands of their own care, let alone the needs of a high-strung, difficult-to-soothe, unhealthy infant.

Community groups and business leaders are now collaborating with early childhood professionals in calling for greater funding and the establishment of partnerships among varied constituencies to ensure high-quality programs for America's young children. The reasons for these collaborative efforts are inadequate support during the 1980s from the federal government, greater numbers of families living in poverty, and an increase in the percentage of working mothers and dual-income families who need quality child care services that they can afford. Successful government, business, and educational collaboration occurred in the past during the Depression, World War II, and in the 1960s, when Head Start began. The lessons learned from those interagency efforts have clearly shown both the necessity and effectiveness of early childhood programs that are comprehensive and high quality. In "Where Did Our Diversity Come From? A Profile of Early Childhood Care and Education in the U.S.," Patricia Olmsted traces the history of programs offering care and education to young children in America.

Public perceptions about our investment in young children in general, and at-risk and minority children in particular, are gradually changing. Today, millions of working parents need quality child-care programs that are consistently and adequately funded, comprehensive in nature to meet the basic needs of children and families, and operated by dedicated and specially educated staffs of professionals. The day-to-day stress that parents face in their jobs has become more intense and complex, and they often have to cope alone due to lack of support from employers, colleagues, family, and friends. This is where alliances formed among home, school, and business can be extremely helpful and comforting.

Still, the majority of child-care centers struggle to be self-supporting, receive only a fraction of their operating budget from outside sources, pay wages far below salaries offered to comparable public school teachers, and provide limited services to children and families. Millions of young children under six years of age never attend quality child care programs, but instead are inadequately cared for by untrained, uncaring, or indifferent persons in centers or homes where quality is difficult to attain. Without national child care standards that address issues such as health and safety, ratios, qualifications of staff, equipment, and materials and programming there will continue to be large numbers of children spending the majority of their days in substandard, dangerous, and nonstimulating settings.

Parents looking for child care often do not know what constitutes quality, or are unable to find or afford it in their community. After looking at seven inadequate child care facilities, one parent remarked that what she was seeing must be o.k., because other parents were choosing it for their children. When will quality be the foundation of all child-care programs?

Many children are cared for in three or more settings during the day, shuffled among relatives, friends, and neighbors. Uncounted numbers of children are left to fend for themselves. This patchwork of ineffective child-care arrangements is having significant developmental effects on today's young children who will be tomorrow's adolescents. Questions must be raised about what these vulnerable young children are experiencing in these varied settings during their formative years. Five years of inadequate care will affect the child and his or her learning ability when it is time to start kindergarten, according to Dr. Edward Zigler of Yale University.

For some, domestic issues and problems surrounding early childhood are overwhelming and it is difficult to look beyond our own country. Yet what is happening internationally will affect us and the ways we interact with children. By studying others, we can often learn more about ourselves. The world is changing rapidly and the increase of children from other cultures into our country occurs daily. Recognizing the value of diversity in the classroom will enable knowledgeable teachers to provide antibias curricular experiences that meet the needs of all the children and adults in the class.

As we examine the living and learning conditions for children today, we see many problems, but there are educators, parents, and community groups ready to assist children and their families. Unfortunately, the number of people requiring assistance is growing at a rapid pace. Preventing problems from occurring in the first place seems to be the one key to ensuring a safe, nurturing, and successful educational experience for all children.

Looking Ahead: Challenge Questions

Describe the beginnings of programs for young children in the United States.

How are children from families headed by young, poor, and single parents at jeopardy for failure in school and society in general? What steps can be taken to assist these children who face poverty every day of their lives?

What can schools do to assist children and their families as they struggle to walk the thin line between economic disaster and a safe and secure life?

What steps are considered more "user friendly" for families with young children?

Why do parents continue to use a child care setting deemed unacceptable?

What unique qualities are present in the preschool programs of Reggio Emilia?

How do standards for quality differ between programs in the United States and France?

What is the role of the teacher in developing a curriculum that is antibias and relevant to the family composition, race, and ethnic background of each child?

Where Did Our Diversity Come From?

A Profile of early childhood care and education in the U.S.

Patricia P. Olmsted

Senior Research Associate

In 1838, *Letters to Mothers* by Lydia Sigourney was published in the United States. It was a book giving the following advice to mothers about early childhood care and education:

> *Who can compute the value of the first seven years of life? Who can tell the strength of impressions, made ere the mind is preoccupied, prejudiced or perverted? Especially, if in its waxen state, it is softened by the breath of a mother, will not the seal which she stamps there, resist the mutations of time, and be read before the Throne of the Judge, when the light of this sun and moon, are quenched and extinct? (p. 89)*

> *The industry displayed in the various trades and occupations, should be a stimulant to the mother, who modifies a material more costly than all others, more liable to destruction by brief neglect. . . . Is the builder of a lofty and magnificent edifice, careless of its foundations, and whether its columns are to rest upon a quicksand, or a quagmire? (pp. 90–91)*

Sigourney's advice clearly reflects the attitudes of that period in America—attitudes about the critical nature of a child's early years, the important role of religion in childrearing, and the pivotal role of the mother. It is perhaps no coincidence that around the year of publication of Sigourney's book, *out-of-home child care by groups and institutions* was just beginning in the U.S.

Any history of early childhood out-of-home services in the United States must trace two major strands of activity. The first strand, with roots in a social welfare tradition, has been associated with the provision of *care* for young children, particularly for those from poor and troubled families. The second strand, with roots in Friedrich Froebel's kindergarten movement, has been associated with the provision of early *education*, especially for children from affluent families. To understand the major events forming these two strands, it is helpful to first consider American attitudes towards childrearing and personal fulfillment.

ATTITUDES FORMED BY OUR HISTORY

The history of the United States has contributed in a unique way to a national set of attitudes including beliefs about the primacy of the family with regard to childrearing and beliefs about the value of personal fulfillment through work. Cochran (1982) discussed the former beliefs by noting that "There is a strong feeling that childrearing is a family affair, to be carried out by the mother, with help from the father, separate from public life. A national commitment to pluralism, stimulated by successive waves of immigration, has carried with it an agreement that different peoples rear their children differently, and reinforced the belief that childrearing practices are the private province of family members" (Draft, pp. 3–4). Regarding beliefs about personal fulfillment through work, Cochran pointed out that both church and state have promoted the value of work throughout the history of this country. Furthermore, with the industrial revolution, work has increasingly implied paid employment, for both men and women, away from home.

The historical movement of American women (including mothers of young children) into the labor force can be related to the combination of the growing mechanization of household tasks, the desire for more consumer goods, and a desire for personal fulfillment through paid employment. Cochran stated, "The tension created by combining the belief that childrearing is a private affair, to be carried out primarily by the mother, with a desire to maximize human potential, individual freedom, and socioeconomic participation through work for pay, is being felt both inside the family and at every other level of American society" (pp. 4–5). This tension manifests itself both in the individual arrangements made by families for child care (often informal, family-based arrangements)

"Where Did Our Diversity Come From?" by Patricia P. Olmsted, *High/Scope ReSource*, Vol. 11, No. 3, Fall 1992, pp. 4-9.
Reprinted by permission of High/Scope Press, Ypsilanti, MI.

and in the diverse views found among people in the United States about who (family, community, or government) should be responsible for child care.

THE CARE STRAND

The care strand of early childhood services began with **day nurseries,** the original social welfare day care centers. These first appeared shortly after the flood of immigration that brought more than 5 million foreign families to the United States between 1815 and 1860 (Clarke-Stewart, 1982; Kahn & Kamerman, 1987). As Kahn and Kamerman stated, "The early cases . . . involve instances of 'day orphans' who were to be protected while their mothers worked or of charitable groups that were responding to alleged or potential child neglect" (p. 121). During the 1870s and 1880s philanthropic agencies began sponsoring day nurseries, seeing such child care assistance for poor or immigrant mothers as the best way to help preserve the family (Steinfels, 1973).

THE EDUCATION STRAND

The beginning of the second strand, early childhood education, can be traced to the nineteenth-century development of the kindergarten. "The idea that some form of education outside the home might be appropriate for children before they entered the first grade paved the way for the later development of nursery schools" (Almy, 1982, p. 479). Specific elements of early childhood education in the United States can be traced to earlier programs developed in Europe by Friedrich Froebel and Maria Montessori (Spodek, 1973). For example, Froebel's ideas that the role of education was to support the child's natural development and that play was an essential part of the educational activity of childhood have been maintained in many U.S. early childhood programs. Similarly, such U.S. program features as prescribed sequences of activities, self-correcting materials, and indirect teaching styles can be traced to the work of Montessori.

During the 1930s middle-class families began to enroll their children in early childhood education programs in large numbers (Clarke-Stewart & Fein, 1983). Most of these early education programs were based on Froebel or Montessori or were derivatives of the nursery school programs developed in England by such educators as Robert Owen and Margaret McMillan.

COMBINING THE STRANDS—THE GREAT DEPRESSION AND THE WAR YEARS

The first large-scale early childhood care *and* education programs occurred in the 1930s, when such programs were authorized under the federally sponsored Work Projects Administration (WPA) to provide jobs for unemployed professionals. (Clarke-Stewart, 1982; Scarr & Weinberg, 1986). By 1937 there were 1,900 programs established and approximately 40 thousand children being served. Located mainly in public schools, the year-round, all-day programs were basically viewed as child care, although they clearly had educational components. With the demise of the WPA, most of the programs were phased out because of a lack of funds.

The variety of care and education settings available is a direct reflection of the variety of needs of families.

During World War II, early childhood care again attracted public attention as many women went to work in defense-related industries. In 1941 Congress passed the Lanham Act, which provided matching federal funds for states to establish day care centers and nursery schools. In 1945 between 105,000 and 130,000 children were enrolled in Lanham centers (Zigler & Goodman, 1982). Following the end of World War II, the Lanham centers and other wartime child care programs were dismantled everywhere except in California and New York City. As men returned from the battlefield, there was a general assumption that women would return to the home. For the most part they did—but not for long.

THE 1960S AND 1970S

In the 1960s women began participating in the labor force in large numbers once again, and thus the need for child care increased—for all families, not just for poor or troubled families, which was the earlier focus of the social welfare movement (Kahn & Kamerman, 1987). This brought renewed interest in early childhood care and education, with one result being a closer meshing of the two strands, child care and early education programs.

There was also an academic rediscovery of early childhood education during this time, as evidenced by the increased interest in the work of Jean Piaget, Jerome Bruner, J. McVicker Hunt, and others (Almy, 1982). More families began to see early education programs as helpful for their children, as a routine part of children's experience. During the 1960s several studies of the effectiveness of early childhood education, particularly for children in low-income families, were launched. Examples of these studies include the High/Scope Perry Preschool study (Berrueta-Clement, Schweinhart, Barnett, Epstein, & Weikart, 1984), the Early Training study (Gray, Ramsey, & Klaus, 1982), and the Mother-Child Home program (Levenstein, O'Hara, & Madden, 1983).

In 1965 the Head Start program, which is still the largest national effort in the area of early childhood education, was initiated. One important aspect of the Head Start program is that its development is based on the premise that early education and enrichment are important for *all* children, not just for children from affluent families (such as those served by the nursery schools of the 1930s). Also, Head Start has a strong educational emphasis, and therefore it has continued the trend (started in the Lanham centers) towards the provision of early education as well as daytime supervision for children from low-income families.

During the 1970s family use of early childhood care and education programs increased still more as American mothers entered the labor force in even greater numbers and as more families saw early education programs as beneficial for their children. During this period different models of early childhood education were tested in the national Head Start Planned Variation program. Most of the models being tested had been developed by child development scholars or early childhood education researchers at universities or research institutions (Miller, 1979). Some examples of planned variation models were the Behavior Analysis Model (University of Kansas), the Cognitively Oriented Curriculum (High/Scope Educational Research Foundation), and the Bank Street College of Education Model (Bank Street College of Education, New York).

In the area of child care during the 1970s, many professionals in the field consider the major event to be President Richard Nixon's veto in 1971 of the Comprehensive Child Development Bill. This bill, sponsored by Senator Walter Mondale and Congressman John Brademas and passed by both houses of Congress, would have established a national child care program for the first time in the United States. In vetoing the bill, President Nixon stated that the legislation "would commit the vast moral authority of the National Government to the side of communal approaches of childrearing over against the family-centered approach" (Nixon, 1971). Government policy since this watershed event has indeed steered a course far shy of any national child care program.

THE BEGINNING OF DECENTRALIZATION, PRIVATIZATION, AND DEREGULATION

According to Kahn and Kamerman (1987), "**Decentralization, privatization,** and **deregulation** became the guiding principles in federal child care policy in the 1980s" (p. 3). The **decentralization** occurred through a combination of federal funding cutbacks and the elimination of matching-fund requirements for states. Federal funds for child care services (Title XX) were converted into Social Services Block Grant funds in 1981 and were passed through to the states. Under this latter funding mechanism, policy and program decisions were made by the individual states. **Privatization** included open support for a diverse child care market: providing incentives to employers,

easing requirements regarding for-profit providers, and giving tax benefits to families. These forms of support were accompanied by a decrease in federal funding and policymaking.

The major instance of **deregulation** involved the failure to enact the Federal Interagency Day Care Requirements. These regulations, developed by federal agency experts and child development advisers in the late 1970s and based on research, would have established minimum standards for child care services, at least for those receiving federal funding, and would have served as general guidelines for all child care services. However, Congress has never adopted these standards, and consequently U.S. child care services are subject only to state standards. These standards vary considerably from state to state, and in some states certain forms of care (for example, family day care homes or church-based programs) are subject to *no* licensing requirements.

With decentralization, privatization, and deregulation characterizing the federal involvement in child care during the 1980s, the roles of state and local agencies became increasingly important. Some states created new child care programs, generally targeted to serve the children of special populations (such as low-income working families or adolescent parents), with state or combined state/local funding. Other states allocated no additional state or local funds for child care, and the federal funds (Title XX through Social Service Block Grants to states) failed to keep pace with inflation, resulting in the provision of services to fewer children each year. During 1988 twenty-nine states provided some funding for early childhood education programs (Children's Defense Fund, 1990). Some states made concerted efforts to integrate early childhood education and child care into one system, while others continued to have the two parallel strands. The resulting overall picture of early childhood care and education was one of great variation from state to state.

Today the United States continues to have a highly decentralized system of early childhood care and education services. The *federal government* does provide funding, organization, and guidelines for some special programs (Head Start, for example). Other federal financial support for the provision of child care comes in the form of tax credits for families, tax incentives for employers, and block grants for states. However, *state* governments set general policy, regulations, and licensing standards for most services and programs. Individual providers—for-profit as well as nonprofit, center-based as well as home-based—organize, administer, and operate their own programs. As a result of this decentralized system, various forms of early childhood care and education exist.

THE FORMS OF EARLY CHILDHOOD CARE AND EDUCATION

Child care arrangements for America's preprimary-aged children (3 to 6 years old) vary widely and may involve one or more of the following types of care. (Families in which all adults are employed often use multiple care-arrangements.)

• *Care in the child's own home, by a relative or nonrelative.* In this arrangement, an adult comes into the child's home to provide care and supervision. The in-home sitter is often a relative who may or may not be paid.

• *Care in another home by a relative.* A common child care arrangement is care of a child by a relative in the relative's home. In some cases, these services are provided without cost, while in others, money, goods, or an exchange of services may be involved.

• *A family day care home.* This arrangement involves care of one or more children on a regular basis by a nonrelative in a home other than the child's home. Family day care home arrangements can vary from an informal, shared-caregiving agreement between friends to a highly formal network of licensed homes.

• *A part-day educational program.* These programs, which can be under private or public sponsorship, are housed in a variety of settings, such as community centers, public schools, churches, and buildings specifically built for this purpose. Educational programs generally consist of a large group of children with two or more adults and are traditionally concerned with children's growth in several areas (social, cognitive, creative). There are likely to be scheduled activities, clearly defined play areas with associated routines, and a specific curriculum (for example, Montessori or High/Scope). Most educational programs for 3- to 5-year-olds, including public programs, are limited to half-day sessions, usually 3 hours a day on weekdays during the school year. However, there are many institutional efforts currently under way to coordinate educational programs with other child care arrangements, to better meet the child care needs of families throughout the entire working day and throughout the entire year.

• *A child care center.* In this arrangement, care is provided either full- or part-time, by groups or by individuals, in facilities devoted to child care. The average number of children served by a center is 50, but the number may range from 15 to 300. In large centers, children are usually divided into groups according to age. There are several types of centers, including: (1) *private for-profit,* (2) *private nonprofit,* (3) *publicly operated,* (4) *parent cooperative,* and (5) *employer-provided.*

Private for-profit centers may be either proprietary or commercial. Proprietary centers are usually small, serving approximately 30 children, and are typically family-run. They are often located in converted shops or homes and may accept only children within a specified age-range (for example, 3- to 5-year-olds) whose families can pay the fee. Commercial centers are generally operated as franchises: A specific program is developed and replicated on a large scale, which results in uniform facilities and procedures. Such centers may accommodate as many as 70 to 100 children in groups of approximately 20.

Private nonprofit centers are usually operated by churches or by private community or charitable organizations and are often located in churches, schools, or community halls.

Publicly operated centers serve children from low-income families who receive government subsidies for child care, as well as children whose parents pay for child care. Because they receive public funding, these child care centers must meet required standards that insure adequate physical facilities, equipment, staff, and educational programs. For many centers, adequate parent-involvement is another requirement.

Parent cooperative centers are those in which parents play a major role in providing child care, management, and decision making, usually with the guidance of a paid director and teachers. As a result of this in-kind service by parents, fees tend to be lower than those for other types of centers, but cooperative centers tend to attract high-income families because the parents must have the time flexibility to work at the center. Parent cooperative centers typically offer part-day programs for young children.

Employer-provided centers are offered by a small number of corporations, factories, hospitals, universities, and trade unions to provide child care as a fringe benefit for their employees. These centers are typically large (approximately 80 to 100 children, divided into appropriate groups) and are usually located close to the parent's workplace.

WHAT EARLY CHILDHOOD SERVICES DO FAMILIES USE?

In 1987 approximately 80 percent of America's 5-year-olds attended public or private kindergarten programs (National Center for Education Statistics, 1990). Data on child care arrangements for 5-year-olds not attending kindergarten is limited. Therefore our analysis here of the children's services that American families use covers only services for children 3 and 4 years of age.

Willer et al. (1991) reported on a survey that provides the most-recent information about the use of various types of early childhood services. Although the survey had two drawbacks (it was conducted by telephone, thus excluding families without telephones from the findings, and its response rate was lower than that usually obtained in surveys), the resulting information is useful in a general way. The survey found that families in which the mother is employed are most likely to choose child care centers for their 3- and 4-year-old children (43 percent use this type of care). This type of family less frequently chooses care by a parent with no supplemental care (21 percent), care in a family day care home (17 percent), and care by relatives (16 percent).

Families in which the mother is not employed most frequently (58 percent) choose care by a parent in the home and less frequently (30 percent) choose care in a center. These families use the other forms of early childhood services (such as family day care or relative care) infrequently.

HOW AVAILABLE ARE SERVICES?

A family's choice of a care or education setting for their child seems to be the result of several factors, including parents' income and education levels, parents' preferences about setting characteristics, and availability of care and education settings within a community. The variety of settings available for child care and early education in the United States is a direct reflection of the variety of needs of families.

When we examine changes in the availability of various types of child care settings over the past 10 to 15 years, we find a large overall increase but variations in size of increase among the different settings. We can provide data for two major settings, both of which are licensed—family day care homes and child care centers. In 1978 there were over 100,000 licensed or regulated **family day care homes** with an estimated total capacity of 400,000 children, based on an estimate of 4 children per licensed home (Ruopp, Travers, Glantz, & Coelen, 1979). By 1990 the number of licensed or regulated family child care homes had increased to approximately 118,000 (Willer et al., 1991) with an estimated total capacity of 860,000 children. Exact figures were not available, but Willer et al. gave indirect estimates of nonregulated family day care homes, which they based on parental reports of child care arrangements and on respondents identifying themselves as family day care providers. These estimates suggest the total number of non-regulated family day care homes to be between 550,000 to 1.1 million. This child care setting typically serves both preschool-aged children (full-day or part-day) and school-aged children (before and after school).

In 1978 the number of licensed or regulated **child care centers** was estimated to be 18,300 with a total capacity of 1.0 million children (Ruopp et al., 1979). By 1990 the number of licensed centers had increased to an estimated 80,000 (Willer et al., 1991) with a total capacity of 4.2 million children.

STATE LICENSING OF CARE AND EDUCATION SETTINGS

As mentioned earlier, in the United States, regulation of early childhood care and education is a *state* rather than a *federal* responsibility. All states have regulations for child care centers and regulations for preschool educational programs that are part of the public school system. The latter are typically included under regulations for regular public school programs. For child care centers, a typical licensing procedure consists of an initial inspection visit and additional visits prior to renewal of the license (the license period may be 1, 2, or 3 years).

The states vary widely, however, in their licensing of family day care homes. Eight states do not regulate homes or regulate only for subsidized care; 3 states have voluntary registration; 13 states register but do not license homes; and 26 states license homes. The minimum enrollment requiring a family day care home to be licensed also varies among states, with half the states requiring licensing when one or more children are enrolled and the other half requiring licensing when from three to six children or more are enrolled (Morgan, 1987).

By 1995 an estimated 66% of children under age 6 will have mothers in the labor force.

Also, individual states have various categories of settings that are exempt from regulations. Twelve states exempt all church-sponsored day care centers; 21 states exempt all nursery schools and other part-day or full-day educational programs other than those affiliated with the public schools. Additional examples of settings that one or more states choose not to regulate include programs run by private colleges and universities, programs in which the parents are on the premises (parent cooperatives), and programs run by the military (Morgan, 1987).

Regulation of settings typically involves requirements concerning these program characteristics:

• **Child-staff ratios and group size.** Research has indicated that staff-child ratio and group size are strongly related to program quality (Ruopp et al., 1979; Whitebook, Howes, & Phillips, 1989). Guidelines for staff-child ratios and group sizes for children of different ages were developed from the National Day Care Study (Ruopp et al., 1979). For 4-year-olds, according to the study, group size should not exceed 20 children, and there should be at least 1 staff member for every 10 children. However, 32 states do not regulate group size at all for preschool children, and of the states that do regulate it, only a small number fall within the range recommended by the research study. For 4-year-old children, only 1 state sets the child-staff ratio at 7 to 1 or 8 to 1; 16 states set the child-staff ratio at 10 to 1; 10 states set a 12 to 1 ratio; and the remaining states set ratios ranging between 13 to 1 and 20 to 1 (Morgan, 1987).

• **Space requirements for centers and family day care homes.** Most states require centers to have 35 square feet of indoor space and 75 square feet of outdoor space. For family day care homes, 21 states have no space requirements. In states with space requirements for day care homes, the minimums are generally similar to those for centers (Morgan, 1987).

• **Age-appropriate program content.** Nearly every state requires centers to provide a written plan for a developmental program, and 34 states have similar requirements for family day care homes. In addition, 24 states require centers to express their educational philosophy in writing (Morgan, 1987).

STATE EDUCATIONAL QUALIFICATIONS FOR EARLY CHILDHOOD STAFF

Educational requirements for early childhood staff are another part of state regulation. Tied in with those requirements is the issue of the salaries of those who work with young children, which is an issue now receiving great attention in the United States.

Although there are large variations among states, salaries of teachers in public school pre-school programs are basically equivalent to those of other teachers in the school system. (For state-funded preprimary programs, the 1988 salary range for a beginning teacher was $12,000 to $20,000; the range for an experienced teacher was $16,000 to $24,000; Mitchell, 1988.) Salaries of teachers in private preschool programs are generally about half of what is earned by public school teachers. Salary levels and certification procedures are related; that is, for public school preschool programs, a college-educated, certified teacher is required, whereas for private preschool programs, certification requirements are a program-specific decision (Morgan, 1987; Schweinhart & Mazur, 1987). At present, some states have a separate certification for early childhood education; other states have programs for this specific certification under development (Seefeldt, 1988).

States tend to have two basic types of educational requirements for staff in child care centers: education prior to employment (preservice) and ongoing training (inservice). In addition, many states recognize the Child Development Associate (CDA) credential, which is a national competency-based credential that usually involves a training program and a competency assessment. The duration of CDA training ranges from 2 months to 2 years, but it is generally 1 year. States differ greatly in the educational qualifications they require for directors, teachers, and assistants in child care centers. For center teachers, 24 states have preservice qualifications, while 26 states do not. Among the states with preservice qualifications, there are 4 different patterns of college course work or previous experience requirements. Among the 26 states with no preservice qualifications, 17 require inservice training, while 9 do not. A few states have entry-level educational requirements for center classroom assistants: Some require a high school diploma; others, only basic orientation given by the center (Morgan, 1987).

For family day care providers, 27 states require neither experience nor any form of education; 13 states require at least preservice training; and 8 states (including 4 of the 13 just mentioned) require some inservice training. The remaining states do not regulate family day care homes and thus have no educational requirements for day care providers (Morgan, 1987).

Considering the minimal educational requirements for child care workers in centers and family day care homes, it is not surprising that they receive very low salaries. According to the Bureau of Labor Statistics, two out of every three child care workers earn wages below the poverty threshold, regardless of their education, training, or experience. In 1988 the median annual income of a full-time child care worker employed in a center was $9,363 (Whitebook et al., 1989). Willer et al. (1991) reported the following hourly wage rates: $7.49 for a preschool teacher, $4.04 for a regulated family day care provider, and $1.25 for a nonregulated family day care provider. Roughly 2 million persons, mostly women, are employed as child care workers. Related to their low salaries are their high turnover rates, in both centers and homes. Whitebook et al. found that annual *staff* turnover in child care centers averaged 41 percent, while Willer et al. (1991) found that annual *teacher* turnover in centers averaged 25 percent.

The issue of staff salaries cannot be addressed, of course, without also taking into account what parents have to pay for early childhood services. With salaries as they are, and with government support as it is, the estimated typical cost to parents for a child's full-time care is $3,000 a year. In a survey of child care professionals in seven major U.S. cities, the yearly cost for a 3- to 5-year-old in a child care center was found to range from $2,600 to $5,200, while the yearly cost for a child in the same age-range in a family day care home was found to range from $2,000 to $6,000. It is reasonable to assume that U.S. child care costs are slightly lower in rural areas than they are in major cities (Children's Defense Fund, 1987).

ISSUES FOR THE 1990S

The information presented in this profile helps to define the early childhood issues that policymakers face in the 1990s. These issues are defined by projecting trends and examining the implications of these trends. For example, although a stable birthrate is predicted for the United States in the near future, the number of 3- to 6-year-old children who will need care will continue to increase as more and more mothers of young children enter the labor force. If recent trends, such as the increasing number of single-parent and "working poor" families, continue, by 1995 the proportion of children under age 6 with mothers in the labor force will reach an estimated 66 percent (Hofferth & Phillips, 1986). This accelerating demand for early childhood services, the complex nature of the present system of services, and the historical roles of federal and state governments in early childhood care and education together raise questions in several areas:

1. PERSPECTIVES: National

Staffing Concerns

Considering past national policies, we can assume it is unlikely that government will provide substantial support for early childhood services for the majority of families in the United States. When this assumption is combined with the increasing need for child care, the following questions must be asked: Who will pay for these services (that is, for the salaries of providers, since staff salaries constitute the largest share of a services budget)? What caregiver (or teacher) training will be required? How can parents be assured of qualified staff in a high-quality early childhood setting?

Earlier in this profile, we noted the very low salaries for most categories of early childhood staff and the accompanying high turnover rate among these workers. Higher salaries might decrease the turnover rate, justify the individual worker's investment in preservice education, and allow states to increase staff educational requirements without creating staff shortages. However, with only limited government support likely for the near future, the families using the services must bear most of the financial burdens related to those services. When we consider that many families in need of services are those in which all adults are working to maintain a desired standard of living and that the salary levels of parents when they have young children are often lower than later in their employment careers, it becomes clear that families will not be able to significantly increase their payments for services to allow for increased salaries for early childhood staff. *This issue of salaries for providers of early childhood services is a critical one for the United States and one with no easy solution.*

Related to salaries is the issue of educational qualifications for providers of early childhood services. With the currently low salaries, what types of training or experience can one reasonably expect a service provider to have? Earlier we presented information about the minimal educational requirements, in most states, for early childhood care and education staff. This information, though understandable in light of the low salaries, is surprising considering that the National Day Care Study found staff qualifications, "especially education/training relevant to young children," to be positively related to both classroom interactions and increases on children's test scores (Ruopp et al., 1979). Also, it is important to remember that even in states with staff requirements, the requirements apply only to licensed settings, which by no means constitute all settings. Thus, even in states that require certain staff qualifications, the requirements apply to only a sub-group of providers. Finally, from a national perspective, the differing requirements among states pose problems for service providers moving from one state to another, as well as for families moving between states. *The issue of qualifications for early childhood staff in the United States is closely linked with the issue of salaries, and it is unlikely that the two issues can be resolved separately.*

Quality of Services

The quality of early childhood services is clearly related to staffing issues (salaries, qualifications). However, there are additional issues related to quality that need to be addressed in the 1990s. Research on the dimensions of quality for different types of settings and different groups of children needs to continue. In addition, we need to determine the best public policies and systems for developing and maintaining high-quality early childhood services. Are the present state systems of regulating early childhood programs adequate? Would a set of national guidelines that states would be required to follow ensure a higher level of quality? In the United States, could a set of national guidelines apply to all early childhood settings—or only to those settings receiving public funding (for example, Head Start or Social Service Block Grant monies)?

The current licensing system used by states serves primarily to set minimum standards. However, in many cases these minimum standards are lower than the levels found to be related to positive child outcomes in research studies. In addition, many states do not regulate certain types of settings or do not regulate specific characteristics within settings (for example, 32 states do not regulate group size for 4-year-old children in centers). Raising minimum standards to levels recommended by research studies, increasing the number of setting characteristics addressed by the licensing system, and including *all* major types of early childhood settings in the licensing system would be steps toward improving the development of high-quality early childhood programs.

During the past several years, the National Association for the Education of Young Children has been working, through its National Academy of Early Childhood Programs, to improve the quality of early childhood services by the development of accreditation criteria and procedures (NAEYC, 1984). The NAEYC accreditation system covers several program components, including curriculum, physical environment, and staff qualifications and development, and specific criteria are established for each component. So far, only a very small portion of the total number of early childhood care and education settings in the U.S. have participated in the NAEYC accreditation procedures. It is a good beginning, but *much more needs to be done to improve the quality of early childhood services during the next decade.*

Parent Information

If government fails to provide substantial support for early childhood services in the near future, parents will continue to assume the major responsibility for supporting, locating, and evaluating early childhood services. *A major issue for the 1990s, therefore, will be the development and dissemination of information to parents to allow them to become more-informed consumers of early childhood services.*

In communities where parents have few early childhood service alternatives, locating services is not a complex process. However, in communities where a variety of types of settings are in operation, many parents spend vast amounts of time searching out information about appropriate, available settings and possible openings in those settings. The process is further complicated by the high turnover rate of providers, which can produce unpredictable fluctuation in the quality or availability of care.

Over the past 15 years "resource and referral" agencies funded by various sources (state, local community, employers) have provided information to parents, employers, and others about early childhood services within their communities. Some resource and referral agencies prepare a listing of community early childhood services, which they provide upon request. Others prepare information about the characteristics of various types of care and about making a care choice; they are often willing to discuss individual care situations with parents and to assist them in their search process.

During the 1980s resource and referral agencies operated in at least some areas of nearly every state, but the funding of such agencies has been a continual struggle, and many communities still do not have one. Also, since some agencies provide only a basic listing of services, there is a need for preparation and dissemination of other information to help parents better select and utilize existing early childhood services. For example, some parents may desire information about different types of programs and how to make decisions about the "best" setting for their child and family. Other parents may desire information about how to identify a high-quality program, that is, about questions to ask and things to look for when visiting a potential setting. And some parents may desire information about what to expect from a provider (the procedure followed by the provider if a child becomes ill, for example), what their own responsibilities are (whether parents must pay for days when their child is unable to attend, for example), and how to clarify these matters when initially making arrangement with the provider. Those resource and referral agencies that have had sufficient funding have been instrumental in assisting parents and others. However obtaining additional funding to allow for an increase in the number of agencies as well as an increase in the types of assistance provided by agencies is a major issue to be dealt with in the 1990s.

A TIME FOR ASSESSMENT

The U.S. has experienced great changes in the area of early childhood care and education since the time of Lydia Sigourney's book *Letters to Mothers*. In the last 25 years, particularly, vast numbers of various types of care and education settings have developed to meet the increasing demand for services. However, the service system has remained a decentralized one, and to a large degree, each family is responsible for locating and supporting the services for their own children.

Now is the time to step back to assess the current system of early childhood care and education services in the United States. We must assess it in terms of its ability to meet the needs of young children and their families, in terms of its viability as an employment system for adults, and in terms of its relationships with other societal systems, such as employment and education. Most important, we need to assess the impact of the system on the children it is serving, to insure that we have a system that will help children develop and grow into productive adult members of the American society.

REFERENCES

Administration for Children, Youth, and Families. (1992). *Project Head Start statistical fact sheet.* Washington, DC: Department of Health and Human Services.

Almy, M. (1982). Day care and early childhood education. In E. F. Zigler & E. W. Gordon (Eds.), *Day care: Scientific and social policy* (pp. 476–496). Boston: Auburn House.

Berrueta-Clement, J. R., Schweinhart, L. J., Barnett, W. S., Epstein, A. S., & Weikart, D. P. (1984). *Changed lives: The effects of the Perry Preschool program on youths through age 19* (Monographs of the High/Scope Educational Research Foundation, 8). Ypsilanti, MI: High/Scope Press.

Children's Defense Fund. (1987). *Child care: The time is now.* Washington, DC: Author.

Children's Defense Fund. (1988). *State child care fact book.* Washington, DC: Author.

Children's Defense Fund. (1990). *Children 1990: A report card, briefing book, and action primer.* Washington, DC: Author.

Clarke-Stewart, K. A. (1982). *Daycare.* Cambridge, MA: Harvard University Press.

Clarke-Stewart, K. A., & Fein, G. G. (1983). Early childhood programs. In P. H. Mussen (Ed.), *Handbook of child psychology* (4th ed., Vol. 2, pp. 917–1000). New York: Wiley.

Cochran, M. (1982). Profits and policy: Child care in America. In R. Rist (Ed.), *Policy studies annals* (Vol. 6, draft version of article).

Dervarics, C. (1992). *The new federal role in children's programs.* Silver Spring, MD: Business Publishers.

Gray, S. W., Ramsey, B. K., & Klaus, R. A. (1982). *From 3 to 20: The Early Training Project.* Baltimore: University Park Press.

Hofferth, S. L., & Phillips, D. A. (1987). Child care in the United States, 1970 to 1995. *Journal of Marriage and the Family, 49* 559–571.

Kahn, A. J., & Kamerman, S. B. (1987). *Child care: Facing the hard choices.* Dover, MA: Auburn House.

Levenstein, P., O'Hara, J., & Madden, J. (1983). The Mother-Child Home Program of the Verbal Interaction Project. In Consortium of Longitudinal Studies, *As the twig is bent . . . Lasting effects of preschool programs* (pp. 237–265). Hillsdale, NJ: Lawrence Erlbaum.

Miller, L. B. (1979) Development of curriculum models in Head Start. In E. Zigler & J. Valentine (Eds.), *Project Head Start: A Legacy of the war on poverty* (pp. 195–221). New York: Free Press.

Mitchell, A. (1988). *The public school early childhood study: The district survey.* New York: Bank Street College of Education.

Morgan, G. (1987). *The national state of child care regulation, 1986.* Watertown, MA: Work/Family Directions, Inc.

National Association for the Education of Young Children. (1984). *Accreditation criteria and procedures of the National Academy of Early Childhood Programs.* Washington, DC: Author.

National Center for Education Statistics (1990). *The condition of education.* Washington, DC: Author.

Nixon, R. M. (1971). *Veto message—Economic Opportunity Amendments of 1971.* (S. 2007), 92nd Cong., 1st sess., Senate Doc. 92–48.

Ruopp, R., Travers, J., Glantz, F., & Coelen, C. (1979). *Children at the center: Summary findings and their implications* (Final report of the National Day Care Study, Vol. 1). Cambridge, MA: Abt Associates.

Scarr, S., & Weinberg, R. A. (1986). The early childhood enterprise: Care and education of the young. *American Psychologist, 41,* 1140–1146.

Schweinhart, L. J., & Mazur, E. (1987). *Prekindergarten programs in urban schools* (High/Scope Early Childhood Policy Paper No. 6). Ypsilanti, MI: High/Scope Press.

Seefeldt, C. (1988). Teacher certification and program accreditation in early childhood education. *The Elementary School Journal, 89,* 241–252.

Sigourney, L. H. (1838). *Letters to mothers.* Hartford, CT: Hudson & Skinner.

Spodek, B. (1973). *Early childhood education.* Englewood Cliffs, NJ: Prentice-Hall.

Spodek, B. (Ed.). (1982). *Handbook of research in early childhood education.* New York: Free Press.

Steinfels, M. O. (1973). *Who's minding the children?* New York: Simon & Schuster.

Thompson, W. R., & Grusec, J. (1970). Studies of early experience. In P. H. Mussen (Ed.), *Manual of child psychology* (3rd ed., Vol. 1, pp. 565–657). New York: Wiley.

Whitebook, M., Howes, C., & Phillips, D. (1989). *Who cares? Child care teachers and the quality of care in America* (Final Report, National Child Care Staffing Study). Oakland, CA: Child Care Employee Project.

Willer, B., Hofferth, S., Kisker, E., Divine-Hawkins, P., Farquhar, E., & Glantz, F. (1991). *The demand and supply of child care in 1990* (Joint Findings from the National Child Care Survey 1990 and A Profile of Child Care Settings). Washington, DC: National Association for the Education of Young Children.

Zigler, E. F., & Goodman, J. (1982). The battle for day care in America: A view from the trenches. In E. F. Zigler & E. W. Gordon (Eds.), *Day care: Scientific and social policy* (pp. 338–351). Boston: Auburn House.

CHILDREN *in* PERIL

GEOFFREY COWLEY

**American kids
remain
the most
neglected
in the
developed
world
—**

Children have never had it easy. A fair proportion have always been beaten, starved, raped or abandoned, and until quite recently even the loved ones faced daunting obstacles. At the beginning of this century, one American child in 10 didn't live to see a first birthday. Today, thanks to major strides in nutrition, sanitation and medical care, 99 out of 100 survive infancy. Yet astonishing numbers continue to die or suffer needlessly. Nearly one child in four is born into poverty, a formidable predictor of lifelong ill health, and a growing number lack such basic advantages as a home, two parents and regular access to a doctor. Every year thousands die violently, from abuse or preventable accidents. Millions go unvaccinated against common childhood diseases. Millions more are poisoned by cigarette smoke or household lead.

Decrying the situation has become a national pastime. Panels are assembled, studies conducted, articles written, speeches made. Yet by vital measures, American children remain the most neglected in the developed world. Their health and welfare are simply "not high on the agenda of this country," laments Dr. Reed Tuckson, a former Washington, D.C., health commissioner and now a vice president at the March of Dimes Birth Defects Foundation. "The federal government doesn't think this is as important as the savings and loan crisis." Here's proof.

Infant mortality

According to newly released government figures, 9.1 out of every 1,000 American babies died during infancy last year (down from 9.7 per 1,000 in 1989). Such rates are a far cry from India's 97 deaths per 1,000 or Guinea's 143, but they're among the highest in the industrialized world—and they don't apply equally to all Americans. The death rate for black infants (17.6 per 1,000 births as of 1988) is more than twice

that for whites (8.5 per 1,000). And some regions remain what the National Commission to Prevent Infant Mortality calls "disaster areas." Washington, Detroit and Philadelphia suffer higher infant-death rates than Jamaica or Costa Rica. Parts of the rural South fare even worse. "What we have here in the Mississippi delta is a Third World situation," says Mike Gibbs of Mississippi's Sharkey-Issaquena Health Alliance. Indeed, a baby born in Sharkey or Issaquena county is less likely to survive infancy than one born in Chile.

The main reason children die during infancy is that they're born too soon or too small. Babies with low birth weights (under 5.5 pounds) are 40 times more likely than others to die during their first month, and 20 times more likely to die within a year. Those who survive often grow up deaf, blind or mentally retarded. The problem has eminently preventable causes, including drug and alcohol abuse, smoking, poor nutrition and a lack of prenatal care. Yet low birth weight is as common today as it was a decade ago. Nearly 7 percent of all U.S. babies—a quarter million a year—are born too small. The rate is far higher, and rising, among minorities. In 1988 fully 13 percent of all black children came into the world dangerously underweight.

Substance abuse

Low birth weight is not the only effect of parental substance abuse. Fetal alcohol exposure is the nation's leading known cause of mental retardation, surpassing both Down syndrome and spina bifida. Cigarette smoke not only poisons developing fetuses—causing a quarter of all low birth weights and a tenth of all infant deaths—but disables children who breathe it growing up. Smokers' kids are at increased risk for many respiratory diseases, including asthma. And babies born to cocaine users suffer devastating neurological problems.

From *Newsweek*, Special Edition, Summer 1991, pp. 18-21. Copyright © 1991, Newsweek, Inc. All rights reserved. Reprinted by permission.

1. PERSPECTIVES: National

The number of fetuses exposed to tobacco and alcohol hasn't changed much lately; America produces 5,000 to 10,000 children with full-blown fetal alcohol syndrome each year, and 10 times that number may suffer the similar but less severe symptoms of fetal alcohol effect. By contrast, cocaine use rose ominously among young women during the 1980s. Though recent findings suggest the problem has peaked, experts guess that a million women of childbearing age use the drug and that 30,000 to 100,000 deliver cocaine-exposed babies each year. At New York's Harlem Hospital, the frequency of cocaine use among expectant mothers jumped from 1 percent in 1980 to 20 percent in 1988. A 1989 survey suggested that 17 percent of Philadelphia's babies were born exposed.

Contagion

Syphilis, gonorrhea and AIDS may sound like adult afflictions, but children are paying dearly for the surge in sexually transmitted diseases over the past decade. They're paying, too, for the decline of childhood immunization efforts. For less than $100 a child can gain immunity against polio, whooping cough, diphtheria, tetanus, measles, mumps and rubella. Virtually all America's kids receive these basic vaccines by the time they start school. Yet vast and growing numbers of 1- to 4-year-olds remain unvaccinated, especially in poor areas. Dr. Antoinette Eaton, president of the American Academy of Pediatrics (AAP), calls the situation "disastrous."

The government stopped tracking early-childhood immunization rates six years ago, but signs of trouble abound. As of 1985 the proportion of preschoolers receiving particular vaccines was 23 percent to 67 percent lower in this country than in Europe. Only half of America's 1- to 4-year-olds were being immunized against polio, according to the AAP, and a quarter received no vaccinations. Recent studies have identified inner-city neighborhoods where 50 to 70 percent of preschool children are unvaccinated. Not surprisingly, these lapses have triggered a major resurgence of once rare childhood diseases. Whooping cough is twice as common today as it was in 1970. Measles cases rose from 1,500 in 1983 to an astounding 25,000 last year.

Lead poisoning

This summer federal health officials are expected to acknowledge formally what researchers and activists have long maintained: that 3 million youngsters—one in six children under 7—have dangerous levels of lead in their blood. A standard ingredient in wall paint until the late 1970s, lead still pervades many households, and mounting evidence suggests that blood levels once considered safe can cause neurological damage. Many experts now consider it the nation's foremost environmental hazard.

Children don't have to eat paint chips to be poisoned; a more common source is the dust that falls from old walls and window panes. Experts are also wary of water systems, lead crystal and imported cans and ceramics. Babies exposed to low doses of lead in the womb tend to be underweight and underdeveloped at birth. During grade school, lead-exposed kids exhibit behavioral problems, low IQ and deficiencies in speech and language. And research has shown that teenagers with histories of lead exposure drop out of school seven times as often as their peers.

Lead poisoning is most prevalent among the least privileged—a 1988 study suggested that more than half of low-income black children are afflicted—yet the hazard extends far beyond the ghetto. The study found that in the group with the *lowest* risk—whites living outside central cities—one of every 11 children had high levels of lead in his blood. Officials at the federal Centers for Disease Control in Atlanta have recommended lead screening for all children under 6, yet only one in 10 receives it. If the agency redefines lead poisoning as expected, the demand for a national testing program will surely grow.

Injuries

No disease, drug or environmental hazard rivals traumatic injuries as a killer of children. Every year mishaps claim the lives of 8,000 American youngsters and permanently disable 50,000. Car and bicycle accidents are the main menace, with a death toll of 3,400. Burn injuries kill 1,300—and 1,200 drown. Others die from choking or falls or gunshot wounds. Though most of these injuries are unintentional, child advocates resist calling them accidents. "Our contention," says former surgeon general C. Everett Koop, now chairman of the national Safe Kids Campaign, "is that 90 percent of permanent childhood injuries can be prevented."

The challenge is simply to make parents more vigilant. Koop's campaign stresses such basic precautions as installing smoke alarms (9 out of 10 fire deaths occur in houses that lack them), keeping toddlers away from swimming pools, turning pot handles toward the back of the stove where kids can't reach them and getting children to wear bicycle helmets. According to the National Center for Health Statistics, nearly 70 percent of all hospitalized bicyclists are treated for head trauma. Helmets reduce the risk of brain injury by almost 90 percent—yet only 5 percent of young bike riders wear them.

Injury would seem an equal-opportunity hazard, yet black children die from injuries at nearly twice the rate of others. Koop blames inadequate supervision and a lack of medical care—which is to say he blames poverty. "When I look back on my years in office," he says, "the things I banged my head against were all poverty."

Poverty

Kids under 5 suffer more poverty than any other age group in America. Roughly one in four is poor, versus one in eight adults, and the consequences are manifold. Poor children are more likely to suffer from low birth weight, more likely to die during the first year of life, more likely to suffer hunger or abuse while growing up and less likely to benefit from immunizations or adequate medical care. Moreover, notes Dr. Peter Boelens of the Sharkey-Issaquena Health Alliance, poor kids grow up without ever "understanding what is necessary for healthy living."

Infant Mortality Rates

As of 1988, infant death was twice as common in the U.S. as in Japan. American black children were dying at twice the rate of whites. Selected rankings:

Country	Deaths per 1,000 live births
Japan	5.0
Switzerland	6.8
Singapore	7.0
Canada	7.3
France	7.7
East Germany	8.1
U.S. Whites	8.5
United Kingdom	8.8
All U.S.	10.0
Czechoslovakia	11.9
China	12.0
Nigeria	13.8
U.S. Blacks	17.6

SOURCES: STATISTICAL OFFICE OF THE UNITED NATIONS; NATIONAL CENTER FOR HEALTH STATISTICS

The First to Suffer

Young children endure more poverty than any other age group in the population.

Percent of children under 6 years who are poor

Percent of all people in U.S. who are poor

SOURCE: NATIONAL CENTER FOR CHILDREN IN POVERTY

Healthy People 2000, the federal government's public-health blueprint for the rest of the decade, seeks to reduce the nation's infant mortality rate to 7 deaths per 1,000 (from today's 9.1), to reduce the frequency of low birth weight to 5 percent (from today's 7 percent) and to ensure that 9 out of 10 (instead of 3 out of 4) expectant mothers get early prenatal care. Modest goals, yet few children's advocates expect them to be met. Too many better-armed interests are competing for the available federal dollars. "Children don't vote," says Florida Gov. Lawton Chiles, chairman of the National Commission to Prevent Infant Mortality, "and they do not contribute to political campaigns."

There are glimmers of hope. The Bush administration recently proposed a five-year, $171 million initiative to reduce infant mortality by half in 10 hard-hit cities—but proposed paying for it by taking money away from existing maternal and child-health programs. Congress blocked that move and has appropriated $25 million to fund the 10-city effort next year. No one is complaining, but the effort is only a start. "We want to encourage and celebrate Mr. Bush's initiative," says Tuckson, of the March of Dimes. "But if we recognize that reducing infant mortality is important, why not 20 cities?"

Or 40? There is no economy in neglecting children's health. Kids born underweight end up in intensive-care units, often at state expense. Many remain lifelong burdens to society. "Forget the humane reasons for providing prenatal health care," says Jennifer Howse, president of the March of Dimes. "There is a cold, hard business reason. It saves money."

With LARRY WILSON *in New York,*
MARY HAGER *and* STEVEN WALDMAN *in Washington*
and JOE DELANEY *in Carey, Miss.*

Homeless Children: A Special Challenge

Linda McCormick and Rita Holden

Linda Perkins McCormick, Ph.D., is professor of special education at the University of Hawaii. She has had a variety of jobs with children who have special needs.

Rita Holden earned her master's degree in special education at the University of Hawaii and is now working for the Hawaii State Planning Council on Developmental Disabilities.

K imo Kealoha is obviously very excited at the prospect of starting his first day of preschool. When asked what he wants to do at school, the tiny boy with large dark eyes says he wants to swing and to play in the sand. He shyly shows us a sheet of paper with a crooked "K" on it. "See, I can almost do my name."

Like other children across Hawaii, Kimo is eagerly looking forward to his first day of school. There is one difference where Kimo is concerned, however: Kimo is homeless. He lives with his mother and older sister in a

The authors acknowledge the Governor's Office of Children and Youth, State of Hawaii, and Homeless Aloha for their support for the survey and preparation of the report that generated the information for this article.

"tent city" in a city park. For six months, before the family was able to find space in the tent city, they lived in a car parked near one of the beaches. His mother feels lucky that they now at least have a canvas roof over their heads, but she doesn't know from one day to the next how long her family will be able to stay in the tent city or whether Kimo will be able to continue attending preschool. Sometimes Kimo goes to sleep hungry and arrives at preschool hungry and dirty, but it isn't because his mother doesn't care. She cares fiercely about giving her children what they need; however, she has little time to search for a job. Her priorities at this time are ensuring that her children are safe and trying to make sure that they have food and access to someplace to sleep and wash.

Every day in America, hundreds of thousands of children wake up homeless, through no fault of their own. There is no single cause of homelessness; there are many contributors. The decreasing supply of low-income housing is most often cited as an important contributor (Children's Defense Fund, 1988; Eddows & Hranitz, 1989).

The McKinney Act* defines a homeless person as "an individual who lacks a fixed, regular, and adequate nighttime residence; or has a primary nighttime residence that is a publicly operated shelter, an institution providing temporary shelter, or a public or private place not designed for the accommodation of human beings." The definition provided by La Gory, Ritchey, and Mullis (1987) is more succinct. They describe a homeless person as "anyone whose night residence is in a shelter, on the street, or in another public place." It can be argued that this definition should be broadened to include persons who are "precariously housed" (e.g., living in doubled-up families).

It is unfortunate that opinions concerning the homeless seem to be based more on prejudice and misinformation than on fact. The notion that the problem has roots in bungled deinstitutionalization policies is an example of questionable information. In reality, the problem is much broader than lack of community services for the mentally ill. Mentally ill adults are only 1 of 10 subgroups that Marin (1988) has identified within the homeless population.

While Marin's list is not inclusive, it shows the diversity of the homeless population. (Keep in

* The McKinney Act, passed in 1987 (amendments passed 1988), provides states with funds to assist the homeless, including assistance to schools to assure that each child of a homeless family has access to free public education.

From *Young Children,* Vol. 47, No. 6, September 1992, pp. 61-67. Reprinted by permission of the publisher, the National Association for the Education of Young Children.

Homeless parents say they need preschools that provide transportation or assistance with transportation, acceptance of their children without lots of red tape, "more than babysitting"—e.g., a developmental and educational program, and respite care (evenings and weekends).

mind that the subgroups are not mutually exclusive.) The subgroups are (1) veterans (primarily from Vietnam); (2) persons with mental retardation or mental illness; (3) persons who are physically disabled or chronically ill; (4) elderly persons on fixed incomes; (5) skilled persons (singles and families) without a source of income because of a recent loss of job; (6) unskilled single parents (often women who have been abused); (7) runaway children (many of whom have been abused); (8) alcoholics and drug-dependent persons; (9) immigrants (legal *and* illegal); and (10) traditional tramps, hobos, and other transients.

Researchers disagree on the actual number of homeless families in the United States; however, there is universal agreement that the number is growing everywhere (Bassuk & Rubin, 1987; Rossi, 1990). In Hawaii, where the interviews in this survey took place, the count was 1238 homeless families in 1989 (SMS Research and Marketing Services, Inc., 1990). This may not seem like a large number until you consider that Hawaii has a population of only slightly over one million people.

This article considers three issues: (1) developmental and behavioral characteristics of homeless young children and their parents, (2) how states and communities are attempting to meet the early education and care needs of young children in homeless families, and (3) the needs or problems that early education and care programs should address. Sources of information for this article included a literature review, a survey of programs across the country that are attempting to meet the early education and care needs of children in homeless families, and interviews with major stakeholders concerned with services for young children in homeless families. These stakeholders were parents who are homeless, teachers in preschools serving children in families who are homeless, and directors of shelters for the homeless in Hawaii. Finally, the article presents recommendations that were generated from interviews with homeless families, shelter directors, and preschool personnel. These recommendations include establishing early childhood services for children and families who are homeless and modifying staff development to prepare early childhood personnel to better meet the needs of this population.

Characteristics of the population

Most of the growing body of literature on the homeless deals with health concerns. Relatively few studies consider the educational needs and characteristics of homeless children, and fewer still specifically address the needs of infants and preschoolers. We decided not to review studies dealing with battered women and their children or low-income families. Certainly these groups are not mutually exclusive; however, there are not sufficient data at this time to risk generalizing across the three populations. That common issues exist across the groups seems likely, but it is equally likely that the condition of homelessness may create distinct characteristics and problems that need specific attention apart from the problems of either poverty or family violence.

While most of the available data describe school-age children, there *are* data dealing with preschoolers (particularly preschoolers who are living with their parents in shelters). Data collection methods and sample sizes varied widely in the studies that generated these descriptive data. The information presented in this article summarizes the many studies that were reviewed. A proportion of the young children in homeless families have been observed to have the following characteristics:

• higher levels of problem behavior than children their age who are not homeless *and* higher levels than older children in the same shelters (Hughes, 1986);

• one or more developmental delays serious enough to warrant referral and further evaluation (Bassuk & Rubin, 1987);

• severe depression, anxiety, and learning difficulties (Bassuk & Rubin, 1987);

• more sleep problems, shyness, withdrawal, and aggression compared to same-age peers who are not homeless *and* diagnosed emotional disturbance (Bassuk & Rubin, 1987);

• severe separation problems, characterized by panic states, hysterical crying, vomiting, and severe anxiety interfering with the ability to participate in routine activities (Grant, 1990);

• poor-quality (superficial) relationships, sleep disturbances (many children engaged in oppositional and disruptive behavior in an effort to avoid napping), and short attention span (Grant, 1990);

• signs of emotional disturbance, including severe tantrums, dangerously aggressive and destructive behavior, extreme withdrawal, elective mutism, violent mood swings, and oppositional and manipulative behavior serious enough to interfere with peer relationships and readiness to learn (Grant, 1990); and

• significant delays in gross-motor development (particularly problems in movement through space and spatial relationships), speech and language development (particularly restrictions in expressive language and vocabulary development), and cognitive development (particularly with tasks requiring sequencing and organization) (Grant, 1990).

Bassuk and Rubin (1987) reported that almost 90% of the families in their sample were headed by a single mother. The median age for the mothers was 27 years of age. Others' studies (e.g., Wood, Valdez, Hayashi, & Shen, 1990) report that one-half or more of their sample of homeless families is composed of two-parent families. The reason that some studies underestimate the proportion of two-parent families may be related to the tendency to question only shelter directors or other "key" informants rather than the homeless family members. Two-parent families may falsely report themselves as single-parent families in order to qualify for services, including emergency shelter.

Among the characteristics associated with parents in homeless families are the following:

• maternal drug and alcohol abuse and psychiatric problems much greater than are found among mothers living in public or private subsidized housing (Bassuk & Rosenberg, 1988);

• a history of abuse as children and battering as adults (Bassuk & Rosenberg, 1988);

• fragmented support networks (Bassuk & Rosenberg, 1988); and

• a greater likelihood of having no health insurance coverage, having no preventive health care, and be-

Shelter directors say many parents are afraid that their children will be taken away from them, that homeless children are especially in need of help with social skills, and that many parents may not seem to be nurturing because, as children, they weren't nurtured themselves.

ing smokers than is found among nonhomeless poor (Winkleby, 1990).

What states are doing

A request for information about programs and services for preschoolers in homeless families was posted on SpecialNet (an electronic bulletin board) on three separate dates in the fall of 1990. Most of the responses to the SpecialNet message were referrals to other sources; all of these were followed up with requests for program information. The fact that these efforts were not very productive may be an indication that not many programs exist that identify themselves as specifically for preschoolers in homeless families. Despite many queries over a four-month period, we were able to collect information on only seven programs: three in Massachusetts, two in Georgia, one in Washington, and one in Missouri.

The information accumulated from these programs indicates wide variability in funding sources, community location, and programming. Some programs are on-site at the shelters, while others are located elsewhere. The major commonality across programs is the focus on the family as a whole, as evidenced by the availability of a range of services for parents and the opportunities for parent involvement in the programs. Services for families are directed to helping them meet broad family needs (either by providing these services directly or by providing information and referral services). Several of the contacts

yielded information with helpful programming suggestions, which influenced formulation of the recommendations presented below.

What stakeholders want

Three groups of persons were interviewed to determine the needs or problems that early education and care programs should address: homeless families, shelter directors, and staff members in programs presently serving young children from homeless families. Parents residing in four shelters were interviewed individually and in small groups at shelter sites. Also, a significant number of nonsheltered homeless parents were identified and interviewed. Contact with these parents was made through an organization serving nonsheltered homeless persons. (In Hawaii, most of these families are living on one of the beaches.) Directors of most of the state shelters were also interviewed.

The interview format was altered somewhat depending on the interviewees, but the issues were the same. Stakeholders were asked

• What is needed/wanted in the way of preschool education and care for children whose families are homeless?

• What do preschool personnel need to know or be able to do to best serve children whose families are homeless?

Parents' responses. There was consensus among the parents when asked what they need (or what they want) in the way of preschool education and care. They want/need the following:

- **Assistance with transportation.** Problems associated with arranging transportation came up repeatedly. One suggestion was monthly bus passes or bus tokens.

- **Day care with a developmental child care orientation.** Parents emphasized that their children need "more than babysitting."

- **Respite care.** Parents would like respite available in the evenings, during the day, and after school. They would like immediate respite help when they need it, and they felt that they should not have to always explain why it is needed.

- **Preschools that take children without "red tape."** Parents noted the need for "streamlining" the program intake process (doing away with complicated forms). Services should be available as soon as assessment requirements have been satisfied.

- **On-site schools.** This was the only issue on which there was some difference of opinion among parents (and some difference of opinion between parents and teachers, as discussed below).

- **Opportunities to share with one another.** Parents expressed a desire for meetings and other opportunities to share feelings and generally "talk story" with other parents.

- **Flexibility related to involvement/participation.** Parents want the opportunity to be involved, and they also want the freedom *not* to be involved with whatever program is provided for their preschoolers. They would like the flexibility to sometimes use the time when their children are in an early childhood program to do other things, such as take classes, do grocery shopping, go on job interviews, and so forth.

- **Mental health services.** Parents emphasized the need for mental health services for their children and for themselves. One parent mentioned the need for "self-esteem groups."

- **Information about available services.** Parents said they have a difficult time finding out what is available for their children. They want information about available preschool, day care, and respite services (e.g., costs, how to qualify, and so forth), particularly about funding options and transportation arrangements.

- **Classes.** Parents asked for classes on parenting, CPR, birth control, first aid, and nutrition.

As noted above, the only difference of opinion had to do with on-site versus off-site early childhood programs. Interviewees typically gave a reason or reasons for their preference. Parents' reasons for preferring early childhood programming at the same location as the shelter tended to center around their concerns about transportation. Some teachers who stated a preference for early childhood services to be provided in a location away from the shelter seemed particularly concerned about maintaining health and safety standards. Other teachers were concerned with providing opportunities for children to learn to separate from their parents. Another concern about setting up on-site programs related to the drawbacks of homogeneous grouping. There was concern that young children (*and* parents) classified as homeless not be segregated in such a manner that they could be stigmatized and denied opportunities for interactions with peers who are not homeless.

The "tone" of responses related to the issue of on-site versus off-site programs was perhaps more important than the words. The general impression was that location

---

Parents were very specific when asked what preschool personnel need to know or be able to do in order to provide quality services. Parents want preschool staff to know that

- children are embarrassed about being homeless;
- parents are dealing with many problems in addition to homelessness and their child's care (e.g., spouse abuse, depression, no money);
- even parents who may seem distracted really care about their children (just as much as do parents who have permanent housing);
- it is very stressful, difficult, and time consuming to have to organize transportation every day;
- most questions seem unnecessarily intrusive, and they make parents feel uncomfortable (because the reasons for the questions are usually not clear);
- children (and parents) should not be asked about absences or length of stay in a program (because they do not want to discuss these things, and they may not know when relocation will be necessary);
- parents would prefer—for whatever special educational and developmental services children need—to "just be provided" without blaming anyone or making a big issue of the problem;
- requests for children to bring baked goods or other goodies and school supplies often constitute a great hardship for families; and
- being homeless does not necessarily mean that a family is dysfunctional.

Shelter directors were asked what they would like to share with early childhood program personnel. They want early childhood professionals to know that

• many parents are afraid that their child(ren) will be taken away from them;
• homeless children are especially in need of help with social skills; and
• the reason many parents may not seem to be nurturing is that they do not know how to nurture (because they were not nurtured themselves as children).

Preschool personnel who have dealt with homeless children made some important points. They wanted to share this information with early childhood colleagues:

• Homeless children are more similar to their peers than they are different. The same basic good teaching practices and activities are generally effective with these youngsters.
• Peer friendships have to be actively encouraged. Do not assume that they will occur naturally.
• Play is particularly important. These children typically have no time or place for play when they are not at the center.
• Homeless children (like their peers) need a feeling of being competent and in control. Provide appropriate choices *and* challenges in a maximally supportive atmosphere.
• Stress is unavoidable when you are homeless. Some children may seem to be coping, but none are impervious to the stresses that being homeless places on the family.
• Even the most basic health and safety concerns may seem overwhelming to already overstressed parents. Be patient and sensitive or they will withdraw.

---

is not as much an issue as ensuring a high-quality program that serves families from diverse socioeconomic backgrounds and does not segregate the homeless.

Recommendations

The following recommendations for early education and care programs reflect input from all three stakeholder groups.

Persons working with homeless children and families need a mechanism for networking and sharing. One possibility would be task forces at the state level and at the district or community level in which people concerned with early childhood services for homeless children could build partnerships with one another and with parents.

Programs must be maximally flexible about scheduling. They need to open earlier and perhaps remain open later so as to meet the needs of parents with nontraditional work schedules. In addition to early education and care programs, there should be a range of available respite care options.

Funds must be made available to help with transportation expenses (if transportation cannot be provided). It will be necessary to seek more creative solutions to transportation problems (e.g., "taxi-pooling" and vans).

Programs must provide (or arrange for) social and case management services. Families need help to work out arrangements for resolving family problems, securing permanent housing, and preventing future homeless episodes. If programs cannot provide these services, they need to advocate for them and give full cooperation to whatever initiatives other agencies have in place for the family.

The following were recommendations for individuals and agencies concerned with providing preservice or in-service training for early childhood personnel who will serve children of homeless families. The stakeholders felt that staff development should
• **Emphasize the nature of the problems faced by homeless persons and their children.** Training should include viewing a tape that depicts life in a shelter or visiting sites where there are homeless families. Most important is understanding what life is like for these children when they are not in the early childhood center.
• **Emphasize that homeless children are similar in most ways to their peers who are not homeless.** Homeless children should not be singled out because of their homelessness. Support each child's individuality and help the child to feel that she is a part of the group. A major goal is to learn how to provide a secure and predictable environment where homeless children feel as psychologically safe and appreciated as do their peers. Quality early childhood services enhance the lives of all young children. These services are absolutely imperative for children when there are multiple risk factors in the family's environment.

• Emphasize that homeless children may need special attention for specific developmental delays and emotional problems. Teachers must be alert to signs of poor self-esteem, feelings of helplessness, anxiety, depression, and problems related to making friends. Teachers should be encouraged to make the effort to establish a special relationship with the homeless child—help the child feel important and worthwhile. Self-esteem-building activities are especially important for these children, who tend to have fragile self-concepts. Provide safe outlets for the child to express his feelings through art, music, puppets, clay, and other creative modes.

• Emphasize that parents may need a great deal of support and encouragement to participate in the program or in self-help classes. Early childhood personnel have a critical role in the lives of homeless children and their families because they can provide a buffering social support. The quality and stability of the support they provide can go a long way to mediate family stress.

• Emphasize that children and parents especially need the support of center staff when the family moves to more permanent housing arrangements. Change is stressful. Once the family has made the transition to permanent housing, the person who is coordinating social services will assist the family to form a support network in the new community and will help to get the children enrolled in appropriate early childhood and/or school programs. Early childhood personnel can smooth this transition by preparing the child for the new program and remaining available as friends for the child and the family.

• Emphasize skills for collaboration and communication among professionals as well as parent-professional partnerships. Unlike most housed families, homeless families typically have a number of past and present service providers who may not necessarily be apprised of one another's activities. The only solution to fragmented services and service overlap is communication.

• Emphasize the importance of sensitivity and vigilance so as not to embarrass children or their families. All training in early childhood education stresses the importance of sensitivity; it must continue to be a primary focus in staff development. Help these children by (1) using every opportunity to model self-control and coping skills; (2) helping children (and their parents) to see that they are not alone in having uncomfortable feelings; (3) letting children know that it is okay to feel angry, scared, lonely, or sad; (4) giving children the words to express their feelings; and (5) enhancing each child's (and parent's) self-esteem.

Conclusion

We enter the twenty-first century with a heightened sensitivity to family issues, including the plight of homeless families. Early childhood personnel have a critical role in the lives of young children and their families. Because of this we have an opportunity (and an obligation) to begin a program of action for young children and their families who are homeless. Homeless children have special needs, as do all children at one time or another in their lives.

References

Bassuk, E.L., & Rubin, L. (1987). Homeless children: A neglected population. *American Journal of Orthopsychiatry, 57*(2), 279–286.

Bassuk, E.L., & Rosenberg, L. (1988). Why does family homelessness occur? A case-control study. *American Journal of Public Health, 78*(7), 783–788.

Children's Defense Fund. (1988). A children's defense budget (FY 1989). Washington, DC: Author.

Eddowes, A.E., & Hranitz, J.R. (1989, Summer). Educating children of the homeless. *Childhood Education,* 197–200.

Grant, R. (1990). The special needs of homeless children: Early intervention at a welfare hotel. *Topics in Early Childhood Special Education, 10*(4), 76–91.

Hughes, H.M. (1986, March–April). Research with children in shelters: Implications for clinical services. *Children Today,* 21–25.

La Gory, M., Ritchey, F., & Mullis, J. (1987). *The homeless of Alabama* (Final Report of the Homeless Enumeration and Survey Project). Birmingham, AL: University of Alabama at Birmingham, Department of Sociology.

Marin, P. (1988). Helping and hating the homeless. *Harper's Magazine, 1*(87), 40.

Rossi, P.H. (1990). The old homeless and the new homelessness in historical perspective. *American Psychologist, 45*(8), 954–959.

SMS Research and Marketing Services, Inc. (1990). *Hawaii's homeless.* (Report prepared for Hawaii Housing Authority).

Stewart B. McKinney Homeless Assistance Amendments Act. Public Law 100–628. (1988).

Winkleby, M.A. (1990). Comparison of risk factors for ill health in a sample of homeless and non homeless poor. *American Journal of Public Health, 80*(9), 1049–1052.

Wood, D., Valdez, R.B., Hayashi, T., & Shen, A. (1990). Homeless and housed families in Los Angeles: A case study comparing demographic, economic, and family function characteristics. *Public Health Reports, 105*(4), 404–410.

Teachers who have had experience with homeless children say that of course they are more like other children than different from them, but that they have some special needs that must be met, particularly emotional needs.

Prenatal Exposure to Cocaine and Other Drugs: Developmental and Educational Prognoses

Mr. Griffith reminds us that "crack babies" are not some new breed of children that we have never seen before; they are simply children. Moreover, their problems are ones that creative teachers have successfully handled for many years.

By Dan R. Griffith

CHILDREN exposed to cocaine prenatally have become a major focus of the national media and a major concern for educators across the country. To put the matter bluntly, the media have sensationalized the problems these children present and have shown worst-case scenarios as if they were the norm. Television and news-

DAN R. GRIFFITH is a clinical associate in the Department of Psychiatry and Behavioral Sciences, Northwestern University Medical School, Evanston, Ill. He was formerly a developmental psychologist with the National Association for Perinatal Addiction, Chicago. He does independent consulting from his office in Park Ridge, Ill.

paper accounts of so-called crack babies describe — and sometimes display — tiny, premature, tube- and wire-laden infants screaming and trembling uncontrollably. Media accounts of older "crack kids" describe them as unable to learn, unable to love, hyperactive, hyperaggressive, and without a conscience.

The media coverage to date has served a positive role in increasing public awareness of the potential harmful effects of substance abuse during pregnancy. However, the narrow focus on prenatal cocaine exposure as the sole cause of the problems experienced by the most severely affected children has created a faulty perception of the problems of most children who were exposed to drugs before birth. Three erroneous assumptions, are common: 1) that all cocaine-exposed children are severely affected, 2) that little can be done for them, and 3) that all the medical, behavioral, and learning problems exhibited by these children are caused directly by their exposure to cocaine.

The truth of the matter is that there has been too little research done to date on children exposed prenatally to cocaine to make any firm statement about the long-term prognosis for them. A few other researchers and I have found differences between cocaine-exposed infants as a group and nonexposed infants as a group. But when such differences are reported, it is

extremely important to realize that these are "group differences," not stereotypical descriptions that fit every cocaine-exposed infant. In fact, the effects vary dramatically from infant to infant and child to child and may be moderated considerably or exacerbated by other risk factors to which an individual child has been exposed.

In this article I will try to dispel some of the myths and stereotypes surrounding cocaine-exposed infants and children. I will also provide readers with tools to enable them to become better consumers of information concerning this problem, whether from researchers or from the media.

MAJOR RISK FACTORS

During the prenatal period it is common for chronic substance-abusing women to receive little or no prenatal care and to have inadequate prenatal nutrition. Each of these factors increases the likelihood of problems during pregnancy and is predictive of developmental difficulties for the child. Lack of prenatal care and poor prenatal nutrition together often lead to low birth weight and/or significant prematurity, factors that further reduce the infant's chances for optimal development.

In addition, a number of postnatal risk factors are related to substance abuse. Probably the major one is continued use

From *Phi Delta Kappan*, September 1992, pp. 30-34. Reprinted by permission of the author and *Phi Delta Kappan*.

of drugs by one or both parents after the birth of the child. Continued drug use by parents may affect the consistency and predictability of parental behavior toward the child. Parents may interact very differently with their children depending on whether they are intoxicated, sober, or recovering from a binge. Chronic heavy drug abuse is associated with an increased incidence of neglect or abuse of the child. This neglect may include poor postnatal nutrition for the child, poor medical care, and an impoverished learning environment. The potential for postnatal drug exposure in the forms of passive inhalation of smokable drugs and/or the accidental oral ingestion of drugs is a final major risk factor associated with the parents' continued drug use. We have no information to date on how these postnatal exposures may affect the development of children.

Many states have attempted to avoid the risks to children of continued parental substance abuse by placing the children in foster homes. However, this solution is not without risk. The systems of foster care in most parts of the country are already overwhelmed by the numbers of children who need placement. Consequently, infants and children are spending significant portions of their lives in "boarder nurseries" or so-called temporary shelters, where they are unable to form lasting attachments because of staff shift changes and high ratios of children to caretakers. Those children lucky enough to be placed in foster homes may go to foster parents who have not been adequately trained to meet the children's special needs. The untrained foster parents are often overwhelmed by the demands of caring for children with special needs, and many of them ultimately return the children to the child protective agency.

Because of the scarcity of suitable placements, those foster parents who have received special training are often given more children than they can handle, so that even trained foster parents become frustrated and eventually burn out. As a result, many drug-exposed children are shifted through multiple placements. It is not uncommon for children to have several placements within the first few years of life. This trauma of attachment, separation, loss, and grief — repeated again and again — results in emotional and behavioral problems for children who have never been exposed to drugs. Sorting out the additional impact of drug exposure is problematic.

DEVELOPMENTAL PATTERNS OF DRUG-EXPOSED CHILDREN

Since April 1986 my colleagues at the National Association for Perinatal Addiction Research and Education and I have been following the developmental progress of more than 300 cocaine/polydrug-exposed children as part of a research study funded by the National Institute on Drug Abuse.

This research project represents a best-case scenario of the impact of prenatal exposure to cocaine on the fetus and developing child. In order to isolate the effects of prenatal exposure to cocaine, other major risk factors have been reduced or eliminated. Because of these special conditions, it is difficult to generalize this research to the entire population of "cocaine-exposed" infants. It may also be a misnomer to describe these infants as "cocaine-exposed," because the majority of women in the study abused other drugs in addition to cocaine. Therefore, I will refer to the children in our research project as "cocaine/polydrug-exposed" children.

Cocaine/polydrug-abusing women were recruited into this project during the early phases of their pregnancies and were provided with prenatal care, nutritional counseling, and therapy for chemical dependence. As a result of receiving good prenatal care and adequate prenatal nutrition, the majority of the infants in this project were carried to full term. Even those infants who were premature were seldom born more than three or four weeks early.

Group differences between the cocaine/polydrug-exposed infants and the nonexposed infants are most apparent during the first few weeks following birth. The drug-exposed infants display disorganized nervous systems that interfere with their ability to regulate their own states of arousal. In particular, drug-exposed infants may have difficulty reaching and maintaining the "quiet alert" state during which infants are best able to process and respond to their external environments. Caretakers can be taught to help these disorganized infants achieve alert states using a variety of comforting techniques, including swaddling, pacifiers, and vertical rocking.

Once drug-exposed infants achieve a state of quiet alertness, they may display low thresholds for overstimulation. Normal levels of environmental stimulation, including caretakers' efforts to interact

socially with the infants, may overwhelm their abilities to regulate themselves. Once overstimulated, some drug-exposed infants withdraw from the offending environment by entering a state of deep sleep as a form of self-protection. Other affected infants are unable to protect themselves and will continue to attend until they are pushed into a hyperaroused, disorganized state of crying.

Recognizing the threshold of overstimulation has proven to be one of the single most important concepts in dealing with the early problems of drug-exposed infants and in developing appropriate treatments. Once the threshold for overstimulation has been exceeded, many drug-exposed infants become the disorganized, chaotic, screaming infants often presented by the media. These same infants, however, can be kept below the threshold of overstimulation with careful regulation of the levels of stimulation surrounding them. When kept below this threshold, the infants can maintain their alert states and practice and improve their abilities to self-regulate while attending to the environment.

The key to assisting drug-exposed infants in their development of self-regulation skills lies in teaching caretakers how to read the distress signals that indicate that the infants are approaching the threshold of overstimulation. When caretakers are overstimulating infants during social interactions, for example, the infants will avert their eyes in an effort to give themselves time to recover from the stimulation. If the caretakers continue to push the infants, the infants may yawn (indicating further distress), then sneeze, hiccup, breathe faster, change color, increase motor movement, and finally begin crying. If the caretakers respond to the early cues by allowing the infants to take a time-out and thus regain their composure, the infants are able to sustain longer interactions, and the caretakers receive the rewards of responsive infants.

At this point, it is important to emphasize several points concerning the characteristics of and interventions for drug-exposed infants. First, not every drug-exposed infant has self-regulatory problems or a low threshold for overstimulation. Second, not every infant who displays these characteristics is drug-exposed. There are many factors other than prenatal drug exposure that may contribute to self-regulation difficulties in infants. Third, the techniques described here for calming and engaging drug-exposed infants are useful for any infant with similar problems. Fourth, with these techniques and highly motivated mothers, even the most severely affected of the drug-exposed infants in this project improved in their abilities to self-regulate while interacting with the environment. Finally, positive side effects of these techniques are increased feelings of competence, confidence, and self-esteem among the caretakers, combined with a greater affection for and enjoyment of the infants.

In our project we have followed the cocaine/polydrug-exposed infants into their preschool years. Assessments using the Bayley Scales of Infant Development at ages 3, 6, 12, 18, and 24 months have indicated very little difference between the average scores of the cocaine/polydrug-exposed group and those of the nonexposed group. By age 3 there were no differences in the overall performance of the cocaine/polydrug-exposed children and the drug-free children on the Stanford-Binet Intelligence Scale (4th edition).

Just as it is important not to overgeneralize negative outcomes for cocaine/polydrug-exposed children, it is equally important not to overgeneralize positive findings of our study. As I mentioned above, the children in our study have not been exposed to the same risk factors as other cocaine/polydrug-exposed children. Their mothers had good prenatal care and nutrition. The children themselves had good postnatal nutrition and health care; received regular screening, diagnosis, and treatment for any medical or developmental problems; and were in stable caretaking environments.

Our research project has found that, with early intervention and the reduction of other major risk factors, the majority of cocaine/polydrug-exposed children seem completely normal with regard to intellectual, social, emotional, and behavioral development through age 3. This is not to say, however, that none of the drug-exposed children displayed problems. The average head circumference of cocaine/polydrug-exposed children was significantly lower at birth than that of nonexposed children and continued to be lower through the first three years. Head circumference is the best single indicator of normal brain growth and development. A small head size at birth that fails to catch up is a significant predictor of poor development.

INDIVIDUAL DEVELOPMENT

When one looks beyond global test scores into the individual behavior and development of each child, it becomes obvious that a number of the cocaine/polydrug-exposed children display problems. By the age of 3 about one-third of the drug-exposed children in our study displayed delays in normal language development and/or problems in attention and self-regulation.

Of those children showing language delays, there was considerable variation in the severity and specific nature of the language problems. However, most of the children have responded well to speech therapy. Research is currently under way to explore in detail the type and severity of speech and language problems in this population.

The majority of attention/behavioral problems seen in cocaine/polydrug-exposed preschoolers are quite similar in appearance to the self-regulatory problems seen in drug-exposed infants. Those children who display problems have low thresholds for overstimulation and low levels of tolerance for frustration. They are able to post normal scores in one-to-one testing situations, but they have difficulty regulating their behavior in more complex situations. When overwhelmed by environmental stimulation, some children with self-regulatory problems withdraw from the stressful situation either physically or emotionally. Others lose control, displaying heightened activity and impulsivity. Still other children may display both extremes of behavior. These bipolar children appear to recognize their oncoming loss of control and try to avoid it by withdrawing from the situation that is causing them stress. This works effectively if the children withdraw soon enough in their arousal cycle, but if the children are already too near threshold or if someone or something prevents them from withdrawing, they will lose control.

Withdrawal or loss of behavioral control in children with self-regulatory problems may be triggered by a number of environmental situations and stimuli. Anything that increases the inconsistency and decreases the predictability of a child's environment (e.g., multiple caregivers, multiple placements, or continued substance abuse by a caregiver) will probably exacerbate the self-regulatory difficulties of children with problems and create such difficulties in children who were

> The most useful tool for developing intervention strategies for the individual child is the behavioral log.

previously good self-regulators. Children who have difficulty regulating themselves also have a hard time coping with transitions and changes in their lives. Such children may display adequate regulatory abilities in a familiar environment, but they can lose those abilities when presented with new environments or new demands or routines in an otherwise familiar environment.

As was the case with infants with self-regulatory difficulties, for the majority of older children with these problems the threshold of loss of control is the major focal point for intervention. It is not that the older children have no ability to self-regulate. However, they often require environments that help them stay below threshold, as well as caretaker assistance in developing self-regulation strategies.

The first step in helping children learn self-regulation is to provide them with consistent and predictable environments. With stable routines, rules, discipline, and nurturance — whether at home or at school — children know what to expect from caretakers and others around them. This confidence in the environment frees them to concentrate on controlling internal states of arousal and impulses. During those times when they must be exposed to new environments or new tasks, it is essential to anticipate their problems and assist them in maintaining control by providing more one-to-one attention, guidance, and structure.

These general techniques will improve the self-regulation abilities of all children. However, children differ considerably with regard to which environmental events trigger difficulties and which interventions are most effective. The most useful tool for developing intervention strategies for the individual child is the behavioral log. The first step in keeping such a log is to define a target behavior to be tracked by an observer. Once the target behavior has been selected, the observer should record every occurrence of it over a period of several days. In order to have a realistic chance of recording every instance of a behavior, it is essential to select only those behaviors that are clearly defined, easily observable, and important indicators of the problem.

Along with each occurrence of the target behavior, the observer should record as much information as possible concerning what was happening prior to the target behavior. Special attention should be paid to environmental events that may have triggered the target behavior, as well as to those behaviors that may be early signs of an impending loss of control. By discovering behavioral triggers, one can reduce the occurrence of problem behaviors either by removing the trigger or by desensitizing the child to that trigger. By identifying early warning behaviors, one can intervene before the child has lost control.

Many caretakers make the mistake of waiting to intervene until a child's behavior is so severe that it cannot be ignored. This strategy is especially problematic with children who have self-regulatory difficulties. Their most severe behaviors occur after their level of arousal has exceeded their threshold of self-regulation. Once a child has passed this threshold, most interventions will be ineffective, and the child is likely to be incapable of understanding the caretaker's attempts at intervention. This sets up both the child and the caretaker for frustration and further loss of control. Conversely, when the caretaker intervenes early in the child's arousal cycle, more severe behavioral problems will be avoided, and the child is still at an arousal level conducive to learning.

Finally, the observer should record the caretaker's responses to the target behaviors, as well as the effectiveness of each response in controlling the child's behavior. This will provide a record of which caretaker responses are effective and which may actually increase the child's frustration and arousal level.

SOME ILLUSTRATIONS

The following case should serve to illustrate these points. A 2½-year-old child

whose development I was following was having severe behavioral problems every evening. His mother reported that he became uncontrollable every afternoon. He ran around the house, breaking and destroying things and engaging in behaviors that were likely to harm him or other members of the family. From the onset of these behaviors until he fell asleep from exhaustion several hours later, he had to be monitored continually by one or both parents.

Keeping a behavioral log made it apparent that this child's behavior was under reasonable control most of the day, while he was home alone with his mother. His loss of control was triggered by the return of his older siblings from school. When the older boys came home they would roughhouse and generally "blow off steam" from having been cooped up in school all day. Once they had acted out for a while, they would calm down and be ready for normal family activities. Their little brother, however, was getting caught up in this rough play and was quickly exceeding his threshold of self-regulation. Once he had passed his threshold, he could not regain control, no matter what his parents did. His mother was able to stop his loss of control by creating structured activities for the three boys to engage in when the older boys arrived home. By adding structure and predictability to the transition period at the end of the school day, she was able to assist her youngest son in maintaining control.

A further benefit that emerged from the behavioral log for this same child was that the mother learned to recognize the early warning signs for his loss of control. During the day, he occasionally lost his ability to self-regulate, and the log demonstrated that such losses were usually preceded by increases in both the rate and the randomness of the child's activity. The mother discovered that, if she sat him down at the first signs of increasing arousal and played a game with him, she could help him avoid most of his severe behavioral outbursts.

One intervention that was particularly effective at calming this child was playing with toy cars and a toy garage. After a few weeks of using this intervention to control the child's behavior, his mother noticed that he began to use this strategy to self-regulate. If he was playing and felt himself becoming overaroused, he would sit down and play with his cars and garage until he felt calm.

> It is important to help children develop new coping strategies before removing their current strategies.

This illustrates two principles that are important in dealing with children with self-regulatory problems. First, the child does not want to be out of control any more than a caretaker wants him or her to be. Second, by intervening early in the arousal cycle, one can catch the child while the arousal level is low enough not to hinder learning. The child is thus able to learn to recognize warning signs and to learn adaptive self-regulation strategies.

A final consideration in constructing a behavioral log is what function if any the target behavior serves. Sometimes what is perceived as "bad behavior" is actually the child's method for coping with increasing arousal levels and for avoiding further loss of control. For example, a 4-year-old child was referred to me because he was "out of control in the classroom," had been cocaine-exposed prenatally, and was becoming increasingly aggressive toward the teacher.

When this little boy arrived for testing, my first impression was that he was nothing like what the teacher had described. He was friendly, polite, and, during the early phases of testing, extremely cooperative. However, after about five minutes of testing had been completed, the child announced that he was done. I tried to persuade him otherwise by redirecting his attention to different items, pushing the table a little closer to him, and asking him to try a few more things. This attempt to make him continue when he wanted to quit was met with a behavioral outburst, including screaming, kicking, and shoving at the table. I immediately pulled the table away, at which time the child ran out of the room.

I assumed that the testing phase of the evaluation was over and started writing notes on the child's behavior. A few minutes later, however, the little boy returned to the room and said that he was ready to continue. After another 10 minutes or so of testing, the child again said, "I'm done now," to which I replied, "That's fine." The child calmly got out of his chair, walked around the room for a minute, and then sat down to resume testing. This pattern was repeated several times, all testing was completed, and the child scored in the superior range for intellectual reasoning.

It was easy to see in a one-to-one testing situation that this child recognized the limits to his concentration and coped with increasing frustration by briefly removing himself from the frustrating situation. It is equally easy to see, however, how this behavior created problems in the classroom. By wandering around, he would be disrupting the learning of other children. When the teacher tried to make him sit back down, she was increasing his frustration by removing from him the one method he had developed for coping. The result was that the teacher and the child became locked in a power struggle. Each repeatedly frustrated the other to the point that the teacher was exasperated and angry with the child and the child lost control and would hit or kick the teacher.

This example highlights two important points to consider when dealing with cocaine-exposed children who have self-regulatory problems. First, it has been said that cocaine-exposed children are hyperaggressive. But the truth of the matter is that some cocaine-exposed children are easily frustrated because of their low thresholds of overstimulation and their self-regulatory problems. It is also true that *any* child will, if frustrated severely enough, try to hit or kick the source of that frustration. Second, it is important to help children develop new coping strategies before removing their current strategies. In the present example, the teacher could have placed the child in the back corner of the room and marked out a walking space with masking tape within which he could pace. This would have allowed him to use his coping strategy with minimal disruption to the rest of the class, and it would have provided concrete boundaries for his behavior. Over time, the child could then be taught other, more subtle ways to take a time-out when he was feeling overwhelmed.

The research project I have described above presents an optimistic picture of the possible outcomes for drug-exposed children when other major risk factors are reduced or eliminated and when early screening, diagnosis, and intervention are provided. Under such conditions, the majority of drug-exposed children seem to have the resilience to recover from the effects of prenatal drug exposure. Unfortunately, however, the majority of drug-exposed children in our country today are exposed to numerous risk factors in addition to their drug exposure and receive no intervention until they reach school. There is no research to date on the outcome of these "multi-risk/no intervention" children. We can assume that their emotional, behavioral, and learning problems will surface more frequently and be more severe than those seen in our study population. However, we cannot assume that prenatal drug exposure alone is the cause of their problems. Furthermore, I have yet to find a child who cannot be helped with thoughtful, nurturing intervention.

As research findings and anecdotal accounts of children prenatally exposed to drugs filter in, it becomes clear that we must evaluate each child according to that child's specific characteristics and learning needs. When this is done, it becomes clear that "crack babies" are not some new breed of children that we have never seen before; they are simply children. Some have behavioral and learning problems; some do not. To date, the problems that have been reported are problems that creative teachers have successfully handled for many years. The major task facing our society and our education system may be providing classroom teachers with the time they need to address the individual needs not only of the cocaine-exposed child, but of every child in the classroom.

Good Things, Small Packages

In a time of gloom and doom about U.S. schools, early-childhood education is something different, a cauldron of fresh and innovative approaches

STEFAN KANFER

Some of the best education in America goes on below the adult eye level.

—Philip Coltoff, executive director, the Children's Aid Society

Coltoff's observation is being echoed in every region of the country. Allan Bloom decried *The Closing of the American Mind* in his 1987 best seller, referring largely to college students. But in the two-to-six age group, American minds are rapidly dilating. So is the interest in early-childhood education—ECE to the trade. "This is a wonderful time to be in the field," says Sara Wilford, director of the Early Childhood Center at Sarah Lawrence College in Bronxville, N.Y. "Interest in ECE has never been more intense."

The moment small children step into their first classroom, they enter a new world of learning. Early childhood education has become a cauldron of fresh and innovative approaches, a place where research is applied with dramatic effect. The days of too much control, overstructured hours and too many "punish mechanisms"—difficult children forced to take naps—are going. The old "teacher-directed" activities are also on their way out. So are elements of rote learning: reciting the alphabet and learning the early stages of reading through memorization.

Building on research that proves children learn more rapidly, and with more sophistication than authorities thought, educators increasingly use tools like one-on-one conversation and drama. Interaction and imagination are settling in. Preschools are bright and inviting; so are the teachers and staffs. They have to be. Close to 60% of U.S. mothers with children under age six are out of the house and on the job. Child care has had to grow up fast.

Although the content and curriculum are as varied as the settings, most ECE centers adhere to guidelines set down in 1986 and revised last year by the National Association for the Education of Young Children. The 60-year-old association is early-childhood's powerful lobby and accrediting body; its membership has doubled in the past decade and now numbers 77,000 professionals. Today it examines teachers and administrators, demands that early-childhood programs meet criteria of health and safety and continually reviews facilities to make sure its standards are being met. When the association outlines the future it wants, it often points to the Perry Preschool Project in Ypsilanti, Mich. Back in 1962, this project selected 123 children ages three and four to take part in an experimental program. All came from families at the poverty level. Half the group was given two years of preschool instruction, 2½ hours a day, five days a week for 30 weeks. The aims were increased self-esteem, socialization and curiosity. Formal learning was not a high priority. The "control " half was given no preschooling. After the preschooling program ended, the kids were tracked through the rest of their school careers to adulthood.

The results, published in 1984, seemed to validate the Head Start program, launched in 1965 as part of the Johnson Administration's War on Poverty. Often located in public school facilities, Head Start provided quality early-childhood education for disadvantaged children. But would it bring any long-lasting benefits?

The Perry Project offered a solid yes in reply. Its preschool group enjoyed a 15 point rise in IQ rating per student after one year. Only 15% of the preschoolers required special education in later years; 35% of the control group needed aid. Of the preschoolers, 67% graduated from high school, vs. 50% of the control group. By age 19, only 31% of the preschoolers had been arrested for some crime, vs. 51% of the others.

The implications for society are as plain as chalk marks on a blackboard: the relatively high cost of the original program—$5,000 a year for each preschooler—was actually a bargain. The results at Ypsilanti are echoing louder across the country, not only in facilities for the underprivileged but also in preschools everywhere. Twenty-seven states now fund prekindergarten facilities—a huge jump from only seven in 1979. And the early-childhood boom goes on unabated. Some 1,700 nationally accredited public programs operate in the U.S.; an additional 4,300 are actively seeking accreditation.

The private sector is even more active. About 5,600 firms provide some kind of day care, and a small but growing group offers on-site or near-site ECE centers. The Lotus Child Center, situated at the company's Cambridge, Mass., headquarters, is an impressive example. The software giant employs 2,000 people, and 60 of their children are currently enrolled. Costs vary according to income. Some parents pay the going rate for private preschools, while other employees are subsidized and pay as little as $20 a

From *Time,* July 29, 1991, pp. 54-55. Copyright © 1991 by The Time Inc. Magazine Company. Reprinted by permission.

WHAT TO LOOK FOR IN A CHILDHOOD CENTER

WARNING SIGN Too many tantrums

■ Do the kids like the teachers? Do the teachers like the children?

WARNING SIGN Cramped quarters

■ If you were a child, would you look forward to coming here every day?

WARNING SIGN Teachers who can't articulate school aims

■ Does the school have a written statement of its educational philosophy?

WARNING SIGN Sweeping personnel changes

■ Is the staff happy? Look for schools where teachers have been working for at least three years.

WARNING SIGN Assurances that overcrowded classrooms are "temporary"

■ What is the pupil-teacher ratio? 12:1 is about the limit, 8:1 is ideal.

WARNING SIGN Too many kids spending "quiet time" in the corner

■ How does the school handle problems? A good school will work to redirect a misbehaving child.

week. "In the future," says program director Mary Eisenberg, "we're going to see a lot more of these centers, as companies calculate the gains for two generations: the employees and their kids."

Whether children are at their parents' workplace or in the basement of a public school or in an idyllic country setting, the approach to learning is undergoing a mini-revolution. Today imagination and play are being stressed as never before. Observes Chicago kindergarten teacher and author Vivian Gussin Paley, winner of a $355,000 MacArthur "genius" grant in recognition of her books about young children: "Essentially, everything you learn in school can be broken down into a story. If you allow children to talk about the little worlds they've created, they'll be able to take on everything."

In other words, play is children's work, and finding the right materials—stories, drama, clay, blocks, sand, water, paints—really means finding the tools for reasoning and maturing. "What's basic and important to any young child's education," says Shelley Lindauer, head of the Lab School Preeducation Program at Utah State University, "is curiosity and observation. It's much more important to know how to go about finding *an* answer—not a *right* answer."

At the Pacific Oaks School in Pasadena, Calif., while the kids seek answers, they are encouraged to see how their individual actions affect the world around them. Children at the school range in age from three months to nine years. Two-year-olds spend two hours twice a week there, and their parents have to come too. While the kids experiment, the adults get lessons in childhood perception. To develop pre-reading skills, older children tell stories and dabble with writing.

The same philosophy pertains at the Early Childhood Center of Sarah Lawrence, where director Wilford finds that her charges learn by imitating, by pretending to be Mommy or Daddy. "In that process, they are developing language and knowledge of symbolic things—the basis for reading and writing."

In the University of Alabama in Birmingham programs, older kids stage plays and operettas; younger ones play with blocks as a means of learning how to add and subtract. Says director Virginia Marsh: "We have never had a discipline problem. The children are so busy doing things that they don't have time to get bored."

The children in Birmingham—and everywhere else in the country—are going to be a lot busier in the coming decade. And so are their instructors. Yale Professor Edward Zigler, director of the Bush Center for Child Development and Social Policy, predicts that "by the year 2000, the number of working women will rise to 75%. We will see full-day programs for children from the age of three." It will take thousands of new preschools to meet that demand, and many more thousands of new teachers and assistants. The prospect is inviting and daunting: the millennium is only nine years away.

Listen closely and you can hear the future banging its spoon on the high chair. —**Reported by Karen Grigsby Bates/ Los Angeles and David Thigpen/New York, with other bureaus**

THE BEST DAY CARE
There Ever Was

CAROLINE ZINSSER

Caroline Zinsser is an educational consultant and former school director who writes and lectures on childhood in America.

In 1943, in Portland, Oregon, two massive shipyards had begun to build a "bridge of ships"—tankers and cargo ships to carry the men, ammunition and supplies that were desperately needed in the war in Asia. It was possible to build the vessels, from keel-laying to launching, in an unbelievable four days. To help accomplish this miracle of production, 25,000 women—5,000 of them mothers—worked not only as secretaries and clerks, but as welders, chippers and burners in the yards and at the ways. Women worked the day shift, the swing shift and the graveyard shift, for the shipyards operated day and night, seven days a week, racing against time to turn the tide of war.

It was in this atmosphere of wartime emergency that Edgar Kaiser, general manager of the yards, launched a plan for the world's largest day care centers. To help mothers on their jobs, he planned two centers to serve 1,125 children each, open 24 hours a day, 364 days a year. He enlisted the backing of his good friend Eleanor Roosevelt and set about building

the finest facilities for child care that this country has ever known.

As the word went out that anybody who wanted to work at the Kaiser Shipyards could have a job, women from all parts of the country flooded into Portland. They rented every spare room, they jammed the buses, they depleted the stores, and they looked for places to leave their children. Many of the women, from farms and small towns, had never seen the ocean, had never left home before, had never been on their own. To the conservative Portland residents, these newcomers, unwanted and unwelcomed, often appeared to be "riffraff."

In the midst of this uncertainty and upheaval, Kaiser moved his plans forward with the same urgency and efficiency that characterized his production line. Used to cutting through delays by finding top people who would get the job done, he hired leading Portland architects to design the children's centers. The architects produced two buildings unlike anything anyone had seen before, huge, round wheel-plans with 15 large rooms in

the spokes and a protected playground at the central hub. Instead of being separated from the shipyards, the centers were placed at the plant entrances so that every worker passed by and mothers could drop their children off in the most convenient way.

To find a director, Kaiser asked government agencies to name the best-qualified people in the country. Using this advice, he hired Lois Meek Stolz, a pioneer in child-development theory, and today a still-lively 93-year-old, as consulting director and James Hymes, Jr., as on-site manager. Kaiser gave Stolz and Hymes only two months to find staff, get equipment, set policy and begin operation. They still remember those days with awe. "Things happened so quickly," recalls Hymes, "we had no time to be apprehensive. We were plunged into implementing the plan."

The most important job was to recruit staff. Only the best professionals would do—teachers with degrees in child development and with three or more years of experience. The directors sent two-page telegrams to every major teacher-training institution, describing the urgent need for teachers and the dramatic location and huge size of the nurseries. The telegrams caused great excitement (some were kept and framed) as nursery-school teachers found themselves in the unaccustomed spotlight of a wartime emergency. One hundred adventurous teachers responded to the call.

An additional lure, as it was for all war-workers, was pay. Stolz and Hymes had assumed they would pay teachers the going rate for nursery-school work. "But," recalls Stolz, "when Kaiser heard how low the figure was, he nearly exploded. 'You can't pay college graduates that,' he said. 'You won't hold them a week. All the administrative offices in the yards will steal them away from you!' "

Salaries were raised to compete with those of other Kaiser workers. Ruth Berkman, one of the teachers who responded to the recruiting telegram, remembers, "I had earned two hundred dollars a year as a teaching apprentice. As a head teacher, I was earning sixty dollars a month. At Kaiser the salary was *five thousand dollars* a year. I had never even had a Social Security number before! They made us feel like treasured members of the profession."

Equipping the centers was another challenge. Materials were scarce and wartime transportation nearly impossible. But once again the Kaiser Company used its expertise. Accustomed to speeding up shipments of steel to meet production schedules, the company now pushed and urged carloads of children's play equipment westward across the country. The numbers were staggering: For a planned 2,000 or more children, 30 rooms were equipped with nonbreakable juice glasses and self-feed bibs, with cots, sheets, blocks, puzzles, easels and everything else needed for round-the-clock care. Because metal was scarce, children made do with awkward wooden scooters constructed in the shipyards, and teachers scrounged scrap material from the docks.

The buildings were a teacher's delight. Classrooms were large and each had storage space and a bathroom with child-size sinks and toilets. Windows on two sides gave the children views of the shipyards. Covered porches provided a place to play outdoors on rainy days. At Stolz's suggestion, two bathtubs were added, built high enough so that adults did not have to bend over, and big enough so

that children could splash and play in the water. Many children who arrived tired, hot and dirty from their cross-country trip were to receive their first bath in days in these famous bathtubs.

The full staff of 100 teachers, six group supervisors, 10 nurses, five nutritionists and two family consultants formed an astonishing concentration of experts in child care. Here was an unprecedented opportunity for pooling ideas to produce the finest facilities possible, and out of excited discussions came many more innovations.

Like other nursery schools of the time, the Kaiser Centers had a policy of having each child go through a health test every morning before being admitted to class. Instead of asking mothers to take mildly sick children home, Lois Stolz suggested converting a room in each center into an infirmary. Nurses and a consulting pediatrician who made a daily visit took care of the children in isolated glass cubicles, and teachers working in the infirmary developed forms of quiet bed play with the children.

Since not all the mothers who worked at the yards enrolled their children in the center, a Special Service Room was set up to care for children on a temporary emergency basis. Fathers could also use the service when they would otherwise have had to stay home to care for their children. Because working parents weren't able to take their children to public-health clinics during the day, the nursing staff offered to immunize children; 3,606 immunizations were given in the first year.

The centers' kitchens provided the children with breakfast, a midmorning snack, a hot meal at noon, an afternoon sandwich with milk, and supper in the evening. The aim was to supply two thirds of each child's daily nutritional requirements. The chief nutritionist sent parents a weekly list of meals served and suggestions for additional food to complete an adequate day's diet. Free booklets, *Recipes for Food Children Like* and *Good Meals for Children on the Swing Shift,* were distributed.

Perhaps most helpful of all was Home Service Food. Eleanor Roosevelt, on a trip to England, had seen women war-workers buy precooked food for their families right at the factory. She persuaded Kaiser to set up a similar service. By selecting from a weekly menu, a mother could order her family's evening meal, to be picked up—precooked and

packaged—at the center's kitchen when she collected her child at the end of the day shift. The kitchen specialized in food that required long cooking, such as a fresh salmon loaf, which came with an avocado-and-lemon gelatin salad and sold for 50 cents a serving.

As the centers began operation, it became clear that mothers needed group care for infants as well as for preschoolers. Group infant care was almost unknown at the time, and the center's decision to admit children as young as 18 months became one of its most closely studied activities. The teachers, who had no training or experience with younger children, worried about the possible traumatic effects of separating infants from their working mothers. However, the teachers found that children adjusted "happily and comfortably."

Elizabeth Oleson Garvais, who kept a journal, wrote of her experiences as a "babies teacher" on the swing shift, which began at 2:30 p.m. and ended near midnight: "At 11:30 the yard whistle gives a long blast. At 11:45 the first parents come in, walking quietly in their heavy shoes, lowering their voices as they collect their children's belongings. Big men in metal helmets gently pick up sleeping babies. Mothers help wrap them in blankets. Many children manage a sleepy smile and hug. Some, wide awake, are carried from the room looking back over Dad's broad shoulders. Some go out still sleeping soundly. Finally the last helmet and the last lunch pail have gone along with the last child, Ruthie, who blinks at me like a sleepy owl. I turn on the overhead lights. The room is a mess of unmade beds, wet sheets, and screens at crazy angles. Ronny's panda lies on the floor beside his cot. The graveyard-shift housekeepers come in. It is 12:05. It is a new day."

In addition to caring on a daily basis for children from 18 months to six years, the centers expanded their services: They cared for school-age children after school, on Saturdays (which were working days at the yards) and during summer vacations. A commissary provided small but necessary items like toothbrushes and shoelaces. For a short while, a Mending Service was in operation. The centers also sent home a biweekly newsletter describing the children's activities; free booklets on child care, written by the staff, suggested toys, holiday activities and shopping ideas and advised parents on how to talk to children about the war.

In addition, parents could borrow children's books from the center's library.

Some ideas were discussed but never fully developed: a dormitory for mothers and infants with a community kitchen and a nursery, a shopping service where parents could leave their orders in the morning for food and household items and pick up the packages after work, a barber service and a photographer who would take informal pictures of the children to send to their fathers overseas. As James Hymes puts it, "We thought that anything that saved the working mother time and energy meant she would have more to give to her child."

The Kaiser Centers were in operation for only two years. They closed in 1945, as the war in the Pacific was winding down, having served 3,811 children, provided 249,268 child care days and freed 1,931,827 woman-work-hours. When the staff was disbanded, the members hoped their work would provide a model for an ongoing effort toward excellent day care. Portland women, as well as those in other cities where wartime day care centers had been established, deluged Congress and the President with protests against closings.

But the Kaiser Centers were never to be replicated. When James Hymes prepared a report to be distributed to other industries, he made a crucial point: "All education is deficit-producing. Child Service Centers are no exception. The greater the number of children served, the greater the deficit." Parents at the centers paid a fee of five dollars for six days of child care, but this covered only a small part of the cost. The deficit was paid by Kaiser, who in turn passed the cost on to the government. In effect, the centers were federally supported through industry.

The Kaiser Centers demonstrated that day care can be good for children and mothers. But it took a special set of circumstances to bring about full support for working mothers. Only the urgency of wartime, with every woman needed on a job, broke down the traditional barriers against caring for children on a large-scale basis.

The centers stand on record as a reminder of what can be done when the need is great. The many people who worked together in Portland over 40 years ago, in the midst of war, brought about a level of excellence in day care that has not been matched. Eleanor Roosevelt was one of those most instrumental in backing the plan, and it is particularly fitting to remember this month, on the centennial celebration of her birth, that the Kaiser Centers would never have been possible without her deep and intelligent commitment to the welfare of women and children.

Who's Taking Care Of The Children?

*Seeking answers to one of the most important issues
facing our nation, PARADE went to the heart of the country
to see what the problems are and what can be done*

Michael Ryan

ENERGETIC AND OUTSPOKEN, Angela Roffle, at 31, is halfway toward her college degree and fulfilling her dream of climbing out of welfare. Nothing has come easily to her. She is a single mother with a 10-year-old and 2-year-old twins living on the economic brink in a crime-ridden area. But for Roffle, those are not the biggest obstacles to achieving her goal. Child care is.

"This is a bad day to talk about child care," she told me the afternoon we met in St. Louis. "A neighbor usually takes care of my kids while I'm in school, but she had to take today off. I have two backups, but my second babysitter is in the hospital, and I couldn't get to the third because my car broke down." Because of her difficulties, Roffle missed several classes and lost previous study time. Still, she is not defeated. "You know," she said, "there are plenty of women who go through this, just like me, at least once a week. You just have to."

Every day in America, millions of parents struggle to find ways and means to provide care for their children while they go to work or school. Today, two-thirds of mothers work outside the home. One-quarter of the kids in this country live with only one parent. An estimated 23 million children require child care.

Of those kids, 8.3 million go to licensed day-care settings that are inspected and required to meet minimum standards for health, safety and educational content. That leaves 14.7 million children in unlicensed settings. Some will get first-rate care with highly motivated caretakers. But others will go to substandard settings where they may run the risk of fire or accident and, in some cases, abuse. Still others have no regular care. Their parents must depend on a shifting network of friends and relatives, and sometimes, in desperation, even leave their children unsupervised.

Child-care experts report that obtaining good day care is a nationwide problem. It is frequently either in short supply, not up to standards or out of reach financially. "I call it a 'trilemma,'" said Arlyce Currie of Bananas, an Oakland, Calif., resource center for parents.

For many parents, the cost is the biggest problem. "Affordability is big issue," said Nancy Travis of Atlanta's Save the Children agency. "Child-care costs here range from $46 to $160 a week." Even for many in the middle class, such costs are prohibitive.

As Kathy Doellefeld-Clancy discovered, however, even having a good income does not guarantee quality care. She and her husband both have good jobs, and she took great care in choosing a day-care center for her son, Jonathan. Almost immediately, though, she started to worry. "One day, I went in and there were about 40 kids with only four teachers watching them," Doellefeld-Clancy said, "I had to stop a piece of equipment from falling on one of the children. I called the director, and she said it was just a fluke. But I went back another time and found one teacher supervising 14 kids."

The last straw came when Jonathan, then 16 months, bit another child. A trained child-care worker would have understood that this behavior can occur at a certain stage. Instead, Jonathan was left in a playpen for an entire day without toys or human contact. One teacher, appalled by this "punishment," reported it to Doellefeld-Clancy. She quickly moved her son to another center.

There are other problems. In some states and localities, the backgrounds of child-care workers are checked. In Georgia, owners of day-care centers are vetted by the Georgia Bureau of Investigation. But in states such as Missouri, church-related day-care centers are exempt from virtually all regulation—as a parent we will call "Dave" discovered to his horror.

Dave thought he had solved the day-care problem when he found a responsible-looking church-affiliated center for his son, then 2. "Then one day when I suggested we go outside and play," Dave recalled, "my son said, 'Are we going to play Pull Your Pants Down?' I said, 'What do you mean?' and he said, 'That's a game we play at school.'"

Dave and his wife sat down with their son and elicited the information that an adult at the day-care center involved the children in "games" that included taking

 From *Parade* magazine, August 30, 1992, pp. 3-5. Copyright © 1992 by Michael Ryan. Reprinted by permission of the author.

their pants down and touching them. They reported their findings to state authorities, who questioned their son, found him credible, and said they would investigate.

"They went to the center and asked, 'Is there someone here who abuses children?'" Dave recalled with indignation. "What do you think the answer was? No action was taken against the center."

Dave and his wife have since put their son in another day-care center, and they have taken him to a counselor. "We think we found out in time," Dave said. "We hope that no permanent damage was done."

Most children, of course, probably will never be injured or molested in child care. But, as Barbara Reisman, Executive Director of the Child Care Action Campaign (CCAC), an advocacy group, points out, "Of course you want children to be in a place where they're not in danger, but that's not enough. All children should be cared for in a bright, engaging space by well-trained, well-qualified people who love children."

That kind of child care is not a luxury but a practical necessity for the economy, Reisman argues. Some studies show that early childhood education of the kind provided in quality day-care settings can help keep kids from dropping out of school later.

Advocates argue that good child care can also benefit employers. Richard Stolley, president of CCAC, was instrumental in the development of a day-care center at Time, Inc., the large media company where he is editorial director. "It's a productivity issue," he explained. "The number of employees who don't show up or who show up harried because child-care arrangements have fallen through is enormous. Child care is not a women's issue. It has an effect on productivity of men and women, on the whole working family."

Angela Roffle, Kathy Doellefeld-Clancy and Dave are three faces of the national problem of child care. Each has struggled to find quality care—each is, somehow, finding a way to solve the problem.

Other countries take a different approach. If Angela Roffle had been born in France, she would have received free pre-natal health care, been granted maternity leave and her children would have been eligible for government-sponsored preschools. In more than 100 countries, Dave and Kathy Doellefeld-Clancy would be entitled to parental leave from their jobs to ensure their children were properly cared for.

In the United States, parents can get a tax credit of up to $1440 annually for child care (which, typically, can cost two times that). Can our government afford to do more?

"The real question," Reisman argued, "is, 'Can it afford not to?'" One study shows that 25% of mothers on welfare can't take jobs because they can't find adequate child care. The social costs of not having good preschool and after-school care, Reisman said, may be far greater than the expense of providing them.

Some communities and businesses are working to find solutions to the day-care dilemma. The Hilltop Day Care Center in Florissant, Mo., was begun a generation ago by the School of Social Work of Washington University. It was designed to provide educationally enriched day care for low-income children. Today, Hilltop—headquartered in an old bank building—is a subsidiary of Lutheran Family and Children's Services and has about 90 children, mostly from low- and middle-income families, enrolled.

"It's a place where our kids can interact with other children," Valerie Joyner told me when she and her husband, Thomas, stopped by the center. "They prepare kids for reading and learning." Two of the Joyner's three children attended Hilltop, and their 6-year-old is thriving in kindergarten after a year there.

Not far away, in an old public-school building in St. Louis, is McCare, a day-care center for employees of McDonnell Douglas, the aircraft manufacturer. "We are completely self-supporting," Steve Zwolak, the center's director, told me proudly. "We charge from $85 to $145 a week, and we have 61 staff members for 186 kids." At McCare, infants get personal attention; older kids get educational play and parents are encouraged to stop in during their breaks.

When I visited, Ann McMahon Piening was dropping off her two kids. Formerly an engineer, she was laid off by the company, but her husband still works there. She says that McCare has helped her establish herself in a new career. "I couldn't do it without McCare," she said. "I wouldn't be willing to leave my children unless I was sure they were safe and getting the kind of attention I would give them myself. My husband and I can go to work ready to do our best, happy that our children are well taken care of."

Choosing Child Care

WHILE THERE ARE NO NATIONAL standards for child-care providers (and 80% to 90% of day-care settings are unlicensed), experts agree that settings should be evaluated according to some general criteria. When selecting a care provider, look for the following:

●**Staff size**. In family day care—that is, day care offered in private homes—one adult should supervise five children at the most. No more than two of them should be less than a year old. In day-care centers, there should be one adult for every three to four infants or toddlers; every six 2-year-olds; every eight 3-year-olds; every nine 4-year-olds; every 10 5-year-olds; and every 10 to 12 school-age children.

Staff continuity is also important. Young children need the security of knowing they will be cared for by the same staffers week after week.

●**Licensing**. In states which license day-care centers, be sure that the setting you choose is licensed.

●**Staff training**. The first five years of life are crucial for a child's development. Although many who offer family day care have good natural teaching skills, it is desirable that day-care staffers have some training in early-childhood education.

●**Surroundings**. A day-care setting should be more than a parking place. It should be bright and cheerful and offer a variety of toys and activities.

●**Safety**. All fire, building and safety codes should be met. Check for multiple exits, fire escapes and fire extinguishers. Some jurisdictions require that day care be restricted to the ground floor of buildings for ease of escape in case of emergency.

●**Staff background checks**. Some day-care centers voluntarily check the police records of their staff members, or are required to by regulations. In other areas, you may be able to obtain a background check by requesting it from authorities.

The Day-Care Delusion

When Parents Accept the Unacceptable

Michael Hoyt and
Mary Ellen Schoonmaker

Michael Hoyt is associate editor of "Columbia Journalism Review" in New York City. Mary Ellen Schoonmaker is an editor at "The Record" in Hackensack, New Jersey.

When the police arrived at her neat brick house in Oxon Hill, Maryland—a middle-class suburb of Washington, D.C.—Nannie Marie Pressley was not at home. The operator of a family day-care business, she was out with six of the children in her care, unaware that a parent had called in a complaint. The police found 22 children, ages 2 to 11, sitting quietly on rows of benches in the basement, and 12 others, 3- to 7-year-olds, lying on a sheet in another room, where an infant was propped on a sofa. Upstairs, in a dark room that reeked of urine, the officers discovered eight infants strapped into car seats, and one lying face down on the floor. In another room were two infants sharing a crib. Pressley had left her teenage stepdaughter in charge of the children—all 46 of them.

• On a recent hot day in a wealthy suburb in New Jersey, police found an 18-month-old boy locked in a car. He was sweating and screaming by the time a passerby noticed. According to the baby's father, a New York-area writer, the child's sitter had developed a serious toothache and driven to her dentist's. Not knowing what to do with the baby, she left him locked in the car.

• Last year, at Wil-lo Haven Day Care Center, a city-run facility that serves working parents in the Crown Heights section of Brooklyn, New York, a tile from the ceiling fell and hit the center's director on the shoulder, leaving a bad bruise. Given the center's condition—broken windows, no heat, dirty plastic sheeting for window shades—the accident was not a surprise. The director was just thankful that the tile hadn't hit her head. Or a child's.

Child-care conditions like these could easily lead to tragedy. But what is more troubling is the reaction of many of the parents involved. For example, at Pressley's family day-care home, some mothers and fathers, even after learning of the overcrowded conditions there, did not object. "I'd take my kids back today except that she was shut down," one father told a reporter for *The Washington Post.* "I saw children there, but I never took the time to count them. She was a very good baby sitter, and that's all I cared about," said the mother of a 7-year-old.

"Fire her? Are you kidding?" said the New York writer of the sitter who left his infant son in a hot locked car. Although he told her never to do such a thing again, he still believes, "She's great with the kids."

> "If we just provide vouchers for every crummy day-care situation, we're accomplishing nothing."
> Rep. George Miller
> (D.-California)

The Brooklyn parents, afraid budget cuts would cause Wil-lo Haven to close defended even that crumbling facility. "I depend on it to help me keep working and stay off welfare," the mother of a 3-year-old explained.

Often, parents do not see what is right in front of their eyes. They tell themselves that the day-care situation they have found is good, even when down deep they may know better. If you criticize it, they get defensive.

Call it the Day-Care Delusion: The mind rationalizes so that the body can go to work. "Some parents have a

Reprinted from *Family Circle*, October 15, 1991, pp. 81-87. Copyright © 1991, The Family Circle, Inc.

Day-Care Checklist | Name of Program _____

Use this list of questions as a scorecard. Make several copies and fill one out for each program you are considering. Answer each question using a scale of 1 through 5 (5 is the highest rating; 1, the lowest). Total each sheet so that you have a score for each facility you visit. (Questions are not listed in order of importance.)

How Do You Feel About:

1. The cleanliness and safety of the day-care environment? ____
2. The safety of the neighborhood? ____
3. The quality of the toys? ____
4. The amount of space available per child? ____
5. The meals and snacks served? ____
6. The procedures at mealtime and the diapering routines? ____
7. The time spent on physical activities? The amount of quiet time? ____
8. The gender and racial balance (both staff and children)? ____
9. The way rules are enforced? ____
10. The opportunities for family involvement? ____
11. The degree to which staff members are prepared to teach children? ____
12. The amount of one-to-one attention children get from the staff? ____
13. The amount of affection children get from staff? ____
14. The ratio of staff to children? ____
15. The availability of the program to parents—can you make unannounced visits? ____
16. The distance of the site from your home? Your workplace? ____
17. The hours of operation? ____
18. The cost of enrollment? ____
19. The overall philosophy? ____
20. The overall quality of the program? ____

Total score for this program ____

Other considerations:

Many other matters are important when choosing day care. Among them:

☐ In addition to low adult/child ratios, look for small group sizes.

☐ Sit in for a morning or drop in unexpectedly and watch how the children relate to the care provider and how she relates to them.

☐ Check the program for current license and liability insurance.

☐ Inquire about the history of the facility—how long has it been in operation, how much turnover has there been among children and staff?

☐ If the program rents or leases space, what is the duration of the rental agreement or lease?

—*Angela Browne Miller*

---

need not to see because they feel so desperate," says Mary Babula, executive director of the Wisconsin Early Childhood Association. "They have to choose what they can afford. Or maybe there's only one center that's open at 7:30 A.M., when they need child care."

Are these parents—the same people who fire off letters of complaint if a box of cereal doesn't have enough raisins—just lousy consumers of child care?

"Some of us go to more trouble in buying a car than in choosing child care," says Angela Browne Miller, who holds master's degrees in social welfare and public health and a Ph.D. in both social welfare and education. For her book, *The Day Care Dilemma*, Dr. Miller recently studied hundreds of different day-care settings and found that parents did not know how to evaluate the quality of the programs; nor did they take the time to find out. Whether from desperation or a lack of knowledge or money, parents are accepting the unacceptable.

To many, child care is still consid-

ered to be a woman's issue. But it's not. If all the working mothers in the United States suddenly quit their jobs to care for their children full time, the economy would crumble. Deprived of that income, hundreds of thousands of families would fall right out of the middle class, some to the poverty level.

With more than 10 million children in day care today, someone must take responsibility for lowering the risk to their well-being and raising the standards of care. Some say it should be the parents; others say it should be the Government. And the battle lines are drawn. Many people—including some mothers who choose to stay home with their children, senior citizens and childless couples—don't want their tax dollars spent on raising other people's kids. But with the growing number of single parents and women who work outside the home, it's clear that day care is here to stay.

Although the Federal Government sets standards for everything from food labels to nursing homes, it plays a minor role in child care, leaving regulation up to the states. As a re-

sult, there is a tremendous variety in the laws and enforcement of rules governing child care.

One of the leading proponents of Federal involvement, Congressman George Mill (D.-Calif.), points out that children are our most valuable asset, our future: "Government must take an active role, to make sure children's needs are met and their safety protected while in child care. There's no evidence that the marketplace will perform that function."

While there is a need for financial assistance, like tax credits and the new child-care vouchers the states are now offering, Miller says money is not enough: "If we just provide vouchers for every crummy day-care situation, we're accomplishing nothing. We have to go to the issue of quality. We have to have skilled, trained people who are properly paid, so we don't get massive turnover rates."

Congresswoman Patricia Schroeder (D.-Colo.) also calls for Federal action. If Government would see to it that child-care workers were better paid, she says, many of the problems concerning quality would clear up: "A lot of good people want to go into child care, but they also like to eat."

Miller and Schroeder would like to see the Federal Government establish national child-care standards that would address such issues as safety, child-developmental needs and training of care providers.

But quality child care is expensive, leaving some parents with little choice but to conclude that the kind of care they're able to buy is all right because it has to be.

After Jessica McClure fell into a backyard well and was trapped for 58 hours in Midland, Texas, in October 1987, it was clear there had been a safety hazard at the family day-care center run by Jessica's aunt and mother. If the Government had set minimum safety standards, that accident might have been prevented. (Other regulations are needed to insure that wastebaskets, cleaning supplies and medicines are covered and out of children's reach, and that all day-care providers frequently wash their hands, particularly after changing diapers or wiping runny noses, to prevent the spread of infection.)

Yet the dangers of inadequate care are usually not so obvious as open wells, falling tiles or one teenager left in charge of scores of children. The dangers may be more subtle, more psychological than physical. But they are real.

"The average quality of child care in this country is poor," says Edward Zigler, Ph.D., Sterling Professor of Psychology at Yale University and co-author, with Mary E. Lang, of *Child Care Choices* (The Free Press, 1991). Dr. Zigler has been visiting day-care centers and studying children for 35 years, and his findings are alarming: "My feeling is that at least one-third of the children in America are having child-care experiences that will compromise their development, by inhibiting their ability to trust, to relate to other children and adults, and to learn." If a child has had five years of inadequate child care, Dr. Zigler believes—ignored for long periods of time, lost in the crowd of other infants and toddlers, or left in a crib or playpen for hours on end—that child may not be ready to learn when it comes time to start school.

"We can tell by 9 months of age which kids are on a failure line or on the success line," says T. Berry Brazelton, M.D., FAMILY CIRCLE contributing editor and professor emeritus of pediatrics at Harvard Medical School. "So what we have to do is get to children early—get them feeling good about themselves, feeling self-confident—then they'll be ready to learn."

"Children learn for the same reasons birds fly—they are learning machines," Dr. Zigler says. One way we turn off that machine is by failing to provide early nurturing. Yet evidence is mounting that many American parents are settling for care that is just not good enough and fooling themselves into believing everything is O.K.

> One father found his family day-care provider's teenage son watching *Dawn of the Dead* on TV as toddlers ambled by the screen.

In her research, Dr. Miller focused on six day-care centers in California. She found programs that ranged from poor to mediocre; only one was rated "good." What is remarkable about Dr. Miller's study, however, is that the 241 parents she interviewed uniformly judged their programs as "excellent," despite Miller's much poorer ratings. Her findings exemplify the Day-Care Delusion.

In his book *Working and Caring* (Addison Wesley, 1985), Dr. Brazelton explains that a parent who shares a small child with another caregiver may grieve, feel guilty, inadequate, hopeless, helpless and even angry at having to give up the child. The parent pulls out emotionally—not because he or she doesn't care, but because it hurts so much to care. As a New Jersey mother of two laments, "Nothing is harder than leaving a baby. Even if you know you have to, and even if you know she's in good hands."

Day-care providers often report that parents at all income levels rush out the door when they drop their kids off in the morning, and rush out again after picking them up in the afternoon. They ask few questions beyond "Did everything go O.K.?" They don't want to know any more, to be reminded that the child spent all day without them.

And in fact, not many parents will admit to having doubts about the place where they leave their child. One Brooklyn couple remembers leaving their 2-year-old daughter with a neighborhood woman who ran a family day-care home, despite having doubts from the beginning. "But we figured if other people like us liked her, she must be O.K.," the father remembers. Yet when he dropped his daughter off one morning and found the woman's teenage son watching the graphic horror movie *Dawn of the Dead* as the toddlers ambled past the TV screen, that was the end of the line. Other neighborhood parents, however, continued to rave about the woman.

Parents need to learn how to find all the child-care options available to them in their communities, and how to choose among them. This means knowing how to evaluate a child-care situation instead of relying on word-of-mouth references from other parents in the neighborhood, what questions to ask and what to look for, and their own rights and responsibilities. (*See "Day-Care Checklist."*)

One stumbling block for parents is that even in the worst situations, they find it hard to be critical of people to whom they have entrusted their children. Meryl Frank, who analyzed and spoke on child-care issues for five years while doing graduate work at Yale, came to know this dilemma well, but only after she had children of her own. "You rationalize," she says. "Parents are busy, harassed. They don't want to know what's wrong. It's a defense mechanism. You say, 'My children are not going to become mass murderers just because they go to this day-care center.'"

"The problem is that it's a provider's market," says Marilyn Ward, executive director of Everywoman's Resource Center, which handles child-care referrals in Topeka, Kansas. For many parents, the simple dearth of quality day care is the problem. "Parents have to work so hard to find something, they want to believe what they've found is a good program," Ward continues. "They don't want to start all over again."

Consider the situation faced last year by families on Orcas Island, a small community near Seattle, Washington, where instances of alleged sexual abuse of toddlers were reported at two local child-care facilities, one a day-care center and the other a family day-care home. When the day-care center in question was closed as a result, six parents wrote a letter to state officials asking that it be relicensed and reopened. Its closing left more than a dozen parents with nowhere to leave their children. They said the state had overreacted in shutting the center down.

n "Variations in Early Child Care: Do They Predict Subsequent Social, Emotional and Cognitive Differences?" Deborah Lowe Vandell of the University of Wisconsin and Mary Anne Corasaniti of the University of Texas at Dallas studied 236 Texas 8-year-olds, all white and mostly from middle-class families. The idea was to trace their early child-care histories and determine the effects of day care on them. The disturbing result was that children with more extensive day care were rated by teachers and parents as harder to discipline. They had poorer work habits, poorer peer relationships, and poorer emotional health than other children.

Vandell points to a similar study of 8-year-olds recently completed in Sweden, a study that came up with nearly opposite findings. In the Swedish study, children with extensive day-care histories were found to be less anxious, more independent and persistent; they also had better verbal skills than home-reared children.

Vandell suspects the difference in the two studies can be found in the quality of care. Sweden has some of the highest standards for child care in the world, with specialized training for caregivers and low child-to-adult ratios. Texas, on the other hand, has no educational requirements for family day-care providers and minimal requirements for caregivers at centers. In Texas, a single family day-care provider may be responsible for up to 12 children; in center-based care, one caregiver may have to watch as many as six infants, or up to 18 toddlers (4-year-olds).

Experts agree that the most important factor for all children is having a stable relationship with warm and skilled caregivers who have enough time to give them the attention they crave.

"If children don't have a relationship

BY THE NUMBERS

More than 10 million children under the age of 6 have mothers in the work force, according to the U.S. Department of Labor. Latest figures from the Census Bureau show that 29.9 percent are cared for in their own homes by a relative or sitter; 35.6 percent are in family day care or are cared for in a relative's or sitter's home; 24.3 percent are in organized child-care programs.*

The Children's Defense Fund reports:

● *Of the more than 6 million children who spend part or all of their day in child care outside their own home, nearly half—2.6 million—are not protected by any state regulations at all.* For example, 22 states do not require even minimal standards in family day care if fewer than five children are involved. Fourteen states do not regulate, or only partially regulate, child-care centers run by religious institutions, even though one-third of all child-care centers are run by religious groups.

● *When child care is regulated by the state, the standards are often inadequate to insure the safety and health of small children.* Nineteen states, for example, allow child-care centers to have a ratio of five or more infants to one adult. In Idaho, it's legal to have one adult for every 12 infants. Louisiana does not regulate family day-care homes serving fewer than eight children. Amazingly, 22 states have no group size limits whatsoever. As for basic health requirements: 13 states do not even require children in licensed or registered family day-care homes to be immunized against such preventable diseases as measles, polio, rubella, or mumps.

● *Regardless of regulations a state may have on its books, many fail to enforce them or to monitor child-care facilities.* Licensing officials in 18 states admit they lack the enforcement staff to see that their laws are being followed. Thus, a license on the wall can give parents a false sense of security. Sometimes complaints are not acted upon. Eight states report that they are unable to respond to all complaints. Do you think you have the unqualified right to visit your child's family day-care facility unannounced? Better check. Parents in 29 states currently do not have that right spelled out in law; yet it is crucial to insuring a child's safety and well-being. (Experts agree that more states are now beginning to pay attention to this issue.)

*The remaining 10.2 percent of children are either in kindergarten or in other forms of child care.

FAMILY CIRCLE evaluated each state based on statistics from "Who Knows How Safe?"—a report by the Children's Defense Fund on state policies as of April 1990. The five categories reviewed were regulation and inspection standards, child-to-staff ratio, group size, parental access, and staff training requirements. We also spoke with Gina Adams of the Children's Defense Fund, Gwen Morgan of Work Family Directions and Barbara Reisman of the Child Care Action Campaign—all experts on the states' role in child care. Their comments plus the results of our evaluation indicate that most states mandate mediocre child care at best.

The following ratings tell which states are doing well and which should be doing better. It should be noted that our rating system is based on an evaluation of laws currently on the books; it does not take into consideration the degree to which they are enforced, the amount of money the states are putting toward child care, or how recent budget cutbacks may have affected states' ability to insure quality programs.

GOOD
Calif., Colo., Conn., Del., Hawaii, Ill., Kan., Md., Mass., Maine, Minn., Mo., Utah, Vermont, Wash., Wis.

FAIR
Ala., Ark., Alaska, Ariz., Wash. D.C., Ind., Iowa, Ky., Mich., Miss., Mont., Neb., Nev., N.H., N.J., N.M., N.D., N.Y., Ohio, Okla., Oreg., Pa., R.I., S.Dak., Tenn., Tex., Va., Wyo.

POOR
Fla., Ga., Ind., La., N.C., S.C., W.Va.

Some states listed as fair or poor are doing well in other categories not addressed in these ratings.

FOR MORE INFORMATION . . .
To help you in choosing the best day care for your child, send for: "How to Choose a Good Early Childhood Program" or "Finding the Best Care for Your Infant or Toddler"—two free booklets from the National Association for the Education of Young Children, 1834 Connecticut Ave. N.W., Dept. HC/FB, Washington, DC 20009 (include a self-addressed stamped envelope with your request). ● The National Association of Child Care Resource and Referral Agencies will refer you to local resource and referral programs. Write: 2116 Campus Dr., S.E., Rochester, MN 55904; 507-287-2220.

[with a caregiver], they feel very insecure. They feel abandoned by their own parents," says Dr. Albert J. Solnit, Sterling Professor Emeritus in pediatrics and psychiatry at Yale and senior research scientist at the university's Child Study Center.

The number of children per caregiver is another important factor. The younger the children, the lower the ratio ought to be. (The National Association for the Education of Young Children recommends the following child-to-staff ratios: ● From 0 to 24 months, 3 to 1; maximum group size, 6. ● From 25 to 30 months, 4 to 1; maximum group size, 8. ● From 31 to 35 months, 5 to 1; maximum group size, 10. ● For 3-year-olds, 7 to 1; maximum group size, 14. ● For 4-year-olds, 8 to 1; maximum group size, 16.) Also, the smaller the size of the group the better, since children tend to feel lost in groups that make them compete for attention.

The results of too-high ratios and too-large group sizes are predictable. The National Child Care Staffing Study, a major study published by the Child Care Employee Project in 1990, observed a typical day-care situation in Atlanta, Georgia, a state that allows very high ratios and group sizes. The researchers found that preschoolers spent close to one-fourth of their time in aimless wandering and were ignored by caregivers for more than three-quarters of the observation period. Less than one in 10 of the preschoolers observed could engage in the complex pretending games that children of that

age should be able to play.

"It all fits together," Dr. Solnit says. "Good care produces something attractive. With poor care, the child functions as if everything is an effort—eating, relating to adults or to playmates. They are like little ghosts."

If child-care conditions are to improve, parents must realize that no government agency or state licensing inspector can be as vigilant as they themselves can be. Maryland's child-care regulations are better than many others. Yet despite the fact that Nannie Marie Pressley flouted state rules in caring for 52 children by herself in an unlicensed day-care home, her only punishment was a $175 fine. Her facility was closed, but no charges were filed against her.

Parents need to ask specific questions when checking out child care: How many children are cared for? What activities are provided? How much weight is given to parents' wishes and their requests for time to talk about how the child is doing? Is the caregiver genuinely interested in both child and parents, and forthcoming with information?

"Look for a place where the care provider wants to know more about you," says Dr. Brazelton, "and where you can stop in at unexpected times. Be sure the provider will sit down with you—at least once a week, but even every day—to talk about your child."

Dr. Edward Zigler believes he has a solution to the Day-Care Delusion, a

plan to insure that parents no longer have to accept the unacceptable. He envisions what he calls the "School of the 21st Century," built around the local public school (programs are currently under way in Missouri, Colorado, Wyoming, Kansas and Connecticut; sites in the works include Kentucky, Arkansas, Iowa and Oklahoma). It includes all-day, year-round, on-site child care for all preschoolers from age 3 to prekindergarten, as well as before- and after-school and summer care for children from kindergarten through at least sixth grade. The school offers a network of family day-care providers, training and support, gives referrals to parents, and helps find substitutes when an individual caregiver is sick or on vacation. Dr. Zigler's program would benefit children of stay-at-home mothers too, because he calls for the Federal government to provide cash allowances for new parents so they can either stay home or use the money to pay for quality day care.

Right now, parents in many parts of the country can only dream about such a program. "Finding [any kind of] child care is a struggle," says a mother with two boys in day care since infancy. "You feel you have to reinvent the wheel." And so parents continue to grapple with real problems, hoping to be able to convince themselves that they're doing their best for their children. *(See preceding page for day-care statistics and for additional sources of information.)*

Meeting the Challenge of Diversity

Elizabeth Jones and Louise Derman-Sparks

Louise Derman-Sparks has worked for 25 years with the many-faceted issues of child development, diversity, and social justice as a preschool teacher, child care center director, parent, college teacher, researcher, and activist. Author of Anti-Bias Curriculum: Tools for Empowering Young Children, *published by the National Association for the Education of Young Children, and of a number of articles discussing aspects of antibias curriculum, Louise also conducts in-services and workshops with early childhood educators across the country.*

Elizabeth Jones, Ph.D., is a member of the faculty in Human Development at Pacific Oaks College, where she has taught both adults and children. Her most recent writing on issues in teaching appears in The Play's the Thing: Teachers' Roles in Childrens' Plays *to be published by Teachers College Press in 1992. She is currently working with a diverse group of preschool teachers in the Pasadena schools in The Partnership Project, funded by the Ford Foundation. She recently joined Louise Derman-Sparks in discussing the challenge of diversity with teachers in Australia.*

As the NAEYC accreditation criteria (National Academy of Early Childhood Programs, 1984) make clear, meeting the challenge of diversity is an essential component of quality early childhood programs. We live in a diverse society in a multicultural world; not to understand and value diversity is to shortchange oneself and others. Experience with the accreditation process has thus far shown that this criterion is among those least likely to be fully satisfied by programs applying for accreditation (Bredekamp & Apple, 1986).

What do the accreditation criteria ask for? Under "Interactions among Staff and Children". . .

Staff equally treat children of all races, religions, and cultures with respect and consideration. Staff provide children of both sexes with equal opportunities to take part in all activities. (1984, p. 9)

. . .and under "Curriculum". . .

Developmentally appropriate materials and equipment which project heterogeneous racial, sexual, and age at-tributes are selected and used. (p. 12)

"Of course," you may say. "That's what we believe and that's what we do." It sounds easy, but it isn't. In teaching young children and teachers and observing a wide variety of programs, we have seen several types of inappropriate approaches to diversity provided intentionally or unintentionally in early childhood programs.

Can any of these inappropriate approaches be found in your center?

1. Teachers believe they're not prejudiced.

At the personal level it may well be true that an individual does not hold bigoted beliefs; however, we all learn prejudices beginning in our childhood (Derman-Sparks & the A.B.C. Task Force, 1989). The practices and stereotypes that support institu-

From *Young Children*, Vol. 47, No. 2, January 1992, pp. 12-18. Reprinted by permission of the publisher, the National Association for the Education of Young Children.

tional racism are all around us, even in curriculum materials in early childhood education. As one example, inaccurate, hurtful images of "Indians" abound in alphabet books, cartoons, and Western movies. They permeate our daily language.

At an AEYC conference, a workshop presenter said, "But what can you do when the children are running around like wild Indians. . .?"

A Native American woman in the audience stood up. "What you've just said is offensive to me," she said.

"And did any of the White women present say anything?" asked the educator to whom this story was told by a White member of the audience.

"No, none of us did," was the reply. "I hadn't really noticed the words when the speaker said them. . . ."

We don't notice. Our unawareness and the lack of actions that challenge bias help to perpetuate oppressive beliefs and behaviors. Prejudice is real for its recipients, regardless of whether it was intentional.

2. Teachers are proud of being "colorblind."

Asked about the racial/ethnic composition of her class, the teacher proudly declared, "I don't know what color my children are. I never notice. They are all just children to me. I treat them all alike."

The children in her class are predominantly African Americans. The pictures of nursery rhyme characters on the walls, the dolls, and the books are nearly all white and reflect only the dominant Euro-American culture. The teacher is sure, however, that she is teaching all the children equally.

This teacher reflects a color-denial philosophy of education. Originally a progressive argument against racial bigotry, it implicitly establishes the dominant (Euro-American) culture experience as the norm and ends up equating "we are all the same" with "we are all White." Moreover, "colorblindness" ignores what we know about children's development of identity and attitudes as well as the realities of racism in the daily lives of people of color.

3. Teachers believe that White children are unaffected by diversity issues.

I don't see why I have to do multicultural curriculum. My class is all White. We don't have any problems with prejudice like teachers do in classrooms that are mixed.

All children are living in a society in which diversity is an ever-increasing reality. And all children are exposed to the biases still pervasive in our country—biases based on gender, age, and disability as well as race, language, and culture. Curriculum that does nothing to counter the biases that dominant-culture children absorb as they go about their daily lives ill-equips them to live effectively and fairly with diversity.

4. Teachers assume that the children they teach are "culturally deprived."

"My children come from deprived homes. Their parents don't even teach them good English before they come to school. They don't know how to be an American. My job is to teach them how to fit in," said one teacher to another.

Her colleague agreed. "You should see the homes they come from," she said. "They're so much better off here at the center. I don't think these parents really care about their children."

These teachers believe that "these children" need experiences that fill the void left by inadequate or inferior parenting; therefore, sharing different families' lifestyles, language, and values is not part of the curriculum. Children's behaviors, including language, that reflect their home culture are stopped and corrected.

Where children are defined as culturally deprived, curriculum is often developmentally inappropriate. Learning through play and spontaneous language is seen as an unaffordable luxury for children who must work hard to "catch up." Working with parents, these teachers give advice on childrearing, leaving no room for questions about the desirability of some of the dominant culture's values or

for examining the value of other cultures' childrearing practices.

5. Teachers seek out resources to develop multicultural curriculum.

Many teachers are making conscientious efforts to introduce multicultural activities into their classrooms. Their intent is positive: Let's teach children about each other's cultures so they will learn to respect each other and not develop prejudice. In practice, however, activities frequently deteriorate into a tourist approach to diversity: "visiting other cultures" from time to time by way of a special bulletin board, a "multicultural" center, an occasional parent visit or holiday celebration, or even a week's unit—and then a return to "regular" daily activities that reflect only the dominant culture. Paradoxically, these curricula usually do not study the Euro-American culture because that is what happens in the regular curriculum.

Tourist curriculum emphasizes the "exotic" differences between cultures by focusing on holidays and ignoring the real-life daily problems and experiences of different peoples. When activities about diversity are only occasionally added to the curriculum, rather than integrated on a daily basis, such limited exposure misrepresents cultural realities and perpetuates stereotyping.

How can you make changes?

Antibias Curriculum: Tools for Empowering Young Children (by Louise Derman-Sparks and the A.B.C. Task Force, 1989) addresses both the daily-life realities of diversity and the biased attitudes and unfair behavior that are part of this reality. It recognizes that children begin to develop awareness both of differences and of socially prevailing biases by the time they're two or three. It asks adults to challenge children to practice critical thinking and activism, while integrating diversity into the daily program.

Teachers who begin to question their previous perceptions and behaviors face several potential obstacles when they consider implementing an antibias approach. Issues of bias stir up painful feelings, threatening both self-esteem and existing relationship patterns. Teachers may have feelings such as these:

1. "It sounds like everything I've been doing is wrong."

This is an awful feeling. It's faced by everyone who comes up against a new set of assumptions governing behavior. In many public schools these days, it's being faced by traditional kindergarten and primary teachers who are being encouraged to adopt developmentally appropriate practice.

Challenged to examine our biases, many of us become defensive, especially if we have always seen ourselves as unbiased and fair to everyone. Disequilibrium is never comfortable, but as Piaget has made clear, it's a necessary condition for constructing new ways of thinking and doing. Colleagues need to nurture each other through this process, just as they do children. It's OK to not be perfect, to be a learner.

2. "But what if I say the wrong thing?"

A public school teacher challenged to move beyond her annual classroom Christmas celebration protested, "I don't really teach about Hannukah because I just don't know how to pronounce all those words." A teacher who habitually diverted rather than confronted racial name-calling explained, "I'm embarrassed and I don't know what to say." It's important to teachers to be knowledgeable, to feel competent. Practicing new behaviors, we may indeed say the "wrong thing." It is hard to know what to say in the face of bias; we don't have many

models. It is hard to broaden the cultural base of our curriculum when what we know and love best are the stories and songs and customs of our own culture. If we try introducing new ideas, we'll be learning with the children instead of teaching them.

3. "I want my classroom to be a happy place."

Many women have been socialized to be nice, to be nurturing, and to keep relationships running smoothly. We are very comfortable reminding children that we're all friends here and helping them solve problems peacefully. We are comfortable with a multicultural curriculum that emphasizes the attractive differences among celebrations, food, and music. We are not at all comfortable with an antibias curriculum that asks us to examine negative attitudes toward differences, including our own. We have no wish to make waves or take risks. If confronted by colleagues or supervisors, we are likely to feel both pain and anger at the threat this poses to pleasant, cooperative relationships among staff and with parents.

4. "I'm ready to address antibias issues with children, but I worry about my relationships with other staff, parents, and administration if I do. What will they say about me?"

A teacher who is the only adult in a classroom may have some privacy to try new curriculum and new dialogues. If she is a member of a team, negotiation becomes necessary. And what about parents? How will they react if familiar holidays aren't observed, if race and disability are talked about openly, if boys are encouraged to play with "girls' things"? Unlike young children, who are willing to explore differences and to think critically about bias, many adults have learned that these are things we don't talk about. In *The Emperor's New Clothes*, no adult had the cour-

age to mention the emperor's nakedness; it was up to a child to make the observation.

Implementation of antibias curriculum sometimes produces conflict situations. Teachers skilled in conflict resolution are aware of the ingredients necessary to make it work: (a) a caring relationship with the children; (b) practice in using problem-solving strategies that empower all the parties to the conflict and enable them to generate creative solutions; and (c) the ability to accept strong feelings, appropriately expressed. Working in this way with young children provides an excellent base for undertaking encounters with other adults around issues likely to generate conflict. It is important that adults have established caring relationships with each other that provide the base of safety from which it is possible to challenge each other.

5. "I'd like to develop antibias curriculum, but I just don't have the materials I'd need."

It's true that there are large gaps in the range of appropriate materials available; but there are more than you might think, especially from the smaller suppliers (see Derman-Sparks & the A.B.C. Task Force, 1989, for resource lists). Some materials can be improvised; families can be invited to share others. Stories can be collected from parents, children, colleagues, and your own imagination.

How do you find support for making changes?

If you have faced up to these potential obstacles and still fear that the consequences of *not* broadening your curriculum—thus leaving children ill-equipped to "play fair" with others in a diverse world—will be worse than the consequences of taking action, what could you do next?

1. **Buddy up with a sympathetic colleague or two in your school or community.**

Talk about changes you'd like to create in your classroom. Share your fears of potential obstacles. Commit to working together and help each other get started. Arrange to observe in each other's classrooms (it's amazing how rarely teachers do this) and then raise questions and make suggestions to each other. You might agree to focus your first observation on the room environment or how children are using different materials. Make a commitment to be both caring and direct. Tell each other about new things you try and what happens.

2. **Begin step-by-step in your own classroom.**

Get ideas from reading and from workshops. Identify one thing you want to change—in the environment, in children's behavior, or in your behavior. Decide whether you want to address all the areas of bias or just one, and whether you want to begin with the one easiest for you (for some people that's gender equity) and then go on to a harder one, or start out by tackling the one that is your biggest challenge. Be alert to opportunities offered by things that children say and do. Remember that children are forgiving. If something feels wrong one day, bring it up again the next day: "You know, yesterday I said something that I've been thinking about some more. I'm not sure that was a good idea. What do you think"? As Vivian Paley (1986) has pointed out, children are eager to discuss issues of feelings and fairness; those are their preoccupations, too. They'll help you if you ask them.

3. **Develop strategies for sharing your learning with other teachers, parents, administrators, and the professional community.**

• Before approaching other staff, consider the following: Is there a climate of trust and caring in your

program, among peers and with administrators? If not, that's your first priority to work on, through resolving other issues or just through getting to know each other

better. One relevant approach is to schedule time at meetings for personal sharing of "family albums": Where do you come from? Tell us about your family and culture and

---

Am I Creating An Antibias Environment?

To gain a sense of whether you're creating an antibias environment in your program, score yourself on this checklist. Rather than relying on memory, have this checklist with you in the classroom. If your answer to an item is "a lot," give yourself 2 points; if your answer is "a little," give yourself 1 point; and if your answer is "no," give yourself 0.

Do I use materials/do activities that teach about. . .
• all the children, families, and staff in my program?
• contemporary children and adults from the major racial/ethnic groups in my community, my state, and American society in their families, at work, and at play?
• diversity within each racial/ethnic group?
• women and men of various ethnic backgrounds doing "jobs in the home"?
• women and men of various ethnic backgrounds doing "jobs outside the home" including blue collar work, pink collar work, white collar work, and artistic work?
• elderly people of various backgrounds doing a variety of activities?
• differently abled people of various backgrounds working, being with their families, and playing?
• diversity in family lifestyles, including single mom or dad; mom works, dad's at home; dad works, mom's at home; mom and dad work; two moms or two dads; extended families; interracial and multiethnic families; foster families; families by adoption; families with differently abled members; low-income families; middle-class families?
• individuals of many different backgrounds who contribute to our lives, including participants in movements for justice?

Now total your points and examine the results _____

If your score is between *16* and *18*, you are using an antibias approach.
If your score is between *11* and *15*, you are moving away from a tourist approach in some areas.
If your score is between *5* and *10*, you are using a tourist approach.
If your score is *4* or below, you are using a dominant (Euro-American) culture-centered approach.

neighborhood, your experiences with differences. Anti-bias issues should not be tackled with coworkers unless the existing relationships are emotionally safe and caring.

• If trust exists, bring up the issue with your school staff as a concern you'd like to share. Are others interested? Identify your allies: Who else shares your concern? Is there enough interest for an in-service, or do you need a voluntary study/ task group? Consider whether to identify interested parents and invite them to participate with staff in such a group.

• Agree on a clear structure for study/task group meetings, with rules of order and a designated facilitator for each session. There will be issues of territory and mistrust; you will encounter both personal and institutional obstacles to change.

• Give it time; expect to continue meeting for a year or more. Plan to go back and forth between discussion and action, making a commitment to both learning and change-making. Apply the same rules of acceptance of each person that govern your work with children.

Antibias work begins with the assumption that, like yourself, other early childhood educators want to grow and improve. Most adults working with young children value fairness, self-esteem, and respect for individual differences. This shared value base is a starting point for questioning each other: "I've been wondering about . . .(the pictures on our walls, the holidays we celebrate, the dramatic play props we provide, some of our books)." Are they fair? What messages do they give children about themselves and about other people?

The other important assumption is that growth takes time. Other adults' priorities may be different from yours. Respect and learn from their priorities while advocating for your own. Recognize the slowness of the

process and people's right not to change even though you think they should. Remember that you are creating disequilibrium when others may be seeking equilibrium in their lives and in their work.

Early childhood educators committed to developmentally appropriate practice—in which children's competence and motivation to grow and learn are trusted, developmental and individual differences are respected, and adult-child relationships are more egalitarian than authoritarian—have a solid foundation for meeting the challenges of diversity. Integrating an antibias approach into developmentally appropriate practice takes time, persistence, courage, and the conviction that children are worth the struggle.

For further reading

Beaglehole, R. (1983). Validating all families. *Bulletin, 14*(7,8), 24–26.

Carter, M. (1988, January). Honoring diversity: Problems and possibilities for staff and organization. *Child Care Information Exchange,* 43–47.

Chafel, J. (1990). Children in poverty: Policy perspectives on a national crisis. *Young Children, 45*(5), 31–37.

Clay, J. (1990). Working with lesbian and gay parents and their children. *Young Children, 45*(3), 31–35.

Delpit, L. (1988, August). The silenced dialogue: Power and pedagogy in educating other people's children. *Harvard Educational Review,* 280–298.

Derman-Sparks, L. (1989, Fall). How well are we nurturing racial and ethnic diversity? *Connections,* 3–5.

Derman-Sparks, L. (1990, November/December). Understanding diversity: What young children

want and need to know. *Pre-K Today,* 44–50.

Dorris, M. (1978). Why I'm not thankful for Thanksgiving. *Bulletin, 9*(7), 6–9.

Forschl, M., Colon, L., Rubin, E., & Sprung, B. (1984). *Including all of us: An early childhood curriculum about disability.* New York: Educational Equity Concepts.

Galinsky, E. (1990). Why are some parent/teacher partnerships clouded with difficulties? *Young Children, 45*(5), 2–3, 38–39.

Garcia, E. (1980). Bilingualism in early childhood. *Young Children, 35*(4), 52–56.

George F. (1990). Checklist for a non-sexist classroom. *Young Children, 45*(2), 10–11.

Greenberg, P. (1969/1990). *The devil has slippery shoes: A biased biography of the child development group of Mississippi (CDGM)—A story of maximum feasible poor parent participation.* Washington, DC: Youth Policy Institute.

Greenberg, P. (1989). Parents as partners in young children's development and education. *Young Children, 44*(4), 61–75.

Greenberg, P. (1991). *Character development: Encouraging self-esteem & self-discipline in infants, toddlers, & two-year-olds.* Washington, DC: NAEYC.

Honig, A. (1983). Sex role socialization in early childhood. *Young Children, 38*(6), 37–70.

Katz, J. (1979). *White awareness: Handbook for anti-racism training.* Norman, OK: University of Oklahoma Press.

Kendall, F. (1983). *Diversity in the classroom: A multicultural approach to the education of young children.* New York: Teachers College Press, Columbia University.

McGinnis, K., & McGinnis, J. (1990). *Parenting for peace and justice.* New York: Orbis.

Neugebauer, B. (Ed.). (1987). *Alike and different: Exploring our humanity with young children.* Redmond, WA: Exchange Press.

Phillips, C. B. (1988). Nurturing diversity for today's children and tomorrow's leaders. *Young Children, 43*(2), 42–47.

Ramsey, P. (1979). Beyond ten little Indians and turkeys: Alternative approaches to Thanksgiving. *Young Children, 34*(6), 28–51.

Ramsey, P. (1987). *Teaching and learning in a diverse world.* New York: Teachers College Press.

Sheldon, A. (1990). Kings are royaler than queens: Language and socialization. *Young Children, 45*(2), 4–9.

Slapin, B. (1990). *A guide to evaluating children's literature for handicappism.* Berkeley, CA: Oyate.

Slapin, B., & Seale, D. (1989). *Books without bias: Through Indian eyes.* Berkeley, CA: Oyate.

Sprung, B., Forschl, M., & Campbell, P. (1985). *What will happen if: Young children and the scientific method.* New York: Educational Equity Concepts.

Wardle, F. (1987). Are you sensitive to interracial children's special identity needs? *Young Children, 42*(2), 53–59.

Wardle, F. (1990). Endorsing children's differences: Meeting the needs of adopted minority children. *Young Children, 45*(5), 44–46.

Williams. L. R., & DeGaetano, Y. (1985). *ALERTA: A multicultural, bilingual approach to teaching young children.* Menlo Park, CA: Addison-Wesley.

Zinn, H. (1980). *A people's history of the United States.* New York: Harper & Row.

References

Bredekamp, S., & Apple, P. L. (1986). How early childhood programs get accredited: An analysis of accreditation decisions. *Young Children, 42*(1), 34–37.

Derman-Sparks, L., & the A.B.C. Task Force. (1989). *Anti-bias curriculum: Tools for empowering young children.* Washington, DC: NAEYC.

National Academy of Early Childhood Programs. (1984). *Accreditation criteria and procedures.* Washington, DC: NAEYC.

Paley, V. (1986). On listening to what the children say. *Harvard Educational Review, 56*(2), 122–131.

A Global Collage of Impressions: Preschools Abroad

Leah D. Adams

"What do you think of European preschools?" "Do they have good schools in Yemen?" "What are Chinese child care centers like?" I am always taken aback when asked such questions. Of course, I'm always taken aback when someone asks what I think of kindergarten education in the United States; I never know how to answer that either. Does the question refer to kindergarten classes in the school near my home? Or kindergartens across the United States? Even if the inquirer expected an answer based on the schools which I visit regularly to supervise student teachers I would have to give a general statement, followed by some qualifying statements related to different teachers, different schools, and different school districts — all within *one* county! The old adage that "All generalizations are dangerous, including this one" always comes to mind.

It is also impossible to make simple comparisons between our schools and child care centers and those in other nations. People in every culture tend to think that their way of doing things is the best and the most natural. Many factors, such as cultural traditions, a country's needs and available resources, and the frequency with which children assume all or part of the responsibility as family wage-earners, must be taken into account when examining the educational system of any nation. We must steer clear of the temptation to look at other nations's efforts as good or bad, according to our own views of education and child rearing.

Leah D. Adams is Professor of Early Childhood Education, Eastern Michigan University, Ypsilanti, MI.

I have been fortunate to visit schools and child care centers and talk with educators in many parts of the world, and while keeping the above cautions in mind, there are some generalizations which I feel are reasonable: (1) The teacher is the most important ingredient in any classroom. Bertrand Russell said that teachers are, more than any other class, the guardians of civilization. This appears to be true, regardless of extent to which a system's goals and curriculum are standardized. There are outstanding teachers and poor teachers in every nation. (2) Good physical facilities are always preferred, but facilities alone do not determine program quality; mediocre programs can be found in excellent settings, and some good teaching goes on in woefully inadequate environments. (3) Throughout the world there is need for more child care and for better educational services; the wealthier nations could expand and improve services, and poorer nations need to offer more opportunity for education.

There are other well-founded generalizations which can be constructed, but individual experiences are more likely to offer small, limited insights. The impressions garnered are based on how the programs looked to me when I visited. These impressions are personal, not scientific nor penetrating. Each, however, has made an impact on my thinking. Travel with me through a collage of those experiences.

North Yemen (Yemen Arab Republic)

We begin in Sana'a, the capital city

From *Day Care & Early Education*, Spring 1991, pp. 4-7. Published by Human Sciences Press, 72 Fifth Avenue, New York, NY 10011.

of the Muslim nation North Yemen, in the mountainous southwestern corner of the Arabian Peninsula. The UNESCO-funded program was housed in a single-story building, constructed of the sand-colored bricks used for most buildings there. The director, trained as a nurse, was dressed in white from head to toe, including a white veil across her face. I had talked earlier with the program's UNESCO consultant from Lebanon, who told me that she urges the staff to teach with their faces uncovered. That morning, because a male served as my interpreter, the veils remained in place.

The setting was clean and well furnished. Brightly colored murals decorated the walls, soft pillows were on the floor of the book corner, and blocks and manipulative toys were available. Fourteen four-year-old boys and girls sat at a rectangular table playing with wooden puzzles. They were given verbal encouragement and occasional help by the teachers wearing the traditional black sharshaf. The children, wearing blue and white checked smocks, appeared happy and relaxed, and the director showed us around with justifiable pride. This setting was far superior to the physical environment of a typical school in this poor nation, and staff had in-service training on how to run a developmentally appropriate program. The program seemed quite structured to my Western eyes, and the playground, in this desert setting, was nearly barren. The excitement which I felt during that visit was not because this was a program model which should be emulated elsewhere, but because it represented a beginning. At the end of the visit I left with the hope that the staff was becoming comfortable with this approach to education. It is not traditional in this part of the world for classrooms to have manipulative materials available. Nor is it traditional for children to work with their hands and create with clay and paint. It is giant step in a nation which has a long history of keeping females at home and a relatively short history of providing education much beyond the reading of the Koran. In Yemen, as in the rest of the world, more mothers have entered the work force, and more child care is needed. This program represented a positive step for a nation with many steps to take toward modernization.

For contrast, travel with me next to the capital of an Eastern European nation, Sofia, Bulgaria, to a program, called a kindergarten, which serves over two hundred children three to six years old.

Bulgaria

The large building was built and designed as a child care center and included a spacious outdoor area, a teacher's lounge, a gymnasium and a swimming pool. The Bulgarian hosts explained that they had done research which showed that children who swam at least twice a week had less flu and fewer colds. Their goal was to have a swimming pool in every kindergarten in the city of Sofia. The children eat three meals a day at the center. All kindergartens in the city are under the same authority and serve the same food. The menus are planned not only for a balanced diet but also with an eye to the appropriate number of calories. I do not recall seeing an overweight child at that large center; they all looked rosy-cheeked and physically fit.

The visitors, a group of us attending a conference in Sofia which was sponsored by OMEP, the World Organization for Early Childhood Education, were entertained by five- and six-year-olds performing a series of traditional folk dances. The folk dances required a high degree of agility and coordination as well as considerable stamina. The children performed with grace and enthusiasm, displaying healthful vigor. A conference delegate from Switzerland remarked to the hosts: "Compared to yours, our children are elephants!" The physical fitness and coordination which the children displayed was concrete evidence of the program's concern for health, diet, and exercise. Ethnic identity and the preservation of cultural components such as folk dances are important parts of their curriculum.

The extensive use of the outdoor area was also impressive. It featured gross motor activity areas including a wheel-toy space for learning traffic rules and space for running and playing games. In addition, a wide variety of materials such as dramatic play props and art materials had been brought outside.

The classroom groups were large by our standards, with as many as thirty-five three-year-olds napping in one room under the supervision of two adults. The cots were placed too close together to pass fire inspection in many of our states, but the rooms were clean and attractive.

It was apparent that group participation and adherence to group rules receive more attention there than in our culture, where we put heavy emphasis on individuality. An accent on group behavior is often the most glaring difference we observe when visiting programs abroad. For example, in the People's Republic of China, I watched a class of twenty-five children play a circle game. The children patiently waited for their turns without being reminded by the teacher.

England

There is a church-sponsored day care program in England which I have visited several times over a period of years. I get a good feeling every time I think about my recent visits there. The first time I visited, in 1977, I took a number of photographs. Those slides have served as good illustrations for graduate classes when I want to show how *not* to run a child care program but do not wish to show pictures of a center known to class members. The setting was bleak and underequipped, the staff appeared indifferent and poorly trained, and the children seemed bored and somewhat unruly. I went back nearly eight years later and found the center had undergone a complete restructuring, and I now have both "before" and "after" pictures. The difference could be attributed to the energetic, knowledgeable, and competent director/head teacher. The setting had been redecorated, and the huge room with its horrendously high ceiling no longer seemed dismal. The director had selected excellent staff and had purchased appropriate equipment. The circle time, in contrast to one which I had observed on the first visit, was interesting and fun and invited the children's involvement. It was a graphic example of the impact an administrator can have on a program. It also points out that we cannot make judgments about child care in any nation without a comprehensive analysis.

If I had rated the British center described above on a scale of 1 to 10 during my first visit in 1977, I would have awarded it a 3; but a different day care center which I visited that very same week, located only a few miles away in the same city, would have been given a 9½. While I have visited many wonderful child care centers in Scandinavia, one which would have drawn a rating of about 4 out of 10, at least on the day of my visit, sticks out in my mind. The numerous child care centers within a ten-mile radius of my home would also draw a wide range of scores on the same scale, and the ratings would fluctuate from year to year, possibly month to month, depending to a great extent on the quality of the staff and the volume of staff turnover.

While well-trained, long-term staff are more likely to be found in high-quality programs, volunteer efforts can also have a positive impact on children.

Indonesia

One of my most memorable visits was to a preschool program in Jakarta, Indonesia, run by student volunteers. For this piece of our collage, imagine a small corrugated-steel building, half the size of our average classroom, crowded with preschoolers on long benches. The children sat still for long periods of time. During my visit, both the temperature and the humidity must have been hovering around 95, but as I stood there in that hot room, channels of perspiration running down

my back, I was thrilled by what I saw. That program was run by students from the Jakarta Campus of the Institute for Teacher Training and Education. The year before, some of the students had conducted a survey in some poor sections of the city to find out how many school-aged children were not enrolled in elementary school. The students were appalled by their findings and decided to take some action. They opened weekend preschool programs in several neighborhoods, volunteering their time and furnishing the materials for the activities. Their goals included helping the children prepare for school and taking steps to instill in the parents an appreciation of the value of education.

Parent cooperation was crucial to the endeavor. The benches had been built by the community members. The members of the community were pleased to show off their school to a visiting American, and many of them, and some of their chickens, came out to greet me as I walked down the dusty alley to the school that morning. I felt it was child advocacy at its finest.

Ecuador

Non-industrialized nations have limited resources available for funding, equipping, and staffing educational systems. Ecuador is one of those nations. It is struggling to provide an adequate educational system for a diverse population of about ten million people.

I visited a preschool in Guayaquil which serves as a training center for the university there. The children, ages two to four, attend five mornings per week, and the university students serve as the classroom teachers. Two student teachers are assigned to each classroom, with twenty-five to thirty-five children, for a school year. A director handles all administrative functions, and university supervisors oversee the student teachers. Ecuador's mild climate enables the school to function very differently from schools in less tropical environments. There is no glass in the classroom windows facing the courtyard, and dramatic

play areas are out in the courtyard, protected by an overhang. The student teachers must furnish most of the teaching materials, including paper and crayons. This school shares a problem with schools I have visited in other developing nations: there is no on-site source of water. This contributes to the school's financial problems, as a large portion of the budget must be spent on the drums of water delivered each day.

Student teachers are required to keep extensive records on individual children and to do thorough planning for each day. The parent program is impressive also. I was shown some of the Christmas gifts, ranging from puzzles to beautifully made, fully clothed cloth dolls which parents had made during parent workshops at the center. The toys were age-appropriate, and it was obvious that much love and effort had gone into their construction.

Australia

Australia's special programs for aborigine children are an example of the global efforts to meet the needs of minority populations. Every nation has diversity in its population, and care is needed to counteract biases and to balance the resources and opportunities available to all children. The Kindergarten Head Start program which I visited in Townsville, Queensland, offered a well-rounded, play-based curriculum to children from the aborigine community. The head teacher appeared to be very supportive of parents and their ethnicity and was creative in her ability to integrate community resources into the program. On the morning of my visit a group of adult male students from the local community college landscape architecture program was installing a new patio area, replacing the older paving blocks. The head teacher had arranged for the free labor to be carried out during the time the program was in session so the children could observe the men at work. She seized every opportunity for field trips and activities which would help the children to feel a part of the larger community, while at the same time instilling pride in their cultural heritage.

Summary

The impressions in this collage are based on personal observations and, in many cases, a single day's visit. The programs described have probably changed. Some may no longer be in existence as this goes to print. Others may be dramatically different now.

The intent here is not to draw definitive conclusions or make stark comparisons. Instead, it is to reflect on how looking at other nations can aid us in better understanding ourselves. It helps to look in a mirror, to recognize the importance of meeting local needs and meshing programs with local values. What makes for good preschool or kindergarten program depends in part upon the culture in which the program is located. School classrooms and child care centers in other nations may look barren by our standards. In many nations there is little evidence of the consumable supplies, such as paint and paper, which we take so for granted, and teaching resources such as books and demonstration materials are sparse. The teaching methods are often more rigid than we are accustomed to or what our children would be able to adjust to, but the teachers may be enthusiastic and competent and the children may seem content and attentive.

There are aspects of some of the programs abroad which perhaps we should try harder to emulate: attention to physical fitness and nutrition, developing a sense of responsibility, and perpetuating cultural traditions and ethnic identities.

In our nation we want children to become independent, creative problem solvers. These qualities are not nurtured in programs with high emphasis on conformity. We should not consider putting larger numbers of children together with few adults, even though that approach seems to "work" in other cultures. We know it is not best for children.

Whenever I visit other nations I am reminded that we do not have a monopoly on high-quality programs for children. When I visit schools in developing nations I come away with admiration of the resourcefulness and dedication of both teachers and students. They "make do" with very limited resources and with physical facilities which are far from satisfactory. Nonetheless, the teachers are trying to teach, and the students are trying to acquire an education. That is what is important.

All that we can ask of anyone, including those who run other nations' programs for young children, is that they do their best. We should ask no less of ourselves in our efforts for our own children.

REGGIO EMILIA
A Model in Creativity

Ilene Rosen

Associate Editor of *Pre-K Today*.

It's midmorning in Reggio Emilia, a small city in Northern Italy. A group of preschoolers and their teacher amble through a field near their school. One child notices light, round puffs growing in the grass. They are soffioni—dandelions gone to seed. Delighted, she shares her discovery with the group. Children scatter to collect the flowers as the teacher uses a camera to record the experience.

Back inside, over the following days and weeks, children investigate soffioni. As they explore, using media such as drawing, painting, sculpture, and collage, they become fascinated with the flowers' spoked shape. Hearing their interest, teachers help the group think of other objects with the same structure—bicycle wheels, Ferris wheels, the sun. Together children continue to explore and recreate. This can go on for a very long time.

Is this an isolated, unusually enriched experience? No—in Reggio Emilia preschools, these kinds of events happen every day.

A View of Reggio Emilia

The Reggio Emilia approach grows from the belief that children are rich, powerful people, full of the desire and ability to grow up and construct their own knowledge. Children have not just the need but the *right* to interact and communicate with one another and with caring, respectful adults.

Reggio Emilia educators consider creativity and learning part of the same process. When children explore an object — a poppy, a statue, a lemon slice — they create their own knowledge. They use the many languages of art, words, movement, etc., to communicate their knowledge to themselves and others. Teachers act as resources to and researchers of the learning process by asking thought-provoking questions, offering materials, and documenting children's work.

Most important, they let each child know he or she is understood and accepted for who she is. Of course, this is true of all quality early childhood teaching. What makes Reggio Emilia preschools unique is the way this philosophy permeates every aspect of the program, including the use of space, teachers' interactions with children, and curriculum decisions.

The Environment as "Third Teacher"

Every part of Reggio Emilia schools, including design, furniture, and materials, is carefully planned to be safe, supportive, and wonderfully stimulating. The warm, welcoming entrance area encourages families to come see what's inside. Messages to parents and displays of children's work hang on the walls, making this space both inviting and informative.

The entrance flows into the *piazza,* or "square," which serves as the communal center of the school. The piazza is based on the city's actual center, a place where people gather to shop and socialize. In the school, it's an area where children of different ages can play together, trying on dress-up clothes or playing in giant-sized mirror-structures. Glass walls and skylights provide plenty of opportunities to observe the outdoors and also offer exciting experiences with weather, light, and shadows.

Three classrooms (one each for three-, four-, and five-year-olds), a dining room, and an *atelier* or workshop open from the piazza. The atelier is in many ways the dynamic heart of Reggio Emilia preschools. Children come here to work on projects, investigate, and explore. It also serves as a kind of art-materials library, storing an astonishing array of papers, clay, piping, found objects, tools, and other items children can choose from. The *atelierista*, or artist-in-residence, is available to assist and guide children as they create and explore. Each classroom also has its own "mini-atelier" stocked with a broad range of writing, drawing, painting, and sculpting materials. A light box, a shadow screen, lots of mural paper, and a wealth of other objects and materials offer children plenty of choices.

Teachers as Researchers and Resources

What is the teacher's role? According to Reggio philosophy, children shouldn't be taught anything they couldn't learn themselves. Then how do teachers know what to teach? By listening, observing, asking questions,

From *Scholastic Pre-K Today*, October 1992, pp. 81-84. Copyright © 1992 by Scholastic, Inc. Reprinted with permission.

reflecting on the responses, and then introducing materials and ideas children can use to expand their understanding. Like other aspects of Reggio Emilia, this principle applies in any quality early childhood program. But Reggio Emilia schools are remarkable for the depth of teachers' observations.

Teachers routinely take notes and photographs and make tape recordings of group discussions and children's play. They meet for up to six hours every week, often focusing on their observations. Classroom teachers, atelieristas, and sometimes *pedogogistas* (education coordinators) review the documentation and strive to hear the strongest currents of interest within children's flow of ideas, such as the spoked shape of soffioni mentioned earlier. Teachers use what they learn to plan activities that are truly based on children's interests. Plus, studying children so intently provides ongoing teacher training. By reviewing the documentation, teachers gain insights into children's individual personalities and child development as a whole.

Collaboration, or "collegial teaching," is another key to the teacher's role. Reggio Emilia educators believe it's necessary for several teachers to review documentation, communicate their own perspectives, and together, arrive at a shared interpretation.

The Project Approach

At the core of Reggio Emilia's curriculum are projects. They offer children and teachers opportunities to come together within the environment and deeply investigate children's interests. Small groups work on projects together, and they can last anywhere from a few days to several months. Almost any occasion that intrigues children can inspire a project. Because teachers welcome new possibilities and unexpected ideas, no one knows for certain what direction it will take. But it's sure to include lots of discussion, graphic representation, and real cooperation among everyone involved.

In the opening scenario, children and teachers gathered to talk about the soffioni they'd collected. Children sketched the flowers using markers, then set out like detectives, searching for materials to represent the round, fluffy dandelions. Eventually they selected pieces of rice paper and tracing

---

Applying Reggio Principles at Home

U.S. interest in Reggio Emilia schools is growing. Here are ways to adapt aspects of this approach in your program.

■ Make your entrance area an inviting place. Consider adding a potted plant, and hang notices for parents and samples of children's work.
■ Place plants around your setting to bring the "outside in." (Call your local poison control center to make sure plants you choose are safe.) Try experimenting with natural light that comes in through windows, doors, or even skylights.
■ Use unbreakable mirrors in creative ways to stimulate interest. Try standing two tall mirrors facing each other, placing a horizontal mirror against a wall at floor level, and lining the inside of cardboard boxes with reflective tiles.
■ Offer "personal paper bags" for children to take home over weekends or vacations. Inside each bag, suggest activities family members can do together based on topics that interest their child.
■ Consider making mealtimes more sociable occasions. Set the tone by using plates and utensils similar to those children use at home. Encourage them to set their own tables, including centerpieces they create themselves, and perhaps even washable tablecloths!
■ Be sure one teacher is always available to greet families when they arrive.
■ Invite family members to bring in real "props" from their workplaces for children to explore. They might also want to demonstrate how the items are used.
■ Encourage children to ask their families for ideas, as well as materials, to use in their play.

Editor's note: Merrill-Palmer, a family and education institute, will sponsor a newsletter for educators interested in the Reggio Emilia approach. For information about subscribing or contributing to the newsletter, write to Dr. Patricia Weissman, Merrill-Palmer Institute, 71A East Ferry Street, Detroit, MI 48202.

---

paper and crinkled them into small balls. The result was a cloud of crackling white flowers that were displayed in the room.

When children draw using light, they express their feelings and ideas to themselves and others.

Teachers supported by children by encouraging, observing, and organizing their ideas as well as supplying materials. Of course, teachers also showed how highly they value children's work. But at Reggio, children's pride in their own accomplishments is what counts.

On Reggio Time

Children are not rushed at Reggio Emilia; instead, their individual paces are respected. Reggio Emilia days have a sequence, but not a schedule. Within the framework of arrival, meeting time, lunch, nap, and departure, children's interests determine how their time is spent. Mornings begin with a free choice of activities. A meeting follows in which children and teachers talk about events that happened at home and memories of yesterday at school, then exchange ideas about how they'll spend the day.

The next two hours or so overflow with possibilities. Teachers work with small groups on projects while other children play within the environment. Often children and teachers take this time to play outside, take walking trips, look at books, or do almost anything else that draws their interest.

Lunch is next, eaten in a dining room where children sit at small, inviting tables they set themselves. Then comes a long rest period, fol-

The piazza — an exciting place to investigate the outdoors, light, and shadows

comed but expected because families and schools share the responsibility of education. This attitude, together with frequent, ongoing interaction between parents and teachers, develops a strong sense of community within the schools.

Reggio educators are quick to point out that these kinds of relationships are, and should be, challenging. But they believe it's essential to serve and work with families in order to serve children. Only by working together can teachers and parents bring young children the best experience possible. And "the best" is what Reggio is all about!

A Reggio Biography

Reggio Emilia began its municipal early childhood education program in 1963. Today, 12% of Reggio Emilia's total town budget supports 22 pre-primary schools for three- to six-year-olds and 13 infant-toddler centers for children aged three months to three years. An elected official heads the schools with the assistance of early childhood professionals and an advisory board composed of parents, educators, and other citizens. Ratios in pre-primary classrooms are 25 children to two teachers of equal status. An *atelierista* and support personnel also work with children. All staff members receive ongoing in-service training.

Editor's Note: A million thanks to Lella Gandini, Reggio Emilia's liaison in the U.S., for her help in preparing this article.

Public Preschool From the Age of Two:
The *Ecole Maternelle* in France

Ian D. McMahan

Ian D. McMahan, Ph.D. is assistant professor in the Department of Psychology at Brooklyn College, CUNY. This article is based on research conducted during a year's fellowship leave spent in Montoire (Loir et Cher), France. The patient assistance of Mmes. Sylvane Beauvy, directrice, and Nicole Pondicq, institutrice, helped make it possible.

A t a time when many people in the United States are engaged in a wide-ranging search for ways to meet the growing need for early childhood care, a rich source of information lies abroad—in countries that have already found solutions to the problem. France is a particularly notable example.

In the *ecole maternelle* (loosely translated as *nursery school*), France has one of the most ambitious and comprehensive systems of free public preschool education in the world. A network of 18,000 schools enrolls more than two million children between the ages of two and five. When an additional 300,000 children in private—mostly religious—preschools (also publicly subsidized) are taken into account, 84% of all two- to five-year-olds in France attend school (Ministere de l'Education Nationale [MEN], 1989a).

In the early 1980s the French Ministry of Education set two important goals for the ecole maternelle (MEN, 1986). The first was to provide a place for every three-year-old whose parents wished to enroll her. This goal has now been met; by the 1987–88 school year,

France has one of the most ambitious and comprehensive systems of free public education in the world, starting with two-year-olds.

more than 96% of French three-year-olds were enrolled. The second goal, which depended partly on fulfillment of the first, was to offer as many places as possible for the two-year-olds.

At a time when proposals to enroll four-year-olds in half-day kindergartens cause controversy in the United States, the notion of two-year-olds attending preschool on what amounts to a full-time basis may seem bizarre. This concept has aroused controversy in France as well (Zazzo, 1984; Arrighi-Galou, 1988), but on the whole it is accepted as a logical step on behalf of children's welfare.

In what follows, I give a brief history and description of the ecole maternelle and then focus more specifically on its classes for two-year-olds. How widespread are these classes? What are they like? And what are their effects on the children in them?

History and purposes of the ecole maternelle

The ecole maternelle in France traces its ancestry to the *salles d'asile* (halls of refuge) set up in Paris in the 1820s and 1830s (Prost,

1968). These were seen more as a means to shelter the young children of working parents from the dangers of the streets than as educational institutions, but gradually they took on an educational role as well. By the 1880s the laws governing the setting up of public schools specifically mentioned the ecole maternelle as the first level of public schooling.

These laws established several important principles that, elaborated over the last century, continue to govern the ecole maternelle. Although noncompulsory, the ecole maternelle is open, available, and free to all preschool-age children residing in France, regardless of means, background, or citizenship. It is a secular institution with a primarily educational mission: to foster the child's transition from the home to the primary school. Its teachers must have the same degree of training as do primary school teachers (the equivalent of a master's degree in early childhood education), and their status and salaries within the national education system are comparable.

The most recent official statement on the role of the ecole maternelle (MEN, 1986) sets three principal objectives:

From *Young Children*, July 1992, pp. 22-28. Reprinted by permission of the publisher, the National Association for the Education of Young Children.

1. help the child adjust to the school settings—its customs, rules, rhythms, and habits—and to show the child that this setting offers its own activities and satisfactions that are very different from those of the family

2. help the child learn to establish cooperative social relationships with other children

3. awaken the child's interest in a broad spectrum of areas that include physical skills, language and communication, artistic production and appreciation, and scientific/technical activities

The ecole maternelle is specifically *not* geared to teach young children to read, a mission that is entrusted to the *cours preparatoire,* the equivalent of first grade in the United States (MEN, 1986, p. 10), although "reading-readiness" activities are an important part of the curriculum, especially in the last year.

Organization and staffing

In sparsely populated rural areas, all of the preschool-age children may be enrolled in a single "baby class" that is attached to the local primary school. Most often, however, the ecole maternelle is a separate institution in its own building, although it may be adjacent to and share some facilities with a primary school.

The typical ecole maternelle has one class for each age level, from the *tout-petits* (two-year-olds) to the *grands* (five-year-olds). Occasionally, depending on the local age mix and demand, the two-year-olds and three-year-olds are grouped together in a single class. Classes in the ecole maternelle are large by United States standards. During 1988 and 1989, the average number of children enrolled per class was nearly 28 (Direction de l'Evaluation et de la Prospective,

1989). This number has been falling steadily; 10 years earlier, it was more than 31 children per class (MEN, 1986, p. 105).

This large class size is one of the most obvious differences from preferred practices in the United States (Bredekamp, 1987). French educational psychologists agree that smaller classes and better staffing ratios are desirable (Celeste, 1987), but they argue that the stability gained by paying professional salaries to a highly qualified staff is a reasonable trade-off for the problems created by large classes. The extremely low staff turnover ensures that children can count on adults not to disappear and that teachers get to know children well.

Each class has its own teacher, who usually has a teacher's aide (paid by the municipality rather than the national education system) to help with dressing and cleaning children, preparing

A class of two-year-olds at the ecole maternelle *in Montoire-sue-le-Loir (Loir-et-Cher) during free play.*

Ian D. McMahan

Teachers have the same training as do primary teachers—the equivalent of a master's degree in early childhood education. Their status and salaries within the national education system are comparable, too.

snacks, and keeping play materials in order. Typically, the director of the ecole maternelle also teaches a class. A number of ecoles maternelles in an area share a support staff that includes physicians, psychologists, and specialists in psychomotor and learning problems.

The National Association for the Education of Young Children defines quality of child care as having low child-staff ratio, low staff turnover, high educational levels among staff, and appropriate settings and equipment. Although the ecole maternelle clearly falls short on staffing ratios, on the other characteristics it comes out very well. Its highly trained staff is extremely stable, and its buildings and facilities are specifically designed and outfitted for a population of two- to five-year-olds (Richardson & Marx, 1989, pp. 34–35).

Regional variations in enrollment of two-year-olds

Even though the ecole maternelle is noncompulsory, for children age three and older, enrollment is essentially universal. Among two-year-olds, the percentage enrolled in school has grown steadily in recent years—from 18% in 1970 to almost 36% in 1987 (MEN, 1989a).

This growth is partly a result of the increased availability of classes for two-year-olds, but the increased availability is itself partly a response to increased demand from parents. Availability for two-year-olds is also a response to demographic changes; in the 1970s, as the number of children in preschool began to drop, administrators faced the prospect of laying off teachers. Instituting classes for two-year-olds was a way of keeping overall enrollments stable by drawing on a larger pool of children (Arrighi-Galou, 1988).

There are important regional differences in the proportion of two-year-olds enrolled in the ecole maternelle. In Brittany, and in a geographic band that extends from Languedoc, near the Spanish border, to the region of Lyon, the proportion is around 50%; in some areas, almost 67%. In Normandy and the Paris region, however, the proportion hovers around 20% (MEN, 1989b). These differences appear to stem from both educational and political choices. In Paris and its suburbs, where enrollments of three- to five-year-olds have remained high, administrators managed to maintain staffing levels without needing to set up classes for two-year-olds, although paren-

tal demand is just as high as in other regions (B. Celeste, personal communication, June 14, 1990).

The ecole maternelle is not the only child care choice that parents of two-year-olds have. In the Paris region and in some other areas, *creches* (infant-toddler centers) offer high-quality day care from shortly after birth until the age of three. However, these centers are financed by municipalities rather than by the national education system, and parents have to share the cost of running the centers. The fees for sending a child to a creche are relatively high, despite a sliding scale.

Another option in most areas is family day care, which is licensed and overseen by the government, but this too is relatively expensive. As a result, parents tend to shift their children from the creche or family day care to the ecole maternelle, which is free, soon after they turn two—*if* the local school offers a class for two-year-olds and has room for them (Celeste, 1987).

Schedules and links with day care

The school day at the ecole maternelle is broken into two 3-hour segments, typically from 8:30 A.M. to 11:30 A.M. or from 9:00 A.M. to 12:00 P.M., then from 1:30 P.M. to 4:30 P.M. or from 2:00 P.M. to 5:00 P.M., four-and-one-half days a week (Wednesdays are school holidays in France, and schools are in session on Saturday morning). In principle, children may attend half-

Classes in the ecole maternelle are very large by United States standards. French educational psychologists agree that smaller classes and better staffing ratios are desirable, but they argue that the stability gained by paying professional salaries to a highly qualified staff is a reasonable trade-off for the problems created by large classes.

The ecole maternelle is not the only child care choice that parents of two-year-olds have. In the Paris region, and some other areas, *creches* (infant-toddler centers) offer high-quality day care from shortly after birth until the age of three. These centers are financed by municipalities, however, rather than by the national education system, and parents have to share the cost of running them.

time, and 40% of two-year-olds do so. However, more than 80% of three-year-olds and essentially all four- and five-year-olds attend full-time (Malegue, 1987).

Most ecoles maternelles make lunch available to children, either in the school or in a separate section of the canteen of the adjoining primary school. About one-half of the children—of all ages—eat lunch at the canteen, then spend the remaining time before school resumes on the playground, supervised by school aides. The teachers use these two hours for lunch and for class preparation. Counting the lunch break, then, the typical French preschooler, whether two or five years old, spends between eight and eight-and-a-half hours a day at school.

For many children, however, even this is an underestimate. At least one-third of the ecoles maternelles, especially those in urban areas, are associated with a *garderie,* or day care center, run by the municipality. Some municipalities charge parents for using the garderie; other municipalities provide this service free. Garderies typically are available to children one to two hours before school in the morning and for as long as two-and-one-half hours in the afternoon, as well as full-time on Wednesdays and during the shorter vacations. Forty percent of the children who attend the garderie are two- and three-year-olds (Malegue, 1987).

Children who attend the garderie are escorted to their classes in the morning by a teacher's aide or a child care worker from the garderie. At the end of school, children who will be staying are taken as a group to the garderie. Several points make this transition easy. The ecole maternelle and the garderie are generally close together and may share facilities such as play yards; and the children, even if they are of different ages and in different classes, know one another from the ecole maternelle. The result is that the garderie seems a continuation of school, although with a looser regime. Of course the 100% change of staff would be of concern to many early childhood educators in the United States.

The day of a two-year-old

What do two-year-olds do at the ecole maternelle? Here is the morning schedule of a typical class (S. Beauvy, personal communication, June 1989):

Time	Activity
8:45–9:00	Individual welcome, toilet
9:00–9:15	Group activities—songs, finger plays
9:15–9:45	Gross-motor activities, gym
9:45–10:00	Toilet
10:00–10:15	Snack
10:15–10:45	Individual play: painting, collage, waterplay, puzzles, and so forth
10:45–11:00	Toilet, coats
11:00–11:30	Playground
11:30–11:50	Welcoming parents, toilet for children lunching at school

When school resumes in the afternoon, practically all of the two-year-olds take a nap of one-half hour to an hour. This is often followed by an hour of story-reading and singing, then another playground session to finish the day.

The most important curricular goals of classes for two-year-olds

Another option in most areas is family day care, which is licensed and overseen by the government; but this, too, is relatively expensive. As a result, parents tend to shift their children from the creche or family day care to the ecole maternelle, which is free, soon after they turn two—*if* the local school offers a class for two-year-olds and has room for them.

Ian McMahan

Madame Beauvy, director of the ecole maternelle *in Montoire, leads her class of two-year-olds in a song with finger play.*

are *acceuil—welcoming* the child by providing a physically and emotionally safe, stable classroom environment—and *eveil—awakening* him or her through access to and experience with a wide variety of activities and materials. Although group activities—singing, reciting poems, and finger play—are stressed, children are also encouraged to play alone and in smaller groups and are explicitly taught to cooperate and share.

Research on effects of the ecole

One reason that French parents are willing to entrust even very young children to the ecole maternelle is the widespread conviction that attendance in pre-school—the sooner the better—is an important step to future academic success.

This belief has a lot of empirical support. In 1980 the Ministry of Education identified a sample of more than 20,000 sixth-grade students, with the intention of following their further academic careers (MEN, 1982). One of the first findings was that each year of preschool experience increased the likelihood that a child would be promoted from sixth to seventh grade (MEN, 1983). This same positive effect has now been found for promotion in the high school years (B. Zazzo, personal communication, February 6, 1990).

These data do present certain problems. During the 1970s, when children in the sample were of preschool age, ecoles maternelles were more accessible to children in urban than in rural areas, and children in rural areas were in general more likely to be held back than those in urban areas (MEN, 1983, Table III–6). In addition, children of higher socioeconomic status (SES) are both more likely to spend several years in an ecole maternelle (Desplanques, 1986) and much more likely to be promoted to seventh grade (MEN, 1983); thus, SES may be a confounding factor. Nevertheless, given the size and representative nature of the sample, the link between length of preschool experience and later academic success appears clear.

Shared concerns about socioemotional development

In the United States a major concern about the placement of very young children in settings other than the family, such as child care, has been the possible negative effects on their emotional or affective development (Belsky & Steinberg, 1978; Belsky, 1984). The more than one-third of French children who enter the ecole maternelle while they are still two years old would seem to offer a perfect testing ground for this concern.

Professor Bianka Zazzo (1984) conducted an extensive study of two-year-olds in the ecole maternelle, including lengthy classroom observations and interviews with parents and teachers. One of Zazzo's most important conclusions was that although the first months of school are a difficult trial for most children, the level

The public preschool (ecole maternelle) is not day care. Sixty percent of the two-year-old children enrolled attend morning and afternoon sessions with a "supervised" span of two hours on the playground between sessions. Forty percent attend half-time, but most twos and virtually all three-, four-, and five-year-olds spend eight hours a day in school.

For many children, however, even this is an underestimate. At least one-third of the ecoles maternelles, especially those in urban areas, are associated with a *garderie,* or day care center, run by the municipality.

and duration of the difficulty does not seem to depend on the child's age. The three-year-old entering school for the first time experiences most of the same problems, and to the same degree, as the two-year-old entering for the first time; thus, in her view, the child gains no real advantage from delay. It is the necessary adaptation, not the particular age at which it is made, that presents emotional difficulties. This study, however, does not touch upon the subject of whether or not this extra year either with or largely away from the parent affects the emotional well-being of a child or the depth and quality of the parent-child relationship.

Other investigators have raised different concerns about early school entry. Arrighi-Galou (1988) maintains that although the older children in classes of two-year-olds may be ready to benefit from the extensive peer contact they receive in the ecole maternelle, the younger children tend to hang back and become passive. Arrighi-Galou suggests changes in the curriculum to counter this effect.

According to parents, the social effects of beginning school at age two are what one would expect: Children talk more, express themselves better, and are more autonomous—less timid and more sociable. Parents also report—less happily—a noticeable increase in their children's use of *gros mots* (naughty words) (Zazzo, 1984)!

Interesting as these results are, they leave a number of questions unanswered. For example, does entering school at age two attenuate the parent-child attachment? Does it tend to substitute a peer orientation for a parent orientation? Are five-year-olds who began school at age two more socialized (i.e., more cooperative, more sensitive to others' needs, more able to control their own impulses) than those who began at age three or older? Further research is needed to respond to such questions.

A fresh sense of possibilities for the United States

France, of course, is not the United States. Its traditions and assumptions about the role of government are very different. France has a long history of centralized control of important institutions, including the educational system. It has also accepted the care and welfare of even very young children as a national responsibility, to be guaranteed and paid for by the state.

However, even if it is difficult to imagine the creation of a system of publicly financed, free, universal preschool education in the United States in the foreseeable future, a look at the French experience in running such a system can give Americans concerned with preschool education fresh ideas and a fresh sense of possibilities.

Note: For those people who read French, an excellent introduction to the ecole maternelle is *La Maternelle,* a volume of essays and articles edited by Azemar (Autrement). Celeste's *Les Petits a la Maternelle* (Syros) focuses on the experiences and problems of two- and three-year-olds in the ecole maternelle.

For further reading

Elkind, D. (1986). From our president. A social experiment of enormous significance. *Young Children, 42*(1), 2.

Greenberg, P. (1987a). Ideas that work with young children. Infants and toddlers away from their mothers? *Young Children, 42*(4), 40–42.

Greenberg, P. (1987b). Ideas that work with young children. What is curriculum for infants in family day care (or elsewhere)? *Young Children, 42*(5), 58–62.

Halpern, R. (1987). Research in review. Major social and demographic trends affecting young families: Implications for early childhood care and education. What national trends affect low-income young families? Should society help? How? *Young Children, 42*(6), 34–40.

Hymes, J.L., Jr. (1987). Public policy report. Public school for 4-year-olds. *Young Children, 42*(2), 51–52.

Mitchell, A., & Modigliani, K. (1989). Public policy report. Young children in public schools? The "only ifs" reconsidered. *Young Children, 44*(6), 56–61.

Morado, C. (1986a). Public policy report. Prekindergarten programs for 4-year-olds: Some key issues. *Young Children, 41*(5), 61–63.

Morado, C. (1986b). Public policy report. Prekindergarten programs for 4-year-olds: State involvement in preschool education. *Young Children, 41*(6), 69–71.

National Association for the Education of Young Children. (1987). Public policy report. Guidelines for developing legislation creating or expanding programs for young children. *Young Children, 42*(3), 43–45.

Garderies typically are available to children one to two hours before school in the morning and for as long as two-and-one-half hours in the afternoon, as well as full-time on Wednesdays and during shorter vacations. Forty percent of the children who attend the garderie are two- and three-year-olds.

New, R. (1990). Excellent early education: A city in Italy has it. *Young Children, 45*(6), 4–10.

References

Arrighi-Galou, N. (1988). *La scolarisation des enfants de 2–3 ans et ses inconvenients [Schooling of 2–3-year-old children and its drawbacks]*. Paris: Editions ESF.

Azemar, G.-P. (Ed.). (1990). *La maternelle.* Paris: Autrement.

Belsky, J. (1984). Two waves of day care research: Developmental effects and conditions of quality. In R. Ainslie (Ed.), *The child and the day care setting*. New York: Praeger.

Belsky, J., & Steinberg, L.D. (1978). The effects of day care: A critical review. *Child Development, 49,* 929–949.

Bredekamp, S. (Ed). (1987). *Developmentally appropriate practice in early childhood programs serving children from birth through age 8.* Washington: NAEYC.

Celeste, B. (1987). *Les petits a la maternelle [Little kids in the ecole maternelle].* Paris: Syros.

Desplanques, G. (1986). *Mode de garde et scolarisation des jeunes enfants* [Types of day care and schooling of young children]. *Education et Formations,* 1986–9, 3–14.

Direction de l'Evaluation et de la Prospective. (1989, February). Enquete dans les ecoles maternelles, elementaires, et speciales [Study of nursery, elementary, and special schools]. *Tableaux Statistiques,* No. 5766.

Malegue, C. (1987). La vie a l'ecole des enfants de niveau preelementaire [Life at school for preschool children]. *Education et Formations,* 1987 (11), 11–24.

Ministere de l'Education Nationale. (1982, April 12). Caracteristiques des eleves entrant en classe de sixieme en 1980 [Characteristics of students entering 6th grade in 1980]. *Note d'Information No. 82–10.*

Ministere de l'Education Nationale. (1983, August 8). Situation, durant l'annee scolaire 1981–1982, des eleves scolarises en classe de sixieme en 1980–1981 [The status, during 1981–82, of students in 6th grade in 1980–81]. *Note d'Information No. 83–25.*

Ministere de l'Education Nationale. (1986). *L'ecole maternelle: Son role/ses missions [The ecole maternelle: Its role and missions].* Paris: Centre National de Documentation Pedagogique.

Ministere de l'Education Nationale. (1989a). *Reperes et references statistiques sur les enseignements et la formation* (Edition 1989) [Benchmarks and statistical references on teaching and education]. Paris: Author.

Ministere de l'Education Nationale. (1989b). *Taux academiques des effectifs scolarises en France Metropolitaine, annee 1988–1989 [Percentages and class sizes enrolled in schools in metropolitan France, 1988–1989].* Paris: Author.

Prost, A. (1968). *Histoire de l'enseignement en France, 1800–1967 [History of education in France, 1800–1967].* Paris: A. Colin.

Richardson, G., & Marx, E. (1989). *A welcome for every child: How France achieves quality in child care.* New York: French American Foundation.

Zazzo, B. (1984). *L'ecole maternelle a deux ans: Oui ou non? [The ecole maternelle at age two: Yes or no?].* Paris: Editions Stock.

A Glimpse of Kindergarten —Chinese Style

Geraldine Beaty Shepherd

Geraldine Beaty Shepherd is a member of the Broadoaks School Advisory Council, Whittier College. She has been very involved in community service, especially in the area of health.

About half of China's kindergartners attend boarding schools. This practice enables their parents to work full time.

Twenty screaming 5- and 6-year-olds may not be what most of us would choose to have on our hands, but here I was, in the center of a Beijing kindergarten classroom as these nearly hysterical Chinese boys and girls crowded around their "American friend." I knelt down among them. They pushed and elbowed each other to get close enough to touch me—my clothes, my hair, several times knocking me off balance, causing us all to laugh. They shouted and babbled at me and at each other. Their two teachers, visibly upset, stood off to one side with the school director. The director, however, smiled on and on. I could not read her chiseled features. Perhaps she was embarrassed, or perhaps she was just genuinely amused at the chaos I had caused. After all, it was her daughter, an interpreter and a teacher at Beijing University, who had brought me unannounced to the school.

I embraced the situation wholeheartedly. Beyond walking the Great Wall, my strongest desire while visiting China was to gain access to an ordinary kindergarten. This, I knew, was discouraged by the Chinese government. Visitors to China are taken to see only a select few of Beijing's primary schools. Or they are taken to the Children's Palace, a special school for unusually talented children. Children at these "model" schools are accustomed to foreign visitors and are groomed to behave accordingly. That my visit to China coincided with the Tiananmen Square student demonstrations was in my favor, for the mood in Beijing at this time was one of optimism and hope. Martial law had not yet been imposed. Had the atmosphere been different, I know my friend would not have risked taking me to the school.

In China one quickly learns that there are two sides to everything: the official and the unofficial. Officially I was not "registered" to visit the school. Because I was there unofficially, my host took certain precautions to prevent being reported for conduct against government policy. This included leaving the taxi and walking the last few blocks to the school and a rapid, conciliatory-sounding conversation between my host, the director's daughter, and the school's gatekeeper. The director personally greeted us at the gate and escorted us in. With a sweep of her arm she indicated we could go where we wished and discreetly disappeared. We did this two mornings in a row, spending a total of approximately six hours at the school. My mind hummed as I absorbed and contrasted my observations with my knowledge of our American kindergartens.

The facility I visited served children of workers from one of the government's large social ministries. The 1,000 children were housed at two separate facilities. Infants and toddlers were cared for in a large nursery in the basement of the ministry; this I did not visit. I attended the preschool, located about one mile away, which housed 300 4- to 6-year-olds. Both were boarding schools, as are approximately one-half of the 4,571 kindergartens in China. Most of the children lived there from Monday morning until Saturday afternoon when they joined their parents for the weekend. This system makes it possible for both men and women to fulfill their obligation of working for their country six days a week. The children eat breakfast, lunch, and dinner at their desks. They are cleaned, clothed, taught, and attended to by the teachers and caretakers. The staff of 80, which results in a ratio of approximately 12 adults to 1 child, includes teachers, aides, nurses, cooks, and maintenance people.

I imagine a Chinese teacher arriving at a typical American preschool would be overwhelmed with the wealth of color and material. I found myself struggling to suppress my reactions as I approached the school I was about to visit. It was obvious that what little resources there were did not go into furnishings, maintenance, paint for the brick and concrete block buildings, or grounds upkeep. The walled compound had various old, dirty, small, one-story brick buildings along one side of the perimeter, the administrative office, a kitchen and laundry building, and storage facility. As we entered the compound, we had to detour around the main walkway that skirts the back of the kitchen building because a huge pile of coal used for cooking and heating had been deposited adjacent to the kitchen door. The combination classrooms/sleeping rooms are

contained in two long, one-story brick buildings parallel to each other and about thirty feet apart. It is in this area of sand and weeds that the children play.

Our first stop was at the one-room building that served as a classroom for 30 4-year-olds. This area was fenced separately from the rest of the compound with the building fronted by a play yard approximately 15′ x 30′. One jungle gym/slide, painted bright blue, constituted their playground equipment. Children's laundry hung from clotheslines on the playground and was also laid over the fence to dry.

As I approached the building, it was apparent that guests were expected, for I could hear the excited whispering of children as they quickly moved their chairs into a semicircle. Here were 29 preschoolers (19 boys and 10 girls, perhaps a validation of the importance the Chinese place on having male offspring when adhering to China's one-child policy) sitting quietly with hands folded in their

laps. They greeted us in unison with "Hello American friend!" and, with some giggles and much staring, they sang several songs under the direction of their beaming teacher. The interpreter asked if they had any questions to ask me, but they responded with more giggles and stares. The atmosphere was polite and formal.

As they continued with their songs and dances, I had an opportunity to look around their classroom. There were no tables or desks for the children, perhaps because at this age they receive little formal instruction. Most of the day is spent playing outside. The wainscoting, doors, and window frames were painted pale green, whereas the remainder of the walls and the floor were unpainted plaster/concrete. An automatic washing machine occupied one corner of the room, whereas a wooden cabinet containing teaching materials was in the other. At the opposite end of the room was a wooden teacher's desk and chair with some shelves

Geraldine Beaty Shepherd

I found myself struggling to suppress my reactions . . . it was obvious that what little resources there were did not go into furnishings, maintenance, or grounds upkeep. The rooms were almost colorless, but full of children's warmth and energy.

for odds and ends. Children's aprons, one for each child, hung on a row of pegs along one wall above which was a wall heater connected to exposed pipes along the walls. Two large, colorful cardboard cutouts of Chinese children, one watering a sunflower garden and one dancing, constituted the room's decor. Some children's drawings were displayed, as in the other classrooms, depicting attempts to all make the same drawing.

This colorless room, in such contrast to our preschools filled with blocks and toys and children's art, vibrated with the warmth of the children. They exuded merriment, enthusiasm, and excitement. They were the focus, a point made all the clearer by the complete void of material wealth. We bowed and smiled our thanks and left amid squeals and giggles.

Next, I spent considerable time observing a kindergarten music lesson. Each classroom has its own adjoining sleeping room for the children. By entering this sleeping room, I was able to observe the 5-year-old children who sat in rows on benches behind small, rectangular tables. The children were learning a song about a cat's meow that they would perform for their parents at the upcoming June 1 spring festival. The teacher played the notes on an old, upright piano while the children sang in unison, over and over. For this 20-minute lesson the children sat quietly, hands in their laps or, as is more customary, behind their backs. A few squirmed, and occasionally the teacher gave a reprimand, but, according to my interpreter, most of the teacher's comments were praise and exhortations to do better and sing louder. One little boy could not behave. He would not sing a note, nor sit still, nor stop poking the children in front of him. As his behavior progressed from disinterest in the lesson to bothering the others, an aide moved to stand directly in back of him. When this did not bring compliance and he tried to get off his chair, the aide physically restrained him. When we left some 15 minutes later, the aide was still standing behind this child, her hands on his shoulders, encouraging him to stay seated.

I hoped he would learn his song, as he would be expected to learn a new song the next week and another new song each week of school. This, and the pianos I saw in each classroom, emphasized the importance the Chinese schools place on music as a vehicle of instruction. In this week's song, the cat was not only meowing but was teaching the children that it was not safe to be out alone at night. Although the subjects of other songs I heard varied, most of the themes centered around peer friendship and patriotism.

Communal living is another area that signaled to children the relative importance of their peer group. The sleeping room I was in contained 36 sturdy, wood-framed youth beds, with guard rails on both sides. Each had a thin mattress neatly covered by a clean sheet on which were printed Chinese abstractions of birds. At the head of each bed, in the same or-

Geraldine Beaty Shepherd

Thirty-six children slept together in this neat, bare room.

der, was a neatly folded pile containing a blanket (no pillow), a towel, and the child's clothes. I wondered where clothes were kept while the children slept. Except for a small cabinet and a wooden desk for the teacher, the room was empty. The room's only decor was two picture calendars above the desk, one in Chinese and one in English. The floors were bare concrete, as were the floors in all of the rooms I visited, including the director's office. How cold it must feel to the children tumbling out of bed on winter mornings!

As the director later described it, the children's regime is structured to group living throughout the day, beginning with their first morning activity. The children wake at 7:00 A.M., wash, dress with the help of "nurses" (usually high-school girls studying to become teachers), have a cup of hot chocolate (hot water and cocoa), and together take a half-hour walk outside the school compound. Upon their return, it is time for breakfast, which they eat at their desks in the classrooms. Next, they all visit the bathroom located at the back of the classroom—girls on one side of the room, boys on the other. I did not go inside the bathroom, but a glance showed an unpainted room with concrete floor, barren of any fixtures, partitions, or sinks. I understand that either the Chinese school bathrooms have a trough with running water or the children use individual chamber pots.

The school day begins at 9:00 A.M., with morning classes of math, language, music, and art, interspersed with recesses. Lunch is followed by naptime. Afternoons are unstructured. Children play outside until dinner or they may watch a video cartoon in the classroom, as they did on one of my visits. Bedtime is 7:00 P.M. I did not think to ask if an adult slept in proximity to the children, but I believe perhaps not. I saw no adult-size bed in the sleeping room nor anywhere else. An

For most of the week, young children are living away from their families, in large groups. Still, they apparently thrive. Does this challenge our assumptions about what children require?

event relayed to me by the director, who lives with her husband in two rooms adjacent to her one-room office/conference room/teacher's lounge, validates this possibility. The week prior to my visit, two 5-year-old boys were discovered missing from their beds at 1:00 A.M. Searching the streets of Beijing, the director found one of the boys a few blocks from the school. The other child turned up several hours later at his parents' ministry, having walked the entire way. I understood the boys were not punished but were told they must never do such a thing again.

It is well known that China lags behind the industrialized nations. I saw much to substantiate this throughout my visit, including at the school. The television set, with its tiny curved green screen, reminded me of the 12-inch televisions we had in the early 1950s. The cartoon we watched had stilted animation that jerked from frame to frame. The hero was a Chinese version of Mickey Mouse, who was having to deal with a wolf lurking among the trees. The children, however, were enraptured and sat quietly, intently watching the video.

Observing the outdoor play area, I watched four boys using plastic badminton paddles to wield a small, partially deflated ball about the yard, each boy cooperating to keep the ball moving. Another boy, who had been playing alone with a ball, stood holding his ball and watching the children. Another boy tried to take the ball away, and a scuffle occurred, resulting in the child's losing his ball and crying. We were

not close enough to hear what the aide said when she tried to intervene and adjudicate, but through his tears we saw this boy yell at the aide and hit her with a full arm and fist swing. She turned and walked away without taking any action toward this child except to hold his arm mid-air for a moment when he tried to hit her again. Several girls comforted him. He joined a group of boys and was soon playing again.

There were few toys for outdoor use other than the jungle gym in the preschool section and a small, metal slide, painted bright blue. I saw one tricycle near the director's office, some distance from the play areas. A cardboard box held six or seven balls, all too deflated to bounce. I wondered if they were just old and had leaked or if they were kept deflated to limit play to tossing and rolling. Next to the box was a large metal washtub that held about 15 plastic paddles. A metal, tubular climbing apparatus shaped like a fish had been placed on the grounds near the kitchen's coal repository, some distance from the central play area. An adult-size wooden glider swing, also painted bright blue, was on the playground, but may have been broken because it was turned backwards and pushed up against a building so the children could not climb on it. There were long jump ropes, which the girls were using in groups. I did not see any boys playing with the ropes. Boys were playing roughhouse tag or ball games or were standing around. Except when the girls comforted the boy who cried, I saw no intermingling of boys and girls during the afternoon recess.

In another classroom, identical to the others except for some foil cutout garlands strung across the ceiling, the teacher conducted an English lesson. She would say a word—usually a noun—in Chinese, and the children would chorus an English word. They seemed proud of their vocabulary. I was told that the government chose English over Russian despite their closer economic ties to the Soviets, in recognition of the universality of the English language. As the teacher explained, the kindergartners were not expected to learn English phrases or sentences; they were merely introduced to English object words. At one recess the children had an English shouting match for my benefit. "Airport" seemed to be a favorite word. "American," "truck," "tree," "grass," "pants," "hand," and many others came pouring out as the children suddenly competed to impress me with their English.

Now it was my turn. We went into a classroom and I was seated on a chair facing the children at their tables. A quick count again indicated a predominance of boys—twice as many as girls. The interpreter stood ready. I wondered what they would ask, believing that at their age it would probably be referent to their own lives more than to their perception of me as a foreigner. The answer to the first question was listened to solemnly by all: "What did you eat for breakfast this morning?" There were a lot of "food" questions, but they also asked what work I did and where I lived. They had all heard of Disneyland. In fact, one of the boys was wearing a Mickey Mouse T-shirt. One child asked why I was visiting China. This was the only question that was not about my personal needs. After the first few questions, I found myself holding a questioner's hand or giving a hug

Despite the lack of worldly goods, these children—well-fed and well-dressed, so open and full of enthusiasm, embracing life in an atmosphere so lacking in material things— promise a sturdy future for their country.

as I answered the question. The children were very warm and seemed to like the physical contact. One little boy tried to sit in my lap but was gently chided by the interpreter when he asked his question. I sensed that he had said something wrong. She explained that he had asked an impolite question. I pressed for the question and we all laughed when I answered it: He wanted to know how old I was.

When it was my turn to ask questions, I learned that they liked playing the best and math the least. They liked to eat hot soup with vegetables (and indeed, these children, like the people I saw throughout Beijing, looked well-nourished). Being at school with their friends was the favorite activity of many of the children. Some said they wanted to be teachers, nurses, railroad men, taxi drivers (one of the higher paying jobs in China), and policemen. One beautiful, delicate little girl wanted to be a doctor like her father. The children answered questions readily, showing no self-consciousness nor any dependence on their teachers for approval of their answers. I thought, this conversation would have been similar in any country, in any language.

At times I was reminded of how old China's culture is, relative to ours. The children were going to dance for me. They were jumping up and down in their eagerness to be chosen to perform. While the teacher played the piano and the class sang, the selected children danced the routines with grace and

self-confidence. In one dance, four boys and four girls faced off and did an intricate minuet, never missing a beat. Four girls performed to a song about the importance of being kind to friends and helping others. To carry their "friends," they formed their arms into a cat's cradle chair, just as I had done as a child and had not seen done for forty years.

Everywhere I was reminded of the uneven qualities of this culture that the Chinese seem to handle with such aplomb: modern video machines hooked up to televisions designed 30 years ago; primitive sanitary conditions with immaculate sleeping rooms; coal and coal dust spilling freely onto the play area; a huge, open cauldron of enamel paint left in the corner of the playground, endangering the health of the children who figure so dearly in China's future; the teachers, who begin training in high school and continue for two years at the teachers college, earning one-third (100 Yuan, or approximately $30 per month) what a tour guide or a policeman earns.

I left the school feeling wonderfully uplifted. It seemed to me that, despite the lack of worldly goods, these children—well-fed and well-dressed, so open and full of enthusiasm, embracing life in an atmosphere so lacking in material things—promise a sturdy future for their country. The children of any culture, including our own, are its most precious resource.

Child Development and Families

- Child Development (Articles 14–18)
- Family Life (Articles 19–23)

Unit 2 includes five new articles on child development. "Why Kids Are the Way They Are" and "How Boys and Girls Learn Differently" will appeal to teachers, parents, and any other professionals who interact with children on a regular basis. Both articles examine the effects of nature and nurture on development. Much has been written concerning the ways in which teachers relate to girls and boys in the classroom. Researchers have identi-

fied a portion of the brain that affects the ways adult males and females approach a situation (i.e., what to do when you are out driving and get lost). Learning styles in children are being examined to determine the best approaches for classroom instruction.

Parents who understand child development or have supportive and knowledgeable preschool teachers they can consult tend not to get caught in the "Holding Back to

Get Ahead" trap that is prevalent through the United States. In many communities, parents are making conscious decisions to wait until their child is six before entering kindergarten so he or she will have an easier time in school. What they fail to realize is their child faces other difficulties as a result of being the oldest child in the room. With such major emphasis in the early childhood profession on providing a learning environment and activities that meet the developmental needs of all the children in the class, it is not necessary to provide a sense of false security by holding a child back where there is clearly no developmental delay or other deficit that would prevent the child from learning and socializing with peers.

We cannot separate the child from his or her family or home environment, therefore, for professionals in early childhood education, much of what we do involves the child's family. We know families come in many different arrangements and the more familiar we are with the people that the child sees on a regular basis, the easier communication with those individuals will be.

Families and their child-rearing beliefs and strategies have changed greatly in the last few decades, and so must parent education and the ways in which teachers communicate with families. More than one-half of all American children can be expected to spend part of their childhood in some type of nontraditional family. By the year 2000 it is estimated that 60 percent of children will spend some time before the age of 18 in a single-parent family. These families need to be supported; moreover, they have special needs that require early childhood educators to be especially vigilant to potential complications and problems that may affect the children's learning processes.

The changes taking place in American families have been one of the reasons the field of early childhood education has grown so rapidly in the past decade. Along with more dual-income families and single-parent families in our communities comes the need for quality early childhood programs. Caregivers and teachers who are trained to work with the special problems and situations that families face will enable the school setting to be a consistent force in the lives of young children and will provide them with a safe, exciting, and nurturing environment. The nuclear family can no longer depend on an extended family network to provide care, assistance, or daily support. Families relocate often and do not have direct access to famiiy resources.

It is increasingly necessary for educators to assist children and their parents as they strive to work and learn together. Information we can pass on to parents, such as the reassuring, caring advice given by Dr. T. Berry Brazelton in "Easing Separation," can help parents and teachers solidify the team approach to education. The article, "A Child's Cognitive Perception of Death," was included in order to assist teachers and parents in their work with young children during a difficult time in their lives.

Professionals who are aware of the enormously varied life circumstances that children and parents experience today are mindful not to offer magic formulas, quick remedies, or simplistic suggestions to complicated, long-standing problems of living and growing together. What many parents do seem to appreciate is a sense that they are respected and given up-to-date objective information about their child. The problem that educators face is that some families are neglecting their responsibility of assisting the schools in educating their children. Parents also greatly appreciate collaborative efforts among school and community agencies when assisting them to meet the needs of their young children

Looking Ahead: Challenge Questions

Do parents really treat girls and boys differently? What can parents do to ensure equal treatment for all their children?

How is learning affected because of the sex of the child?

What are the effects of divorce on children of different age levels? Why are boys especially vulnerable to divorce?

Explain the practice of "redshirting" in kindergarten.

What considerations should directors of programs take when providing for nutritional needs of young children?

How is illiteracy perpetuated from generation to generation? What can teachers do to aid children and their families who live in print-poor homes?

List several activities that will help children to understand death.

What makes the separation process so difficult? Are there specific steps teachers can take to assist parents and children in this process?

WHY KIDS ARE THE WAY THEY ARE

Children inherit a host of traits from Mom and Dad, but that inheritance
is greatly influenced by their environment.

Julius Segal, Ph.D., and Zelda Segal

Three-year-old Linda, in perpetual motion, is the nerve center of her preschool group. She is enthusiastic and eager and commands the attention of both her teacher and peers. Spunky and self-confident, Linda is viewed by her father as "a future CEO of some big company."

Melanie, Linda's neighbor and classmate, couldn't be more different. She needs constant prodding to join the group and is content most of the time simply to sit on the sidelines and observe. Her mother describes her as a daydreamer rather than a doer, "with the sensitivity and soul of a poet."

How did these children get this way? What caused Linda to be so sociable, Melanie so private? As kids grow, why do some turn out to be cheerful, others glum? Some sensitive, others thick-skinned?

Over the years, explanations have swung like a pendulum from "nature" (heredity is responsible) to "nurture" (upbringing is all that matters)—and back again. While one authority stresses only what the child brings into life, another emphasizes only the experience that life brings to the child.

The clash of these perspectives— the nature-versus-nurture argument—constitutes one of the most strident and enduring controversies in psychology. For parents, the issue is far from trivial. Your opinion about the roles of heredity and environment can greatly affect your view of your child's development and, thus, your approach to child rearing.

If you are persuaded, in one father's words, that "it's all in the genes," you tend to be convinced that for better or worse, your child is destined to carry with him throughout his life the personality patterns that he is born with, and that your own input will count for little. Such a conviction can lead some parents to stigmatize their children unwittingly by indelibly labeling them, for example, "hyper," "lazy," or "aggressive."

If, on the other hand, you feel certain that the environment rules supreme, you are likely to conclude that, if only you knew how, it would be possible to make *any* desired changes in your child's personality and behavior. Such a belief puts the onus entirely on parents, opening them up to unwarranted feelings of anxiety and self-blame.

The truth, of course, is that neither extreme is valid. In recent years, both behavioral geneticists and psychologists have accumulated evidence showing that children's behavior cannot be explained by either heredity or environment alone. Linda and Melanie—and every newborn entering this world—will develop as a result of both nature and nurture. Indeed, the relevant issue is not whether the human personality has innate or environmental roots but how both are intertwined.

The imprint of the genes.

At the instant of conception, the chance combination of the mother's and father's genes eventually produces a unique human being dupli-

> *Differences in home environment are seldom able to erase the similarities between twins.*

cated nowhere on earth. Each human being is distinct not only in the combination of physical characteristics, such as eye color, nose shape, fingerprints, and skin pigmentation, but also in patterns of personality and behavior. Never before, unless by the most unlikely chance, has the same genetic pattern existed; nor, except in the case of identical twins, is it likely to be repeated.

Much of the evidence of heredity's power comes from studies of identical twins who, while sharing the same genetic makeup, have been reared apart from each other. More than a half century of such studies shows that differences in home environment are seldom able to erase the persistent similarities between twins.

From *Parents*, December 1991, pp. 80-84, 86. Copyright © 1991 by Gruner & Jahr USA Publishing. Reprinted by permission.

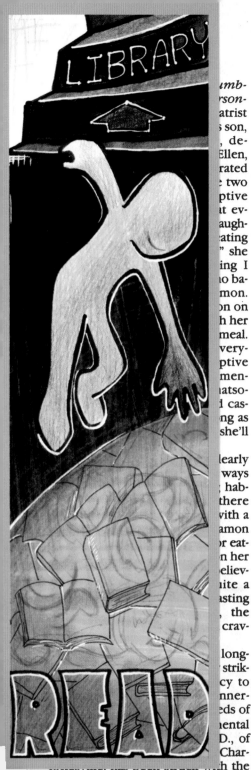

...umb-
...rson-
...atrist
...s son,
..., de-
...Ellen,
...rated
... two
...ptive
...t ev-
...augh-
...ating
..." she
...ing I
...o ba-
...mon.
...n on
...h her
...meal.
...very-
...ptive
...men-
...atso-
...d cas-
...ng as
...she'll

...learly
...ways
...hab-
...there
...ith a
...amon
...r eat-
...n her
...eliev-
...ite a
...asting
..., the
...crav-

...long-
...strik-
...cy to
...nner-
...ds of
...ental
...D., of
...Char-
...h the
uncanny resemblance in the way
they cross their arms, hold their shoulders, and sit. Psychologist Susan L.
Farber, Ph.D., reports in her book,
*Identical Twins Reared Apart: A Re-
analysis* (Basic Books), the case of
Madeleine and Lillian. Each of these
women intrigued her husband with
the habit of rubbing her nose and
rocking to and fro when tired, despite the fact that the women had
never known each other.

Just as specific food preferences
and body gestures can be "pro-
grammed" by genes, so, too, can

much broader characteristics of a
child's personality. Since 1979, University of Minnesota psychologist
Thomas J. Bouchard Jr., Ph.D., and his
colleagues have studied more than
100 sets of twins and triplets who
were reared apart. Their results, published last year in *Science,* confirm
the findings of earlier studies showing that "genetic factors exert a pro-
nounced and pervasive influence"
on such traits as vulnerability to
stress, achievement, motivation, shyness, and even occupational and leisure interests.

The fact that personality characteristics are substantially innate will
come as no surprise to observant parents. Think of the times you have
peered through a hospital nursery
window and beheld the distinct patterns of newborn behavior. Some
new arrivals are constantly squirm-

*Even sociability, a trait
heavily determined by the
genes, can be influenced by
the environment.*

ing, while others are in repose; some
are fussy, others placid; some are sensitive to every sound, others remain
unimpressed.

Once babies come home, the contrasts become even more apparent.
One sleeps through the night and
falls into a routine; another is a night
owl and follows no set pattern in
sleeping or eating. One is responsive
to human stimulation; another is
slow to warm up. One seems to
study the environment in long and
deliberate takes; another has the attention span of a grasshopper. As
soon as a second child is added to
the family, writes behavioral geneti-
cist Robert Plomin, Ph.D., of The
Pennsylvania State University, in University Park, "parents realize that
they did not treat the two children
differently enough to account for
the behavioral differences that are
so apparent between them."

The impact of environment.
Despite the acknowledged influence of the genes, it would be wrong
to conclude that nature can account
altogether for the dramatic differ-

ences in personality displayed by children. Bouchard and his colleagues
are quick to point out that the evidence from their identical-twin studies does not challenge the importance of upbringing and education in
a youngster's development. Indeed,
in any randomly selected group of
kids, the variations in a given personality trait are due at least as much to
the influence of environment as to
heredity.

That influence begins in the
womb, where the physical connection between a woman and her fetus
creates the baby's first environment.
The nutritional value of a pregnant
woman's diet, for example, can help
determine whether her baby will attain the IQ level that his genes may
have made possible. Pregnant wom-
en who use drugs or who smoke or
drink heavily deprive the fetus of

oxygen and nutrients—which can
affect the baby's intellectual, emotional, and social development. Clearly, when babies are born, they have
already undergone experiences that
can govern how the characteristics
they inherited will actually unfold.

From the moment of birth, environmental factors in the real world
also begin to exert their power. Daily
interactions with parents, siblings,
and other significant family figures
help shape the child's motives, values, and ways of dealing with conflict. And later, with the advent of
school, experiences outside the family—especially with teachers and
friends—exercise an influence too.

Surprisingly, even the same parents may provide a dramatically different home environment, with different effects, for each child in the
family. The reasons are explained by
Penn State psychologist Judy Dunn,
Ph.D., and Robert Plomin in their recent book *Separate Lives: Why Siblings Are So Different* (Basic Books).
To begin with, hard as parents may
try, they don't relate to all of their
kids—each of whom has a distinct na-

ture—the same way. And even if parents did, quite miraculously, treat each child in precisely the same manner, each child would *interpret* that approach in a different fashion. Moreover, factors within the family, such as the birth order, number, and sex of children, can make a difference. So, too, can siblings' encounters with different teachers and friends, and unpredictable life events such as accidents and illnesses.

In the view of most investigators today, genes don't establish a fixed end point of development; rather, they set a range over which a trait may evolve. For example, although it can be safely predicted that a child born with genes for average to above-average intelligence is not destined to develop the IQ of a genius, it cannot be predicted where along the broad range of the child's IQ potential the youngster's IQ will actually fall. That depends on the child's experiences in life—among them the extent of parental stimulation, the quality of schooling, and the nature of stressful events encountered.

Similarly, you may not be able to transform a basically self-interested eight-year-old into a little St. Francis. But, as shown in studies of children's altruistic behavior, you can teach children—through exhortation, example, and practice—to move up at least a few notches in their individual potential for caring. It is not uncommon for naturally insecure schoolchildren to slowly gain self-confidence because their parents have missed no opportunity to offer praise and thus boost the children's self-esteem. But in some cases, parents have also heightened their children's insecurities because, as one nine-year-old put it, "nothing I do is good enough for them."

A child labeled "born lazy" becomes achievement-oriented in junior high when a charismatic teacher ignites a dormant passion for science; another child falls far short of her potential because a hostile and punitive teacher constantly ridicules her for being pushy and rude. Such cases bear out an important point made by Plomin: "Genetic effects do not take away free will; they do not determine behavior. Genetic influences are just that—influences, tendencies, propensities."

Even sociability, among the personality traits most heavily determined by the genes, can be significantly in-fluenced by the environment. As psychologist Paul Mussen, Ph.D., and his colleagues explain in their textbook *Child Development and Personality* (Harper & Row), naturally introverted individuals can often be helped to adopt a more outgoing attitude, while painful life experiences can cause buoyant extroverts to become withdrawn.

For a number of years, developmental psychologist Jerome Kagan, Ph.D., and his colleagues at Harvard University, in Cambridge, Massachusetts, have been tracking infants who are genetically predisposed to intense shyness. In the early months of life, such babies show signs of anxiety when exposed to a new toy. After the first year, they stop playing, turn quiet, and look wary—and their physiological responses change: The heart rate goes up, the pupils dilate, and the blood may show higher levels of a stress-related hormone. As they grow, these children continue to respond cautiously to novel situations. As toddlers, they stay glued to their mothers, and as schoolchildren, they consistently remain on the periphery.

In his most recent studies, Kagan has been following up these innately shy kids by visiting them in their homes. Although many remain timid, a sizable proportion are becoming less so. Kagan finds that those who are managing to overcome their inhibited and fearful approach to life are being helped by parents who simply don't accept their youngster's nature as a permanent fixture of his or her personality. Instead, these parents take steps to induce change: They bring other kids into the home, slowly help steer their children into

Responding to Your Child's Nature

Virtually every parent has faced the issue of how to deal with attributes of her child that she finds undesirable. The work of nature-nurture researchers suggests these guidelines.

Give up the notion of blame. Many mothers and fathers, disappointed that their child's personality does not fit the image that they had in mind, end up blaming either the child or themselves. Some feel betrayed and victimized by their youngster and, thus, attribute the problem to "willful disobedience" or "lack of self-discipline," observe psychiatrists Stella Chess, M.D., and Alexander Thomas, M.D., in *Know Your Child* (Basic Books). Other parents condemn themselves for not sufficiently understanding the nuts-and-bolts of child rearing to, say, transform their "baby John McEnroe" into the easy kid they had hoped for. Keep in mind that your child's personality tendencies reflect the chance workings of genetics and are no one's fault.

Avoid making a big deal about innate characteristics that, in the long run, are of no significance. Remember the cinnamon-loving identical twins described on page 82 of this article? The second mother, upset by her daughter's food habit, may well have created more problems than she bargained for by making the "addiction" a do-or-die issue. Preferences in food—or, later on in childhood, in clothes or books—are, after all, matters of taste. In contrast, such issues as learning to get along academically and socially, and having respect for the rights of others, are matters of human adaptation and survival. These issues, therefore, demand parental attention.

Work within the framework of your child's nature. More than fifteen years ago, as part of their pioneering studies of children's temperaments, Chess and Thomas developed the "goodness of fit" principle. They emphasized that parents, in trying to encourage change, should take their child's basic temperament into account. This is what the parents in developmental psychologist Jerome Kagan's studies did in helping their children overcome their extreme shyness. To be sure, these parents encouraged their timid kids to try new social experiences—but they did so "slowly and gently," as Kagan puts it, allowing their children to adapt at their own speed. Parents who demand compliance overnight, or who use punitive methods to enforce change, are inviting trouble, Chess and Thomas maintain. Similarly, easily distracted children should not be forced to concentrate on homework for long, uninterrupted periods; instead, they should be offered short breaks, after which they must return to work. We can bring out the best in our children by respecting their distinct natures. **—J.S. and Z.S.**

social interactions, and help them cope with the stress caused by the experience. (See "Responding to Your Child's Nature.")

Kagan's work illustrates how the environment can act as a creative editor of the child's life story—refining, shaping, and even modifying the basic script submitted by genetics. This is precisely what often happens with adopted children, who grow up displaying patterns of personality and behavior that reflect their upbringing at least as much as their genetic inheritance.

Can such strategies of nurture actually revise nature's script? Child psychologist Lewis P. Lipsitt, Ph.D., executive director of science at the American Psychological Association, in Washington, D.C., says, "you can never predict how big an effect your efforts might have—but this much is clear: Parents should never assume that the child's innate biological makeup irrevocably determines the child's psychological destiny."

Even some abnormal conditions that are known to be purely genetic can be influenced by the environment, Lipsitt reminds us. Phenylketonuria (PKU), for example, is an inherited metabolic defect that causes mental retardation; but if it

is detected at birth and the newborn is maintained on a special diet, the PKU gene turns out to have no impact on the child's intellectual development.

Moreover, even when an undesirable trait persists, parents can affect the *way* that it is expressed. If, for example, you have in your midst a basically aggressive five-year-old, there is a fair chance that he will grow up displaying aggressive tendencies. But over time, he can express this trait in a number of ways. On the one hand, he may be abusive to his friends and get into trouble with the law. On the other hand, he may become a star tackle on his football team or an enterprising salesperson.

In the same way, naturally hyper kids can be inspired to invest their restlessness in worthwhile hobbies or competitive sports. And introspective kids can be encouraged to apply their sensitivities to creative pursuits. As Scarr has pointed out, "We have a responsibility to help our children become the most with what they've got."

Developmental changes.

Parents have a tendency to become discouraged if their child displays problematic traits—such as

impulsiveness, fearfulness, distractibility—that seem fixed and unrelenting. But studies of children followed over the years suggest that such pessimism is unwarranted. Despite the demonstrable force of heredity, the story of our children's development is one of change, not constancy.

It is very difficult to predict how children will behave later on based on their behavior as babies. Even given the strength of genetic traits, we cannot be at all certain which twists and turns their development will take in the months and years ahead. The years between infancy and adulthood are full of unforeseen events that are likely to change the patterns of personality dictated at the start by nature. "Human development," says Kagan, "does not proceed along a single, predictable line. Instead, it comprises a set of transitions and transformations that can advance in many different directions—more like a branching oak tree than a tall, slim palm."

Julius Segal, Ph.D., is a psychologist and lecturer whose latest book is *Winning Life's Toughest Battles* (Ivy). **Zelda Segal** is a school psychologist in private practice. Both are contributing editors of *Parents* Magazine.

how boys and girls learn differently

**And what you need to know to make sure your child
has an equal chance to succeed in school**

Susan Chira

Susan Chira reports on education for The
New York Times.

The first day of school—a new
teacher, new friends, new lessons.
And for boys and girls, very different learning experiences to come.

Gender has become the latest buzzword
in education, as recent headline-making
reports have pointed to a great disparity in
the ways each sex is taught and each might
best succeed. What should parents be
watching for to ensure that their child,
whether boy or girl, gets the best from
school?

HOW EACH SEX
MAKES THE GRADE

No matter what parents thought before
they had children, most soon become convinced that boys and girls are distinct
creatures. Whether the traits are inborn,
the result of hormones or different brain
structure—as some experts claim—or the
result of being treated differently—as
others believe—is hotly debated.

But for whatever reason, from the moment they enter the classroom, boys and
girls *do* tend to behave differently. In
experiments at a variety of preschools,
psychology professor Aletha Houston,
Ph.D., of the University of Kansas in
Lawrence, showed that girls were more
likely to choose activities overseen by
adults, while boys were more likely to
wander off and play independently. Young
boys are generally the more active sex;
girls tend to have more self-control and to
be more compliant and sociable.

As they grow, boys tend to have stronger large motor skills—those that help
them run, climb, throw balls. These physical abilities often translate into more developed spatial skills (having good mental
pictures of how shapes fit together, being
adept at puzzles or Lego building blocks),
which lead to an easier time with math.

Girls, on the other hand, tend to have
stronger verbal skills and so, in the beginning, are better readers. They're also generally more attentive listeners and have
more advanced fine motor skills—the ones
that help them hold a pencil.

In many ways, therefore, boys often
start school behind girls. But by junior
high, there's a flip: On standardized tests,
boys just about match girls in verbal skills,
and they start pulling way ahead in science
and math.

The most dramatic change, though,
and perhaps one that affects all future
learning, is how each sex views its own
abilities. During the teen years, boys'
self-esteem rises, whereas girls' plum-
mets. Harvard psychologist Carol
Gilligan, Ph.D., studied preadolescent
girls at two private schools, one in
Ohio, the other in New York State.
Most, she found, had been spunky as
young girls. But by adolescence, they
suffered a dramatic loss of confidence.
Asked their opinions on any number of
even personal issues, these formerly
outspoken girls would answer hesitant-
ly—"I don't know," or "I'm not sure
what I think."

And a survey of 3,000 teens commissioned by the American Association of
University Women (AAUW) confirmed
Dr. Gilligan's findings on a national
scale. This 1991 report showed that
girls emerge from adolescence with far
less self-confidence than boys. These
teenage girls were more likely than boys
to say they wanted to look like someone
else or—of even more concern—to *be*
someone else.

AT THE STARTING GATE

The first time parents may directly
encounter the "gender question" is at
kindergarten enrollment. For the most

From *Redbook*, September 1992, pp. 191-192, 194-195. Copyright © 1992 by Susan Chira. Reprinted by permission.

part, girls' strengths help them adjust to school more quickly. "Being able to sit still and listen will get you further in kindergarten classrooms than running, jumping, and good spatial skills," says Barbara Willer of the National Association for the Education of Young Children.

As a result, parents of boys are increasingly being advised to hold their sons out of school for a year, a practice known as redshirting (from the school-athletics tradition of holding promising young players—in red shirts—on the bench for a year). Not only are five-year-old boys often less mature than their female classmates, the argument goes, but today's kindergarten classroom gives them less opportunity to develop the necessary maturity. These days most kindergartens are more like first grade used to be, with children often expected to be able to recognize the alphabet and to spell and print their names.

Some experts applaud the move to start school later, reasoning that if a child's first experience at school is unhappy, his later years will be, too. But a growing number believe that holding a child back has no impact at best—and can actually be harmful. A recent study of more than 2,500 children by the Gundersen Medical Foundation in La Crosse, Wisconsin, found that children who start kindergarten at age six rather than five do not necessarily fare better. And other researchers argue that boys who start kindergarten at six are often *too* far ahead of their classmates, intellectually and emotionally. They'll get bored, and they can easily turn off school altogether.

If you're not sure what to do, talk to your son's nursery school teacher and to a kindergarten teacher in the school he'll be attending. Think, too, about your son's experience in preschool, play groups, or other classes—has he liked playing with other children? Does he seem to be keeping up with them? Some parents have even been advised to consider their son's height; tall boys might be "pushed" ahead a bit, but shorter ones could feel more comfortable having another year to mature. In the end, your intuition about your own child is the best guide.

BAD NEWS FOR GOOD GIRLS
Because teachers often work so hard to help boys in the skills they lack, the girls get ignored. A recent report by the AAUW reviewed virtually all major studies on girls and education and concluded that girls are being short-changed. Teachers call on boys more than girls, reports Myra Sadker, Ed.D.,

what's hot in sex ed

Seventeen states now require public schools to teach sex education; another thirty encourage it. In 1970, it was required in only one state. That's good news for the nine out of ten parents who say they want sex ed for their kids. But what kind of sex ed schools should provide is still controversial.

Fifteen of the seventeen states call for abstinence to be emphasized, and that has fueled the popularity of Sex Respect, a ten-session program in which middle school students attend "abstinence assemblies," chant chastity pledges ("Do the right thing! Wait for the ring!"), and ponder the pitfalls of premarital sex: pregnancy, disease, and loss of self-esteem. Over the past three years, nearly 1,700 school districts have adopted Sex Respect—and more have chosen one of 15 programs modeled on it.

But parents in several states have fought abstinence-only classes, stating that they teach fear, guilt, shame, sexism, and ignorance. They prefer programs that face up to the reality of teen sexuality—a recent Centers for Disease Control survey reports that 54 percent of youngsters have had sex by the time they graduate from high school. In these classes, students are taught it pays to say no but also learn how to protect themselves if they choose to say yes.

Last October, in an effort to set standards and stem the tide of teen pregnancy and AIDS (now the sixth leading cause of death for 15- to 24-year-olds), the Sex Information and Education Council of the U.S.—with input from the American Medical Association, the National Education Association, and 14 other groups—issued guidelines calling for comprehensive sex ed from kindergarten through twelfth grade. The proposed curriculum covers the basics, such as abstinence and contraception, but also breaks daring new ground: teaching early in elementary school exactly how intercourse takes place and, for older students, explaining that homosexuals have relationships that can be as fulfilling as those of heterosexuals. —LINDA CHION-KENNEY

professor of secondary education at American University in Washington, D.C., and offer them more detailed, constructive criticism. Even the praise is more specific and useful. With girls, more attention is paid to the *appearance* of the work—"This looks okay." But boys are more likely to hear: "Good ideas in the first paragraph, but you need to look more closely at development." Girls seem hesitant to use school computers—and get less encouragement from teachers to try.

It's not that teachers intentionally overlook girls' needs—it's the squeaky-wheel syndrome: Boys speak up when they don't understand, but girls stay silent. When teachers videotape their classes to check for differences in the way they treat boys and girls—as researchers have suggested they do—they're often surprised by what they find. "I realized that a number of the

girls were having some of the same learning difficulties as the boys, but I recognized it more in the boys," says Trini Johannesen, a teacher in Stockbridge, Michigan, on leave to serve as vice president of the Michigan Education Association. "The girls were simply less overt."

A NEW EDUCATION FOR TEACHERS
Taping classes is just one way teachers and researchers are learning to recognize and correct differences in the way they treat boys and girls. Luvenia Jackson, an assistant principal at the Riverdale Middle School in Riverdale, Georgia, who helps train other teachers, also checks seating plans. If boys are placed in front—as they frequently are so teachers can keep an eye on them—girls often receive less attention, she finds. She also suggests that

teachers keep a tally of the number of times they call on boys and girls.

Johannesen has observed that girls take more time to think through their answers, while boys will shout them out, less worried if they're right. She advises teachers to wait longer before calling on *anyone* and to encourage more independence and problem solving on the part of girls. "If a girl is looking into a microscope and she says it's fuzzy," Johannesen says, "the teacher's tendency will be to fine-tune the instrument, rather than asking, 'What part of the microscope do you think could solve that problem?'"

When it comes to math and science, researchers are looking into a number of strategies they hope will close the gender gap. "Cooperative learning"—a hot new teaching method that divides the class into groups, with students working together on math problems or jointly editing each others' writing—has been especially helpful. Teachers find that students thrive in such groups. But girls do particularly well in math with this method, possibly because they feel more comfortable in a supportive environment.

Additionally, researchers suggest that when teaching math and science, teachers avoid using typically male metaphors—such as examples that involve sports. Girls may also respond better if teachers make it clear that math and science are tools for solving everyday problems that affect real people. Teachers should talk about famous women scientists and invite dynamic women scientists and engineers into class.

PARENTS AS COACHES

When it comes to ensuring equal opportunities, both boys *and* girls can benefit from at-home efforts. Since reading to kids is the single best way to prepare them for learning to read, boys especially may benefit from lots of time looking at books.

what kids *won't* be reading this year

Book banning in public schools, which hit an all-time high last year, is expected to increase again this fall, according to People for the American Way, an anticensorship organization in Washington, D.C.

Books believed to contain profanity or sexual material have long been favorite targets, but today censors are even more sensitive. *Laugh Lines,* a collection of riddles by Joan Blank, was pulled from a California elementary school for its "demeaning manner" toward the reader who can't solve the puzzles. Censors in an Iowa district claim *Rolling Harvey Down the Hill,* by Jack Prelutsky, is insulting to chubby people, and Dr. Seuss's *The Lorax* was challenged in a Laytonville, California, school district because it made fun of loggers.

—ROBBIN MCCLAIN

For girls, choosing toys that encourage spatial reasoning—blocks, construction toys, gyroscopes, puzzles—will put them on more equal footing. Making sure that daughters get plenty of running-around and climbing play will also help.

Educators advise that parents exert themselves to bring nature and mini-science lessons into children's lives. Both sexes will profit, but it's especially important to show girls that these subjects can be fun. At the beach, talk about shells, fish, and the ocean, or if your own knowledge is shaky, bring along a children's book that introduces marine biology. A drive over a bridge can spark a conversation about how bridges are built—the beginnings of engineering.

If your daughter complains that the teacher never calls on her or that "the boys get all the attention," try to help her to find ways to change the situation. And bring up the subject at a parent-teacher conference. Even if your daughter doesn't complain, you might be suspicious if her report card shows that she always "listens carefully" or if the teacher is effusive in praising the child's cooperation. You don't want to encourage unruliness, obviously, but it's important to make sure your daughter isn't afraid to speak up or that the teacher isn't neglecting her because she is so quiet and compliant.

The AAUW offers guidelines for parents and teachers to determine if schools are treating girls fairly. It advises that you check statistical results—find out what percentage of boys and of girls take higher-level math and science classes. Are there enough funds for girls' sports? Also, ask teachers and administrators whether they have the same expectations of boys and girls in all subjects; whether both boys and girls are encouraged to play sports; whether guidance counselors and others are sensitive to gender issues, or encourage the girls to take traditionally female classes like home economics and typing, while they push the boys toward computer study.

With the right information, parents and teachers can work together to make sure that boys and girls not only get through school but thrive there.

Holding Back to Get Ahead

To insure success, parents are giving their children an extra year in preschool

Roberto Suro

In the 1950's, when the children of the baby boom were in elementary school, being held back for a year was an indelible mark of failure, while being the youngest in the class was sometimes considered a sign of brilliance. Now that the boomers themselves are parents, everything has changed.

Recent studies show that since the mid-1980's a rapidly increasing number of parents are choosing to send their children through an extra year of preschool so that they enter kindergarten as 6-year-olds, a year after the normal start time in most states.

While the practice is most common among affluent families who are acting voluntarily, it is increasingly being used by public school officials to hold back primarily poor and minority children deemed unprepared for first grade.

Backlash Sets In

Indeed, the extra year has become so common so quickly that a backlash has set in; some prominent educators argue that it is misguided, and some policy makers add that it is a capricious misuse of scarce resources when public schools provide extra-year programs. "Redshirting," they call it, borrowing the term used in college athletics when students are held back to let them develop physically or to give them an extra year of eligibility.

"Education issues tend to go in cycles, and today's parents are holding their children back because they think it is a way to insure academic success, just as parents of earlier decades pushed theirs ahead for the same reason," said Joe L. Frost, professor of education at the University of Texas, Austin.

Both practices, Professor Frost said, "go against a lot of evidence that children do best when they are kept close to their age group."

Critics assert that children do best when left close to their age group.

Proponents of late-start programs say that widespread curriculum changes have pushed the onset of academic work and testing down to kindergarten and first grade—and that some children are not emotionally ready. An extra year, parents say, will also insure that youngsters are more mature when they must contend with social pressures like drug abuse.

They find plenty of support in long-standing education theories concerning children's developmental, as against chronological, age and in the new and growing preoccupation with early-childhood "readiness."

In the 1920's Dr. Arnold Gesell, then a prominent specialist on childhood education, began arguing that young children should be promoted on the basis of their developmental rather than chronological age. His ideas are still being refined by the Gesell Institute of Human Development in New Haven, which teaches school personnel how to conduct a widely used test designed to determine children's developmental age by observing motor, perceptual and language skills and the ability to socialize.

Avoiding Being Pushed

"Rather than start children too early and have them fail, we suggest giving those that need it an extra year before kindergarten or before first grade," said Louise Bates Ames, associate director of the Gesell Institute. "The goal should be to insure that at each stage they receive an education that is developmentally appropriate, rather than being pushed along on a rigid schedule."

At an education conference in 1989, President Bush and the nation's governors dealt less with developmental, appropriateness and more with educational preparedness, listing as the first of six national educational goals that "all children in America will start school ready to learn."

In a report issued last month, the Carnegie Foundation for the Advancement of Teaching estimated that 35 percent of children nationwide—some 1.5 million—are not prepared to enter school on their first day of kindergarten. The report called for all school districts not participating in Head Start to establish preschool programs for all 3- and 4-year-olds.

Extra-year programs have already taken hold in a number of states. A

From *The New York Times*, January 5, 1992. Copyright © 1992 by The New York Times Company. Reprinted by permission.

1990 survey in Texas, for example, showed that 39 percent of all school districts offered some kind of extra-year, pre-first-grade programs, while 10 percent said they planned to start such programs by this year and 13 percent hoped to start them in the future. Conducted by Mary Martin Patton, now an education professor at the University of New Mexico, the survey showed that 80 percent of existing programs had been established between 1986 and 1989.

This rapid growth prompted the Texas Board of Education to adopt a rule change in 1990 that severely restricted prekindergarten and kindergarten retention. But faced with parent protests, the board reversed itself less than a year later. Last spring it modified the rule to allow the placement of children in extra-year programs "with parental consent."

Jack Christie, a member of the state board from Houston, said: "In some districts as many as 27 percent of children were being retained and I thought some of that was unnecessary. It is appropriate when a child is socially immature or is somehow not up to par, but parents are doing it just because their kids are small, because they think that by being older they'll have an advantage in athletics or in getting better grades."

The trend, Mr. Christie warned, may help create a new class system of educational haves and have-nots. "We are heading quickly to the point at which half the children in first grade will be overaged and the other half will have been put at a disadvantage because they did not get that extra year," he said. "There's a question of fairness to start out, but then we are also adding another year to the state education program without any real determination that such a major change is justified."

Samuel J. Meisels, an education professor at the University of Michigan, is among the most prominent experts arguing that extra-year programs are a response to an excessive emphasis on academic achievement and testing in the early years of school, and that such programs often aggravate this emphasis rather than correct it.

Harmful Effects

"The intentions of the framers of such programs may be well founded," Professor Meisels said, "but the programs' effects—unintended or not—may have harmful consequences."

Professor Meisels says that public schools can too easily use extra-year programs as a means of forcibly retaining students, in effect flunking them in preschool or kindergarten. Extensive research on forced retention shows not only that it is applied disproportionately to minorities, especially boys, but also that children who are old for their grades are much more likely to drop out before completing high school.

Of course, it is parents who ultimately decide on voluntary retention, and they tend to base the decision on personal considerations, not educators' theories. "I thought our son David was ready academically to go on to kindergarten, but he wasn't ready emotionally," said Mary Powell of Houston, referring to her son, then 5 years old. "Also, he was tall for his age and teachers always expect more from big kids, so we decided to give him another year so he could meet expectations."

David was attending preschool at St. Francis Episcopal School, which offers a prekindergarten transitional program for 5-year-olds. The principal, Kay Walther, said it was designed "to let children do a lot of listening, discussing, feeling, cutting and touching, but not lots of sitting and writing."

Now that her son is in fifth grade, Mrs. Powell said, "It was a life decision to send him to pre-K, but we've never regretted it, and we think that having that extra year is going to benefit him all the way through college, because at every step he'll be a little older, a little more mature than if we had pushed him ahead."

With 780 students who range from preschool to eighth grade, St. Francis is a small private school that emphasizes parental involvement and individual attention.

But Professor Meisels says the practice can be self-defeating nonetheless. "As the kindergarten group grows older through holding out," he said, "the focus of instruction typically shifts upward in response to the needs of the older students and the expectations of their parents. Ironically, this contributes to the escalation of academic demands that brought parents and some professionals to recommend holding out originally."

As early retention in various forms gains in popularity, Professor Frost said, some grave problems are going unaddressed. "An extra year is an easy way for parents to sidestep their responsibility to spend a lot of time with small children," he said, arguing that if children are not ready for kindergarten it may be because parents have not made the effort to prepare them. Also, he said, an extra year is an easy solution for schools unable or unwilling to provide individualized teaching.

"The real answer is not to force kids to accommodate to the schools," Professor Frost said, "but to have schools that can keep children of the same age together and accommodate to each child's needs."

Feeding Preschoolers: Balancing Nutritional and Developmental Needs

The preschool years present unique opportunities, as well as challenges, for parents and other adult caregivers. This article presents an overview of the relationship between the developmental and nutritional needs of the preschooler.

MADELEINE SIGMAN-GRANT, Ph.D., R.D

Dr. Sigman-Grant, Assistant Professor, Department of Food Science at Penn State University has for over 25 years worked as a clinical and adminstrative dietitian and a public health nutritionist. She serves as technical resource for cooperative extension programs in the College of Agricultural Sciences. Her research interests include children's fat intake and other feeding issues, food safety in child care programs and appropriate handling of infant formula.

The years between a child's second and fifth birthdays represent a period of rapid social, intellectual and emotional growth. At the same time, overall physical growth rate is decelerating while motor skills are being fine-tuned. Preschoolers, busy exploring their environment, are typically described as being pleasant, independent, trusting, helpful, inquisitive, cooperative, positive, delightful and purposeful.

PHYSICAL DEVELOPMENT

The preschooler's height and weight are not increasing as rapidly as they did during the first 12 months of life when a weight gain of 12–15 pounds or more is common. Between 3 and 5 years of age the child probably will not gain more than 4 pounds per year. Thus, a monthly weight gain of about 1/3 pound is common. This slower growth rate is reflected in a decrease in appetite and less interest in food, a phenomenon which frequently generates the common concern of caregivers that preschoolers are "poor" eaters.

The shift from large motor to fine motor skills development at this age provides an opportunity for caregivers to encourage preschoolers to participate in food preparation (Hertzler, 1989). Many of the basic skills involved can be mastered by children during this period (Table 1). As well as enhancing fine muscle coordination, food preparation can be used to teach colors, shapes, sizes and size comparisons, cultural differences and mathematical concepts.

Paradoxically, while American adults worry that their preschoolers may not be eating enough, the incidence of childhood obesity continues to rise (Dietz, 1986). Sedentary lifestyles and genetic predisposition as well as caloric overconsumption, particularly of high sugar and/or high fat foods, are implicated in this increase. Television viewing is also seen as a risk factor in the development of childhood obesity, due to the limitation it imposes on physical activity along with concurrent exposure to product advertising which often promotes the use of foods of low nutrient value and high caloric density.

Leaving Toddlerhood. The time between 18 months and 3 years can be difficult for both adults and children alike. This is the period when infants begin to recognize themselves as separate from the adults in their life. In an attempt to enhance this separateness, toddlers

From *Nutrition Today*, Vol. 27, No. 4, August 1992, pp. 13-17. Copyright © 1992 by Williams & Wilkins. Reprinted by permission.

often exhibit egocentric behaviors. They enter into power struggles with their adult caregivers; at the same time, they are fearful of new experiences. These behaviors are particularly evident in feeding situations. Recognizing adult concerns when they refuse to eat, toddlers may refuse food until they get whatever it is they decided they wanted. Adults, on one hand, feel threatened by the lack of control and, on the other hand, feel pressure to be certain toddlers are well nourished and healthy. Many toddler mealtimes end in tears and anger for both parties.

Between 3 and 5 years of age the child probably will not gain more than 4 pounds per year.

The Preschool Years. While toddlers struggle to exert self-control, preschoolers are ready to stretch their limits and explore the world. Many parents and child care providers enter the world of feeding the preschooler still reeling from the wounds of trying to feed the toddler—an experience often characterized as a "war zone." These preceding struggles may leave adults "on guard" and uncertain about interacting with the preschooler. Caregivers who recognize the emotional maturity of the preschooler will be better equipped to expand preschoolers' eating experiences.

Feeding the preschooler must be viewed in juxtaposition to feeding the toddler. Although feeding preschoolers may appear as a continuum, caregivers should be guided to view it as separate from the erratic patterns noted during the toddler years. This distinction is critical in achieving the nutritional and developmental goals of the preschool years—learning about, and living in, the world. A synopsis of common emotional, eating and feeding behaviors observed in preschoolers appears in Table 2.

NUTRITIONAL DEVELOPMENT

Food Preference. Children younger than four may have distorted concepts of accepted and rejected foods (Rozin et al., 1986). The children in this study believed that if something is edible, it can be safely consumed in any amount and will support growth. They also believed if any two foods, such as spaghetti and bananas, are acceptable then the combination of the two is also acceptable. And finally, contact of an acceptable food with a disgusting (grasshopper) or inedible food (paint) does not make the acceptable food inedible. By the time children reach the age of 4, they make the same edible-inedible distinctions that adults make.

Parental influences on food patterns are critical in the development of food preferences (Dietz, 1986). Nicklas et al. (1991) reported that young children with high intakes of selected dietary components asso-

ciated with the risk of cardiovascular disease (total fat, saturated fat, dietary cholesterol) continue to have higher intakes of these foods as they mature than do their peers. The authors conclude that persistence of eating behaviors appears to begin as early as age 2.

Using foods as rewards or presenting them paired with adult attention increases a child's preference for that food (Birch et al., 1980). When foods are simply presented at snack time or when given without a social context, food preferences do not appear to be influenced. Thus, using dessert as a reward for eating broccoli only in-

---

Feeding preschoolers may appear as a continuum, but it should be viewed as separate from the erratic patterns noted during the toddler years.

---

creases the desire for the dessert, not the broccoli! If caregivers wish to increase preschoolers' consumption of broccoli, they should use broccoli as the reward. Yet, when asked, parents thought that rewarding the ingestion of a target food would be at least as likely to produce an increased liking for that food as using the target food as a reward itself (Casey and Rozin, 1989). When these parents were asked to provide suggestions for creating food likes, they suggested involving children in food preparation, presenting foods in an acceptable form, mixing the target food with a highly desirable food or eating the food themselves. They believed that coercive methods were ineffective.

Another influence on children's food preferences is the frequency with which children see a particular food. The neophobia of toddlerhood may persist into the preschool years. It is critical for caregivers to present new foods frequently. Continued exposure promotes acceptance. When preschoolers observe adults consuming a food, it is more likely the children will begin to consume the food. And finally, peer

Table 1
Physical Abilities of Preschool-Aged Children in Relationship to Food Preparation

Age (yr)	Food Preparation Skills*
2	• Can scrub, tear, break, snap and dip
3	• Can pour milk and juice and serve individual portions from a serving dish if given instructions
	• Can wrap, mix, spread and shake
	• Feeds self independently, especially if hungry
4	• Can wipe, wash, set table, pour premeasured ingredients
	• Can peel, spread, cut, roll and mash foods; crack eggs
5	• Makes simple breakfast and lunch
	• Can measure, cut, grind and grate

* Adapted from Hertzler (1989).

Table 2
Observed Emotional, Eating and Feeding Behaviors of Preschoolers

Age (yr)	Emotional Behaviors	Eating Behaviors	Feeding Behaviors
1–2	• Neophobia • Sharing is difficult • Requires constant supervision • Enjoys helping but can't be left alone • Curious • Often defiant • Eager for attention	• "Finicky" eater • Food jags • Holds food in mouth without swallowing	*One-year-old* • Uses spoon with some skill (especially if hungry) • Has good control of cup—lifts, drinks, sets it down, holds with one hand • Helps self-feed *Two-year-old* • Masters big arm muscles movements
3	• The "me too" age—wants to be included in everything • Responds well to options rather than demands • Sharing is still difficult • Somewhat rigid about the "right" way to do things	• Eats most foods except for certain vegetables • Dawdles over food when not hungry • Comments on how foods are served	• Uses spoon in semiadult fashion; may spear with fork • Medium hand muscle development • Feeds self independently especially if hungry
4	• Shares well • Needs adult approval and attention—shows off • Understands; needs limits • Follows rules most of the time • Still rigid about the "right" way to do things	• Eating and talking get in the way—prefers to talk • Strong food likes and dislikes • Refuses to eat to the point of tears	• Uses all eating utensils • Small finger muscle development
5	• Helpful and cooperative with family chores and routines • Still somewhat rigid about the "right" way to do things • Very attached to mother, home and family	• Likes familiar foods, prefers most vegetables raw • Latches on to food dislikes of family members and declares these as own	• Fine coordination in fingers and hands

influence, even during the preschool years, can affect food preferences.

Food Intake. Caregivers appear to be more concerned with the amount of food consumed rather than the type of food fed or even the feeding environment (Satter, 1987). Statements such as, "My 3-year-old just doesn't eat enough," or "My 4-year-old would rather talk than eat," are frequently heard. Satter recommends allowing children to determine how much, and even whether, they eat. However, she also stresses that caregivers are responsible for selecting and buying food, setting timing of meals and snacks, making meals, presenting foods in appropriate forms, maintaining standards of behavior at the table and making mealtimes pleasant.

Allowing children to determine how much they will eat is quite different from allowing children to freely select what they eat. The classic study of Davis (1928) demonstrated that young children select a variety of foods in amounts sufficient to promote growth and health when they are presented with healthful food choices. The study by Klesges et al. (1991) suggests that if given choices between non-nutritious and nutritious foods, preschoolers are not apt to independently choose nutritious foods. Predominately Caucasian children from a high socioeconomic group selected foods that were high in sugar, saturated fatty acids and sodium. However, when these children were informed their parents would be monitoring them, they modified their intake by decreasing their food selections or by choosing fewer foods high in sugar. It is not known if these children had frequent access to the non-nutritious food or if the children were denied these foods. Denial of these foods may have influenced the children's selection. When mothers were allowed to intervene, the children tended to reduce non-nutritious food intake rather than increase intake of nutritious foods.

Birch and Deysher (1985) demonstrated the ability of young children to show caloric compensation in response to changes in caloric density and food cues. When children, ages 3 to 5, were given a high-calorie pudding prior to being offered other snack foods, they responded by consuming less of the snack than when given a low-calorie pudding.

> **Allowing children to determine how much they will eat is quite different from allowing children to freely select what they eat.**

A more recent study measured food intake of 15 preschool children on 6 different days (Birch et al., 1991). Children were presented with two different menus at predetermined feeding times. Menus contained nutritious and familiar foods. Children were free to consume whatever they wished at a particular meal or snack. Although there was considerable variation in individual and meal-to-meal energy intakes, daily energy intake for each child remained relatively constant.

In most cases, high energy intakes at one meal were followed by low energy intakes at subsequent meals and vice versa.

These two studies support the idea that when preschoolers are presented with nutritious food choices, they appear to be able to self-regulate their intake to meet energy needs without adult inter-

> **When preschoolers are presented with nutritious food choices, they appear to self-regulate their intake to meet energy needs without adult intervention.**

vention. The critical issue is for the caregiver to provide adequate amounts of healthful food choices. Caregivers should then step aside and allow the children to self-select without undue pressure or interference.

Current Dietary Considerations. Recent dietary recommendations for all healthy Americans over the age of 2 have been issued by several health and scientific organizations (NCEP, 1991; USDA, 1992). It is anticipated that initiation of these recommendations early in life will lead to the reduction in the risk of developing chronic diseases. Additionally, early introduction of a variety of healthful foods may positively influence food preferences and taste. General guidelines include eating a variety of foods in amounts sufficient to promote growth and maintain healthy weights. They also suggest eating a diet that is low in fat, saturated fat and cholesterol as well as consuming plenty of fruits, vegetables and grain products. Finally, they suggest use of foods containing high amounts of sodium, salt and sugars only in moderation. In essence, these guidelines are suggesting a shift in energy sources from high-fat to high-carbohydrate foods.

A word of caution must be given to caregivers concerning any attempt to reduce dietary fat intake for growing children. When sources of fat are eliminated from the diet,

it is critical to replace the "lost" calories with other, healthful foods, such as grain products, fruits and fruit juices. If this energy is not replaced in the diets of growing children, growth failure can occur. Changes in the energy sources contained in the typical preschooler diet should be initiated very slowly. Growth should be routinely monitored.

Preschoolers appear to be consuming diets which meet, or exceed, two-thirds of the Recommended Dietary Allowances for micronutrient and energy (McNutt, 1991). Thus, the concern expressed by caregivers for inadequate food intake does not appear to be justified. However, concern about caloric distribution and type of fat ingested may be warranted. Food consumption patterns of preschoolers do not meet suggested profiles (Table 3). Cholesterol consumption does meet the recommended level of less than 300 mg/day. Therefore, the primary nutritional concern in feeding preschoolers is the redistribution of energy from high-fat foods to those higher in complex carbohydrates.

Nutrition Knowledge. The nutrition awareness of preschoolers were recently assessed (Anliker, 1990). Children were asked questions in four areas: food groups (i.e., "Which three foods are fruits?"), food transformations (i.e., "Which food is made from potatoes?"), food origins (i.e., "Which food comes from a chicken?") and energy balance (i.e., If you exercise a lot, will you become fatter or thinner?"). Preschoolers showed significant levels of nutrition knowledge. They demonstrated knowledge in each of the areas examined. They were able to identify foods of higher nutrient density as being ones to use to make their doll "grow big and strong."

Further examination of the messages the parents had communicated revealed a significant and positive relationship between the messages given and the children's nutrition knowledge scores.

CAREGIVER "DEVELOPMENT"

Health professionals and nutrition educators would probably agree that it is the adult caregiver who presents more feeding challenges

> **Preschoolers showed significant levels of nutrition knowledge.**

than the preschoolers for whom they care. Adults receive a variety of messages regarding their role in the feeding situation. They are told they should foster a nurturing environment, make certain their child gets adequate amounts of nutritious food for proper growth and development, offer diets that are low in fat, limit non-nutritious foods, set "good" examples, provide nutrition education, expand the child's world with new experiences and so on. Often adults receive conflicting information. Bombarded with a host of expectations, parents and caregivers can easily become confused and unsure. Limited nutrition knowledge and food preparation skills may negatively affect caregivers' abilities to feed preschoolers appropriately.

The responsibility of nutrition educators and health professionals is to assist caregivers in recognizing the biological, physical and social environments associated with feeding preschoolers and to enable caregivers to develop personal feeding and food selection strategies without unwarranted feelings of guilt.

Table 3
Summary of Preschooler Dietary Fat Intake

Current Dietary Guidelines*	Reported Consumption Patterns†
<30% calories from total fat	35% calories from total fat
<10% calories from saturated fat	14% calories from saturated fat

* Based on recommendations issued by the National Cholesterol Education Program.
† Based on data from the Continuing Survey of Intakes of Individuals, 1985.

Since preschoolers appear to have biological controls that influence their total energy intake and food preferences, caregivers should be encouraged to follow the traditional adage of balance, variety and moderation. Foods are intrinsically neither good nor bad; moderate amounts of all foods can be eaten by adults and children. Acceptance of new foods, new textures and new tastes takes time and patience. Caregivers should be encouraged to maintain their responsibility to provide preschoolers with adequate amounts of a variety of nutritious foods and to allow the children the freedom to select the amounts needed from these foods.

REFERENCES

Anliker JA, Laus MJ, Samonds KW, Beal VA. Parental messages and the nutrition awareness of preschool children. *J Nutr Educ* 1990;22: 24–9.

Birch LL, Deysher M. Conditioned and unconditioned caloric compensation: evidence for self-regulation of food intake in young children. *Learning Motiv* 1985;16:341–55.

Birch LL, Johnson SL, Andresen G, Peters JC, Schulte MA. The variability of young children's energy intake. *N Engl J Med* 1991;324:232–5.

Birch LL, Zimmerman SI, Hind H. The influence of social-affective context on the formation of children's food preferences. *Child Devel* 1980; 51:856–61.

Casey R, Rozin P. Changing children's food preferences: parent opinions. *Appetite* 1989;12:171–82.

Davis CM. Self selection of diet by newly weaned infants: an experimental study. *Am J Dis Child* 1928;36:651–79.

Dietz WH. Prevention of childhood obesity. *Pediatr Clin North Am* 1986;33:823–33.

Hertzler AA. Preschooler's food handling skills-motor development. *J Nutr Ed* 1989;21:100B-C

Klesges RC, Stein RJ, Eck LH, Ishell TR, Klesges LM. Parental influence on food selection in young children and its relationship to childhood obesity. *Am J Clin Nutr* 1991;53:859–64.

McNutt K. Are we pickin' on the kids? *Nutr Today* 1991;26(3):42–6.

National Cholesterol Education Program. *Highlights of the Report of the Expert Panel on Blood Cholesterol Levels in Children and Adolescents.* Washington, DC: National Heart, Blood and Lung Institute, 1991.

Nicklas TA, Webber LS, Berenson GS. Studies of consistency of dietary intake during the first four years of life in a prospective analysis: Bogalusa heart study. *J Am Coll Nutr* 1991;10:234–41.

Rozin P, Fallon A, Augustoni-Ziskind ML. The child's conception of food: the development of categories of acceptable and rejected substances. *J Nutr Educ* 1986;18:75–81.

Satter E. *How to Get Your Kid to Eat . . . but Not Too Much.* Palo Alto, CA: Bull Publishing Company, 1987.

U.S. Department of Agriculture. *Building for the Future: Nutrition Guidance for the Child Nutrition Programs,* FNS-279, 1992.

A Child's Cognitive Perception of Death

Modern technology and health practices of people today have resulted in people living longer than ever before. Also, the institutions of the hospital and funeral home today make death more physically distant from the child's world. It is not uncommon for the past two generations to have grown up to middle adulthood and not to have experienced the death of an immediate family member (Lerner, 1976). As a result, death today is viewed more as an intrusion on normal reality (Gordan & Klass, 1979).

Catherine Goodwin
and Phyllis M. Davidson

Catherine Goodwin is Special Education Coordinator, College of Human Ecology, The University of Tennessee. Phyllis M. Davidson is Associate Professor, School of Home Economics, Tennessee Technological University.

Historically, children were common witnesses to death in their family. During the great plague of the Middle Ages, the chant "Ashes, ashes, all fall down" from a children's game called ring-around-the-rosie conveyed children's awareness of the death of many people at that time (Kastenbaum, 1981). Children's awareness of death as a constant possibility was further widened by the first prayer a child usually learned — "Now I lay me down to sleep, I pray the Lord my soul to keep. If I should die before I wake, I pray the Lord my soul to take" — and by children's games such as peek-a-boo, hide-and-seek, and also rope skipping chants (Crase & Crase, 1976; Kastenbaum, 1981).

Before the 1900s, the infant mortality rate was high. A significant number of infants could be expected to die before adulthood (Gordon & Klass, 1979). Since death commonly oc-curred at home, children very likely helped with the care of the patient, were present at the time of death, were included in the planning of the funeral, and attended the funeral.

Professionals who work with young children are recognizing the importance of teaching the concept of death to young children (MacIsaac & King, 1989; Riley, 1989). As teachers, it is important for us to understand how young children perceive death in order to have competence in teaching children about death and assisting those who have been touched by death personally. This paper reviews the literature on work conducted on how children perceive death. It also provides teachers with practical ideas which they can use to facilitate the discussion of death in the classroom.

The majority of research on children's perceptions of death has been conducted with children three years and older. For the child three and under, it has been found that the child's concern is with the separation from the parent (Bowlby, 1969; Brenner, 1985; Kersey, 1986; and Kübler-Ross, 1969). The child's reaction to this separation is greatly influenced by adults who care for the child.

A study conducted with Hungarian children (Nagy, 1948) has provided the foundation from which most work on children's perceptions of death has originated. Nagy studied 378 children, three to ten years of age, who expressed their thoughts and feelings on death. Nagy discovered three phrases in the child's awareness of mortality, which blended well with Piaget's last three stages of cognitive development.

According to Piaget, children pass through four cognitive stages as mental structures mature and they interact with the world around them. Piaget's stages of cognitive development are sensorimotor (birth to two years), pre-operational (two to six years), con-crete-operational (seven to eleven years), and formal-operational (twelve years to adulthood). Consequently, if we use Piaget's model, a child of three would not react to or understand the death of a friend or relative in the same way as a child of twelve (Wass, 1979).

In the first phase of awareness of death (three to five years), the child views death not as final, but as a temporary state like sleeping (Kane, 1979; Kersey, 1986; Kübler-Ross, 1969; Lonetto, 1980; Nagy, 1948). Nagy

From *Day Care and Early Education*, Winter 1991, pp. 21-24. Copyright © 1991 by Human Science Press, Inc., 72 Fifth Avenue, New York, NY 10011. Reprinted by permission.

concluded that the child viewed death as a continuation of life, but on a reduced level. Being dead and being asleep are viewed as similar conditions.

Children between five and nine years of age begin to comprehend that death is final but that it is also something that happens to other people and not themselves. At this stage, children may personify death as being a man, skeleton, monster, or "bogeyman." Since death is viewed as a person, it may be fought; thus, a clever person may not be caught by death. Death captures and takes away only those who are too old or weak to conquer it (Kane, 1979; Kersey, 1986; Kübler-Ross, 1969; Lonetto, 1980; Nagy, 1948).

The third phase starts at nine or ten years of age and continues onward to adulthood. In this stage, the child begins to grasp the concept that death is universal and not reversible, which is consistent with Childers and Wimmer (1971), who found that by age ten, 90% of the children recognized death's universality. The child begins to realize that he or she will one day die and that it may even be a painful process. The child at this stage shows adult reasoning (Kane, 1979; Kersey, 1986; Kübler-Ross, 1969; Lonetto, 1980; Nagy, 1948).

This cognitive developmental approach for understanding a child's perception of death was reinforced by Koocher (1973), who used developmental tasks developed by Piaget to study seventy-five children's (six to fifteen years) perceptions of death. He concluded that children's understanding of death seemed fairly consistent with their overall way of understanding the world.

Other factors which have been found to influence children's perceptions of death have been socioeconomic class (Tallmer, Formaneck, & Tallmer, 1974) and the culture in which the child was reared (Gartley & Bernasconi, 1967; Melear, 1973).

The following is information from experts who have worked with teaching young children about death. One

of the best times to discuss death with a young child is when he or she has had a direct or indirect experience with death, such as the death of a family pet or a death on a television program. The timing of questions from young children might not always be at appropriate times for discussion; however, if the question cannot be answered immediately, it should be made clear to the child that you are not avoiding the subject and that you will deal with it at a more appropriate time.

Guidelines for Caregivers

Communication Strategies (Crase & Crase, 1976) has identified five principles for effectively communicating with children about death. Following are those five principles and concepts from other professionals which reinforce those communication principles:

1. Children's questions need to be answered truthfully, factually but with few details, and at a level which they can understand. According to Grollman (1967), children don't need to fully comprehend the answers to their questions about death. Simply talking about the subject makes it less mysterious and fearful. Furman (1975) has identified three basic underlying questions which children are attempting to answer:

a. What is "dead"? Developmentally this question lays the foundation for a child to understand that death is not life or a reduced level but means no life, breathing, pain, sleeping, or eating.

b. Can it happen to me?

c. Can it happen to you?

2. Make sure you understand what the child is asking before giving an answer. Children ask questions using both direct and indirect approaches for the purposes of cognitive information (seeking clarification to confusing experiences) and emotional reassurance (seeking comfort and a lessening of anxiety). In order to gain more infor-

mation to appropriately answer a child's questions about death:

a. Ask the child how he or she would answer the question (Wass, 1984).

b. Communicate with the child's parents about situations at home which might precipitate the question.

c. Observe the child at play for clues to his or her concerns.

3. Avoid ambiguous answers explaining death. In an attempt to protect young children, adults often give confusing explanations of death. Grollman (1967) has identified some common unhealthy explanations:

a. "*Mother* has gone on a long journey" (p. 10). A child might interpret this to mean that he or she was abandoned or deserted without a good-bye. As a result, the child may feel anxiety, or resentment or develop a false hope that the lost person may return.

b. "God took *Daddy* away because he wants and loves the good in heaven" (p. 11). This could result in a child's developing fear, resentment, and hatred toward God as well as fearfulness about being good.

c. "*Daddy* is now in heaven" (p. 11). Cognitively, young children cannot understand the spiritual connotation of someone residing in heaven when he or she saw the physical body placed in the ground.

d. "*Grandma* died because she was sick (p. 12). Young children may become fearful of death because of an inability to distinguish between serious illnesses and common childhood diseases.

e. "To die is to sleep" (p. 12). Young children may be fearful of taking naps and going to sleep because of a fear of never waking up.

4. Respect a child's view of death irregardless of how inaccurate the perception may be. This will enable a child to develop trust in an adult and will facilitate adult–child communication.

5. Avoid answering children's questions based on religious and philosophical beliefs. If a child is persistent in seeking an answer within

those domains, parents should be encouraged to share their personal beliefs with the child.

Activities

The advantage of experiences in the classroom:

Have live pets in the classroom so that children can experience death in a simple, nonpersonal, objective manner. When death occurs, use it as an opportunity to talk about death. Invite children to participate in the disposal of the dead animal.

Have children take responsibility for keeping live plants in the classroom. Children need to learn that in order to live and grow, all living things need elements such as food, water, and light.

Introduce young children to the cycle of life. In the spring, plant sunflower seeds with the children. Let the children water and watch the sunflower grow. When it dies in the fall, discuss the benefits obtained from the sunflower seeds (food for birds and people).

Allow children to learn from experience by taking them on a field trip to a cemetery (Riley, 1989).

Plan the curriculum to provide experience for children to become aware of their feelings and emotions. The use of puppets can be helpful in getting children to express their feelings in nonthreatening ways. Use active listening such as "You are feeling_____ now because_____" to help children label and understand their feelings.

Plan the curriculum to provide opportunities for children to develop body awareness. Help children to learn parts of the body and their function, as well as physical changes which occur after death, such as loss of hearing, sight, and breathing. These types of experiences can also be related to class pets.

Use bibliotherapy for the purpose of providing information after death. Stories with a death-related theme should be occasionally read to children. Books with accurate pictures concerning death should be made available for children to look through at their leisure.

In summary, death does not have to be foreign to a child's world. Children's perceptions of death appear to grow though developmental levels similar to Piaget's stages of cognitive development.

Along with these basic stages, factors such as life experiences, religious background, environmental influences and language also play a role in each child's understanding of the concept of death.

References

Anthony, S. (1972). *The discovery of death in childhood and after.* New York: Basic Books.

Bowlby, J. (1969). *Attachment and loss: Vol. 1. Attachment.* New York: Basic Books.

Brenner, A. (1985). *Helping children cope with stress.* Lexington, D. C. Health.

Childers, W., & Wimmer, M. (1971). The concept of death in children. *Child Development, 42,* 1299–1301.

Crase, D. R., & Crase, D. (1976); November–Helping children understand death. *Young Children,* pp. 21–25.

Furman, E. (1975). Helping children cope with death. In J. F. Brown (Ed.) (1982), *Curriculum planning for young children.* Washington, DC: National Association for the Education of Young Children.

Gartley, W., & Bernasconi, M. (1967). The concept of death in children. *Journal of Genetic Psychology, 110,* 71–85.

Gordon, A. K., & Klass, D. (1979). *The need to know: How to teach children about death.* Englewood Cliffs, NJ: Prentice-Hall.

Grollman, E. A. (1967). Prologue: Explaining death to children. In E. A. Grollman (Ed.), *Explaining death to children.* Boston: Beacon Press.

Kane, B. (1979). Children's concept of death. *Journal of Genetic Psychology, 134,* 141–153.

Kastenbaum, R. J. (1981). *Death, society, and human experience.* St. Louis: Mosby.

Kersey, K. (1986). *Helping your child handle stress: The parent's guide to recognizing and solving childhood problems.* Washington, DC: Acropolis Books.

Koocher, G. (1973). Childhood, death and cognitive development. *Developmental Psychology, 9,* 369–375.

Kübler-Ross, E. (1969). *On death and dying.* New York: Macmillan.

Lerner, M. (1976). Why, when, and where people die. In E.S. Shneidman, (Ed.), *Death: Current prospectives.* Palo Alto, CA: Mayfield.

Lonetto, R. (1980). *Children's conceptions of death.* New York: Springer.

MacIsaac, P., & King, S. (1989). What did you do with Sophie, teacher? *Young Children, 44* (2), 37–38.

Melear, J. D. (1973). Children's conceptions of death. *Journal of Genetic Psychology, 123,* 359–360.

Mills, G. C., Reisler, R., Robinson, A. E., & Vermilye, G. (1976). *Discussing death: A guide to death education.* IL: ETC.

Nagy, M. (1948). The child's theories concerning death. *Journal of Genetic Psychology, 73,* 3–27.

Riley, S. S. (1989). Pilgrimmage to Elmwood cemetery. *Young Children, 44* (2), 33–36.

Tallmer, M. Formanek, R., & Tallmer, J. (1974). Factors influencing children's concepts of death. *Journal of Clinical Child Psychology, 3,* 17–19.

Wass, H. (1979). *Dying: Facing the facts.* Washington; DC: Hemisphere.

Wass, H. (1984). Parents, teachers, and health professionals as helpers. In H. Wass & C. A. Corr. (1984). *Helping children cope with death: Guidance and resources* (2nd ed.). Washington, DC: Hemisphere.

Beyond Parents: Family, Community, and School Involvement

Teachers and administrators are not adequately prepared to address the range of children's social and psychological needs. They know what ought to be done, but not how to do it. Fortunately, as the authors point out, there are others who can help.

Patricia A. Edwards and Lauren S. Jones Young

Patricia A. Edwards and Lauren S. Jones Young are associate professors of education at Michigan State University, East Lansing.

A child lives in many worlds. Home, family, school, neighborhood, and society shape the contours of childhood and adolescence. Action in one sphere ripples through the others. In the best of circumstances, these realms are complementary and reinforcing—guiding children's positive development into informed citizens and economically independent adults. The best of circumstances, however, elude large numbers of children, especially poor children of color who live in the inner city.

Recent hopes for successfully launching U.S. children into the 21st century have been pinned on reclaiming a part of our past—the involvement of parents as partners in the education of their children. The importance of parent involvement in children's schooling has been a persistent theme in the research and school reform efforts of the last three decades.[1] Studies point to higher student achievement when parents participate in school activities, monitor children's homework, and otherwise support the extension into the home of the work and values of the school.[2]

Family/school involvement is a two-way street. Children are more likely to make smooth transitions between home and school when they see aspects of themselves and their experiences reflected in the adults who teach them. Parent voices can strengthen the school program and mediate tensions between school and community; open exchanges hold the possibility of aligning the expectations of schools and families. Many of us who grew up in stable, close-knit neighborhoods knew that many eyes—including those of our teachers—watched us and would tell our mamas when we misbehaved.

In the past, neighbors, teachers, and parents spoke in a common voice. James Comer, a professor of child psychiatry at Yale University, likes to tell a childhood story about how his mother and his teacher would meet at the local A & P. They would talk about his progress and behavior in school, sharing and reinforcing family and school values. He comments: "When schools were an integral part of stable communities, teachers quite naturally reinforced parental and community values. At school, children easily formed bonds with adults and experienced a sense of continuity and stability, conditions that were highly conducive to learning."[3] For many children today, those kinds of communities and the ready support of nearby relatives and friends have vanished.

That parents no longer run into their children's teachers at the local grocery store says much about the changes that have taken place in poor urban neighborhoods and in growing numbers of poor rural communities. Teachers—black or white—rarely live in the same economically depressed neighborhoods as the children they teach. Many middle-income and working-class African-American families have also moved out, assisted in large part by eased racial restrictions in housing.[4] Gone too are many of the businesses and social institutions—the foundation and vitality of community life—that these families supported.

At the same time, transformations in the urban economy have limited the kinds of jobs available to high

From *Phi Delta Kappan*, May 1992, pp. 72, 74, 76, 78, 80. Reprinted by permission of the authors and *Phi Delta Kappan*.

school graduates and dropouts. While it was once possible to find good-paying jobs in automobile, steel, and other kinds of heavy manufacturing, the kinds of jobs available in the inner city today pay wages that fail to keep pace with the costs of raising a family. In the inner cities, those with little economic security are concentrated in the same areas, living with the daily stresses that accompany economic hardship and desolate neighborhoods.

Once the norm, the married-couple household, with father employed and mother at home caring for the children, is a disappearing pattern. Economic concerns drive mothers to work long hours outside the home. The number of children affected by unwed parents, divorce, and separation continues to rise. From 1970 to 1989 the proportion of children living with one parent jumped from 12% to 24%, and many of them were living with mothers struggling to make ends meet.[5] At any given time, one-fourth of American children live with one parent, usually a divorced or never-married mother; among African-American and Latino children, that figure skyrockets to 55% and 30% respectively.[6]

Adults other than a child's parents are taking on significant child-rearing roles. While the extended family's involvement in child rearing is not new among African-Americans, for example, the scope of that involvement is growing. Parents who thought that their child-rearing days were over are increasingly raising their grandchildren. In the last 20 years, the percentage of black children being raised by a grandparent has risen from 3.2% to 12.5% (or one in eight).[7] Households with children under 18 years of age now commonly include foster parents, extended families, children living with other relatives, adoptive parents, or reconstituted and blended families.

One of every five children in the U.S. lives in a family whose income is below—often far below—the poverty level; that rate doubles among blacks and Latinos.[8] While poverty levels rise and fall, children remain the most impoverished age group, and obstacles to their well-being continue to mount. The realities of impoverishment should horrify a wealthy nation, but we shut our eyes to the social context of childhood in the inner city. Poverty brings a host of risk factors in addition to empty pockets. Lack of immunizations and health care, poor nutrition, inadequate housing, homelessness, acquired immunodeficiency syndrome (AIDS), substance abuse, and violence become regular features of poor children's lives. The crack-cocaine epidemic is touching every corner of low-income urban African-American communities, manifesting itself in babies exposed prenatally to drugs, mothers too strung-out to see to the needs of their children, and neighborhoods under siege. The problems are complex and interrelated, but together they undermine the strength and frustrate the efforts of poor families and their communities.

The resilience of families is impressive. Contrary to popular images—and irrespective of family structure—most families today are not in disarray and are not failing to meet their child-rearing responsibilities.[9] It is necessary to sort out the group called "parents," noting the range in their experiences, in their relationships with their children, and in their feelings about school. Some have a high regard for education; for others, their children's schooling is a relived struggle amid more pressing concerns. The goals and values of individual families will vary and may differ from those of the teacher and the school. It is this individuality that parents bring to parent involvement efforts. Yet too often parent involvement strategies are developed as if these important variations did not exist, and the results are disappointing. Until schools acknowledge the range in dispositions, backgrounds, experiences, and strengths among families, efforts to establish sound home/school communication and partnerships will continue to falter.

JUSTIFYING FAILURE

Students' home lives are both blamed for children's low achievement in school and seen as children's salvation.[10] In growing numbers of communities the significant adults and institutions in children's lives pull in opposite directions.

As the two major institutions that socialize children, families and schools share a long history—often one of tension and mistrust.[11] While most schoolpeople stress the importance of parents as their children's first and primary teachers, in reality large numbers of parents are excluded from routine exchanges with schools. Meetings scheduled during working hours, few communications to parents from school, few opportunities to observe in classes, and a variety of other factors make parents feel unwelcome and uncomfortable in their relations with schools.

Just as most schools have not yet figured out how to facilitate strong parent involvement, neither have they adjusted well to new family and community realities. Teachers are among the first to witness the human costs of society's wider failures, but, while cognizant of those changes in their classrooms, they and other educators have been slow to question the "one style fits all" pattern of home/school practices.[12] Family/school practices are steeped in assumptions about childhood, family, community, and school roles. When conceptions of what should be don't mesh with what is, educators often attribute that failure to parents' irresponsibility, lack of interest in their children, and lack of skills.[13] Tensions rise, and blame is volleyed back and forth between school and home. An example from a rural southern school illustrates this point.

Donaldsonville Elementary School had been recognized for its "good curriculum," even though teachers were disappointed with the progress of their students. Eighty percent of the student population were African-American children, and 20% were white children; most were members of low-income families. Teachers felt that they were doing all they could to help these children at school. Without parental assistance at home, the children at Donaldsonville were going to fail. The teachers' solution was to expect and demand that parents be involved in their children's education by reading to them at home.

To the teachers this was not an unreasonable request. There is good evidence of positive gains made by "disadvantaged" elementary students when parents and children work together at home on homework and learning packets.[14] What the teachers did not take into account was that 40% of the school's parents were illiterate or semi-literate. When the parents didn't seem willing to do as the teachers asked, teachers mistook parents' unfamiliarity with the task being asked of them, coupled with low literacy skills, for lack of interest in their children's education. The continued demand that parents read to their children at home, which had a particular meaning in teachers' minds, sparked hostility and racial tensions between teachers and parents. Each group blamed the other for the children's failures; each felt victimized by the interaction. Children were caught between their two most important teachers—their classroom teacher and their parent.

The principal and the teachers recognized that they had to mend the serious rift between them and the parents. The principal stated that she wanted to "unite the home, school, and community." Creating a process for parents to become integral and confident partners in their children's schooling was the first step. But how to begin? Should the process be expected to emerge from traditional—and failed—interactions between home and school? Five other cases will allow us to explore this matter further.

Case #1: The drug bust. A first-grade student was absent for 16 consecutive days. The student's concerned teacher did what most teachers would do: she attempted to contact the child's parent. She sent several letters home and telephoned the parent, but the number was no longer a working one. The teacher even called one of the parent's neighbors to inquire if the neighbor would inform the parent of the need to arrange a conference. None of these efforts to reach the parent proved successful.

Sharing her concerns with the principal, the teacher learned that the mother had previously been arrested for drug use and that a baby had been removed from her home during her last incident with the police. The principal's fear that the mother might have resumed her involvement with drugs was borne out when the mother was arrested a few days later. The children were placed in foster homes; the mother faces a 20-year prison sentence.

Case #2: My sister's children. A teacher's attempt to contact a third-grader's parent led to the discovery that the parent was missing. The child's 17-year-old aunt stated that she had not heard from her 22-year-old sister and did not know where she was.

Case #3: Caught in the middle. A mother who had custody of her 5-year-old son suspected that her former husband had been sexually abusing the boy. Consequently, the mother did not want the school to contact her former husband about their son's performance in school. The father, however, demanded that he be kept informed by receiving the same communications from the school that were sent to his former wife. He further charged that the mother was an alcoholic and that he was in a better situation to respond to the child's needs.

Schools must do more than merely refer students to social services and health departments. They must become multiple-service brokers for children.

Case #4: The school as a battleground. The faculty in a large urban school felt that it was under siege. Drug paraphernalia littered the school grounds. Gang fights were common occurrences. Tensions between teachers and parents had reached the point that teachers felt their lives were in jeopardy.

Case #5: Bewildered in kindergarten. A kindergarten teacher with more than 20 years of experience was at a loss as to how to develop a workable instructional program for a young child who was acting, according to the teacher, "strange." The child's learning style did not fit any pattern that the teacher had observed in all her years of teaching. She arranged a conference with the parent to better understand how best to work with this child. During the course of that conversation, the parent revealed that her daughter had tested positive for the virus that causes AIDS. The mother added, "I want the best for my child, but I just don't know what is going to happen to her schoolwise." While the teacher did not verbalize her feelings at the time, she later confided to a colleague that she did not know the best way to develop the child's learning potential.

A DIFFERENT FRAMEWORK

Like the situation in Donaldsonville, each of these cases raises significant questions about the appropriate role of schoolpeople in the lives of children and their families and communities. How far into the home and neighborhood should the school's responsibility extend? What forms should home/school partnerships take? How are teachers to be helped with designing instructional programs for children with neurological disabilities stemming from viruses, addiction, and environmental pollutants?

Schoolpeople are going to have to think differently about what they want for children and what they expect from families and communities. In Donaldsonville the missing link was forged by a program created by a local university professor who never accepted the assumption of parents' lack of interest in their children's success. She solicited community support to attract parents to a reading program, where they would be assisted in learning how to read and how to read with their children. She called on community leaders to recruit parents they knew in contexts outside the school. Church leaders black and white, agreed to preach from their pulpits about the importance of helping children learn to read. They regularly urged parents to attend the weekly reading sessions to learn to help their children in school, noting the importance of literacy as a tool of faith.

A local bar owner emerged as a strong supporter of the reading program, informing mothers who patronized his establishment that they would no longer be welcome unless they put as much time into learning how to read to their children as they spent enjoying themselves at his bar. He provided transportation to school and back home for participating mothers and secured funds from the city social services department for child care for parents who otherwise could not attend. A grandmother organized a campaign to telephone program participants each week. In sum, the bridge that connected home and school was found in the broader community.

In poor rural communities like Donaldsonville and in inner-city neighborhoods, the social context calls for re-thinking the definitions and processes of home/school interactions. Boundaries separating the responsibilities of home, school, and community are blurring, calling into question traditional conceptions of parent involvement as a one-to-one relationship between parent and teacher. Despite the research on the benefits of parent involvement, traditional practices will continue to fall short for a wide band of children in poverty. John Blendinger and Linda Jones, among others, advise us to reach out to parents in new ways, to help parents connect to resources, to create environments where parents feel welcome, and to organize various avenues for participation.[15] Each of these steps is important, but they are insufficient for many poor communities. What these strategies typically lack is an ecological approach to strengthening all aspects of the child's development—a perspective underscored by Shirley Brice Heath and Milbrey McLaughlin, who question the adequacy of schools as social institutions, "because they are built on outmoded assumptions about family and community."[16]

Where should schools draw the line? Are schools the new place to accommodate the interwoven needs that children bring with them to the classroom? If we believe that schools have an obligation to assist students with aspects of their social and personal lives that interfere with their cognitive and social development, then we must rethink our structures, practices, and purposes.

Schools must do more than encourage parent involvement isolated from the broader social context; they must do more than merely refer students to social services and health departments. They must become multiple-service brokers for children.

Social, emotional, physical, and academic growth and development are inextricably linked. As the social supports for children weaken, teachers have to devote much more time and energy to non-instructional demands. Teachers' and administrators' primary responsibility is instruction, but, as a practical and moral matter, they cannot ignore the social and psychological dimensions of their students' lives. Changing social contexts demand changing practices. This view not only stretches the boundaries of parent/school involvement but redefines its purpose: not just higher academic achievement, but the well-being of children in its fullest sense.

Several efforts currently under way are redefining the relationships of school, family, and community. Schoolpeople are forging alliances with an array of community organizations and agencies.[17] They are extending notions of the "family," making room for single parents, working parents, foster parents, grandparents, and others having significant responsibility for children. They are challenging the separateness of systems designed to support children and their families. And they are devising strategies to meet a fuller range of children's needs, using family and community resources.

This work is a lot to ask of educators whose professional education did little to prepare them for it. Yet many individual teachers and administrators today are up to their elbows in such tasks, trying to respond to children's physical and social needs as they are pulled away from other responsibilities. Addressing the deepening needs of urban poor children today will tax all available resources both in and outside of schools. One thing is clear: teachers and schools cannot do it alone. An ecological approach and shared responsibility through multiple partnerships could free educators to better focus on learning needs. Donaldsonville is an example of how one school mobilized resources within families and the community to build positive learning experiences for children.

Schoolpeople will need to develop repertoires of styles and strategies that acknowledge the interrelationships of the social and the individual, they will need to reconceptualize the networks of community organizations and public services that might assist, and they will need to draw on those community resources. Developing an integrated, accessible system of support for children and their families requires adopting different philosophies of service provision and removing the boundaries separating services—a prospect made more difficult as agencies compete for scarce public dollars. Yet, until such partnerships are formed, schools will not be able to sponsor the kinds of home/school/community relationships considered so important to children's inschool growth and development.

Moving to broader notions of community alliances means moving beyond incremental tinkering or simply assessing deficiencies of parents, teachers, schools, and communities. The framework that we propose calls for a coordinated network of multiple resources that builds on family and community strengths. Experience shows that teachers and administrators desperately want to be successful, but, because they are not adequately prepared to address the range of children's social and psychological developmental needs, they are left frustrated. They know what needs to be done, but not how to do it.[18] There are others who can help.

This discussion leads us to offer five recommendations:

1. Home/school strategies should be founded on the strengths of families and their understandings of their children.

2. Efforts should be organized around preventive strategies. Thus school personnel must understand the children and families that they serve—including the wide range of social, personal, economic, and psychological stresses that families may be encountering. They will need to assess how this information will facilitate closer relationships with families to support children's in-school and out of school development.

3. Schools should explore multiple models for reaching out to families and to agencies involved with the families that they serve.

4. Drawing on community resources should become part of the school's daily routine, enabling speedy responses to children's immediate needs.

5. Prospective educators should encounter these issues in their professional preparation programs.

These proposals call for greater inclusion of adults who are important in children's lives and in vastly different ways from our traditional conception. Illustrating some of those different kinds of involvement—the convergence of school, family, and community in full support of children—has been the aim of this article. The time has come to reframe home/school relations diligently and seriously in light of the old African saying: "The whole village educates the child."

NOTES

1. Urie Bronfenbrenner, *The Ecology of Human Development: Experiments by Nature and Design* (Cambridge, Mass.: Harvard University Press, 1979); and Anne T. Henderson, ed., *The Evidence Continues to Grow: Parent Involvement Improves Student Achievement* (Columbia, Md.: National Committee for Citizens in Education, 1987).

2. Joyce L. Epstein, "Toward a Theory of Family-School Connections: Teacher Practices and Parent Involvement," in Klaus Hurrelmann, Franz-Xaver Kaufmann, and Friedrich Losel, eds., *Social Intervention: Potential and Constraints* (New York: Walter de Gruyter, 1987); and Shirley Brice Heath and Milbrey Wallin McLaughlin, "A Child Resource Policy: Moving Beyond Dependence on School and Family," *Phi Delta Kappan*, April 1987, pp. 576–80.

3. James P. Comer, "Home, School, and Academic Learning," in John I. Goodlad and Pamela Keating, eds., *Access to Knowledge: An Agenda for Our Nation's Schools* (New York: College Entrance Examination Board, 1990), p. 23

4. William Julius Wilson, *The Truly Disadvantaged: the Inner City, the Underclass, and Public Policy* (Chicago: University of Chicago Press, 1987).

5. U.S. Bureau of the Census, *Martial Status and Living Arrangements: March 1989* (Washington, D.C.: U.S. Government Printing Office, Current Population Reports, Series P-20, No. 445, 1990).

6. Ibid., p. 3.

7. Ibid., p. 4.

8. Children's Defense Fund, *The State of America's Children, 1991,* (Washington, D.C.: CDF, 1991), p. 24.

9. *Speaking of Kids: A National Survey of Children and Parents* (Washington, D.C.: National Commission on Children, 1991), p. 41.

10. Virginia Richardson and Patricia Colfer, "Being At-Risk in School," in Goodlad and Keating, pp. 107–24.

11. Sara Lawrence Lightfoot, *World's Apart: Relationships Between Families and Schools* (New York: Basic Books, 1978).

12. Joyce L. Epstein, "How Do We Improve Programs for Parent Involvement?" *Educational Horizons*, January 1988, pp. 58–59; and Barbara Lindner, *Family Diversity and School Policy* (Denver: Education Commission of the States, 1987).

13. Anne C. Walde and Keith Baker, "How Teachers View the Parents' Role in Education," *Phi Delta Kappan*, December 1990, pp. 319–22.

14. Jim Cummins, "Empowering Minority Students: A Framework for Intervention," *Harvard Educational Review*, February 1986, pp. 18–36.

15. John Blendinger and Linda Jones, "Parent Involvement in Schools," unpublished manuscript prepared for Boulder (Colo.) Public Schools, 1989.

16. Shirley Brice Heath and Milbrey Wallin McLaughlin, "Community Organizations as Family: Endeavors That Engage and Support Adolescents," *Phi Delta Kappan*, April 1991, pp. 623–27.

17. Lisbeth Schorr, *Within Our Reach: Breaking the Cycle of Disadvantage* (New York: Anchor Press, 1988).

18. Lauren S. Jones Young, "Restructuring Institutional Arrangements: Toward a Comprehensive Child Policy," in Gary A. Griffin and Anna Lowe, eds., *Creating an Agenda for Urban Educational Research and Development: Proceedings of a Wing-spread Conference* (Chicago: College of Education, University of Illinois, 1989), pp. 25–35.

PRE-K TODAY TALKS WITH

T. BERRY BRAZELTON, M.D.

T. Berry Brazelton is clinical professor emeritus of pediatrics at Harvard Medical School and founder of the Division of Child Development Unit at the Children's Hospital in Boston. Dr. Brazelton is the author of many books about childhood and parenting, a columnist for The New York Times *and* Family Circle, *and an advocate for children.*

This month, Pre-K Today*'s Dr. Adele M. Brodkin spoke with noted pediatrician and family advocate Dr. T. Berry Brazelton about his views and experiences in helping parents and children cope with separation.*

Pre-K Today: Dr. Brazelton, for many years you have been helping children and their parents meet the challenges of growing up. You know an awful lot about their feelings. Is separation frequently difficult for parents as well as children?

Dr. Brazelton: It's very difficult for parents, particularly in the earlier years. And, unfortunately, unless parents handle their side of it, any difficulties the child may have in separating are reinforced. You see, parents hate to give a baby up. The kind of love affair you get into with a baby is such an amazing surprise that I think it's almost frightening to share it with someone else.

Are those feelings similar for parents of infants, toddlers, and preschoolers?

They are different at each age, probably less each time. By toddlerhood you know that these children are going to benefit from peer interactions and learning about other people. And you know that, by preschool age, it's really time for children to have experiences with other kids.

What sort of effect does separation have on the parent/child relationship?

I think early separation causes a kind of grief reaction on the mother's part and probably, maybe to a lesser extent, the father's part. What I call grieving is a tendency to feel depressed, unhappy, a little bit helpless, and guilty. So you defend yourself in three ways: 1. *Denial*—this means denying that it matters. 2. *Projection*—Projecting on to the caregiver that his or her behavior and judgment are negative and the parent's are positive *or* vice versa. 3. *Detachment*—The parent detaching himself or herself, not because he doesn't care, but because it hurts. These defenses are unconscious but they are liable to exist when there are repeated separations, such as a working parent leaving a child at a center or

From *Scholastic Pre-K Today,* August/September 1991, pp. 44-46. Copyright © 1991 by T. Berry Brazelton, M.D. Reprinted by permission of Lescher & Lescher, Ltd.

school. We need to be ready for that with parents and help them.

How can we do that?

By helping parents understand that their feelings and reactions are normal and healthy; that this experience doesn't lead to real loss or permanent separation; and that the defenses that are surfacing are not necessarily mechanisms one needs to live with, because if they are aware of these defenses then they aren't at the mercy of them.

Some teachers and parents may feel competitive. If so, the person in charge at the center needs to take time to sit down with each and acknowledge that the feelings are normal and healthy.

You have observed that teachers can feel resentful toward parents. How can we address that?

I think many teachers feel mothers ought to be home with their kids and these feelings often reflect a deep-seated bias. But remember, a bias needs to be brought to light and talked about, so teachers can then say, "Hey, of course she has to go off to work. Thank goodness she's leaving that child with me — I can do a good job with her."

Let's move up in the age scale a little bit to when children are toddlers or even preschoolers. What's your feeling about how separation should be handled. Should it be gradual?

Yes, ideally. And it should be with people the children know and trust, particularly people who the parents know and trust, and who the child learns to know and trust—giving the child a chance to adjust at his or her own pace.

Let's say that there's a program in which the parent is encouraged to stay for a period of time—days or weeks. When the time comes, how should the parent go about leaving?

Saying goodbye means telling the child ahead of time about what is going to happen, preparing her at home, then saying, "I'm going and I'm staying away for ten minutes (or twenty minutes — a certain amount of time). Then I'll come right back."

The parent, then, comes back in just that amount of time, saying, "Remember, I said I'd be gone ten minutes and now here I am." Repeat this until a child is comfortable.

Sometimes parents have let us know that when they are in an early childhood setting in those early days, they're not really sure what their roles should be. What can teachers do to help them?

Give parents clues about what is acceptable and what isn't. Parents are there to help the child with separation, so whatever works best in that setting is the goal. Unless the program is a cooperative, and I think those are wonderful, I think the teacher should encourage what would help her manage the group.

How else can a teacher, in the case of younger children, make it easier for the parents and the children during this time?

By forming relationships. That's the first job of any center— seeing and forming relationships with the whole family, not just the child. NAEYC's philosophy about healthy early childhood development is really aimed at trying to focus on the family rather than just the child.

Let's look at several common parent reactions to separating. How about the parent who leaves without saying goodbye?

That's really deserting the child at a time when she needs the parent very much. The parent's inability to face his own grief may be influencing her actions.

How can the teacher, then, avoid that situation?

The teacher can say to the parent, "You don't need to leave without saying goodbye. It will be better for both of you to tell her you're leaving. Please come back."

What about the parent who may drag out goodbyes?

It's so hard for parents to make the separation. The teacher, at that point, could step aside with the parent and say, "One or two goodbyes is enough. More than that isn't fair to your child."

Then there's the parent with the stiff-upper-lip approach who sees the quivering lip on the child and says, "You're fine. Mommy's got to go to work. This is your work." What can the teacher do in that case?

The teacher can come over to the child and say reassuringly, "I'm going to be right here with you. I'll help you." We all need to remember that there's a lot to be learned, and a lot is learned from separation. Parents may need to be helped to see it this way. And kids, too, when they've made it for a short time. You can congratulate children and say, "Look what you did. You really did it."

The way a parent separates affects the way a child separates. When a parent is ambivalent, the child is bound to pick up on it, and play on it and get caught in a kind of morass of feeling sorry for herself, wondering if Mommy has put up a big enough fight, rather than turning to the coping systems that would help her get used to the new situation and learn that she can have fun with the other kids and caregivers. I think this is one reason that I would suggest that parents prepare their children at home so that when they get to the center, they can begin to look outward and see the things that would help them make it.

And in preparing them at home, the parent would tell them all the wonderful things there are in school.

A parent might say, "I'm going to miss you and you're going to miss me, but this is a pretty special time. You're going to have some kids to play with and a teacher who cares about you, and I'll come back to get you and you can tell me all about it when I do."

I know that the infancy period is especially important to you. Do you want to say anything more about that time in a child's life?

Yes. I think it's harder to separate in that period because you do feel the tendency and the need for that dependency much more acutely than you do when the child gets older and you know they have coping systems they can fall back on. In infancy, I don't think you ever quite think they do. In fact, you don't even want them to have them. Separating from an infant is very complex for both the parent and the child.

What about that growing bond or relationship that they have? Is it impaired by this?

It doesn't need to be. It can be enhanced by it. You learn to separate and learn how critical your relationship is, but also how strong it is. You can separate successfully and come back together, and the passion is still there, which is very reassuring.

EDITOR'S NOTE: *In 1989, T. Berry Brazelton and Bernice Weissbourd (founder of the Family Resource Coalition), helped to set up a national advocacy organization to represent the interests of parents and families. Officially titled Parent Action, the organization speaks out for parents "whenever Congress is considering action on tax policies, health care, child care, and employment regulations that affect America's families," and "links parents with other organizations and publications to build a network of support for those who have America's most important job: raising the next generations of American citizens." Find out more about this membership organization to share with the parents in your program by contacting Parent Action, P.O. Box 1719, Washington, DC 20013.*

How Schools Perpetuate Illiteracy

To break the cycle of illiteracy—how "the poor get poorer"—schools must help parents understand how to help their children at home.

LA VERGNE ROSOW

La Vergne Rosow is a literacy volunteer, a community college literacy and ESL instructor, and a literacy consultant. Her address is P.O. Box 85, Huntington Beach, CA 92648.

"**W**hat's this word?" 9-year-old Mitzi asked her mother.

"What word?"

"This one," she said as she crashed her finger down on the first of 10 words she had to do for homework.

"Uh, well, you know you're supposed to sound it out. Now sound it out."

"I did! *Do or. Do or. Do or!*" She'd learned her lessons well. "D-o" spells *do* and "o-r" spells *or*. Both child and mother knew how to sound out a word they couldn't read, and Mitzi was skillful at finding the little words in the big words, too. "How do I make a sentence with 'do or'?" she asked as she turned over the packet of papers.

"Um, well, I can think of it, but when I try to tell you it, it don't come out right. Just do the best you can. I'm not supposed to tell you *everything*," the young mother said, trying to maintain some semblance of dignity before her child.[1]

The little girl turned the packet over again to try the next word. She was supposed to write a sentence with each of the 10 words on the mimeographed list. By Friday, having done each of 4

activities with the words, she was expected to be able to spell all 10 words on a test. This was only day 2 of a 4-day homework assignment. (Later Mitzi's mom explained that just figuring out what the words on the list were was only part of the problem. Then they had to construct sentences that had only words they could already spell. The proposed sentences always grew shorter and shorter as the struggle progressed.) Ten minutes had passed, and Mitzi still hadn't written the first sentence.

Suddenly she said, "Is it *door?*" and then turned the packet over to start writing.

"Um, no, I don't think so. I think that's spelled another way," her mother answered thoughtfully.

"Well, then, how do you spell *door?*"

"I think it's dore, you know, *dore.*"

A True Life Drama

The little girl seemed to be trying to take in the logic of her mother's phonetic performance. I leaned forward, hoping to be invited into the dialogue, but heard instead the echo of a literacy and language lecture by Steve Krashen on how the rich get richer. Those who are rich in literacy fortify their children with good stories and beautiful books long before they enter school; the poor readers don't even understand that process and so per-

petuate illiteracy from generation to generation.[2] Now, having no invitation to intervene, I was forced to witness this true life drama of what Krashen calls how "the poor get poorer."

Having already repeated the 1st grade, Mitzi was facing the dreaded prospect of failing the 2nd, due to poor performance in language arts. Her mother was an adult nonreader. "I can read the words," she had explained, "but when it comes to explaining it, it's just like a wall goes up, and I can't say what I mean." By a wall going up, I'd immediately figured she was talking about stress, the *Affective Filter*[3] that stops learning and performance. But Mitzi's mom meant instead that she couldn't comprehend text. I was there to help her learn to read when Mitzi had come home from school. Not knowing whether the child knew why I was visiting her mom, and having gotten no introduction, I was not free to move in on the mother/daughter ritual that served only to teach Mitzi that schoolwork is tough and she is never able to do it well.

Krashen had lectured about the ease with which students accustomed to print-rich environments breeze through schoolwork on words they had already learned through pleasure reading. "Those who are readers typically know what most of the words mean already. They have seen them before, in Judy Blume's novels or in Dungeons and

By La Vergne Rosow, "How Schools Perpetuate Illiteracy," *Educational Leadership*, Vol. 49, No. 1, September 1991, pp. 41-44. Reprinted with permission of the Association for Supervision and Curriculum Development. Copyright © 1991 by ASCD. All rights reserved.

When children of the literate elite need help, their parents can fill in the blanks the school has missed. When children of the print poor need help, they have nowhere to turn.

Dragons. . . ."[4] Meanwhile, children from nonprint homes and classrooms are left to flesh out the loser's end of the bell-shaped curve. When children of the literate elite need help, their parents can fill in the blanks the school has missed. When children of the print poor need help, they have nowhere to turn. The girl who already knows 9 of the 10 assigned spelling words from pleasure reading will make a 100 percent if she studies the 1 unknown word and 90 percent if she does nothing. The girl who can't read will be faced with 10 new words, an almost overwhelming task of memorization. If she really struggles, she'll earn a C-. In school, that is how the rich get richer and the poor get poorer. They'll imagine that if they had just studied a little harder or worked a little longer they would have done better. "And like the victims of child abuse, they blame themselves."[5] I'd heard the lecture . . . more than once. School is a test . . . to see who already knows the most and to see whose parents can do the best job. Now I was witnessing the demonstration.

From One Generation to the Next

After 30 or 45 minutes of guesswork, Mitzi ran out to play, knowing that her faithful mother would be waiting to help her with another hour and a half of homework when she came in.[6] She couldn't know that the production of sentences is a test, a call for *output* that shows what the reader already knows; output is simply anything the learner can say or write. Sentence production

was not *input* designed to give the new or nonreader information.[7] Based on what is understandable and relevant to the learner, input becomes acquired without learner effort. Nor could Mitzi's mom know that this assignment was difficult because it employed a bot-

tom-up strategy. It required that the learner remember all sorts of meaningless little pieces of the language, like "do," and put them into bigger pieces: sentences. She had been told that if she did this enough, she would know how to spell, and that would then help her

---

Teachers Can Foster Family Literacy

Illiteracy does run in families, but we can end it in our classrooms. And, with funds for extra supplies, books, released time, and help from our schools, K-12 teachers can extend a hand to the parents of the "Mitzis" in our classrooms. We can:

- Make our classrooms examples of "print-rich environments" by providing plenty of books, magazines, posters, and notes.
- Invite parents to story times or other literacy events and help them to enjoy these occasions with their children. Help parents to understand that good questions are designed to stimulate thought, not extract correctness.
- Send books home that we have read to the children. Tell parents that talking about books will help their children learn to appreciate literature.
- Communicate with parents in clear language; find speakers of their languages when they are not proficient in English.
- Tell parents about adult literacy services such as Adult Basic Education and Literacy Volunteer programs. Encourage them to seek help, assuring them that it is never too late to learn to enjoy reading; but forewarn people of possible disappointments like the numbers of months on waiting lists, so that initial problems don't seem like personal affronts.
- Tell parents about local library story hours and services, and invite the librarian to meet them.
- Teach parents how to identify good book features such as: predictable text, Caldecott and Newberry Medalists, their own children's recognition and delight over books made familiar at school. Perhaps a very simple, large-type checklist can help.
- Teach parents not to fall for gro-

cery and drug store workbooks and other skill-level materials. Then point out where they can buy inexpensive books in the neighborhood, such as used book stores, flea markets, library sales, school purchase bargains (Scholastic Books), and chain stores.
- Visit children and parents in their homes to gain insights into their interests. In the process, you may find resources for the entire classroom, such as a parent who can sing folksongs.

For *homework*, teachers should assign enrichment tasks—not activities that ask students to finish incomplete classroom work, use materials that are not available, or obtain teaching at home when none may be available. Instead, the school-related homework should foster love of learning and build a bridge between classroom activities and life at home. For example, teachers can:

- Encourage children to read nursery rhymes or songbooks already made familiar at school.
- Suggest family projects such as handprint collections or pressed flowers, which will be used for school writing; in turn, the writing projects will then be returned to the home as reading materials.
- Give directions for making finger- and hand-puppets that match poems learned at school, and invite students to roleplay or dramatize stories from home for their classmates at school.

Making school/home connections with the parents of the Mitzis in your classrooms is a tough task—but a very good investment. Breaking the cycle of illiteracy continues to pay off generation after generation. □

—La Vergne Rosow

reading: in reality, only those students who are already readers can back into this kind of task successfully. She couldn't know that no struggle would have been involved in pulling a part (a word) out of a whole, such as a real story.

For Mitzi and her mom, there was never any storytelling or picture book enjoyment. But because Mitzi's mother was bent on not having her child do poorly in school the way she herself had, night after night, they labored over writing sentences for sounds like "door."

Finally, Mitzi had hit the word *floor,* and when she said it, her mother realized there was a pattern connection. "Yes, now, if that one's *floor,* what's this one?" she asked pointing back to word number one.

"But you said . . . " Mitzi, a very bright child, had already learned in one lesson the spelling "d-o-r-e."

I wondered what if, instead of *floor,* the familiar word had been *look* or *poor* or *boot.* What other reasonable and wrong connection might have been triggered? How many little transfers of poverty occur in the name of homework each night across this land as illiteracy passes from one generation to the next?

Keeping Secrets from the Have-Nots

Who is accountable when all the mothers of all the Mitzis just don't measure up? Without knowing the futility of their efforts and the waste of their scarce funds, how many take the cue from this kind of school assignment and buy grocery store workbooks to occupy what would be pleasure book times for the literate elite?

Why aren't mother and child seeing beautiful pictures in books brought home from school and sharing favorite stories that Mitzi has heard again and again in class instead of impoverished little mimeographs with lists of meaningless words? Who profits when the values of the literate haves are kept secret from the illiterate have-nots? Surely we know too much of the reading process to pretend this disparity is created in ignorance. The assignment to sound out "do or" and to produce a sentence from it robs Mitzi of real reading time, but Mitzi doesn't know that. And Mitzi's mother doesn't know that. Can this kind of "literacy lesson" pass as a naive accident in our bountiful domain where consistently "the poor get poorer"?

21. Schools Perpetuate Illiteracy

[1] A 1988 survey of adult nonreaders showed that the biggest reason adults seek literacy help is self-esteem. L. Rosow, (November 1988), "Adult Illiterates Offer Unexpected Cues into the Reading Process," *Journal of Reading:* 120-124.

[2] S. D. Krashen, (1988), USC lecture notes (unpublished).

[3] Krashen describes the *Affective Filter,* the metaphor for the stress barrier that prevents new information from coming into the brain and appropriate known information from being accessed. S. D. Krashen, (1985), *Inquiries and Insights: Second Language Teaching, Immersion and Bilingual Education, Literacy,* (Hayward, Calif.: Alemany Press, a division of Janus Book Publishers, Inc.), pp. 10-11.

[4] Ibid, p. 108.

[5] Ibid.

[6] Not every nonreading mother is so faithful. The mother of another 9-year-old child, Arthur, had a thousand important things to keep her from having to face working with her child on school assignments. L. Rosow, (November 1989), "Arthur: A Tale of Disempowerment," *Phi Delta Kappan* 71, 3: 194-199.

[7] For a comprehensive discussion of input vs. output, see S. D. Krashen, (1989), "We Acquire Vocabulary and Spelling by Reading: Additional Evidence for the Input Hypothesis," *Modern Language Journal* 73, IV: 440-464.

Author's note: I am pleased to report that through subsequent tutoring, Mitzi's mother has just finished reading the first book of her life.

I would like to thank Professors David Eskey and William Rideout, Jr., for help with the Mitzi case.

How Teachers Can Help Ease the Pain

Children of Divorce

Candy Carlile

Candy Carlile is Assistant Professor of Education, University of Mary Hardin-Baylor, Belton, Texas.

The structure of the American family is rapidly changing. In the 1960s 60 percent of American families could be described as traditional, with two parents, one at home, and two or three children. Only about 7 percent of U.S. families are now considered to be "traditional" (Elkind, 1986). Today we can expect 50 percent of all first marriages to end in divorce (Glick, 1984; Weitzman, 1985), with an even higher rate of divorce for remarriages (Berns, 1985). By the year 2000, it is expected that 60 percent of all U.S. children will spend some part of their lives in single-parent homes (Jellinek & Klavan, 1988).

Literally millions of children in classrooms across America are desperately trying to adjust to the personal tragedy of divorce. This process can be made easier for these children when sensitive, caring teachers work to create a safe, nurturing classroom environment that promotes the recovery and healing necessary for a child's well-being.

The Pain of Divorce

Even in the best of situations, divorce is a painful process for every-one. Although children of all ages are affected, perhaps the most vulnerable are those at the elementary school level. Ironically, when these children need parental love, assurance and support the most, their parents are least able emotionally to provide it. Unfortunately, the turmoil often does not stop after the divorce is final. Parental hostility and bitterness may escalate through the years and continue to cause needless pain and suffering that could result in psychological damage to the child.

A 10-year study of children of divorce conducted by Wallerstein and Kelly (1980) cited a number of symptoms that children in such cases might experience. Of these behaviors, the following might be observed in the elementary school classroom: anxiety, depression, regression, asthma, allergies, tantrums, daydreaming, overaggressive behavior, withdrawal from relationships, poor school performance, frequent crying or absence of emotion, and difficulty in communicating feelings. If any of these symptoms persist, professional counseling should be sought immediately for the child.

Children are remarkably resilient, however. Although they experience a great deal of pain and feelings of loss, most can and will recover from the trauma of divorce (Bienenfeld, 1987). With the help of an understanding teacher, the classroom can become the brightest spot in a child's life during this difficult time.

Things To Know About Divorce
Although children react differently to divorce depending upon age, maturity and individual situations, teachers need to be aware of some generalities to fully understand the plight of their students.

■ Children of divorce, as well as parents, go through a classic mourning process after divorce, much like after a death in the family. They experience disbelief, then anxiety, anger, sadness, depression and eventually, if given reassurance, acceptance of the divorce (Bienenfeld, 1987).

■ 80 to 90 percent of children recover from the initial shock of divorce in about a year (Jellinek & Klavan, 1988).

■ Boys react more intensely than girls to the loss of their fathers from the home. They are sometimes angry with their mothers for either causing the divorce or driving their fathers away (Dodson, 1987). From elementary school right through high school, boys from single-parent homes were more often classified as "low achievers" than children from intact families (NAESP & Charles F. Kettering Foundation, 1980).

From *Childhood Education*, Summer 1991, pp. 232-234. Reprinted by permission of Candy Carlile and the Association for Childhood Education International, 11141 Georgia Avenue, Suite 200, Wheaton, MD. Copyright © 1991 by the Association.

■ A common reaction of children of divorce who have been rushed into adult roles and responsibilities is to seek early escape from their childhoods. In such cases, these feelings can result in girls becoming sexually precocious and contemptuous of the parent who has been overdependent on them (Hetherington, 1981).

■ 95 percent of divorced parents with custody are mothers (Dodson, 1987). On an average, divorced women and their minor children experience a 73 percent decline in their standard of living in the first year after divorce (Weitzman, 1985). This may result in children having to move into less expensive dwellings and perhaps assume new or increased latchkey responsibilities as mothers struggle to make ends meet financially.

■ Children of divorce are more apt to be late to school or late more often and to miss school altogether. They are also more likely than their counterparts from intact families to spontaneously skip school (NAESP & Charles F. Kettering Foundation, 1980).

■ Teachers have discovered that Mondays and Fridays are especially difficult days for children of divorce (Francke, 1983). Leaving one parent at the end of the week and the other on Sunday can often be too much of an emotional overload for a young child. Anxiety, sadness and tears in the classroom on those days may be a result of the added stress.

A Place To Heal

If children are to recover from the trauma of divorce, they must have a buffer zone between them and parental conflict. Bienenfeld (1987) encourages parents to establish such a neutral zone by refraining from fighting and arguing when their children are present. Unfortunately, this doesn't always happen, and the classroom provides the only "conflict-free" haven for these children. With a little extra effort and planning, we can make

our elementary school classrooms much more than simply havens. We can make them places where children can begin to heal and become whole again.

What Teachers Can Do To Help

■ *Know your children*. Children of divorce are usually not eager to talk about their family problems for fear of being perceived as different. It is a teacher's responsibility to identify children of divorce at the beginning of each school year, either through school records or information derived from other teachers. It's also helpful to know when the parents separated to determine approximately where the child is in terms of the healing process. Confer with parents of all students as often as possible to remain aware of other family crises that may occur during the school year.

■ *Talk about feelings*. In a survey of approximately 100 children of divorce, preschool through teen, two emotions were discovered to be predominant in interviews with the children: anger and sadness (Francke, 1983). Guilt, grief, loss, helplessness, loneliness, rejection and anxiety are also common emotions experienced by children before, during and after divorce. Children need to know that it's okay to have these feelings and

that they are not alone. If they hesitate to verbalize their feelings, they should be given the opportunity to express themselves in other ways. The use of puppets and dolls (Francke, 1983), unstructured drawings (Bienenfeld, 1987), role-playing and creative writing are a few of the strategies found to be successful in the classroom.

■ *Bibliotherapy*. Using fictional books to help children through difficult times in their lives is certainly not a new strategy for elementary school teachers. Fortunately, a number of noteworthy juvenile books deal with the topic of divorce. Some are for independent reading by children, but I have found the most effective use of these books is to read them aloud to students and then discuss them together. This way the teacher is able to reach everyone—those who are dealing with divorce on a personal level and the other children who can always benefit from a lesson in understanding and kindness. (See Figure 1 for titles.)

■ *Make children aware they are not alone*. Through instructional activities, teach children about the many different types of family structures in today's society. Have children make individual booklets that tell about their families. Construct a class bulletin board using photos of family members. As a

---

Figure 1. Children's Books and Other Sources

Bienenfeld, F. (1980). *My mom and dad are getting a divorce*. St. Paul: EMC Corporation.

Blue, R. (1972). *A month of Sundays*. New York: Franklin Watts.

Brown, L. K., & Brown, M. (1986). *Dinosaur's divorce*. New York: Atlantic Monthly.

Cain, B., & Benedek, E. (1976). *What would you do? A child's book about divorce*. Indianapolis: The Saturday Evening Post Co.

Goff, B. (1969). *Where is daddy? The story of a divorce*. Boston: Beacon.

Kindred, W. (1973). *Lucky Wilma*. New York: Dial.

Lexau, J. (1971). *Me day*. New York: Dial.

Perry, P., & Lynch, M. (1978). *Mommy and daddy are divorced*. New York: Dial.

Pursell, M. S. (1977). *A look at divorce*. Minneapolis: Lerner.

Sitea, L. (1974). *Zachary's divorce*. In M. Thomas & C. Hart (Eds.), *Free To Be You and Me* (pp. 124-7). New York: McGraw-Hill.

Stanek, M. (1972). *I won't go without a father*. Chicago: Albert Whitman.

Zolotow, C. (1971). *A father like that*. New York: Harper & Row.

cooperative learning activity, have children cut pictures from magazines illustrating different types of family structures. These pictures can be placed in a classroom story-starter file or glued to a piece of posterboard to make a collage.

■ *Modify your language.* Be sure home correspondence, assignments, classroom assignments and school events allow for the variety of family structures represented within your classroom. A child may want to bring a grandparent to Open House or create a Mother's Day card for an aunt, a stepmother or the teacher down the hall. While divorce is no longer considered a social stigma, a child who attends Parents' Night with someone other than a parent can needlessly experience a great deal of personal embarrassment due to unthinking school personnel and children's insensitivity.

■ *Be tolerant of behavior changes.* The majority of children trying to cope with divorce experience a change in behavior. An increase in anxiety, restlessness, decreased concentration and daydreaming may be observed. The change may be immediate or gradual—with children responding to their own internal timetables (Wallerstein & Kelly, 1980). Lonely children may arrive at school early and stay late to receive as much time and attention from the teacher as possible (Francke, 1983).

Teachers must be patient with these children and deal with each case individually. When a child has had an especially bad day, extra time may need to be given for work that was not completed, or perhaps the child might be granted a "time out" from the classroom. Sometimes, a few classroom rules may need bending in order for children to regain some control of their emotions and their lives.

■ *Keep communication open with parents.* Divorce tends to complicate communication between teachers and parents. Simply scheduling parent-teacher conferences can become a major ordeal. Both parents may demand separate conferences, or neither parent may be able to come for the time you have scheduled. For the child's sake, it's important to make the extra effort necessary to keep parents informed of what's happening at school and to stay informed yourself. If necessary, make adjustments in conference times, or make evening telephone calls when parents are home from work.

Also keep in mind that the child may be having to adjust to two households now; books, homework assignments and notes about school progress or upcoming events may be left one place when they are needed at another. An additional matter to consider is that the child's transportation to and from school may also change with parental separation. With the increase in kidnappings by noncustodial parents, it is helpful for school personnel to be informed of which parent has been awarded legal custody of the child. Then, at least, it is possible for the custodial parent to be notified in case someone else arrives to pick the child up during school hours.

The Classroom and Beyond

The trend toward divorce in America is definitely not on the decline. Female-headed families are increasing 10 times as quickly as two-parent families. As a result, the number of emotionally troubled children in classrooms continues to grow with each new semester. In many cases, teachers are providing the only safety net for these children (Francke, 1983). Schools can no longer ignore the problem and must begin to support teachers by providing training that en-

ables them to better understand and deal with children of divorce. In addition, budgets must be stretched to ensure that guidance counselors are in place at the elementary school level. Unless more progress is made toward reaching out to these children, some predict that as many as three out of four children of divorce will themselves get divorced. Can we afford having this prediction become a reality?

References

Berns, R. M. (1985). *Child, family, community.* New York: Holt, Rinehart & Winston.

Bienenfeld, F. (1987). *Helping your child succeed after divorce.* Claremont, CA: Hunter House.

Dodson, F. (1987). *How to single parent.* New York: Harper & Row.

Elkind, D. (1986). Helping parents make healthy educational choices for their children. *Educational Leadership, 44*(3), 36-38.

Francke, L. B. (1983). *Growing up divorced.* New York: Linden Press/ Simon & Schuster.

Glick, P. C. (1984). Marriage, divorce and living arrangements: Prospective changes. *Journal of Family Issues, 5,* 7-26.

Hetherington, E. M. (1981). Children and divorce. In R. W. Henderson (Ed.), *Parent-child interaction: Theory, research and prospects* (p. 52). New York: Academic Press.

Jellinek, M., & Klavan, E. (1988, September). The single parent. *Good Housekeeping,* p. 126.

National Association of Elementary School Principals & Charles F. Kettering Foundation. (1980). One-parent families and their children: The schools' most significant minority. *Principal, 60,* 31-37.

Wallerstein, J. S., & Kelly, J. B. (1980). *Surviving the breakup.* New York: Basic Books.

Weitzman, L. J. (1985). *The divorce revolution.* New York: The Free Press.

Single-Parent Families: How Bad for the Children?

K. ALISON CLARKE-STEWART

Alison Clarke-Stewart is a professor in the Program in Social Ecology at the University of California, Irvine. She has written extensively about the various environments that influence children's development, including the family and day care. Currently she is doing research on how divorce and child custody affect children. Her books include: Daycare *and* Child Development in the Family.

Researchers know many factors that make divorce harder for children to endure—and the school can't do much about them. But teachers can help keep school from being one more problem.

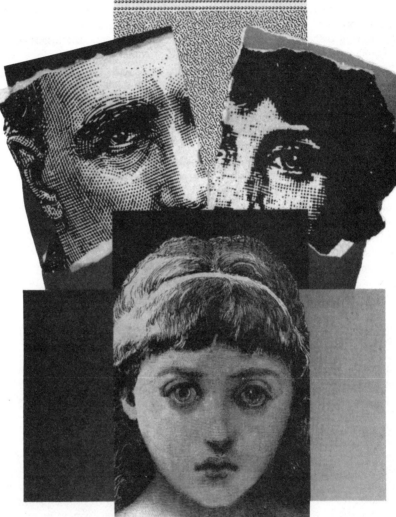

Six-year-old Nathaniel makes his own lunch before he goes to school. Nine-year-old Katherine comes home to an empty house and spends the afternoon watching television. Twelve-year-old Jason does the shopping, babysits for his younger sister, and sighs a lot. There's no question, children today do not live the protected, dependent existence that most of their parents—and teachers—did as youngsters. Responsibilities are thrust upon children at earlier and earlier ages. Expectations for their independence and achievement are high. Many of them experience daily stress.

One contributing factor in the complex web of contemporary economics and life-styles is the increased frequency with which children are growing up in single-parent families. A high proportion of these families are the result of divorce, and it is specifically on the distinctive situation of such families that this paper will focus.

Today, in the United States, one schoolchild in three has parents who are divorced. Thirty percent of these children live in stepfamilies. The other 70 percent live with their mothers or fathers alone.

What are the consequences of their parents' divorcing for children's lives, development, and achievement? Are these children "at risk"? If so, how much, and for how long? Should unhappy parents have stayed together "for the sake of the children"? Behavior problems observed in children from "broken homes" are often attributed to the parents' divorce, but is this always an accurate assessment? Are

From *NEA Today*, January 1989, pp. 60-64. Reprinted by permission of the National Educational Association of the United States.

there ways that schools and teachers can help children with problems rooted in their parents' divorce?

As divorce has become more and more common in this society, researchers have asked these questions, and the answers they have come up with are both worrying and encouraging. Worrying, because their observations show that children do indeed suffer, and suffer severely, when their parents get divorced. Encouraging, because they also show that negative effects on children's psychological well-being are not inevitably long-lasting. Children can be helped through the painful transition of their parents' divorce to a healthy, happy, and well-adjusted life.

How Divorce Hurts

The effects of divorce begin long before the divorce itself, for both parents and children. In one study, observations of children as long as 11 years before their parents separated showed the effects of predivorce family stress. Boys in families in which the parents subsequently divorced were more impulsive and aggressive than boys in nondivorcing families. For parents, the effects begin to show in the years before the separation, through such symptoms as headaches, fatigue, weight loss, depression, anxiety, and mood swings—and these symptoms intensify after the separation. On a scale of stressful life events, separating from a spouse is second in intensity only to the death of a spouse. Over 40 percent of the adults going through a divorce report suffering from at least five physical or psychological symptoms; one-fifth need psychiatric help or hospitalization.

For children, too, the initial reaction to their parents' separation is traumatic. Children whose parents get divorced are initially distraught, shocked, afraid for their own futures. It doesn't make it any easier that one in three of their friends may be in the same boat. Losing *their* mother or *their* father is devastating. Their world turns upside down. Divorce is most devastating for "innocent victims"—those who have no control over its initiation—and children never initiate divorces.

In one study, interviews with children whose parents were getting divorced showed that none of them were happy about their parents' di-

vorce, even if the parents were often in violent conflict with each other. More than three-quarters of the children opposed the divorce strongly, and even five years later one-third were still disapproving, dissatisfied, and intensely unhappy. The nuclear family is all the child knows, so children inevitably experience a strong feeling of loss—of the family unit, of security, and of their fairy-tale fantasy of "happily ever after."

After the divorce, the losses continue. For some things in life—and par-

Not one child was happy about a family divorce, even if the parents were often in violent conflict with each other.

ents may be among them—two is always better than one. One parent can be in only one place at a time, and for parents going through a divorce, that place is most often work, therapy, or the lawyer's office. One parent can have only one point of view, and for divorcing parents that point of view is most often their own. One parent can model only one gender role, give only so many hugs, offer so much discipline, and earn so much money.

Parents going through a divorce and the period following it are overwhelmed, overworked, and disorganized. There is not enough time for work or for themselves. They are absorbed in their own problems of survival, in their involvement in work (for many women, for the first time), in dating, in self-improvement, and in the search for support.

The children are often neglected. In the first couple of years after the divorce, children have less regular bedtimes and mealtimes, eat together as a family less, hear fewer bedtime stories, and are more often late for school. Discipline is less consistent, positive, and affectionate. And perhaps most salient of all, the aftermath of divorce brings economic disaster for most mothers and children.

Recent studies in a number of states have shown that after a divorce women suffer a drastic drop in income and

standard of living—in California, for example, a drop of 73 percent. Men's standard of living improves—42 percent in the states included in this study. Most women are not prepared to support themselves financially, even if they worked before the divorce. They commonly receive inequitable divorce settlements, no lifetime alimony, and a limited amount of spousal and child support (often not paid). They have few job prospects, no job histories, limited earning potential, and no careers. Because 90 percent of children in divorced families live with their mothers, this economic disaster directly affects the children. No-fault divorce has created a new impoverished class. More than half of poor families are made up of single mothers with children—and a sizable proportion of these mothers are divorced.

But it's not just the poverty that's hard to live with. It's the *drop* in income—and the more affluent the family, the harder that is to handle. Giving up Junior League friends to live on Hamburger Helper and food stamps is not only economically stressful, it's demoralizing as well.

Small wonder that children from divorced families are more likely than others to become juvenile delinquents, psychiatric patients, suicide victims. More than half have trouble in school—the result of depression, anxiety, guilt, loneliness, low self-esteem, low achievement, and bad behavior.

Getting over Divorce

The good news is that these effects are not inevitable and they don't have to be long-lasting. Divorce is a painful, negative experience for everyone involved. But people—children especially—are resilient, and time heals. The first year after the divorce is the worst emotionally, and it gets worse before it gets better. But by two or three years after the divorce, in most families, routines are back to normal, physical symptoms have disappeared, the intense psychological stress is over, and adults and children have improved self-esteem and are functioning competently.

The process of adjusting to divorce and subsequent life in a single-parent family is smoother and easier for some adults and children than for others. Some individuals bounce back within a year or two. Others never really get over the experience. Although children whose parents get divorced are "at risk" for psychological and behavioral problems, these problems are not *inevitable*. Researchers currently are probing into the conditions and personal qualities that determine whether a child makes a quick and complete recovery from divorce and a positive adjustment to life in a single-parent family. They have found a number of factors that seem to be critical.

Age. One important determinant of children's reactions to their parents' divorce is age. The younger a child is, the better the prognosis for a complete adjustment. Preschool children don't know what "divorce" is. They don't understand what's going on, and they react to their parents' separation with bewilderment, fear, and regression. But in the long run, they are the most likely to be emotionally unscathed.

Very young children have spent less time in a conflicted family. Their familiarity with and attachment to the family unit is less. And the parents themselves are younger, which makes their recovery easier.

Children who are 6 to 8 years old when their parents divorce understand what is going on better than younger children, but they hurt more. They yearn for the lost parent, and they feel rejected, torn in two, angry at the custodial parent. They don't have a well-developed sense of time, nor do they understand the nature of blood ties. So when they are with one parent they miss the other. They are afraid that while they're apart, the missing parent will find another son or daughter and forget them.

Over the long run, a bare majority of these children adjust fairly well. In a study of 60 divorced families in California by Judith Wallerstein, for example, 10 years after the divorce, 40 percent of the children who had been in this age range at the time of divorce were still functioning poorly.

Children who are 9 to 12 years old when their parents divorce are more upset than younger children. Their parents tell them more about the reasons for the divorce. They often align with one parent (usually the custodial parent) against the other. They are the most likely of all to suffer psychosomatic symptoms of stress and suppressed anger and to have problems in achievement and conduct at school.

One parent can model only one gender role, give only so many hugs, offer so much discipline, and earn so much money.

An increase in household responsibilities and the need to make money often thrust these children into a precocious independence that may include premature sexual awareness or sexual activity.

Similarly, young adolescents, 13 to 16 years old, may be pushed too fast into independence by their parents' divorce. At the best of times, early adolescence is a vulnerable period of shaky self-esteem and conflicts over autonomy. A divorce may precipitate an adolescent's dropping out of school, getting pregnant, or getting into trouble with the law. Young adolescents react to their parents' divorce with unrealistic anguish, anxiety, and outrage: How could you do this to me? Along with the children who are 9 to 12 at the time of the divorce, they have the bleakest long-term outlook. In Wallerstein's study, slightly over half the children in this age range were doing poorly 10 years later.

Sex. For a variety of reasons, divorce is harder on boys than on girls, and boys are more likely to have problems. Boys are more vulnerable in general, and boys—who, like girls, are usually in a mother's custody—are most likely to lose the parent who is their gender-role model and the stronger authority.

Family competence and confidence. Adults who are more intelligent, assertive, self-assured, well-educated, creative, imaginative, mature, emotionally stable, tolerant of frustration, good at coping, willing to take risks, and socially bold are better able than most to deal with divorce and single parenthood, and so are their children.

Similarly, children with strong personal qualities tend to handle the divorce situation more easily. Ironically, however, the children who are most likely to need such strong personal qualities, because their parents are getting divorced, are least likely to possess them, because they are more likely to have grown up in an unharmonious family environment.

Economic situation. Perhaps the single best predictor of the long-term consequences of divorce is the family's financial situation. The drastic drop in income and economic insecurity that accompany many divorces present severe challenges for both parents and children. Stories of single-parent families struggling for survival—living on cold cereal for dinner and trying to keep up the mortgage payments or moving from opulent abodes to tiny apartments in impoverished neighborhoods—are common. These changes inevitably lead to depression and resentment. For children, the economic drop packs a triple whammy: they lose material objects and opportunities, they lose status with their peers, and they are victims of their mothers' distraction and depression. Economic factors have a powerful effect on parents' and children's adjustment to divorce.

Parents' caring and availability. Children's relationships with both their parents after the divorce are very important for a healthy adjustment. These relationships, researchers have found, depend in large part on the child's continuing contact with both parents and on the ability of both parents to provide adequate supervision and consistent, authoritative discipline balanced by ample affection.

Because good relations with both parents have been found to be important for children, many states now award joint or shared custody of children to divorcing parents. Such arrangements sound ideal. The children do not "lose" a parent. They receive a more balanced exposure to two adults. Both parents continue to contribute fully to childrearing. And there is a greater likelihood that the expenses of child support will be shared. For the parents, there is regular and reliable relief from child care as well as the opportunity to make important decisions about the child and to offer daily, not Disneyland, care.

Little is known, however, about whether children really do better in joint custodial arrangements. Existing research is based on small, self-selected samples, and the results of different studies are not entirely consistent. There do seem to be some benefits of joint custody in terms of stress, satisfaction, self-esteem, and symptoms—if joint custody was the choice of the parents rather than of the courts. There is also some evidence that parents with joint custody are less likely than parents with sole custody to return for relitigation of the custody arrangement—again, if they themselves originally chose joint custody.

Court-ordered joint custody, however, may not have any of these benefits. Recent evidence, again collected by Judith Wallerstein, suggests that two years after the divorce, children in court-ordered joint custody arrangements are not doing as well as children in families where the court ordered sole custody. A possible reason is that in the families with court-ordered joint custody, the parents retained a rigid (court-ordered) 50-50 custody split, while only half the couples who had chosen joint custody were still following a 50-50 split. The others had slipped into the more conventional weekday/weekend division of time.

Whatever the legal arrangement, what is most important from the children's perspective is the *quality* of their relationship with both parents. If either parent disappears from the family, if either parent is rejecting, the child will suffer. To promote their children's satisfactory adjustment, parents must look out for the children's needs as well as their own, and not become overly self-absorbed—a challenge when they, too, are hurting.

Parents' current relationship. Children also suffer more if their parents are hostile toward each other. Some divorce researchers have gone so far as to suggest that the reason children of divorced parents have problems is not that they are separated from one of their parents but that their parents continue to fight overtly—sometimes violently—in front of them. In numerous studies, parental conflict or cooperation before and after the divorce has been found to predict both parents' and children's psychological well-being. It is most damaging to children when parents go on fighting and neglect the child or use the child as a pawn in their continued battling—

for example, through custody relitigation or child-snatching.

Stability of circumstances. Another factor that makes adjusting to a divorce difficult for children is the number of changes that inevitably accompany divorce. Moving to a new town and leaving old associations behind immediately upon separation may be the best thing for the parent, but it is not usually best for the child. The more changes children experience—moving to a new neighborhood, starting a new school, having mother start a job, going through repeated separations and reconciliations, living with changes in the custody arrangement—

What is most important from the child's perspective is the *quality* of his or her relationships with both parents.

---

the harder it is to adjust. When parents remarry and the child becomes part of a stepfamily—which happens 1,300 times every day in this country—the change may, again, be good for the parent's mental health but not necessarily for the child's, since it adds new relationships, new conflicts, new rivalries, new uncertainties, and new complexities.

Despite the problems of separation and transition to a new family form, in certain limited ways children can benefit from change. Children who move to a new class or a new school a year or two after the divorce, for example, have had a chance to adjust to living in a divorced family. The change gives them the opportunity to shed any bad reputation they may have made for themselves during the time of emotional crisis and go on to more positive relationships and achievements.

Access to outside help. Finally, the parents and children who adjust best to divorce are those who get help. Divorce is a trauma it's hard to go through alone, and adults and children alike benefit from the opportunity to talk about their experiences to sympathetic and supportive listeners. These listeners may be family members,

friends, teachers, counselors, therapists, or other people who are going through divorce. Social support, from either a network of emotionally supportive and accepting friends or participation in social or professional groups, has been found to buffer stress. What's important is that divorcing parents and children be assured that they are worthy, that they are loved, and that things will—eventually—get better. If they can be given advice about how to speed the process of things getting better, or if they are provided with tangible services, from laundry to loans, this also is helpful.

What Can Teachers Do?

In any year, in any class, the odds are high that there will be some children who are going through some phase of a parental divorce or remarriage. Teachers may be puzzled, annoyed, or completely frustrated by the effects of these events on the children's behavior in school. What can they do to assist these children and allay their own frustrations?

For one thing, teachers should try to be well-informed about what to expect from children under these circumstances. They should know that children, especially boys, are likely to act up and act out, to be distracted and withdrawn, to let their schoolwork slide, for as long as two years after their parents separate. During this time, these children, and their parents, need support and sympathy, not judgmental evaluations and criticism.

Teachers can attend workshops, read books, talk to their colleagues about the problems divorce creates and about possible solutions to those problems. Many schools now offer group programs for children whose parents are divorced, and there is growing evidence that these programs are helpful in children's adjustment.

Children whose parents divorce go through a slow and painful process of coming to understand and cope with the divorce and their new lifestyle and often reduced circumstances. This process can be guided—and children's adjustment can be eased—but time and support are necessary.

Children need to acknowledge the reality of their parents' separation, disengage from the parents' conflict, resolve their own feelings of loss and anger, accept the permanence of the divorce, and achieve realistic hopes and dreams for themselves. All this takes time. Classroom teachers can give children whose parents have just split up a break for some period of adjustment and transition, reducing their stress with lighter assignments and extra attention. Being patient and sympathetic is likely to pay off in the end.

Another way teachers can alleviate the problems created by divorce is by raising the consciousness of their other students about what divorce means and about what children whose parents are divorcing might be experiencing. Later on, teachers can help children whose parents are divorced by offering them a fresh start after they have made the initial adjustment to the divorce. In new classes or workgroups, their fellow students won't be biased by any bizarre or disruptive behavior they may have shown in the immediate aftermath of the divorce.

Looking more toward the future, teachers should do as much as they can to prepare their students for adult life in the twenty-first century. Two points are particularly important here. Students need preparation for the difficulties and challenges of marriage and family life, so that they won't take lightly the decisions they'll be making about when and whom to marry and when to have children. Girls need preparation to pursue lucrative careers and to be self-supporting. This is no longer a feminist issue alone. It is an issue of economic survival.

Divorce is a social phenomenon that affects us all. It is up to all of us, then, to help children and their parents cope with it as well as they can.

For Further Reading

Divorce. Sharon J. Rice and Patrick C. McKenry. Sage Publications, 1988. A systematic summary of recent research on the sociological and psychological processes involved in divorce.

Growing Up Divorced. Linda Bird Franke. Linden Press/Simon & Schuster, 1983. This is one of the many books available for parents—to inform, to educate, and to assist in their challenging task of rearing children after divorce. It provides an excellent review of the research demonstrating how divorce presents a series of crises for children, depending on their age and sex.

Interventions for Children of Divorce: Custody, Access, and Psychotherapy. Walter F. Hodges. Wiley, 1986. For those who are interested in the kinds of therapy and support programs currently available for children of divorce, this book offers an introduction. It also gives a thorough review of research showing the effects of divorce on adults and children.

Mothers and Divorce: Legal, Economic, and Social Dilemmas. Terry Arendell. University of California Press, 1986. *The Divorce Revolution.* Lenore Weitzman. Free Press, 1985. The sociologist authors of these books explore the dire economic and social consequences of divorce for modern middle-class single mothers. Both call for drastic reforms to make divorce legislation more equitable for men and women and to provide adequate support for child rearing.

"Single Parent Families: A Bookshelf: 1978-1985." Benjamin Schlesinger. *Family Relations*, vol. 35, pp. 199-204, 1986. This article lists 80 books and special issues of journals on single parents that appeared between 1978 and 1985. A hint of the vast literature available on this subject, this annotated list suggests where to start reading.

"Single Parenting: A Filmography." Lee Kimmons and Judith A. Gaston. *Family Relations*, vol. 35, pp. 205-211, 1986. This annotated listing of films provides teachers with a description of a broad range of available films, filmstrips, and videotapes that deal with the single-parent experience. All would be useful for classes, support groups, or workshops.

Appropriate Educational Practices

- **Preschool and School-Age Programs (Articles 24–29)**
- **Assessment (Articles 30–32)**
- **Special Needs Programs (Articles 33–37)**

Instruction versus guidance, systematic versus emergent, teacher-chosen versus child-initiated. These are some of the ideas around developmentally based education that are currently debated by caregivers, teachers, parents, and school boards. The principles and philosophies behind these discussions are complex. Those involved in the discussions are firm in their views.

Some people hold that young children must be prepared for the twenty-first century, which is arriving soon as the post–industrial information/technology-based era. They sense the urgency of transformed skills and abilities that will be necessary to function effectively in society. To be next century's adults, today's children require an infusion of powerful instruction and many believe that early childhood is the time to begin. Those on this side of the debate believe direct instruction, based on visionary goals, and use of academic tools (such as workbooks, basal readers, sequenced tasks, and paper/pencil) are appropriate practice to prepare young children for entry to the next century. Achievement is verified by testing, an important measurement to advocates of national standards.

The other side of the debate, while affirming the necessity of preparation, emphasizes young children's learning for the present rather than for the future. To them, the path to effective adult skills and abilities is developmental. Young children learn through exploration of physical objects, and their instruction is embedded in the activity itself. Appropriate practice, to developmentalists, is child-initiated activity, based on emergent goals, using objects of the physical world as tools of learning.

The strength of today's debate over appropriate practice in early childhood indicates another swing of the educational philosophy pendulum. This time, it involves an early childhood community that is more sure of its knowledge and more mature in its practices. It is also a community more divided over its philosophy than on earlier swings.

As knowledge and practice expand, a seeming paradox may be occurring that causes a rupture in philosophy. When any professional community grows, it divides its tasks. The early childhood education community is no exception: one groups studies children, another designs curriculum, still another teaches. Knowledge of children is built by some, while practice with children is perfected by others. Early childhood philosophy is further influenced by opinions from other fields (e.g., political and economic) when state or national conditions shift attention to education.

One vital component of appropriate practice is authentic assessment of children's progress. Reliance on testing as the only measure of achievements is too narrow when practice is developmentally appropriate. So, more inclusive techniques become necessary. Teachers find that it is useful to develop skill in a variety of observational formats. One technique currently being used by teachers is the assessment portfolio, which preserves the work done by children. Keeping periodic records of children's development along with their work aligns well with appropriate practice. This variety of assessment methods provides a much broader picture of children's performance than is available in programs that are test-driven.

Appropriate practice always involves all children, regardless of handicapping condition. Teachers are finding assistance in providing for special needs children by partnering with special educators and families. Early intervention programs are making use of family service plans that link the partners in coordinating and delivering the services that children need. This is maximum inclusion for children, rather than exclusion by handicapping condition. Teachers in a program that is designed to include all children will find themselves reexamining their roles and practices. They will be learning how to work alongside special educators and personnel from other agencies as well as with the whole family.

Authentic appropriate practice, based on children's development, has no shortcuts and cannot be trivialized. By working out specifics of routines, procedures, materials, and assessment suitable for young children, the early childhood profession strengthens its identity. It is a helpful exercise to ensure the match of practice with childhood. Putting thought and planning and process behind the words involves using knowledge of child development to inform caregiving decisions and curricular choices. This is also an exercise in teacher autonomy; to own and value the work of the profession.

The current debate on developmentally appropriate practice is a healthy one, calling for knowledge to remain based on young children and practice to resist standardization. How the early childhood community's perception of appropriate practice will evolve by the twenty-first century remains an open question.

Looking Ahead: Challenge Questions

What is involved in the concept of school readiness? How does appropriate curriculum relate to school readiness?

What place do academics have in a developmentally appropriate program?

Before reading the article, "What Good Prekindergarten Programs Look Like," identify five aspects of an effective, appropriate prekindergarten program.

Other than testing young children, how can teachers assess their progress? What is a teacher's role in early intervention for young children with special needs?

READINESS: CHILDREN AND THEIR SCHOOLS

Dr. Lilian G. Katz

Dr. Lilian G. Katz is Director of the ERIC Clearinghouse on Elementary and Early Childhood Education at the University of Illinois.

The readiness of America's children to benefit from schooling was one of the major issues discussed by the President and the nation's governors at the 1989 education summit. The first of six national education goals announced by the President in 1990 was: "By the year 2000, all children in America will start school ready to learn." The following specific objectives were further defined under the goal:

■ All disadvantaged and disabled children will have access to high quality and developmentally appropriate preschool programs that help prepare children for school.

■ Every parent in America will be a child's first teacher and devote time each day to helping his or her preschool child learn; parents will have access to the training and support they need.

■ Children will receive the nutrition and health care needed to arrive at school with healthy minds and bodies, and the number of low birthweight babies will be significantly reduced through enhanced prenatal health sytems.

This article will explore major issues related to readiness that those who are striving to achieve the goal will need to address.

The Concept of Readiness

After considering the readiness goal and its more specific objectives, policymakers, educators, and parents are likely to have questions about the concept of readiness. This concept has been debated for more than a century (Kagan, 1990). The main issue debated is the extent to which development and learning are determined by biological maturational processes versus experience. Maturationists emphasize internal developmental processes that render children more or less able to benefit from formal instruction. Interactionists take the position that inherent maturational processes and experience interact to contribute to children's learning and that virtually all human beings are born with a powerful, built-in disposition to learn. Indeed, the quantity and rate of learning during the first few years of life are nothing short of spectacular. The fact that by 3 or 4 years of age most children can understand and use the language of those around them is just one example of learning that takes place long before children begin school. In other words, children are born ready to learn!

However, *what* children learn during their first few years, *how* they learn, and *how much* they learn depends on many factors. Among the most important factors are the children's physical well-being and their emotional and cognitive relationships with those who care for them. The school readiness goal reflects two broad concerns about these factors. The first concern is related to characteristics of the children themselves, such as the fact that increasing numbers of young

children live in poverty and/or in single-parent households, have limited proficiency in English, are affected by the drug abuse of their parents, have poor nutrition, and receive inadequate health care. These conditions are frequently a source of stress on families and affect how much and how well children's natural disposition to learn is encouraged and strengthened.

The second area of concern involves such matters as the high incidence of retention in kindergarten and the primary grades, delayed school entry practices in some school districts, segregated transition classes in others, increasing use of standardized tests to determine children's readiness to enter school, and the employment of such tests to deny some children entrance to school and to place them in special classes. These trends are due largely to a historic downward movement of the academic curriculum: the college curriculum of a previous generation moves down into the high school curriculum, the replaced high school curriculum moves down into the elementary school, which pushes the elementary curriculum further down to the first years of formal education. This trend means that children are receiving more formal, whole-group academic instruction at increasingly younger ages, which may now be so incompatible with the children's neurological and mental capacities as to produce excessive stress and failure among young children during the first year of school.

These two areas of concern suggest that reaching the school readiness goal will

Reprinted from *The ERIC Review*, Vol. 2, No. 1, 1992, pp. 2-6. The Educational Resources Information Center (ERIC) is sponsored by the U.S. Department of Education, Office of Educational Research and Improvement.

require a twofold strategy: one part focused on supporting families in their efforts to help their children get ready for school and the second on helping the schools to prepare for the children by being responsive to the wide range of backgrounds, experiences, languages, and needs children bring with them to school.

In sum, one of the main issues embedded in the national school readiness goal is that when many children approach their first school experience, they are not ready to learn what most schools want them to learn. The arguments among specialists, educators, and the public at large on these issues are not about whether young children should obtain good grounding in the basic skills; the main point of contention is *when* it should be accomplished.

Some of the causes of the presumed unreadiness of children for school result from the conditions in which they are growing up, and some reside within the school itself. Thus, one of the important problems for communities, parents, and educators to address is how communities and their agencies can help families get their children off to a good start. Another issue to be addressed is how the schools can better respond to the children on their doorsteps. In other words, how can schools respond effectively to the wide range of individual differences in background, development, and prior experience with stories, books, pencils, group settings, and so forth that differentially equip children to adapt to their first school setting?

Getting Children Ready for School

The term "readiness" is commonly used to mean readiness to learn to read. However, children's ability to adapt to the school situation and its demands involves more aspects of their development than the knowledge and skills involved in reading. Children's general social development and intellectual backgrounds should also be taken into account when considering ways of helping children to prepare for experiences they are likely to encounter in school.

Social Readiness

When children enter school they have to be ready to function in an environment different from that of the family, an environment in which individual needs are not well known, in which group norms and expectations prevail, in which there can be a large number of different relationships, and in which one's place is neither clear nor given.

> ❝ *Children are more likely to cope successfully with their first school experience if they come to it with a backlog of positive experiences of being in a group away from home . . .* ❞

Children are more likely to cope successfully with their first school experience if they come to it with a backlog of positive experiences of being in a group away from home with very familiar adults. Children for whom a prekindergarten or kindergarten class is the first group experience outside of the home will require plenty of time and support to adjust to group life and the classroom routines and to be able to function independently in the class. It is rarely helpful to push or cajole a child who is new to the "big school" into conformity. Indeed, it is developmentally appropriate for a young child to be somewhat wary and cautious in an environment full of people who are largely strangers! Young children are also more likely to approach new relationships with adults with confidence if they have already had some previous positive experience with nonfamily authority figures. Participation in a good preschool program affords such experience. However, some children may be wary of the school setting because their previous group experiences have been unpleasant. In either case, the newcomer's hesitation should be treated with respect and patience.

Young children are also more likely to adjust easily to school life if they have experienced satisfying relationships with a few peers. The evidence is now compelling that children who fail to achieve minimal competence in social relationships with their peers during the early years are at risk of developing a variety of social maladaptations, including academic failure, dropping out of school, and later mental health difficulties (Katz and McClellan, 1991).

Parents and preschool teachers can help pave the way for a child's adjustment to school by providing ample opportunities for interaction with peers in which the child can learn such social skills as taking turns, making compromises, and approaching unfamiliar children. A young child who is not yet able to approach peers with confidence will benefit from much support, guidance, and patience from the teacher.

One of the most important influences on children's social development is experience within the family. It should be noted that the whole range of social difficulties identified during early childhood can be observed among children of all social classes and ethnic backgrounds (Katz and McClellan, 1991). However, because not all the children within a particular family achieve the same success in developing social competence, the family does not provide a single environment, and the processes by which individual children within it acquire social competence are not easy to discern. Thus a parent may have a few worries about the social development of one child, whereas for other children in the family, entry into new peer groups went smoothly.

Some young children are unable to meet the expectations of the class because they are having social difficulties, such as feeling rejected by peers. Some children create social difficulties, for example, by starting fights with peers, because they cannot meet the expectations of the class. However, if children are having social difficulties such as being unable to approach unfamiliar peers because their mastery of their peers' language is limited, or because the activities available and topics addressed are unrelated to their own cultural background, their social difficulties may be exacerbated (Katz and McClellan, 1991).

The available evidence indicates that helping families with their children's social development should be put high on the list of strategies to address the readiness goal. Local community agencies, working with groups, individual parents and teachers, and other school personnel (e.g., social workers and psychologists) can help by providing resources for parents that specifically address strategies for fostering their young children's social development.

Intellectual Readiness

Children are more likely to feel competent in school if they can understand and use the language of the peers and adults they meet within it. In many communities, the number and variety of languages spoken is so large that it is not possible for all of the children in a class to have a teacher who speaks their language and materials available to them in their own language. However, communities and school districts must make every possible effort to identify adults who can help children of all language backgrounds in the school.

In a similar way, young children are more likely to have confidence in their ability to cope with school if they can relate to the ideas and topics introduced by the teacher and discussed by other children in class activities. Parents and preschool teachers can help by familiarizing children with a wide range of stories, songs, and linguistic expressions likely to be encountered in the school setting.

"At-risk" children are often assumed to be deficient in experience and to suffer from lack of stimulation and therefore to be intellectually unprepared for school. However, very few children actually lack experience or stimulation. Although the content and nature of the experiences available to children in different settings are likely to vary widely, they are nevertheless experiences that can stimulate children's intellectual development.

For example, children growing up in the inner cities of America have plenty of experience and stimulation. But experience and stimulation are not, in and of themselves, conducive to optimal intellectual development. What young children require is adult help in making sense of their experience and giving meaning and order to the stimulation that surrounds them. A young

> *" The community, working with local preschools, adult education programs, children's librarians, and other similar agency and resource people, can help by providing experiences for preschoolers which help them make sense of their everyday worlds. "*

child in a crowded environment in which many people come and go, often in unpredictable ways, may find it stimulating—especially at first; but without someone's help in explaining and understanding why people come and go, where they go, what they do, what they are planning, and the like, the stimulation can be incoherent and overwhelming. After a few years of incomprehensible stimulation, children give up being able to make sense of their experience, and eventually natural curiosity about their world and the disposition to learn about it are likely to weaken and even disappear.

Although all children are born with the predisposition to learn, in a few cases that predisposition may be weakened by the time a child enters school because of insufficient adult response to the child's explorations and questions. As Rogoff (1990) points out, all significant learning, especially in the early years, occurs in social contexts and is embedded in social relationships.

The community, working with local preschools, adult education programs, children's librarians, and other similar agency and resource people, can help by providing experiences for preschoolers which help them make sense of their everyday worlds. Preschool teachers and others could help familiarize children with songs and stories and provide opportunities for conversation using important words and phrases in English. Adults should also encourage and help children translate songs, stories, and important words and phrases into other languages that may be spoken by children in the neighborhood school. The school district or individual school may have to take leadership for bringing the relevant agencies, specialists, and resource groups together to enable optimal use of the available resources in the community.

Parents and preschool teachers can strengthen intellectual preparedness by providing children ample opportunity for conversation, discussion, and cooperative work and play with peers with whom they are likely to start school. Parents of children not enrolled in a preschool program can help by talking to the staff at the children's future school about the kinds of stories, songs, and special activities and field trips usually offered at the school and by introducing related topics to their children.

Getting the School Ready for the Children

The most important strategy for addressing the school readiness goal is to prepare the school to be responsive to the wide range of experiences, backgrounds, and needs of the children expected to come to the school. Aspects of school practices to be considered in this effort include the curriculum, staffing patterns, and age considerations.

Appropriate Curriculum

A position statement on school readiness issued by the National Association for the Education of Young Children (1990) points out that, given the nature of children's development, "the curriculum in the early grades must provide meaningful contexts for children's learning rather than focusing primarily on isolated skills acquisitions" (p. 22). In other words, the school readiness goal should be addressed by adopting curriculum and teaching practices that are developmentally appropriate. The nature of development is such that curriculum and teaching practices in the early years are appropriate if they take into account the following developmental principles:

■ *Informality.* The younger the child, the larger proportion of time should be allocated to informal versus formal learning experiences. As children grow older, their capacity to benefit from formal, whole-group instruction increases. However, in the case of young children, when a single formal method of instruction is used for a group of children diverse in background, experience, language, aptitudes, interests, and developmental rates, a significant proportion of the group is condemned to fail.

There are at least three kinds of informal activities to be provided for young children: (1) spontaneous dramatic play, (2) arts and craft activities, and (3) cooperative work on extended group investigations and exploratory and constructive projects in which the teacher role is consultative rather than didactic. Although young children benefit from having all three kinds of informal activities on a regular basis, it is the last kind that provides a context for challenging all aspects of children's intellectual and social growth (Katz and Chard, 1989).

An important part of this developmental principle is that the more informal the learning environment is, the more access the teacher has to information about where the learners are in their development, what is easy for them, what confuses them, and what kinds of help they really need. Formal instruction tends to reduce teachers' access to information about the learners they are trying to help. Thus the curriculum during the first years of school must emphasize small-group work. As the children work together on various investigations, teachers are in an ideal position to make observations of individual children's progress and needs. On the basis of these observations, teachers can plan systematic instruction in the basic skills and other learning to

be given to small groups of children or individuals as needed.

■ *Horizontal relevance.* The younger the children, the more important it is that what they learn is meaningful in the present. Horizontal relevance contrasts with vertical relevance, which is characteristic of learning designed to prepare children for the next lesson or the next grade or another future experience and lacks meaningfulness in the

> **❝ . . . the more informal the learning environment is, the more access the teacher has to information about where the learners are in their development . . . ❞**

present. As children grow older, their capacity to benefit from learning that has vertical, or future, relevance increases. The developmental emphasis must be that what the children learn during the early years is designed to help them make sense of their own experiences and environments. Young children might study buildings in their own neighborhoods or animals encountered in their own environments rather than ancient castles or exotic creatures of the past such as dinosaurs. As children grow older, it is the responsibility of schools to help them understand the experiences and environments of others—those who are far away in both time and place. But during the early years, the nature of intellectual development is such that content and skills emphasized should have horizontal relevance.

■ *Interactive learning processes.* The younger the children, the more they learn through interactive processes versus passive, receptive processes. That is not to say young children cannot learn from passive, receptive processes; indeed, young children learn a great deal from experiences in which their role is a passive one, such as tele-

vision viewing or listening to stories. However, the disposition to go on learning, which is a major goal for all of education, is strengthened primarily by engagement in active exploration and investigation as well as interaction with real environments and objects.

■ *Application of skills.* Skills can be acquired and strengthened through a variety of processes—observations, imitation, trial and error, coaching, and instruction. They can be improved with optimum drill and practice. In young children, skills are best developed and strengthened when they are applied in meaningful contexts and free from performance criteria (Katz, 1991).

Appropriate Staffing

Teachers are more likely to be able to accommodate the diversity of experiences, backgrounds, languages, and interests of their pupils if their classes are small and if they have the services of a qualified full-time aide. To address both the social and the intellectual development of children who are potentially at risk for academic difficulties requires the skillful deployment of at least 2 adults for every 18 to 20 children in the kindergarten. Furthermore, having two adults in each class makes it easier to staff classes with adults who speak more than one language. Small child/staff ratios provide teachers with the opportunity to spend unhurried time with every child, to address each child's unique needs, and to develop good relationships with parents.

Age Considerations

The National Association for the Education of Young Children's Position Statement on School Readiness (1990) points out that, contrary to what is commonly assumed, there are no tests by which to determine reliably whether a child is "ready" to begin school. "Therefore, the only legally and ethically defensible criterion for determining school entry is whether the child has reached the legal chronological age of school entry" (p. 22). [For a counterpoint to this statement, see "Early School Entry Is Essential for Many Gifted Children," *The ERIC Review,* Vol. 2, Issue 1, 1992, p. 19.]

this statement, see "Early School Entry Is Essential for Many Gifted Children" on p. 19.]

Some school districts are experimenting with mixed-age grouping in the early grades as a way of reducing grade retention rates and encouraging children to help each other in all areas of learning (Katz, Evangelou, and Hartman, 1990).

Realizing the goal of having all our children ready for school and all our schools ready for the children by the year 2000 will require the best efforts of all involved: parents, teachers, administrators, and everyone in the community who has a stake in the well-being of its children. And that's just about everybody!

References

Kagan, Sharon L. (December 1990). "Readiness 2000: Rethinking Rhetoric and Responsibility." *Phi Delta Kappan*, 72 (4): 272–279. EJ 418 153.

Katz, Lilian G. (1991). "Pedagogical Issues in Early Childhood Education." In *The Care and Education of America's Young Children: Obstacles and Opportunities*, edited by S. L. Kagan. Ninetieth Yearbook of the National Society for the Study of Education. Chicago: University of Chicago Press.

Katz, Lilian G. and Sylvia C. Chard (1989). *Engaging Children's Minds: The Project Approach*. Norwood, NJ: Ablex Publishing Corporation.

Katz, Lilian G., Demetra Evangelou, and Jeanette Allison Hartman (1990). *The Case for Mixed-Age Grouping in Early Childhood*. Washington, DC: National Association for the Education of Young Children.

Katz, Lilian G. and Diane McClellan (1991). *The Teacher's Role in the Social Development of Young Children*. Urbana, IL: ERIC Clearinghouse on Elementary and Early Childhood Education. ED 331 642.

National Association for the Education of Young Children (November 1990). "NAEYC Position Statement on School Readiness." *Young Children*, 46 (1): 21–23. EJ 421 837.

Rogoff, B. (1990). *Apprenticeship in Thinking: Cognitive Development in Social Context*. New York: Oxford University Press.

Myths Associated with Developmentally Appropriate Programs

Marjorie J. Kostelnik

It seems everywhere early childhood practitioners turn these days, people are talking about developmentally appropriate practice and programs. The term 'developmentally appropriate' has become prominent in journal articles, books, the media, professional newsletters, conference presentations, publisher's materials and manufacturer's advertising. Teachers and administrators, theoreticians and researchers, parents and politicians have all become involved in the 'developmentally appropriate' programs discussion. The problem is, not everyone means the same thing when they use the term. In fact, the phrase developmentally appropriate is becoming a catch word people use to describe almost anything and everything associated with early childhood education. The same terminology may be used to justify such incompatible notions as 'readiness' programs for children and programs that advocate giving children the 'gift of time'—structuring children's learning experiences within narrowly defined parameters and not structuring them at all—grouping children by ability and grouping children by almost any criteria other than ability. These inconsistencies have led to much confusion about what developmentally appropriate programs entail (Walsh, 1991). In the absence of true understanding, myths have sprung up to explain what it all means. These myths represent collective opinions that are based on false assumptions or are the product of fallacious reasoning. Some have evolved from people's attempts to simplify complex phenomena, resulting in oversimplification to the point of inaccuracy. Others have resulted from people's intuitive interpretations of child behavior or superficial understanding of child development and learning-related theories and research (Spodek, 1986). Still more myths have been created as a way for people to make finite and absolute, a concept that is in fact open-ended and amenable to many variations. Unfortunately, these myths are widespread; causing misunderstandings and anxiety among practitioners and the public. What follows are a few of the most common ones I have encountered both in this country and abroad.

Myth: *There is one right way to implement a developmentally appropriate program.*

Reality: When talking about developmentally appropriate practice with any group of practitioners it is not unusual to hear statements like, "You always use learning centers." "You never use whole group instruction." "You always let children determine the content of the lesson." "You never correct children." "You always let children figure out their own spellings for words." "You never use lined paper." Likewise, teachers and administrators may ask, "Is it ever okay to show children how to hold a pencil?" "Is it wrong to spell words for children when they ask?" "Exactly when should we introduce cursive writing?" These kinds of pronouncements and queries represent efforts to establish single, correct approaches to instruction. They are based on the belief that one method of teaching suits all children and all situations. Unfortunately, the reality is that teaching is complex; there is no one solution that fits every circumstance. On the contrary, individual teaching episodes can and should be qualified by "It depends" (Newman and Church, 1990). It depends on such variables as what the child's current level of comprehension might be, what experiences the child might have had, and the kinds of previous knowledge and skills the child brings to the situation. Contextual elements including time, human resources, the physical environment, material resources, and the values and expectations of the school and community must also be factored in. The goals, strategies and standards school personnel finally choose are all affected by these constraints. Hence, every educational decision requires judgement—judgements by teachers and administrators—made on the spot or over time, but always with certain children in mind. This means practitioners must continually weigh out what they do in relation to their knowledge about how children develop and learn. To translate that knowledge into actual teaching strategies, they must be willing to explore a variety of practices in the classroom and to allow themselves to make mistakes. Moreover, teachers will have to continually examine their assumptions and learn from the children as they evaluate the effectiveness of their teaching. What meets the needs of several children in a group may not be appropriate for others. What was optimal for last year's class, may not be so this year. One's search then, is not simply for 'right' answers but for the best answers to meet the needs of children representing a wide range of abilities, learning styles, interests and backgrounds. Finally, teachers too, differ from one another and require flexibility to develop an approach to teaching that is compatible with their beliefs and comfortable for them as well as for their students. These variations in both children's and teacher's needs, necessitate differences in the programs designed to meet them. Hence there is no one model that is best for all.

From *The Beacon*, November 1991, pp. 1-4. Reprinted by permission of *The Beacon*, Newsletter of the Michigan Association for the Education of Young Children.

3. APPROPRIATE EDUCATIONAL PRACTICES: Preschool and School-Age Programs

Myth: *Developmentally appropriate practice requires teachers to abandon all their prior knowledge and experience. Nothing they have learned or done in the past is acceptable in the new philosophy.*

Reality: It is not only a daunting prospect, but an affrontive one, for seasoned practitioners to contemplate returning to novice status in their pursuit of developmentally appropriate practice. Those who approach the idea in this frame of mind are understandably discouraged and/or resistant. However, the facts of the matter are, few experienced teachers require a total 'make-over' to become more developmentally appropriate in their practices. The knowledge of children and teaching they have gained over the years, will serve as the foundation from which they can examine their pedagogical beliefs and instructional practices. In addition, since the concept of developmental appropriateness has evolved from past educational trends, most teachers are already implementing numerous philosophically compatible strategies and activities in their classrooms. Some practitioners simply need 'permission' to continue. Others, need help recognizing their own strengths. In either case, teachers are most successful making the transition to more developmentally appropriate practice when they build on what they know.

Myth: *Developmentally appropriate classrooms are unstructured classrooms.*

Reality: Some people make this claim because they equate structure with rigidity and so shun the term. Others envision a classroom in which chaos reigns. Both interpretations are based on misinformation. Structure refers to the extent to which teachers develop an instructional plan, then organize the physical setting and social environment to support the achievement of educational goals (Spodek, Saracho and Davis, 1991). By this definition, developmentally appropriate classrooms are highly structured. Both teachers and children contribute to their organization. Teachers generate educational goals for students based on school-wide expectations tempered by their understanding of individual children's needs, abilities and interests. All of the activities and routines of the day are purposefully planned to promote these goals. Keeping their instructional plan in mind, teachers determine the arrangement of the furniture, what specific materials to offer children, the nature and flow of activity, the approximate time to allocate to various

instructional segments, and the grouping of children throughout the session. As teachers interact with children they observe them, listen to them, instruct them, guide them, support them and encourage them. Consequently, while teachers carefully consider long-range objectives, their moment-to-moment decision-making remains fluid in order to capitalize on input from the children (Newman and Church, 1990). Children ask questions, suggest alternatives, express interests and develop plans that may lead the instruction in new directions. In this way, overall instructional goals are merged with more immediate ones, thereby creating a flexible, stimulating classroom structure. Developmentally appropriate classrooms are active ones in which both teachers and students learn from one another. Such learning requires a constant interchange of thoughts and ideas. As a result, there are times during the day when many people are talking at once or when several children are moving about the room at one time. To the untrained eye these conditions may appear chaotic, but a closer look should reveal children on-task, constructively involved in their own learning. If children are wandering aimlessly, screaming indiscriminately or racing from place to place, the environment is not conducive to learning, and so is developmentally inappropriate.

Myth: *In developmentally appropriate classrooms, teachers don't teach.*

Reality: This myth stems from the stereotypic idea that teachers are people who stand up in front of a group of students, telling them what they need to know. And, that the teacher's most important duties consist of assigning work to children and checking for right and wrong answers. According to this scenario, teachers are always directive and center-stage. People who envision teachers this way, may not recognize all the teaching that is going on in a developmentally appropriate classroom. For example, teachers create physical environments and daily schedules that enable children to engage in purposeful activity. Curricular goals are frequently addressed through pervasive classroom routines such as dressing to go outside, preparing for snack and cleaning-up. Although some whole group instruction takes place, teachers spend much of their classroom time moving throughout the room working with children individually and in small informal groups. During these times,

they influence children's learning indirectly through the provision of certain activities in which the focus is on children's self-discovery and exploration. They also teach children directly, using a variety of instructional strategies. Teachers initiate learning activities as well as respond to children's initiatives. They pose questions, offer procedural suggestions, suggest explorations and provide information. As opportunities arise, instructors present children with challenges that help them move beyond their current understandings and strategies (Newman and Church, 1990). Additionally, teachers constantly reflect on what is happening in the classroom. They make judgements about children's progress and introduce variations or changes in focus as children's needs warrant. All of these activities are essential teaching behaviors.

Myth: *Developmentally appropriate programs can be defined according to dichotomous positions. One position is always right, the other position is always wrong.*

Reality: The dichotomies, Process-focused versus Product focused, Child-initiated versus Adult-initiated, Socially-oriented versus Cognitively oriented, are some of the ones people typically refer to when talking about developmentally appropriate programs. Such discussions tend to treat these variable as polar opposites. As a result, the items on the left, above, are usually defined as 'good', 'desirable' and 'appropriate'; those on the right, as 'bad', 'undesirable', and 'inappropriate'. Furthermore, because the categories are mutually exclusive, they imply that developmentally appropriate programs are 100 percent process-focused with no thought given to products; that children initiate all learning episodes and adults initiate none; that social development is more important that cognition. None of these assertions are true. Developmentally appropriate programming is not an all or nothing proposition. For example, process learning is very important to children and should be highly valued by teachers. The satisfaction a child gains from painting is more important than the degree to which his or her picture represents the adult's notion of reality. However, anyone who has watched young children proudly show-off their work, knows that products are sometimes important too. Likewise, many, many activities in the developmentally appropriate classroom come about through child exploration and initiation. Yet, others are introduced by the teacher as a way to spark children's interest in something new. Furthermore, although social development cannot be ignored, neither can cognitive pursuits. To elevate one above the other denies the integrative nature of child development. Consequently, it is more accurate to envision variables such as these along continuums. Rather than calling to mind issues of all or none, yes or no, good or bad; a continuum suggests that educational planning is really a matter of degrees and balance. Developmentally appropriate programs are both varied and comprehensive. They enable children to engage in the kinds of experiences they need at a given time. Such experiences will fall in different places along the continuum, depending on the child and will differ from time to time.

Myth: *Academics have no place in developmentally appropriate programs.*

Reality: Academics represent the traditional content of the schools. In most people's minds this encompasses reading, writing and arithmetic. Proponents of this myth, believe young children are not 'ready' for academics. They proudly announce that students in their programs are not expected to read or use numbers or write. Opponents, point to the myth as a sign that children who participate in developmentally appropriate programs are not 'learning' the essentials. They worry that such children will lack critical skills necessary for achievement. Both claims are based on an overly narrow interpretation of academic learning. They equate academics with technical subskills (e.g. reciting the ABC's or writing out numerical equations) or with rote instruction (e.g. emphasis on worksheets and drill). Each of these definitions is too narrow in scope. They confuse

concepts with methods and ignore how reading, writing and number- related behaviors and understandings emerge in young children's lives.   Children do not wait for elementary school to demonstrate an interest in words and numbers. They manifest literacy-related interests as infants when they mouth a book or 'pat the bunny', and again as toddlers when they beg, "read it again." Likewise, young children count - one cookie ..two shoes.. three candles on the birthday cake. They compare-" Which has more?"..." Who still needs some?" Children calculate -" Will it fit?" "Now I have two, I need one more." These kinds of activities form the beginnings of literacy and mathematical thinking — the true essence of academics. Children continue on in this manner as they mature, seeking new knowledge and skills as their capacities to know and do increase. Thus, there is no specific time, before or after which, such learning is either appropriate or inappropriate. These evaluative labels are better applied to the parameters within which academics are defined and the strategies teachers use to address academic learning. Programs that focus on isolated skill development and that rely on long periods of whole group instruction or abstract paper-and-pencil activities do not meet the needs of young children. Those that emphasis concepts and processes, that utilize small group instruction, active manipulation of relevant, concrete materials and interactive learning provide a solid foundation for academics within a context of meaningful activity. Using children's interests and ways of learning as guides, early childhood teachers do four things to promote academic learning. First, they understand the broad nature of literacy and mathematics and are familiar with the concepts, processes and content that comprise them. They recognize that reading is more than reciting the alphabet or making letter- sound associations out of context; that writing is not the same as penmanship; that mathematics goes beyond rote memorization

of number facts. Second, they recognize manifestations of academic interest and exploratory behavior in the children they teach (e.g. "Teacher what does this say?" "How many do we need?" "Look what I made." etc.) Third, teachers provide concrete materials and relevant experiences to enhance children's academic learning. (e.g. They read to children often and invite children to respond and interpret the story. They sing songs, read poems, and play rhyming games in which sound associations are addressed. They give children materials to sort, sequence, count, combine or divide and make estimations about. They offer children many ways to express themselves both orally and in writing). Fourth, teachers introduce new information, materials, and problems that stimulate children to make observations and comparisons, to question, to experiment, to derive meaning, to make predictions and from which to draw their own conclusions. In this way academics become an integral part of classroom life.

Myth: *Developmentally appropriate programs are suitable for only certain kinds of children.*

Reality: Some people believe that the notion of developmental appropriateness only fits young children, or middle-class children, or Euro- American children, or children who have no special needs. This is a fallacy. While specific details of what is appropriate for children will vary from population to population and from child to child, the principles guiding developmentally appropriate programs are universally applicable. To put it another way, one might ask, "For what children is it appropriate to ignore how they develop and learn? For what child is it inappropriate to treat him or her as an individual?" If the answer is none, then there is no group for whom the basic tenets of developmental appropriateness do not apply.

What Every Preschooler Needs to Know

The signs of a tot who's really ready and set to go are much more subtle than knowing his ABCs—and can make the critical difference in his long-term school spirit.

Andrea Atkins

Contributing editor Andrea Atkins specializes in education issues.

A 3-year-old who will be starting preschool this fall should be able to:

(a) recognize colors
(b) recognize shapes
(c) sit still for at least 30 minutes
(d) imitate at least three animal sounds

Yes, this is a trick question. The truth is, the average 3-year-old may be able to do all of these things, or none of them, and still be a perfectly competent preschooler. "The academic expectations for a child just beginning school are minimal," emphasizes Bettye Caldwell, Ph.D., distinguished professor of education at the University of Arkansas in Little Rock. "You want your child to come to preschool feeling happy, reasonably secure, and eager to explore and learn."

What a relief! While it's true that recent research indicates that a successful preschool experience can indeed translate to long-term education success, "ready for preschool" has become an overused and overvalued phrase. "The majority of children are ready for preschool," explains Shelley Lindauer, Ph.D., associate professor and director of the Child Development Laboratory School at Utah State University in Logan. "Almost all children can benefit from some quality out-of-home experience from age 2 on."

The range of developmental accomplishments between ages 2 and 4, when most kids start preschool, is wide. Some kids in this age range may talk your ear off while others barely utter a peep. One

5 Ways to Build a Successful Preschooler

1. Read to your child daily.

2. Get down on the floor and play with your child.

3. Provide opportunities for him to play with—or be around—other children.

4. Meet your child's needs quickly—but without stifling her attempts at independence.

5. Respond to your child's verbalizations—even the earliest coos and gurgles—with lots of enthusiastic wordplay and conversation.

child may rush into a classroom with glee; another may cling to you like lint. All such behavior falls within the range of normal to a preschool teacher.

There are certain skills, however, that can *enhance* your child's ability to adapt to preschool. We've pulled together the following developmental barometers that are based on the average 3-year-old—the age when most children begin preschool. Of course, if your child is older or younger, you'll want to adjust your expectations slightly. And remember that a seemingly minor upheaval—such as the arrival of a baby brother or sister, or a move to a new home—can result in some temporary regression. With all that in mind, here are some skill suggestions for preschool readiness. Again, these are guidelines, not musts—take them with a pound of salt.

SOCIAL SAVVY

EMPATHY Your 3-year-old should have some beginning sense of other children's needs. "If two preschoolers are playing with blocks, each needs to be aware that the tower being built by the other child means something to him," says Sara Wilford, M.S.Ed., director of the Early Childhood Center at Sarah Lawrence College in Bronxville, New York. "A younger child won't yet have this capacity, and will be more likely to wreck another kid's tower."

GETTING ALONG Most children are interested in making friends by age 3 and often "play" better with other children in preschool than they do at home. Why? There are professionals to help them handle their disputes and discover how much fun being around peers can be.

 From *Child*, June/July 1992, pp. 64, 66. Copyright © 1992 by Andrea Atkins. Reprinted by permission.

SHARING No one expects a preschooler to be able to share all the time. Teachers will simply compensate by having more toys and letting kids work out their troubles on their own.

DEVELOPMENTAL DETAILS

LANGUAGE A child should have enough language fluency to express what he feels and wants ("I'm hungry"; "I want to play with the truck" as well as to relate to other adults and children, says Lillian Katz, Ph.D., professor of early childhood education at the University of Illinois, Urbana. While children who don't speak at all may indeed become frustrated by their inability to make themselves understood, you need not be concerned if your child isn't yet able to speak in complete and coherent grown-up sentences.

ATTENTION SPAN "There's an awful tendency to stereotype young children as 'having short attention spans,' " notes Dr. Katz. But the truth is, "it's inappropriate activities that make them inattentive," she emphasizes. Good teachers know that a mix of time for free play and short (about 15 minutes) activities keep kids content.

FOLLOWING INSTRUCTIONS Often parents believe their child can't follow instructions, but they're usually giving too many at once or the wrong ones. Your youngster will most likely respond to a specific request like "put away the crayons" easier than the broader "clean up this mess."

ACADEMIC KNOW-HOW

LETTER RECOGNITION It's helpful if a child can recognize her name or at least the first letter of her name, notes Dr. Lindauer. It's *not* necessary for her to be able to recite the alphabet.

COLORS AND SHAPES Many preschoolers know the difference between a circle and square, or can tell red from green. But they need not identify a hexagon or understand that lavender is a shade of purple. No one expects it, and no one will hold it against them if they still don't get it.

STORY-TIME SMARTS Being read to builds a 3-year-old's power of concentration, imagination, and language abilities. If you've been reading to your child at home, then he'll be able to enjoy story time along with all the other kids in his class *who can't read yet* either.

CAN-DO SKILLS

USING THE BATHROOM Most preschools for 3 and above require that a child be toilet trained (programs for 2-year-olds will generally take kids in diapers). If your child is not, talk to the teacher about it. "No child is the first to be in this situation," emphasizes Fretta Reitzes, director of the Center for Youth and Family at the 92nd Street Y in New York City. "Trust that the school can help you deal with that. You don't have to keep it a secret or try to frantically correct it."

GETTING DRESSED It's helpful if a preschooler can put on her own coat, hat, and shoes (if she can't tie her shoelaces yet, simply opt for the easier hook-and-loop fastening type).

IDENTIFYING BELONGINGS Knowing what's his (knapsack, pencil, jacket) can go a long way toward helping a preschooler feel at ease. Help him by affixing tape or fabric labels marked with his first name to all his gear.

CLEANING UP After a snack, a 3-year-old should be able to throw out her plate and cup, and wipe up her spot when directed.

TESTING, TESTING: WHEN TO PROCEED WITH CAUTION

Some preschools require that children be "tested" for certain academic and social skills before admission. Most educators say this practice should raise a red flag for parents. "Research has shown that structured education does not do any good for very young children," says Dr. Lindauer. If you live in an area where all preschools insist on an application and interview process, be especially wary of teachers who don't get down to your child's eye level and speak directly to him. Also, a child should not have to recite or write the ABCs as part of an admissions interview. "The child may be able to do that," notes Wilford, "but it's not a developmentally appropriate practice to be teaching that sort of academics now. A preschooler's work is to play and to learn to get along with others in a group."

What Good Prekindergarten Programs Look Like

Janice Molnar

Janice Molnar, PhD, is a researcher at the Bank Street College of Education in New York. Her article is based on material she contributed to *Early Childhood Programs and the Public Schools,* by Anne Mitchell (also of Bank Street) and Michelle Seligson and Fern Marx (of the Wellesley College Center for Research on Women) and published by Auburn House © 1989, part of Greenwood Publishing Group in Westport, Connecticut. Their book presents the results of a four-year study of early childhood programs carried out by Bank Street and Wellesley with funding from the Carnegie Corporation of New York and the Ford Foundation.

Reprinted with permission.

All parents want their children to get the best possible start in education. And an increasing number of parents want this to happen when their children are only three and four years old.

Parents and taxpayers look to the public schools to make this happen. But we have to ask if the nation's public schools are ready and able today to provide high-quality early childhood education for every child coming through their doors. More particularly, are the schools prepared to introduce children to the world of education with an effective, appropriate, high-quality prekindergarten program?

To answer that key question, the Public School Early Childhood Study carried out a mail and telephone survey of early childhood program directors at the state level and child advocates in all 50 states and the District of Columbia; we also did a pin-point mail survey of some 1,225 public school districts. We then visited 13 public school prekindergarten programs in 12 states to get a sense of what was happening "at ground level." Two people spent five days at each site observing staff and classroom practices and conducting face-to-face interviews.

Programs Are Remarkably Diverse

From all this data, we were able to get a fairly accurate picture of prekindergarten programs in public schools. We learned that, first of all, they are remarkably diverse. They reflect a range of implicit assumptions about young children and how they learn. Even within a given school with a particular approach to the education of young children, shades of difference could be seen between one classroom and another down the hall.

Thus, the one thing we can say without qualification about the classrooms we visited is that it is impossible to generalize. Even in sites which had a clearly articulated philosophy and set of guidelines, the way the program was translated by the teacher in the daily rhythm of classroom activities and social exchange varied considerably. In this respect, at least, they are like early childhood programs everywhere.

Environment and Materials

Across the 13 sites, most classrooms we visited had the kinds of materials traditionally found in any early childhood environment: child-sized tables and chairs, for example, and appropriate shelving and storage space. Large numbers of rooms had child-sized sinks (61 percent) and storage space for children's personal belongings (75 percent), indicating that many of the prekindergartens were housed in space designed specifically for young children.

The vast majority (80 percent or more) of the 76 classrooms on which we had the most complete information had creative play equipment: small toys, construction toys, puzzles, blocks, art and crafts materials, and housekeeping furniture and accessories. Record players and records were observed also in these classrooms (over 80 percent), and over half had additional audio equipment such as tape recorders.

Young children learn best through

From *Streamlined Seminar,* Vol. 9, No. 5, May 1991, pp. 1-7. Reprinted with permission of the National Association of Elementary School Principals.

active engagement with "open-ended" materials—painting easels, for example, or musical instruments—that allow them to explore at their own pace, in their own way, and to the extent of their own interest. Unfortunately, 30 percent of the observed classrooms did not have easels (in a couple of cases, they were present but used as small bulletin boards). Just over half had sand/water tables (though for health reasons state regulations forbade them in a few of the sites). Not even half the classrooms had pets or other nature/science materials (43 percent and 45 percent, respectively). Not quite one-third of the classrooms had musical instruments; only 10 percent had a piano.

Young children also require challenging materials that help them gain mastery over their environment by focusing on a particular concept or set of skills. In the observed classrooms 55 percent had math manipulatives (cuisinaire rods, unifix cubes, number puzzles); 38 percent had language games (picture lotto, story sequence cards, letter puzzles). These kinds of materials extend children's language, reasoning, and conceptual abilities in a focused way, when used in combination with open-ended materials. We know that closed-ended, paper-and-pencil activities are inappropriate for young children. Not only can they be a frustrating waste of children's time, but in many cases they may permanently blunt children's curiosity and desire to learn. Nevertheless, 22 percent of the observed classrooms had commercial textbooks and/or workbooks.

Appearances Can Deceive

Of course, what matters is neither the presence nor the absence of particular materials but rather how materials are used. For example, we visited one relatively new and attractively designed open-classroom environment that, at first glance, was quite impressive: the classroom space was colorful and well organized, materials were new and plentiful.

But a second glance revealed that this "materials catalogue come to life"

(to quote one of our observers) *lacked* life. There was little to suggest that this was a space used by children. Children's work was not displayed. Teachers did not interact freely with children. By the end of our visit, the newness had worn off to reveal a sterile, uncreative, and unattractive environment.

On the other hand, we visited a dark windowless classroom in a 60-year-old, worn-out building. This new prekindergarten was short of commercially produced toys, games, or other educational materials. But it had a highly skilled teacher with many years of Head Start experience, who filled the room with teacher- and parent-made materials and created a language-rich environment full of challenge and stimulation. It was a fertile, creative, and attractive environment.

Cultural Diversity—or Sterility?

The lack of attention to cultural diversity was particularly disturbing in classrooms in which the children and teaching staff were themselves of diverse backgrounds. A southern classroom of young black children was devoid of culturally relevant materials (with the exception of a single picture of an Asian family hung on the wall); its teacher explained, "We celebrate Black History Month and Martin Luther King, Jr.'s birthday. You should be here then."

A northern classroom of black, white, Hispanic, Asian, and Native American three-year-olds offered no clue—whether through materials, bulletin board displays, storybooks, snacks, or songs—of the rich cultural community within its four walls. In this particular classroom of predominantly non-English-speaking children, there were no language games, no communication arts materials, and no cultural or child art displays (the January bulletin board displayed penguins frolicking in a winter scene); and there were only white dolls in the dramatic play areas.

Particularly striking was the fact that across all classrooms, very little children's work was displayed. Nor were

many teacher-made materials present. In general, classroom displays were commercially produced and culturally neutral, using animals or cartoon personalities in place of people (a Thanksgiving display in one classroom featured Walt Disney characters dressed as Pilgrims and Indians).

What About Learning Centers?

Learning centers help organize classroom space to facilitate small-group instruction and independent learning. They allow for individualizing the classroom program through self-selected, child-centered activities.

Usually the "standard" centers—for housekeeping, blocks, library, and art—were present in the observed classrooms. Rarer were the centers for math, nature/science, and enriched dramatic play. Dramatic play areas encourage children to explore well beyond the traditional housekeeping roles, for example, with costumes, real-world objects (firefighters' helmets, suitcases, steering wheels) and other props that support a wide range of fantasy play.

In fact, given the materials we saw at hand, there were nevertheless fewer learning centers than one would expect. The situation regarding blocks is typical. Although almost every classroom (92 percent) had blocks, only 17 percent had areas set aside for blocks. In the remaining classrooms, there was insufficient space for blocks, so that the space more resembled a storage area (several shelves of blocks) than a center designed for concentrated creative activity. Further, although over half (58 percent) of the classrooms we visited had math manipulatives, not even a quarter (22 percent) had them arranged in a math center to facilitate their use.

This lack of organization of the classroom environment does not encourage a child's independent use of materials but instead pushes teachers to direct the way the child will use materials.

In busy and stimulating environments, it is also important for children to have private spaces where they "can get away from it all." Very few classrooms—even among the very best we saw—had planned quiet or cozy areas for children.

Given the importance of gross-motor play in the psychomotor development of young children, we were surprised at the lack of provision for gross-motor activity among the classrooms we visited. The majority of programs evidenced inadequate space, equipment, and time for appropriate attention to gross-motor development.

In many programs gross-motor play was a token part of the schedule or used solely when the children "needed to let off some steam." In one daily half-day program, only 40 minutes of gross-motor activity *per week* was scheduled. This particular program happened to be a very academically structured program. The rationale for the lack of emphasis on gross-motor activity was based on limited time: "We only have an hour of structured [academic] time and we don't want to take away from it."

"Gross-Motor Rooms"

This situation was in stark contrast to the half-day schedule of another site, which gave a very high priority to gross-motor activity. In this three-hour program, there were two daily periods of gross-motor play. The day opened with 30 minutes in one of the program's two "gross-motor rooms." These were open areas, around which several classrooms were clustered. The spaces were carpeted and equipped with climbing equipment, large blocks, and other materials supportive of indoor, large muscle activity. Later in the day, a 40-minute outdoor play period was scheduled.

In inclement weather, children had the use of an indoor gymnasium, which was equipped to allow for the kind of full-scale gross-motor activity that's usually possible only outdoors: tricycling, running, rope climbing, tumbling, swinging, jumping. We observed the teacher, aide, and children together playing number-based tag games; creating imaginary worlds comprised of block towers and tunnels and other stimulating activities. These periods of-

fered far more than just "letting off steam." In this program physical activity is viewed as a creative learning opportunity.

What About Curriculum?

The terms "developmental" and "developmentally appropriate" are widely used in the print and oral rhetoric surrounding the prekindergarten curriculum, but in practice they are not widely understood.

Four sites described their programs as "developmental." However, to borrow the words of a teacher trainer we interviewed, "There is far more talk about developmental philosophy than there is actual developmental education."

Perhaps our biggest shock came in a district whose written philosophy was a well-articulated treatise on developmentally appropriate education; it stressed the uniqueness of each individual child's trajectory of development and the importance of self-selected, experiential activities. We were, therefore, unprepared to see unit-based classroom instruction for four-year-olds. Each teacher followed approximately the same sequence of lessons. Pre- and post-tests were included with each unit, and criterion mastery tests were administered after each series of five units. Children were divided into ability groups based on their scores on the pretests. Lessons were presented according to difficulty "beginning with the lowest order of skills competencies and proceeding systematically to higher level tasks." In a six-and-a-quarter-hour day, only a half-hour was scheduled for independent activity in one of the classrooms we visited.

In another classroom in this site, the "Classroom Rules" were posted on the bulletin board. They read as follows: "Please obey all rules/Listen, teacher is talking/Pay attention/Follow directions/Be quiet when guests are present/Stay in line (hands behind)/Be quiet when resting and testing." This classroom was in direct opposition to the program's philosophy of a child-centered

environment, child-initiated activity, warm adult-child interactions, and expressive language and individuality.

Misunderstandings at Both Extremes

This complete misperception of the meaning of "developmentally appropriate" most commonly resulted in an excessive "academic" orientation. However, we observed one site in which a "play-based" curriculum almost completely excluded materials with an explicitly cognitive orientation. Overall, the classrooms in this site ranged from good to excellent in terms of materials, room arrangement, and activities observed. We would have been hard pressed to find fault, were it not for the virtual absence of math manipulatives, language games, and science materials.

Considered together, these two extremes of misunderstanding reflect a more serious misconception of early childhood curricula. Too often, the choices are conceived on an either-or dimension: either a "traditional" laissez-faire, play-based program, or a formal, academic one. This is a false choice. Lilian Katz' useful distinction between *academic* and *intellectual* rigor helps explain the mistake made by the latter district:[1]

> *Academic* rigor refers to strong emphasis on completion of school-like tasks, exercises, grade level achievement, grades and test scores, following instructions and meeting requirements, conforming to procedures and conduct necessary to succeed in the academy and to fulfill its institutional requirements. *Academic* also suggests being out-of-touch and abstract. In contrast, *intellectual* rigor refers to characteristics of the life of the mind and its earnest quest for understanding, insight, knowledge, truth, solving intellectual puzzles, and the like.

Thus an early childhood program that is developmentally appropriate goes **beyond "just" play to intellectually challenge children through the use of problem-solving materials.**

Home-made Approaches That Work

Between these two points on the continuum, we saw a mix of challenging, age-appropriate, developmentally based curricula. An especially good example is "Changes," an integrated art and science curriculum jointly developed by two teachers in St. Louis. On the day of our observation, the teacher passed around a bowl of clay powder and encouraged the ten children to use their senses and talk about how it looked, felt, and smelled. Next, a wet squishy ball of clay and a dry ball were passed around. Children were asked to compare the two. Each child had a chance to hold the two pieces.

The next step was to compare a piece of clay fired in a "special oven" with a piece that had been air-dried. The teacher asked the children, "What would happen if you put these two pieces in water?" After discussing this for a few minutes, they tried it out, placing first the fired piece and then the air-dried piece into a dish of water. The teacher explained they could leave the pieces in the water and return to them later.

Then the group moved to another part of the room and worked with clay set up on tables. They busily kneaded it with their hands and used rolling pins, clay bricks with designs on them, and other tools. The teacher walked about, asking children what they were doing without disrupting or directing their activity.

Later, the children returned to the two pieces of clay in water to see what had happened to them. The teacher talked to each child, showing respect and encouraging his or her self-expression. The clay was taken out of the water and passed around and again the children were asked to see how they could change it.

In another site, a harvest theme was expressed throughout one classroom. Books and displays on gardening, farming, soil, and similar topics were featured prominently. In the middle of the room a large dirtbox (actually, a child's wading pool) was filled with large root vegetables—rutabagas, potatoes, yams, carrots—which the children repeatedly dug up and reburied with great enthusiasm.

In the classroom down the hall, children strung clay beads, painted at the easel with crushed blueberries, made pottery out of salt dough, and played with log houses, tipis, and hogans in conjunction with a Native American theme.

In yet another site, a "storekeeper" rang up groceries on an adding machine in the dramatic play area, while in another part of the room a small group of children tried to predict what would happen to their "pigs-in-a-blanket" they were about to place in a toaster oven.

Teachers in these programs, however, said it was not easy to convince parents that their children were really learning and not "just playing." When teachers build on children's actual experiences, they often cannot "prove" that specific learning objectives are being reinforced—even though many are. Yet, because they don't get cut-and-dried explanations, some parents can't understand how experiential activities can be more valuable than structured, paper-and-pencil-based "pre-reading" and "pre-math" activities.

Other Curriculum Approaches

Several districts used locally developed or nationally standardized unit-based materials but did not hide behind the "developmental" label. They tended to be urban districts serving largely minority populations.

One district used the Distar program in its double session, half-day prekindergarten program. Distar is a structured, direct-instruction approach to teaching language. We observed an afternoon session that began when the children counted to 30, sang the ABC song, took attendance (the teacher called out each name, and each child responded, "I am here" or "I am present" and put his or her name card on the attendance chart), and discussed the colors and designs on each other's clothes.

The class then began a series of three unrelated 10-minute Distar lessons: one on vehicles, one on the days of the week, and one on the concepts "wet" and "dry." While the teacher worked with the first group of four boys (the children were grouped by ability) on vehicles, a second group of six children worked with the aide. The aide drew different shapes (circle, triangle, square, and rectangle); each child, in turn, copied the aide's drawings. The third group worked independently on puzzles. Every 10 minutes, each group stopped and rotated to the next activity.

Following this highly structured learning period, the class went to group music, followed by a group art activity. Fortunately, it was then time for the children to go home.

Another district used three National Diffusion Network programs: (1) Early Prevention of School Failure, (2) Project STAMM, and (3) Talents Unlimited.

The Early Prevention of School Failure Program follows a diagnostic and prescriptive approach to the following areas: gross motor and fine motor skills, auditory skills, visual skills, and language skills. From a screening done during the first three weeks of school, supplemented by data from parents, a profile of each new incoming child is constructed. On the basis of these profiles, the teachers place children in three ability groups in each classroom, then proceed to introduce new skills and reinforce others for a prescribed set of concepts. Student profiles are updated throughout the year (teachers use checklists for this) and then passed on to each child's next grade-level teacher.

Project STAMM (Systematic Teaching and Measuring Mathematics) is a sequential math program for grades K-2. It encourages the use of concrete materials in mathematical problem solving and is accompanied by a teacher management system for observing and recording each child's performance.

Talents Unlimited is a systematic program to enhance recognition and use of thinking skills. Children develop thinking skills through the "talent" areas of productive thinking, communication, forecasting, planning, and decision making.

The three programs were chosen by

a district-level steering committee as best meeting the learning objectives of the district.

Narrow Objectives

These and several other curriculum approaches we observed in the course of our site visits were characterized mainly by narrow, discrete skill objectives, ability groupings, limited autonomy for teachers, and limited opportunities for initiative, creativity, and spontaneity for the children.

Nonetheless, these standardized curricula were generally well received by parents. "We have statistics on parent satisfaction. They're more than 90 percent satisfied in all categories," said a district administrator. One parent liked the prekindergarten program "because it's pushing my child to learn more and be prepared for the academic rigor of kindergarten." "Children excelling. That's the bottom line," said another parent. Teachers were not surprised by positive parent response: parents like pencil-and-paper activity, they say, because it proves their children are "really learning."

Many teachers also liked the curriculum. However, it must be noted that the more enthusiastic opinions were voiced by teachers with little to no prior experience teaching preschool-aged children. Rather, they tended to be individuals who came to early childhood education with an elementary background and who appreciated a standardized curriculum because it "told them what to do." Moreover, it resembled their teaching styles before being assigned to prekindergarten.

Concern for Continuity

Curriculum is one element of the child's experience in an early childhood program. Continuity is another. If a child is in a stable group of children, with the same staff for most or all of the day in the same location, a high degree of continuity is demonstrated. If the child experiences smooth and understandable changes from year to year, continuity is high. But if changes are abrupt and disturbing, continuity is low.

There is, for example, the problem of *daily continuity*. In one program the child and parent arrive together at 7:00 a.m. and have breakfast. The child then greets his or her teacher and goes off to play with one of the 15 other children in the room. After the teacher and mother converse, the mother leaves for work.

When the child's father arrives at 4:30 p.m., the child is happily playing with the same children and the same teacher in the same room the mother saw that morning. The father is able to talk to the teacher about his child's day.

In another program the child is dropped off at 8:30 a.m. and stays with an aide in a group of 20 "early birds" until 9:00 a.m., when the teacher arrives. The child goes, with a few others, to another room to join the rest of the preschool class (24 children in all). They spend the next three hours there. Then some children go home, while the rest go to a large cafeteria to eat lunch with about 150 kindergartners and first graders. After lunch the prekindergarten children go to the child care room for a nap until 3:00 p.m. Then they wake up and move to another room with other children who have just arrived from all-day kindergarten. They all stay there until 5:00 p.m.: some are then picked up and the rest move to another room for later pick-up. A prekindergartner in this school is passed in and out of six different groups of children.

Being part of a relatively stable group of children and adults is a more beneficial educational experience for young children than being part of a changing and unstable group. Children who form secure relationships with teachers are not only better able to make a smooth transition between home and school but are also able to use the teacher as a source of security during the day. The essential elements of a secure relationship are the availability and predictability of the teacher.

There is also the concern for *long-term continuity*. One goal of a good early childhood program is to ensure a smooth transition from prekindergarten to kindergarten. This assumes a similarity of focus and intent between prekindergarten and kindergarten classroom environments and activities. But this is no longer certain because kindergarten is becoming "what first grade once was": *i.e.,* the real point of entry into the school system, when the child begins academic instruction. We saw that clearly in the kindergartens we visited.

Almost without exception, the kindergarten consisted of a highly structured, academically oriented experience. Time was rigidly scheduled and divided into non-integrated learning periods (reading time, math time, music time, large group time). The majority of the day's activities were teacher directed. Independent activity guided by child choice was generally limited to brief play times—as short as 15 minutes in half-day kindergartens. Learning materials, especially for language arts and math activities, were heavily reliant on workbooks and worksheets that supplemented standardized reading and math series. (We have already noted that 22 percent of the observed *pre*kindergarten classrooms used workbooks; in comparison, 78 percent of the *kindergartens* in those same sites used workbooks.) Even open-ended activities like art tended to emphasize total-group art "projects," in which each child is directed to make the same thing (identical turkeys for Thanksgiving or hearts for Valentine's Day).

Given the more rigid nature of the receiving kindergarten environment, continuity between prekindergarten and kindergarten is not necessarily a good thing. For example, the smoothest continuity occurred in those districts which pushed the structured kindergarten and early elementary curriculum downward into prekindergarten (in short, imposing a developmentally inappropriate program upon the children). Ironically, continuity was poorest in those sites in which the prekindergarten program was developmentally appropriate and the kindergarten program was not.

This pattern is not good. *Both prekindergarten and kindergarten should focus on an upward extension of earlier development* rather than a downward extension of schooling. The research shows that young children learn best through direct, concrete experience of the world rather than through the symbolic manipulations more often associated with formal instruction (particularly with reading instruction).

They're Flunking Kindergarten

There is no evidence that greater long-term gains result from kindergarten programs heavy with academic instruction.[2] In fact, the opposite may be true. Across the country parents are complaining that their children are in danger of flunking kindergarten, and many children are being made to repeat the kindergarten year.

There seem to be four solutions to this problem: three would change the child, the fourth would change kindergarten.

The first "solution" is to make the prekindergarten program more academic, with standardized curricula, teacher-directed academic activities, and play as the reward—not the medium—for learning. It is not a useful solution.

A second "solution" is the growing popularity of the "developmental kindergarten." This only adds a second, "transitional" year of kindergarten, either between prekindergarten and kindergarten (called "developmental" kindergarten or "readiness" kindergarten) or between kindergarten and first grade (called "pre-firsts" or "transitional firsts"). This is a well-intentioned—but generally ineffective—response to the fact that many children today who can't meet the demands of kindergarten and first grade are either held back or referred to special education.[3]

A third "solution" is to push up the entrance age to kindergarten. In the past 30 years, the average age of kindergartners has been creeping up: a child who might have been among the oldest in the class in 1958 would now be one of the youngest.[4] Yet, no matter what the cut-off date for kindergarten

entry, some children would be "older" (born in the first three months of the cut-off year) and some would be "younger" (born in the last three months) and would be grouped accordingly.

The fourth, and optimal, solution to the mismatch between prekindergarten and kindergarten is to re-think the kindergarten program as a developmental, age-appropriate program for meeting the needs of a diverse group of children.

We saw efforts in several districts to improve the kindergarten through upward diffusion of the prekindergarten program. In all cases, some degree of interaction between prekindergarten and kindergarten teachers was involved.

A districtwide, multiyear strategy is being used in one district we visited. Its director of elementary education and the early childhood supervisor want continuity from prekindergarten through first grade. Their long-range plan is to institute a developmentally appropriate curriculum for all children age three through age six.

This district's prekindergarten program is a model of appropriate activities for three- and four-year-olds. A wide variety of materials and equipment is available, teachers are well-trained, and children have many choices. The program philosophy is expressed in the motto, Learning through Play.

When full-day kindergarten was proposed, the planning committee included teachers from prekindergarten, kindergarten, and first grade. Their curriculum was so successful it was also proposed for part-day kindergartens.

Conclusion

Today, the debate over the role of public schools in early childhood education is ready to move beyond the question of *whether* to the question of *how.*

Good programs for children cannot be mandated, but the necessary condi-

tions can be specified. These would include the following:

- children in small groups
- caring and well-prepared teachers who have specific child-related training in their background, as well as experience with young children
- the leadership of principals who are knowledgeable about childhood development and early childhood education and supportive of ongoing staff development
- a clearly stated philosophy of early childhood education
- an underpinning of sound principles of child development and theories of education
- a clear, coherent curriculum, yet one with broad enough goals for teachers to work creatively within it
- and a partnership of teachers and parents.

Leadership is critical. In public school programs, the school and community leadership must be committed to appropriate practice throughout its prekindergartens, kindergartens, and early elementary grades. It must also be committed to providing the financial and human resources for staff development and the retraining of teachers and administrators so that a sound philosophy of early childhood education can be translated into practice.

Notes

1. Katz, L. G., J. D. Raths, and R. D. Torres (1987). *A place called kindergarten.* Urbana, Ill: Clearinghouse on Elementary and Early Childhood Education, p. 29.

2. Spodek, B. (1982). The kindergarten: A retrospective and contemporary view. In L. G. Katz (Ed.), *Current topics in early childhood education.* Norwood, N.J: Ablex Publishing Corporation.

3. Shepard, L.A. and Smith, M. L. (1986). Synthesis of research on school readiness and kindergarten retention. *Educational Leadership*, 44 (3), 7886. In fact, there is no evidence that an extra year of schooling solves the problems it was intended to solve. In what may be the only review of transitional classes, Lorrie Shepard and Mary Lee Smith conclude that "children in these programs show virtually no academic advantage over equally at-risk children who have not had the extra year. Furthermore, there is often an emotional cost associated with staying back." (p. 85).

4. Shepard and Smith (1986), p. 81.

Structure Time & Space
To Promote Pursuit of Learning
in the Primary Grades

Marianne Gareau
and Colleen Kennedy

Marianne Gareau is a first grade teacher at LaPerle Elementary School in Edmonton, Alberta, Canada. She has also worked as an Elementary Consultant with the Alberta Department of Education.

Colleen Kennedy, M.Ed., teaches a combined class of first and second grade children at Richard Secord School in Edmonton, Alberta, Canada. Both authors pursue a continuing interest in the study of child development and applications to classroom practice.

As the bell rang, signaling the beginning of Greenvale School's day, seven-year-old John joined a large group of children who were looking for a place to sit on the stairs that surrounded the open library. When most of the children were seated, Mrs. McNeil, the principal, began reading aloud from a book. After she had finished, several children shared stories they had written and then everyone began moving toward their classrooms. John stayed behind for a few minutes to select new library books. When he arrived at the classroom, a number of children were already engaged in quiet reading activities. John quickly selected an insect book from the science display and nestled down on the rug to read.

At 9:30 the teacher, Mr. Woodland, moved to the story area. John returned his book to the science area and found a place close to Mr. Woodland. As soon as Mr. Woodland finished reading the story, children began leaving the group to collect their writing folders and find a place to write. John preferred to work in the quiet area by the storage cupboard. He opened his folder and reviewed what he had written the day before. A small group of children was talking with Mr. Woodland, and John knew that unless he needed some assistance, he would have a large block of time in which to work on his insect story. Toward the end of the writing session, the teacher came by and John showed him the beginning portion of his story. Mr. Woodland offered a few suggestions. Then it was time for recess.

After recess, John went straight to the planning board. It was learning center time, and he wanted to join the group that was working on a large papier maché dragon in the work area next door.

After lunch, the whole class gathered together for a large-group session. The VIP (a child, identified as the Very Important Person for the day) initiated the afternoon activities by inviting the group to talk about the calendar, while Mr. Woodland wrote on a piece of chart paper at the back of the group. John knew that toward the end of the group session, the class would be invited to read Mr. Woodland's story. He wondered if Mr. Woodland was writing about insects. Later in the afternoon, the children went to gym class and then returned to their classroom to participate in math activities. John and a small group of children worked with Mr. Woodland on two-digit place value, while the rest of the students worked on math activities individually and in small groups.

This vignette gives a glimpse of what we believe to be appropriate educational programming for primary grade children. We base this belief on what we know about young children—their developmental characteristics and the ways in which they learn best—and on our philosophy of education and general goals in primary edu-

> **Children's characteristics should dictate the use of space and time in the classroom.**

cation programs. These two important aspects provide the impetus for a fuller discussion of the appropriate use of time and space to support children in engaging in meaningful learning experiences. Teachers need to be aware of the developmental characteristics of young children and of the overall goals of the primary program. Therefore, we discuss the use of time and space in primary classrooms, referring to what is known about how young children learn

From *Young Children*, Vol. 46, No. 4, May 1991, pp. 46-51. Copyright © 1991 by the National Association for the Education of Young Children, 1834 Connecticut Avenue, NW, Washington, DC. Used by permission.

best and relating this to our introductory vignette.

Organizing the classroom day

For a child in the preoperational stage, time is purely subjective: "A long time" may be a minute or an hour, depending on the activity in which the child is engaged. As young children develop, they move from this subjective concept of time to a more objective one. Being able to put events in temporal order and understanding the possibility of time units, for instance, are later developments. In primary programs, the child must learn to use time; it is through managing time that a child can best gain an understanding of it.

We often hear adults speak of children's "short attention spans" when what they are referring to is that young children who are not interested in certain tasks, or who are not motivated, tend to look for something else to do. If we think instead of a child's "task-orientation time," the time a child will pursue an activity that is interesting and meaningful, we have a more productive approach to facilitating children's learning (Nash, 1979). Our challenge as educators is to discover what we can do to increase task-orientation time, since we know that children will learn more with increased concentration on tasks.

Task-oriented timetables

Research studies reported by Nash (1989) suggest that, in many kindergarten programs, a child's task orientation actually decreases from the beginning to the end of the year. Classroom observations indicated that such reductions were related to interruptions scheduled into the program. Well-intentioned teachers, believing they should accommodate the children's short attention span by planning frequent changes in activity, were in essence contributing to the problem!

Therefore, we need to modify our timetable to place the emphasis on tasks rather than on time. If we continually make decisions for children based on scheduled times rather than on completion of tasks, we discourage growth in attention span. Instead, we should provide children with large blocks of time to engage in meaningful activities and projects, and eliminate routines that interrupt their work. Although children at this age may be easily distracted, they are also capable of periods of intense concentration when engaged in meaningful activities. In the introductory vignette, the schedule is organized according to developmental needs of children in this age group. Learning is accomplished in an integrated fashion, with large blocks of time scheduled for reading, writing, and math activities, and every attempt made to minimize disruptions or interruptions of the children's activities. Children have the opportunity to develop their language skills through naturally occurring interactions with the teacher and with their peers, both on a one-to-one basis and in small groups. Children may also exhibit pensiveness and should be allowed time to ponder and reflect. If John knows that he has a large block of time to work on his insect story, he will feel free to take the time he needs to collect his thoughts, ideas, and information before and as he writes. John also realizes that this is a continuing project that does not have to be finished in one day.

Whole-group routines and activities

Whole-group activities that are likely to interest most of the children can be placed later in the school day. As the time for these activities approaches, teachers should alert children to the need to bring closure to their tasks. In John's classroom, the "traditional" opening activities have been placed in the middle of the day. Such an approach takes advantage of children's strong interest and motivation in getting immediately involved in individual learning activities at the start of the day. After lunch, children are more ready to come together as a large group.

Because they make time and events visible, planning boards can be very useful. They encourage children to recognize the beginning and end of an activity and to develop insight into planning their activities and managing their time. In our classroom at Greenvale School, children assume responsibility for their own learning by selecting their center time activities at the planning board.

If we continually make decisions for children based on scheduled times rather than on completion of tasks, we discourage growth in attention span. Instead we should provide children with large blocks of time to engage in meaningful activities and projects, and eliminate routines that interrupt the child's work.

Figure 1. Sample timetable

9:00 A.M.	Assembly (three times each week)
9:15 A.M.	Quiet Reading
9:25 A.M.	Shared Reading/Read to Class
9:35 A.M.	Writing (whole group conferencing, quiet writing, shared writing)
10:20 A.M.	Recess
10:35 A.M.	Centers (Integrated Curriculum)
11:30 A.M.	Lunch
12:45 P.M.	Opening Activities (story, calendar, number line, time, weather, feelings chart, message, show-and-tell)
1:20 P.M.	Physical Education/Music
2:20 P.M.	Recess
2:35 P.M.	Math Lesson and Math Centers
3:35 P.M.	Dismissal

We should also establish routines that are reasonable and make sense to children. As much as possible, these routines should meet the child's (rather than the adult's) needs. For example, taking off coats and hanging them up when coming in makes sense, but sitting quietly and waiting until everyone completes a worksheet does not. When routines are appropriate, there is a "flow" to the school day that children respond to well and find comfortable. In John's classroom, the children do not have to wait for the teacher to tell them what to do next. Because they have developed meaningful routines, they can move from one learning activity to another with minimal direction from the teacher and little disruption to the flow of daily learning activities. Figure 1 shows the timetable followed in John's classroom.

Organizing the learning environment for children

In discussing ways to organize the classroom, Nash (1979) outlines four basic steps:

1. Develop a philosophy and general objectives.

2. Clarify knowledge of child development and ways of learning.

3. Decide on basic learning areas.

4. Look at children's behavior and arrange the classroom to reduce distractions.

General objectives for primary children

The first step consists of developing a philosophy and general objectives. Many well-known experts such as Katz (1987, 1988), Nash (1976), and Bredekamp (1987) have identified the following fundamental goals for a sound educational program for young children:

- learn about and like themselves
- develop positive feelings about learning through experiencing success
- select, plan, and organize their own learning activities for a significant portion of the program day
- engage in meaningful activities with language and literacy

In providing an environment where children can learn about and like themselves, teachers and other adults must first of all demonstrate true affection for the children. Children who know they are cared for will feel safe enough to talk about themselves and get to know themselves well. Since modeling is one of the most powerful tools for learning, children who are treated with respect and trust will tend to develop a positive self-concept and

a respectful attitude toward others.

The best way for children to develop positive feelings about learning is through achieving success in their tasks. This requires an environment that presents children with a variety of open-ended learning activities to accommodate their different abilities and interests. For example, children in Greenvale School choose stories according to their reading level and interest. They also work on math activities individually or in small groups rather than as a whole class.

Children are capable of assuming responsibility for their own learning. When a teacher organizes the classroom environment to allow children choices in planning and organizing their activities for a portion of the day, they become even more skilled at directing their own learning. John's obvious sense of control over his writing activities is a good example of this.

Finally, it is important for young children to engage in many meaningful activities with language and literacy. Since reading and writing are basic skills of early schooling, much of the school day should be connected to acquiring and practicing language use. Children should have daily opportunities to interact with others, to read and be read to, and to write selections of their own choosing.

These goals recognize the importance of providing children with meaningful experiences that will prepare them to be lifelong learners. Elementary school teachers can achieve these goals by providing a classroom environment that is compatible with developmental characteristics of young children. Children's innate desire to make sense of the world, to experiment, discover, and create, must be reflected in the classroom organization.

Matching the program to developmental characteristics

The second step involves clarifying our knowledge of children's development and ways of learning. Children between the ages of four and seven share many characteristics (Norris & Boucher, 1980; Feeney, Christensen, & Moravcik, 1983; Beaty, 1986). For example, they experience growth spurts, which may cause instability, awkwardness, and an increased need for movement. Small muscles and bones are not completely formed or developed; therefore, fine-motor tasks still present a challenge for many children. Most children of this age are naturally farsighted, and activities requiring close work such as printing are very tiring. Children's hearing is not fully developed, and phonics-related activities requiring close attention to

small details may be inappropriate. In organizing the classroom program, teachers should be aware of these physical conditions.

Touch and movement are crucial to young children's learning. Memory is largely associative and needs to be linked to a particular experience or action. This is one reason field trips and projects are particularly powerful learning activities. Thought does not always precede action; although children may carry out plans made in advance, plans may also evolve during an activity (Norris & Boucher, 1980). Teachers should capitalize on this characteristic and give their children activities open-ended enough to involve both planning and spontaneous innovation.

Learning areas related to children's interests

In the introductory vignette, the teacher applies his knowledge of child development by providing the children with opportunities to learn through activity, in small groups, and on a one-to-one basis. He also recognizes that children learn in different ways and provides a variety of learning areas in the classroom, as well as the opportunity to make choices. The third step in structuring the learning environment is to decide on basic learning areas such as reading-writing, math-science, and fine arts areas. In these areas teachers can develop units of study that capitalize on children's inter-

---

Figure 2. **John's classroom at Greenvale School**

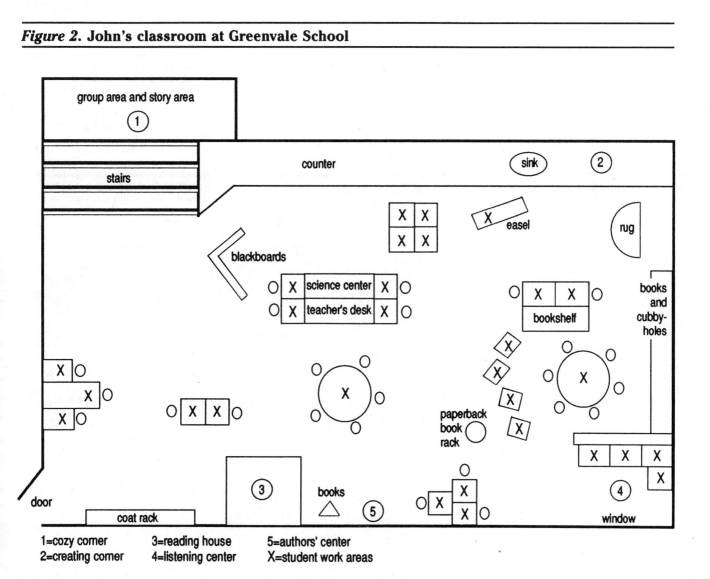

1=cozy corner   3=reading house   5=authors' center
2=creating corner   4=listening center   X=student work areas

Classroom space should be used to complement children's developmental characteristics: The needs to move, touch, experience variety, and make decisions.

ests. John's interest in insects has been incorporated into the science center, which includes live insects brought in by the children. This in turn leads to a writing activity on this topic. Because children learn in an integrated fashion, attempts should be made to connect the learning areas whenever possible.

Children's behavior determines room arrangement

In Nash's (1979) fourth step, she proposes that we look at children's behavior to decide how to set up these learning areas. One of our tasks as teachers is to assist children in making sense of their world, or "making connections." One way in which children grow toward logical thinking is by repeatedly experiencing connections between things. In organizing the classroom space, we should at-tempt to position learning materials close to others with related learning objectives. Children's curiosity will then be a positive feature, since they can add what attracts their attention to their present activity. Finally, space should be arranged to reduce distractions. Grouping can be made according to quiet or noisy activities, clean and messy ones. Figure 2 presents a view of John's classroom at Greenvale School.

Use time and space to support development

If we are to be effective teachers, we must understand developmental characteristics of children and use these as a basis for designing our programs. When we identify children's characteristics as intrinsic to their particular stage of development, we are more likely to view these characteristics in a positive light. Rather than imposing a structure that is counter to children's natural ways of learning, we will design our timetables and our classroom environments to accommodate and capitalize on these ways of learning. The result of such planning is children who retain their innate motivation and interest in learning.

References

Beaty, J. J. (1986). *Observing development of the young child.* Columbus, OH: Merrill.

Bredekamp, S. (Ed.). (1987). *Developmentally appropriate practice in early childhood programs serving children from birth through age 8.* (exp. ed.). Washington, DC: NAEYC.

Feeney, S., Christensen, D., & Moravcik, E. (1983). *Who am I in the lives of children? An introduction to teaching young children.* (2nd ed.). Columbus, OH: Merrill.

Katz, L. (1987). What should young children be doing? *The Wingspread Journal, 9*(2), 1–3.

Katz, L. (1988). Engaging children's minds: The implications of research for early childhood education. In C. Warger (Ed.), *A resource guide to public school early childhood programs* (pp. 35–52). Alexandria, VA: Association for Supervision and Curriculum Development.

Nash, C. (1976). *The learning environment.* Toronto: Methuen.

Nash, C. (1979). *A principal's or administrator's guide to kindergarten.* Toronto: Ontario Institute for Studies in Education.

Norris, D., & Boucher, J. (Eds.). (1980). *Observing children through their formative years.* Toronto: Toronto Board of Education.

School-Age Child Care:

A Review of Five Common Arguments

Mick Coleman, Bryan E. Robinson, and Bobbie H. Rowland

During the past decade, parents and educators have increasingly expressed concern over the potential safety and developmental risks associated with children in self-care, or the care of another child (Garbarino, 1984; Harris, Kagay, & Ross, 1987; Robinson, Rowland, & Coleman, 1986; 1989; Zigler & Ennis, 1988). One result has been a growing interest in school-age child care (SACC) programs.

Unfortunately, implementation of a SACC program is not always an easy task. Different values and beliefs can be held within any given community as to (a) whose responsibility it is to provide SACC; (b) the types of services that should be provided; and (c) how best to manage the day-to-day operation of the program.

In this article, the authors examine five common arguments that they have encountered during their SACC programming work over the past six years. Some of the arguments have come from parents, others from teachers, and still others from community leaders. Programming resources are also given to assist early childhood

Mick Coleman is Assistant Professor, Child and Family Development, and Extension Human Development Specialist, University of Georgia, Hoke Smith Annex, Athens, Ga. Bryan E. Robinson and Bobbie H. Rowland are both Professor of Human Services, University of North Carolina, Charlotte, NC

educators in addressing the arguments so that they might plan for the effective development and delivery of SACC services.

Argument 1: There is no need for SACC programs. They have always existed.

It is true that parents have for decades depended upon relatives, libraries, churches, park and recreation services, and youth clubs as informal sources of SACC. Unfortunately, these services are often unable to meet the growing demand for SACC (Coleman, Rowland, & Robinson, 1989). In some cases, the number of children requiring services is too great. In other cases, the type of services desired by school-age children and parents go beyond the training of the staff or the philosophy of the SACC services; rather, they require a wide range of services. As noted by one parent:

I don't want my child in school all day. He needs to be a kid. He needs to play in a safe environment. The program did nothing more than

help him with his homework and give him books to read.

The authors have also heard the opposite complaint, that a particular SACC program placed too much emphasis on recreation and too little emphasis on helping children complete homework assignments. In fact, there are many SACC options available, each having its own set of potential advantages and disadvantages (see Massachusetts Office for Children, 1988). Each educational facility must consider its own unique values, needs, resources, and barriers in deciding upon the implementation of a SACC program. This process should ideally include a community needs assessment, the results of which should provide guidance on developing a philosophical mission statement (e.g., educational, recreational, support, enrichment, protection), as well as operational policies (e.g., hours of service, schedules, staffing, finances, curriculum). The needs assessment survey need not be complicated. As noted in

From *Day Care & Early Education*, Summer 1991, pp. 13-17. Published by Human Sciences Press, 72 Fifth Avenue, New York, NY 10011.

127

Table 1
Developing a SACC Needs Assessment Survey

Who
- needs SACC? Consider:
  the age or grade of children.
  the sex of children.
  family income.
  the area of residence.
  the needs of children with exceptionalities.
- should staff the SACC program? Consider:
  child care providers.
  trained adult community volunteers.
  professional youth leaders (e.g., Camp Fire, 4-H, YWCA).
  college students.
  retired or substitute teachers.

What
- barriers might prevent parents from using SACC services? Consider:
  cost.
  transportation.
  hours of operation.
  overcrowded program.
  dislike of program policies (e.g., discipline).
  dislike of staff (e.g., not involved with children).
- barriers might prevent children

from using SACC services? Consider:
  dislike of activities (e.g., too "babylike").
  dislike of schedule (e.g., too rigid).
  dislike of staff (e.g., too authoritarian).
  too few children of the same age enrolled in program.
- activities would parents (and children) like in a SACC program? Consider:
  homework time.
  free play.
  snack.
  arts/crafts.
  recreational activities.
  safety education classes.
  drama.
  dance.
  tutoring in special classes (e.g., piano, computers).
  field trips.

When
- are SACC services needed? Consider:
  before school.
  after school.
  during teacher in-service days.
  during school vacation.
  during inclement weather.
  when child is sick.
  at night.

Where
- should SACC programs be located? Consider:
  local schools.
  recreation departments.
  youth club/agency sites (e.g., YMCA).
  churches.
  day care centers.

How
- satisfied are parents with their current SACC arrangement?
- satisfied are children with their current SACC arrangement?
- much are parents willing to pay for SACC services per week?
- many hours per day do children currently spend at home alone?
- many hours per day do children currently spend at home under the supervision of another school-age child?

Why
- provide SACC services?
  The answer to this question should (a) be based on an analysis of responses to the preceding questions and (b) guide SACC program developers in writing a philosophical mission statement, operational policies, curriculum guide, and job descriptions.

Table 1, the survey should revolve around a basic set of who, what, when, where, how, and why questions.

Argument 2: School-age children are old enough to care for themselves.

While school-age children may sometimes appear old enough to care for themselves, their growing independence should not be overinterpreted. School-age children still need adult guidance and support in order to successfully handle self-care situations that demand adultlike responsibilities. This point was recently discovered by one elementary-school teacher who lamented:

I have three children in my class who go home alone every afternoon. "I don't want to go home alone," they cry. How can I help?

One of the first questions that should be asked in a situation like this is whether the parents are fully aware of their child's fears. They may not be.

It is during the school-age years that children first begin to develop friendships and interests independent of their parents. Parents may subsequently place too much trust in their child's readiness to assume self-care responsibilities. Yet, the confident school-age child who left for school in the morning may, like the children encountered by the above teacher, become fearful later in the afternoon when faced with the prospect of returning home alone. Other children may react against their fear by acting out. Even children who enjoy their

newfound independence can quickly find themselves in situations for which they are unprepared due to a lack of self-care information, experience, and/or skills.

All children have the same sense of curiosity that can lead to accidents in the absence of adult supervision. Safety for children in self-care should thus be viewed as a developmental issue rather than a geographic issue. For example, children living in rural areas are sometimes more isolated than their peers living in urban areas and may thus be able to gain help in an emergency. Even parents of children living in "safe" middle-class neighborhoods cannot completely protect their children against the potential hazards associated with a self-care situation.

The safety risks associated with childhood behavior is perhaps best reflected in the fact that between twelve and fourteen million American children (or one in four) under age fifteen require medical attention due to accidental injury each year (National Coalition to Prevent Childhood Injury, 1988). These numbers are greater than for any disease, making injuries the number one health risk for American children under the age of fifteen.

Children in self-care may especially be at risk for in-home accidents. A recent study sponsored by the Whirlpool Corporation found that in 71% of all homes fitting the self-care category, children under age fourteen were using major home appliances on a regular basis, in many cases as part of their household chores (Project Home Safe, 1987).

Less is known about the social-emotional and psychological threats to children in self-care. Some studies report that children in self-care suffer from fear, anxiety, and loneliness, while other studies report that children in self-care are no different in their psychosocial adjustment from their peers under adult supervision (see reviews by Robinson et al., 1986, 1989).

Regardless of their child care arrangement, all children can benefit from learning in-home and out-of-home safety skills (e.g., responding to emergencies and strangers; time management; food safety). School-age child care programs represent an ideal situation in which to demonstrate safety skills, as well as give children the opportunity to practice safety skills. A list of safety curriculum resources is given at the end.

Argument 3: Anyone can care for school-age children. Specialized training is not required.

This is an argument also frequently heard in relation to preschool child care. However, in the case of SACC there is an added twist in that some educators may fail to make a clear distinction between the care and education of preschoolers versus that of school-age children. For example, at a recent workshop on guiding school-age children, one preschool teacher remarked:

I do the same thing with my nine-year-olds in the afternoon that I do with my three-year-olds in the morning. I make them sit beside me and hold my hand when they misbehave.

Apart from adopting a more positive strategy for guiding three-year-olds, this teacher's inability to see other options for guiding school-age children reflects a simplified mind-set of transferring the preschool day into the after-school program.

Effective preschool teachers do not necessarily make effective SACC teachers, since some adults relate better to certain age groups than others. It is thus unrealistic to expect all teachers of three-year-olds to understand or relate to nine-year-olds.

Regardless of their training or work experience, all SACC teachers should have a knowledge of the development of school-age children, their interests and needs. Armed with this knowledge, SACC teachers can plan an after-school schedule that takes into account the previous seven to eight hours of mental, sedentary school work in which children have been engaged. More specifically, the after-school schedule should provide children with maximum independence in choosing and implementing their own activities. A relaxed, flexible after-school schedule is also needed in which children select their own activities. Such a child-centered environment helps children to develop a sense of self-confidence and industry.

SACC teachers help children to develop real-life problem-solving skills by allowing them to negotiate their disagreements, assign meaning to their play activities, and solve dilemmas that arise from their play activities. Put another way, SACC teachers are most effective when they facilitate activities by asking challenging questions (e.g., "What do you think would happen if you used a different color?"), providing information (e.g., "John is using a *legend* to read the map"), and offering supportive suggestions (e.g., "Maybe your kite would fly higher if you tried a different type of paper. What do you think?"). In contrast, formal "teaching" methods transform the after-school program into an extension of the school day, denying children a change of pace and the opportunity to learn on their own.

SACC teachers should also consider the role of school-age children in a SACC program. It is inappropriate to assume that older school-age children are willing or able to help care for smaller children, a situation that can arise when the teacher is unsure of how to plan or implement school-age activities.

Older children do not enjoy the same types of activities or respond to the same types of guidance techniques as younger children. SACC teachers thus need specialized resources and training related to the development and facilitation of activities for school-age children. The staff training and activity resources listed at the end can help SACC teachers to learn developmentally appropriate approaches for working with school-age children of different ages.

Argument 4. There is not enough money to pay for SACC.

SACC programming can indeed be expensive, involving such major expenses as staff, utilities, educational materials, rent, transportation, snacks, and insurance. When confronted with costs, the authors are reminded of a simple but powerful statement made by a colleague when asked about the expense of implementing a SACC program. She replied, "We pay for what we value."

Paying for value should indeed be a central theme in developing SACC programs. Unfortunately, SACC budgets are sometimes developed with insufficient attention given to the types of materials and equipment preferred by school-age children or their use of these materials. School-age children are more likely than preschoolers to use large quantities of materials in creating more complex products; they are more likely to be attuned to commercial products advertised on television; they are accustomed to using more sophisticated (and expensive) equipment in their school classrooms; they use indoor and outdoor equipment that is different from that used by preschoolers; and they have more personalized interests and hobbies that require a wide range of materials (Meritt, 1988).

According to a national survey, the median weekly payment made by parents for child care for children between the ages of five and fourteen was $40.10 (U.S. Department Commerce, 1987). However, variation was found within the survey results, with payments going as low as $10-$19 per week and as high as $70 and over.

SACC programs may be supported by a combination of service fees and private and in-kind support, as well as local, state, and federal grants. Parent fees usually provide most of the operating revenue for SACC programs (Baden, Genser, Levine, & Seligson, 1982). Additional private support may come from individuals, foundations, businesses, or service organizations. In-kind support (e.g., rent, transportation, utilities, custodial service, staff) may come from cooperating agencies.

Fortunately, parents seem to be willing to pay for SACC services. According to one recent national survey, 59% of all parents were willing to pay for after-school educational programs, and 52% were willing to pay for after-school noneducational programs (Harris et al., 1987).

One current source of government support for SACC programming is the Dependent Care Planning and Development Grant (Office of Management and Budget, 1988). This grant provides for a variety of services in two broad areas: (a) resource and referral, and (b) direct SACC service delivery. Funds may be used to assist in the planning, development, expansion, or improvement of SACC services. Some states also have special grants available for SACC programming, such as the "Children's Trust Fund" (1989).

The respective House (H.R. 3) and Senate (S. 5) child care bills would provide additional financial support for SACC programming. The future

of these bills depends upon the House and Senate's reaching a resolution on differences between their respective bills, as well as the President's signing the compromise bill.

Argument 5: Parents are more concerned with affordable SACC than quality SACC.

In fact, and not surprisingly, parents want both. It is thus particularly frustrating when they sometimes find that they can have neither. As noted by one parent:

I don't know what to do. My child refuses to go to the after-school programs that I can afford, calling them "baby-sitting." And those that she likes are too expensive.

Developing affordable, quality SACC programs need not be difficult. The financial cost of operating a SACC program can be accommodated by networking with a local school and/or other community agencies. This arrangement allows for the sharing of materials, staff, and facility space. In fact, many of the most successful SACC programs in the nation have been conceived of and addressed as a community issue in which community resources are shared.

Likewise, developing a quality SACC curriculum is not difficult when we take into account the developmental needs of school-age children within the context of their typical day. After school, school-age children need time to refuel with a nutritious snack, time to let off steam through safe and interesting outdoor games, time to work on homework, time to socialize with peers, and time to pursue their own interests. As mentioned above, a developmentally appropriate SACC curriculum addresses these needs by providing a relaxed schedule and a child-centered environment. A number of organizations can supply SACC administrators and teachers with information on developing such an environment. Five such organizations include the following.

The School-Age Child Care Project
Center for Research on Women
Wellesley College
Wellesley, MA 02181

Project Home Safe
American Home Economics
  Association
1555 King Street
Alexandria, VA 22314

National Association for the
  Education of Young Children
1834 Connecticut Avenue NW
Washington, DC 20009-5786

Georgia School-Age Child Care
  Council
1340 Spring Street, Suite 200
Atlanta, GA 30309

University of Kentucky
College of Home Economics
Department of Family Studies
The Research and Development
  Center for School-Age Child
  Care and Early Education
102 Erikson Hall
Lexington, KY 40506-0050

Conclusion

As interest in SACC continues to grow, educators are being looked to for guidance in the development and implementation of quality SACC programs that contribute to the growth and development of school-age children. The resources given in this paper are provided to assist educators in providing this guidance.

References

Baden, R., Genser, A., Levine, J., & Seligson, M. (1982). *School-age child care: An action manual.* Boston: Auburn.

Children's Trust Fund. (1989). *Children's trust fund of Georgia.* (Available from Children's Trust Fund Commission, 10 Park Place South, Suite 410, Atlanta, GA 30303).

Coleman, M., Rowland, B. H., & Robinson, B. E. (1989). Latchkey children and school-age child care: A review of programming issues. *Child and Youth Care Quarterly, 18* (1), 39-48.

Dodd, C. (1989). *The new school child care demonstration act of 1989 (S. 457).* (Available from Senator Christopher Dodd, United States Senate, Washington, DC 20510).

Garbarino, J. (1984). *Can American families afford the luxury of childhood?* Unpublished manuscript, Pennsylvania State University, College of Human Development, University Park, 1984.

Harris, H., Kagay, M., & Ross, J. (1987). *The American teacher 1987: Strengthening links between home and school.* New York: Metropolitan Life Insurance Company.

Massachusetts Office for Children. (1988, January). *School-age child care technical assistance paper: Getting started.* Boston: Author.

Meritt, P. (1988, October). From one director to another: Tips on school age child care. *Child Care Information Exchange,* 26-28.

National Coalition to Prevent Childhood Injury. (1988). *Safe kids are no accident.* Washington, DC: Author.

Neugebauer, R. (1979, November). School age day care: Getting it off the ground. *Child Care Information Exchange,* 9-15.

Office of Management and Budget. (1988). *1988 catalog of federal domestic assistance.* Washington, DC: U.S. Government Printing Office.

Project Home Safe. (1987). *Whirlpool corporation study shows children regular appliance users.* Washington, DC: American Home Economics Association.

Robinson, B. E., Rowland, B. H., & Coleman, M. (1986). *Latchkey kids: Unlocking doors for children and their families.* Lexington, MA: Lexington.

Robinson, B. E., Rowland, B. H., & Coleman, M. (1989). *Home alone after school: Providing the best care for your child.* Lexington, MA: Lexington.

U.S. Department of Commerce, Bureau of Census. (1987, May). *Who's minding the kids? Child care arrangements: Winter 1984-85.* (Current Population Reports, Household Economic Studies, Series P-70, No. 9). Washington, DC: U.S. Government Printing Office.

Zigler, E., & Ennis, P. (1988). Child care: A new role for tomorrow's schools. *Principal, 68* (1), 10-13.

Selected In-Home and Out-of-Home Safety Curricula

Bower, D. W. (1986). *Care of myself.* University of Georgia Cooperative Extension Service, Hoke Smith Annex, Athens, GA 30602.

Columbia Gas System. (1988). *How to be a key performer.* 200 Civic Center Drive, P.O. Box 117, Columbus, OH 43216-0117.

Corporation for Public Broadcasting. (1988). *What if I'm home alone?* 1111 16th Street NW, Washington, DC 20036.

Cyr, L. F., Holmes, V. J., & Kelly, J. M. (1987). *3 to 5, I'm in charge.* University of Maine Cooperative Extension Service, Roger Clapp Greenhouse, Orono, ME 04469.

Johnson, C., & Pinson, C. (1989). *When I'm in charge.* North Carolina State University Extension Service, P.O. Box 7605, Raleigh, NC.

Labensohn, D. (1986, June). *On my own and ok.* Iowa State University Cooperative Extension Service, Child Development Department, 103 Richards Hall, Ames, IA 50011.

Todd, C. M. (1986). *Operation safe kids.* University of Illinois Cooperative Extension Service, 547 Bevier Hall, 905 South Goodwin Avenue, Urbana, IL 61801.

Selected Staff Training and Activity Resources

Arns, B. (1988). *The survival guide to school-age child care.* Huntington Beach, CA: School-Age Workshops Press.

Bender, J., Elder, B. S., & Flatter, C. H. (1984). *Half a childhood: Time for school-age child care.* Nashville, TN: School-Age Notes.

Blau, R., Brady, E. G., Bucher, I., Hiteshew, B., Zavitkovsky, A., & Zavitkovsky, D. (1977). *Activities for school-age child care.* Washington, DC: National Association for the Education of Young Children.

Dade County Public Schools. (1984). *After-school care activities manual.* Office of Vocational, Adult, and Community Education, 1450 NE Second Avenue, Room 814, Miami, FL 33132.

Fink, D. B. (1985). *An intergenerational adventure: A training curriculum for older adult caregivers working with school-age children during the hours after school.* Wellesley, MA: Wellesley College Center for Research on Women.

Project Home Safe. American Home Economics Association, 1555 King Street, Alexandria, VA 22314.

Rowland, B. H., Coleman, M., & Robinson, B. E. (1987). *School-age child care training manual.* Charlotte, NC: The Council for Children.

School Age Connections Newsletter. University of Illinois Cooperative Extension Service, 547 Bevier Hall, 905 S. Goodwin, Urbana, IL 61801.

School Age Notes Newsletter. School Age Notes, P.O. 120674, Nashville, TN 37212.

University of California Cooperative Extension. (1988). *4-H afterschool program manuals.* 11477 E. Avenue, Auburn, CA 95603.

The Assessment Portfolio as an Attitude

Cathy Grace and Elizabeth F. Shores

The teacher's use of good judgment is a key to effective assessment of young children. Taking time to think about children and their behavior is very important, whether or not a teacher uses an assessment portfolio. It has been estimated that the average first grade teacher makes about one thousand decisions a day and the average preschool teacher makes twice as many (Jackson, 1968; Murray, 1986). There is little time in the teacher's day to think carefully about individual children and their special needs, yet early childhood professionals must incorporate such "thinking time" into their schedules, not just to plan the next day's activities but to reflect upon the events of the current day. A teacher of three-year-olds once said, "I feel like a detective. There is so much to know and three-year-olds can tell me so little. I would have to guess about everything if I didn't have their behavior to give me clues." This is an example of what can be called *the portfolio attitude.*

Teachers begin to assemble an assessment portfolio by *writing down* these clues, along with their observations, thoughts and questions about individual children. As they collect samples of their pupils' work and observation cards about class and small group games and activities, and as they interview the children to gain more information, teachers assess young children in appropriate ways. The assessment process is a vital part of planning, implementing and maintaining developmentally appropriate practice in the classroom.

In the past, a school might have considered a young child "ready to learn" when he made an acceptable score on a standardized test. Today, however, many school and government officials define "readiness" as the student's being prepared to participate successfully in formal schooling. "Readiness" now has multiple dimensions, the most important being that the child has an orientation toward learning and a certain ability to solve problems. Educators no longer consider first grade the child's first learning experience. Rather, they view first grade as a continuation of the learning process that began at birth.

In response to the shift in public policy, teachers are beginning to use instructional practices that reflect what many have known all the time–that children's concepts of reading and counting, their social skills, and their physical and emotional growth occur over time and in predictable developmental stages. Their innovations in early childhood classrooms are another example of *the portfolio attitude.*

Non-graded primary units are being instituted in public schools and multiage grouping has renewed popularity (Charlesworth, 1989). In 1988 the National Association of State Boards of Education released a report, *Right From the Start,* which set forth recommendations for restructuring schooling for four- through eight-year-olds. The report urged that

> Early childhood units be established in elementary schools to provide a new pedagogy for working with children age 4–8 and a focal point for enhanced services to preschool children and their parents.

All of these events signal the admission by those in education and outside the field that children's learning is a continuous process. Thus, the collection and maintenance of information about the child's learning also should be continuous.

For teachers who always have based instruction and curriculum on their observations of their students, the "fuss about assessment" is bewildering.

For those teachers who have always based the majority of their instructional strategies and curriculum plans on the results of standardized achievement tests, criterion referenced tests based on state-mandated curriculum objectives, or student placement tests such as readiness tests, the "fuss" is intimidating. Some of these teachers are suspicious. Others expect that "this too will pass".

For teachers who are new to the field, the debates over testing, placement and other related issues are confusing and frightening. They may wonder, Who is right? What is right? How do I know if what I choose to do will be the best course of action for the children in my room?

To address the concerns and reactions of these teachers, we should reflect on the old saying that "The

From *The Portfolio and Its Use; Developmentally Appropriate Assessment of Young Children* by Cathy Grace and Elizabeth F. Shores (1992, Southern Early Childhood Association). Available from SECA, P.O. Box 5403, Little Rock, AR 72215-5403, for $10 plus $1.25 shipping and handling.

more things change, the more they stay the same". In the early history of preschool and primary education, teachers accumulated student work and used it in planning and instruction. Moreover, parents and communities respected the informed judgments of teachers.

Since then, our society has reacted and overreacted to world and national events—Sputnik, *Why Johnny Can't Read* (Flesch, 1955), integration of public schools, shifts in demographics and in family dynamics. Our educational system has felt the turmoil. By the 1970s and 1980s, *what* was taught, *how* it was taught and *when* it would be taught were largely controlled by curriculum guides, standardized tests and state and federal legislation about school assignments and equal educational opportunities. Teachers, once valued as the experts on children's development, seemed to gradually lose the public's respect and, with that, the authority to plan how to meet their students' needs.

With governmental guarantees of equal educational opportunity has come ever-greater government bureaucracy—until many teachers feel their spirits have been broken and the sense of community within many schools and school districts has diminished.

Standardized testing is one dimensional and only depicts the child's brief engagement with an unnatural set of circumstances. Teachers who are new to the profession or not familiar with alternatives to one dimensional testing should seek out teachers who have and are using a variety of strategies to assess children in their classroom; they should read about alternative assessment; they should watch teachers through video taped segments or visit classrooms where continuous assessment is practiced.

Observational skills are learned by observing. Teachers new to implementing the strategy must gain practice, skill and accuracy over time. When implementing portfolios as a strategy for assessment, teachers may want to depend on the collection of work samples to verify their observations. As they become more experienced the means by which data in the portfolios is collected will become more varied.

The early childhood profession has been and will continue to be accountable for the quality of educational programs children attend. As parents and children will be taking a more active role in curricular decisions, teachers will become decision *facilitators*. In this way accountability will be shared by all parties and not be viewed as an unknown that has driven decisions made by school policy makers and frightened

some teachers into giving up appropriate teaching practices. *This is an example of the portfolio attitude.*

Today, policymakers, the media and the public all seem very concerned about education, especially early childhood education. President Bush and the nation's governors have set forth the readiness goal. Numerous states are providing new educational opportunities for three- and four-year-olds. Congress has appropriated more money for child care for poor families and for parents seeking job training with the intent of becoming self sufficient. The challenge is to see that these new programs and policies are developmentally appropriate and support the development of all children.

With the advent of school-based management programs, teachers are enjoying a new sense of empowerment and professionalism. They have the opportunity to reclaim their true responsibility. They can again become decision-makers or facilitators, planning appropriate learning experiences and assessment measures for children. The assessment portfolio can help teachers as they recreate their role in society and in the lives of children and families.

Since appropriate assessment is a collaborative process involving children, parents, teachers and the community, the portfolio method promotes a shared approach to making decisions which will affect the child's future and attitude toward learning. True partnerships are formed when parents and teachers work together in determining the best course of action for the young child. Portfolios serve as a departure point for parent and teacher communication to begin and to flourish. Again, *this is an example of the portfolio attitude.*

The time is right to expand the classroom horizon and broaden the child's canvas. The assessment portfolio represents an attitude that frees the teacher so that she may focus on the child and develop an intimate relationship with him—one that will remain long after the paintbrushes are put away.

REFERENCES

Charlesworth, R. (1988). "Behind" before they start? Deciding how to deal with the risk of kindergarten "failure". *Young Children.* 44(3), 5–13.

Flesch, R. F. (1955). *Why Johnny can't read.* New York: Harper.

Jackson, P. (1968). *Life in the classroom.* New York: Holt, Rinehart and Winston.

Murray, F. (1986). *Necessity: The development component in reasoning.* Paper presented at the sixteenth annual meeting, Jean Piaget Society, Philadelphia.

National Association of State Boards of Education. (1988). *Right from the start.* Alexandria, VA: Author.

Tests, Independence and Whole Language

*Standardized tests often do more harm than good,
but is there an alternative? Here's what a noted
New Zealand educator has to say*

❝*Whole language is not 'airy-fairy' and neither is whole language evaluation.***❞**

BRIAN CUTTING

Brian Cutting is Educational Director of Wendy Pye Limited, an international publishing consultant and book publisher based in Auckland, New Zealand.

Why should children fail? Is it their fault, or does it have more to do with the educational system?

It would seem difficult to blame the children themselves. After all, most of them learn to talk, with all of language's complexities, well before they go to school (even though their learning continues for some years after that). Why is this learning so successful? Why do children learn to talk so naturally, and with apparent ease? These are some of the contributing factors:

- No one expects children to fail—not the children themselves, not their parents, not even the politicians and administrators concerned with education policy.
- Children are responsible for much of their own learning. Parents don't teach them every day. There's no manual for learning to talk which says: *Step one, tongue movements; Step two, consonants; Step three, vowels.* If such manuals did exist, children would certainly be less successful.
- Children practice for a long time. In fact, we're happy to let them take up to three years before some concern is voiced. And we're tolerant and full of praise for their "mistakes," not even seeing them as mistakes, but (especially at the beginning stages of learning) delighting in their attempts to say words.
- There are no tests of talking. Everyone recognizes that children will learn different things, at different rates and in differ-

ent ways. There are no tests, because children *do* learn to talk.

But imagine what would happen if someone decided that tests of talking were essential. A test would be designed, and talkers tested. For some children, the test items would be easy. These children would be ahead of the test. For some, the test items would match what they know—their stage of development. They would be fine. For others, the test items would be beyond their present competence. They, on the basis of the test, would fail.

What would happen to these failed talkers? Using the model given by learning to read, there would be remedial type classes where the children could practice all the things they didn't know. There would be exercises designed to improve their ability to pass the test, rather than on learning to talk (which the children were doing quite happily until they, and their parents, found out that they couldn't). These would be artificial exercises which someone had identified as important elements in the "learning-to-talk" process.

Even the most elegant of standardized tests of "talking" would show that some children were good (passed) and some children were bad (failed). In fact, there would be an outcry if such a test were given, because of the huge number of children who would be placed behind their more successful peers and who would be removed to attend specially funded "talking" programs.

If we really wanted to make learning to talk a non-success story, the easiest way would be to design tests that would set a standard which all children would be

From *Teaching/K-8,* May 1991, pp. 64-66. Reprinted with permission of the publisher, Early Years, Inc., Norwalk, Connecticut 06854.

expected to reach. We all know that such procedures would be futile for children learning to talk. So why do we use similar procedures for children learning to read and write?

Apart from learning to talk, children have learned many things successfully. It's worthwhile asking how they learned to do all these things. Not from following a manual. Not from learning to do all the parts before trying the whole. Not from artificial exercises divorced from real contexts. And not from tests, which supposedly identify what children know and don't know about a task. (Unfortunately, tests don't free learners; they constrain learning to what test developers believe to be important.)

Dismal cycle. We can't treat children as if some will be winners and others failures, because gradually the children who fail (when they really thought they were doing quite well) will begin to associate learning with failure. After repeated failure, they'll see school as futile. Worse, they'll begin to see themselves as hopeless. They and their parents never question what the test is testing or how how well it tests. Why would any education system fail children in this way, almost guaranteeing that five-year-olds will become habitual failures, doomed to a dismal cycle of practice-test-remediation until the children end up in special education classes?

There has to be a better way and there is. The focus on independent learning implies that the focus should be on independent evaluation as well.

This personal assessment of individual learning is not haphazard or random. (Whole language is not "airy-fairy" and neither is whole language evaluation.) It is systematic, regular and thorough. It can be used by teachers to help individual children learn more effectively about reading. (Is this book too difficult? Which books would help most?)

This kind of assessment caters to children's individual needs, while providing teachers with the feedback needed to help their children become independent. It helps teachers learn about reading and changes their ways of thinking about *how* children learn to read. Evaluation should not be viewed as an isolated chore necessary to give a child some grade, but rather as a natural part of the daily class program—a part that is vital for successful teaching and learning.

Proving failure. The whole point of learning is to be independent. Independence can never be achieved if children have been turned away from learning by repeated failure, no matter how lofty the goals of the original program. It always amazes me that we have to prove failure over and over again. Most adults couldn't face such a system, so why do so many adults seem to support such a system for children, even when they're aware of its consequences?

The recorded observations of reading behavior provide all the information needed to show parents that their children are making progress. They also allow teachers to show parents how they can help their children at home.

Is it too heretical then to ask if we need the tests, the workbooks and the reading materials associated with them? Is it so difficult to replace them with alternative methods of assessment which place the emphasis on individuals and observations?

By the way, I wonder whether the basal workbook test system survives not because of its educational value (which is a proven failure for so many children). I wonder whether it owes its resilience to administrators who don't really trust their teachers to provide effective learning through alternative models of learning like whole language.

The upper grades. There is often an assumption that real learning starts after children move on from the lower grades, that more formal education and evaluation procedures now become essential. No more play! Down to work! Well, such a system may work for the successes of the school system, but for those already disillusioned by repeated failure, more of the same will hardly prove to be the panacea they seek. Why continue a cycle of failure?

If the differences between children entering school are great, so are the differences between children entering a class at the beginning of the year. The implication for teachers is that, just as in the lower grades, independent learning should be the focus of classroom practice. It follows that evaluation should be as individualized as possible. Children's learning can't be constrained by the uniformity that testing brings. The emphasis on individuals and independent learning means that teachers have created classrooms where diversity is recognized and can exist.

If learning in the upper primary and middle school years is to change, teachers and children must be allowed independence from a set, inflexible program of teaching and testing. The principles of whole language learning can help teachers to provide more enjoyable and successful learning for

"The focus on independent learning implies that the focus should be on independent evaluation as well."

"It always amazes me that we have to prove failure over and over again."

all their children. And, the same principles which guided evaluation in the lower grades should guide evaluation for older children.

A balanced approach to evaluation should continue, with emphasis placed on observations, listening to children read, individual responses of various kinds, the children's own evaluation of their learning. Tests just don't give the feedback needed for self-evaluation of learning. They only give feedback on success or failure.

Worthwhile system. Listening to children read (running records, miscue analysis) is essential. You cannot find out what your children really know about reading without doing this. No test can do it more effectively, so it's worthwhile to organize a system where you listen to children read on a regular basis.

There's no reason why you shouldn't extend the "listening" with an individual conference, getting children to read both orally and silently, and then questioning them to find out how to help them understand more (about both the book and the reading process itself).

Also, there's no reason why these individual conferences should not be in the form of informal prose inventories, both published and those made up by you. All you need to make your own inventories are books with a developmental, gradual sequence of difficulty. The information collected can be stored in cumulative records, which will provide all the valid evidence needed by the school and parents about a child's progress.

The responses children make about their learning is one of the most valuable ways of evaluating their learning. If they can read a book and successfully turn it into a play, they have demonstrated their understanding of it. As they read independently, they can construct responses of many kinds to show how well they have understood what they read—information which is not available through other means.

If national comparisons need to be made, the standardized tests used should correlate with the teaching practice and assessment used in schools. Otherwise, the mismatch will guarantee failure for many learners.

It's difficult being a whole language teacher. You often have to work in a system which subverts your beliefs. You integrate language arts and then unravel the strands, teaching and testing tenses of verbs. You teach reading using whole contexts and marvelous materials, and you do worksheets on phonics because that is what will be tested. You evaluate learning by running records and observations (and even some diagnostic tests), only to have a standardized test tell you and your children—children you know are learning to read well, especially in terms of their competence—that they really are failures.

It's hard, but teachers and the parents of the children they teach must look for alternative ways of evaluating language learning, ways that move away from the tests and classroom practices that guarantee, for too many children, failure in school.

I would like to gratefully acknowledge the contribution to this article made by Jill Eggleton, author of Whole Language Evaluation *(available through The Wright Group).*

Tracking Progress Toward the School Readiness Goal

It's time to design new forms of school readiness assessment, forms that do not encourage tracking of students, narrowing the curriculum, or kindergarten retention.

PENELOPE ENGEL

Penelope Engel is a Professional Associate of the Educational Testing Service, Suite 475, 1825 Eye St., N.W., Washington, D.C. 20006.

"By the year 2000 all children will start school ready to learn."[1]

The National Governors' Association (NGA) set this national school readiness goal at its meeting in February 1990. At first glance, the statement may appear to be a call for a nationwide school admissions test for 1st grade, but if you know what lies behind this sentence, you'll see that nothing could be farther from the truth. In fact, this statement helped focus public attention on the compelling arguments *against* group-administered school readiness tests.

Widely publicized in the literature, these arguments have been debated in numerous forums and forged into policy statements by at least a dozen education organizations. Three general premises emerge: group-administered pencil-and-paper readiness tests are inappropriate for preschoolers and lack sufficient validity for making school entry decisions (Meisels 1989, Meisels et al. 1989, NAEYC 1988); their use often has the effect of narrowing the preschool curriculum and making

it excessively academic (Shepard and Smith 1988, Bredekamp and Shepard 1989); and test scores, when used to deny school entry, contribute to the practice of kindergarten retention, which is counterproductive public policy (Shepard and Smith 1989).

At the NGA meeting, the President and the governors warned that an assessment for school readiness should *not* be developed for purposes of measuring progress toward the readiness goal, because of the danger that it could be wrongfully used to determine when a child should start school. "Other current indicators of readiness may serve as proxies," they noted, "and still others need to be developed."[2]

The governors suggested that new methods be developed using teachers' cumulative observations of children.[3] At a minimum, this would yield better information to improve learning. It could possibly produce meaningful data for policymakers as well.

The Limitations of Proxy Measures

Figure 1 lists specific objectives toward meeting the readiness goal. These objectives concern provision of quality preschool programs, prenatal nutrition, and health care, as well as

the involvement of parents as their children's teachers. Policymakers will use "proxies," defined as indicators that do not measure children directly but that indirectly measure factors positively associated with readiness, in order to track national progress toward these objectives.

The National Center for Education Statistics (NCES) is now assembling these proxy data from various government-sponsored national surveys. These include national statistics on prenatal care; low birthweight babies; child nutrition; the percent of eligibles served by subsidized preschool programs; the supply, demand, and quality of preschool services; the kinds of learning experiences provided; the extent of parental involvement; and child retention in early grades. NCES will rely heavily on the National Household Education Survey, a planned triennial telephone survey to a national sample of households, for the ongoing tracking of the education-related information, including data on parents as their children's teachers.[4]

Proxies, however, are not adequate readiness measures. While appropriate now as an interim method for tracking progress toward the readiness goal, they are nonetheless insufficient for this purpose. They provide

By Penelope Engel, "Tracking Progress Toward the School Readiness Goal," *Educational Leadership,* Vol. 48, No. 5, February 1991, pp. 39-42. Reprinted with permission of the Association for Supervision and Curriculum Development.
Copyright © 1991 by ASCD. All rights reserved.

Fig. 1. National Goals For Education Readiness

Readiness Goal 1: By the year 2000, all children in American will start school ready to learn.
  Objectives:
  • All disadvantaged and disabled children will have access to high-quality and developmentally appropriate preschool programs that help prepare children for school.
  • Every parent in America will be a child's first teacher and devote time each day helping his or her preschool child learn; parents will have access to the training and support they need.
  • Children will receive the nutrition and health care needed to arrive at school with healthy minds and bodies, and the number of low birthweight babies will be significantly reduced through enhanced prenatal health systems.

---

an important piece of the puzzle by periodically informing us about factors, including essential services to children, that enhance early learning. But they do not tell us the extent to which our children have the requisite skills, attitudes, or behaviors they need and, therefore, what we need to know to help them succeed in school. Knowing the percentage of low birthweight babies each year is important, but this won't tell us why children aren't learning to read. Making high-quality preschool programs available to all needy children is unquestionably desirable; but paradoxically, to obtain good "proxy" data on the overall quality of such a program, you need an outcome measure of its effect on children.

The Office of Educational Research and Improvement (OERI) acknowledges "the proxy measures based on preschool enrollment, parental involvement, and characteristics of preschool programs do not suffice to make inferences about actual readiness to begin school."[5]

With good, and more direct, measures of children's behavior, we will know better, for example, if certain kindergarten teaching strategies are differentially effective for youngsters with limited English proficiency, a particular type of disability, or a certain learning style. If we increase funding or redesign a program, we need to know the effect of such changes. With only proxy data to report, we can say we doubled the budget and we're serving twice as many, but we can't say if the program made a difference in children's learning.

Real improvement in a child's readiness to learn and a teacher's readiness to teach is enhanced, not by having macro-level data on the national percent of eligible participants in a program, but by understanding behavior within the personal microcosm of that teacher with that child, as they interact with parents and other children.

The Fear and the Need

In discouraging the development of a national readiness test, the governors did the right thing. Their decision reflects concern in the professional community that national use of an inappropriate assessment, even if administered to only a sample of children, could lead to a highly academic preschool curriculum and ultimately to denying children the right to enter school with their age-mates.

Their decision is, in fact, only one of several recent behavioral and policy changes that discourage the use of school readiness tests. Several states have discontinued mandated kindergarten or early grade testing, and pre-K through 1st grade programs were recently granted a statutory exemption from Chapter 1 testing requirements. Further, informal, off-the-record communications with publishers reveal that sales of group-administered tests for the early and preschool grades have either remained flat or started to decline.

Assessment of young children, however, hasn't gone away, and it probably won't, because assessment—*good assessment*—is needed more than ever. In spite of the decrease in legislative requirements and a broad awareness of the dangers of misusing readiness tests, the pressure for "results" from states and districts for accountability purposes is increasing.

The Southern Regional Education Board (SREB), for example, now reporting annually on the progress of its 15 member states toward Year 2000 education goals, includes results of readiness assessments among the indicators of progress toward its school readiness goal.[6] And as one measure of the quality of programs, SREB includes "the use of assessments or tests of readiness for young children."[7] Legislation introduced in the U.S. Senate in 1990 requires that all relevant data on school readiness be considered for inclusion in a national report card on the educational goals.[8] Good readiness measures are needed not only for accountability purposes, but also for diagnosing learning needs, planning appropriate interventions, and evaluating programs.

A Call for Reform

Because of what Sharon Kagan, Yale University's Associate Director of the Bush Center in Child Development

Knowing the percentage of low birthweight babies each year is important, but this won't tell us why children aren't learning to read.

and Social Policy, calls a "fortuitous collision of events," a unique opportunity is now present for a major national reform in the assessment of young children. Our increased need for information to help children begin to learn has combined with our heightened awareness of the failings of readiness tests, so that "the seeds are right for change."[9] Now is the time to invest in a reform of this country's school readiness assessment.

The reform should begin with an effort to separate school entry from readiness. Many other nations have specific school starting points. In Sweden, children start school at age seven; in Japan, West Germany, and Switzerland at six; in New Zealand at five; and in Britain and Australia as early as four. The concept of readiness, wrongly applied, can be used to keep the "unready" out and thus deny those who need it most an opportunity to engage in learning at school. The dangers of

The Magic Tress of the Mind: How to Nurture your Child's Intelligence, Creativity, and Healthy Emotions from Birth to Adolescence. Marian Diamond, and Janet L. Hopson. E.P. Dutton, New York: 1998.

Endangered Minds. Why Children don't Think and What We Can Do About It. Jane Healey. Touchstone Books: California, 1991.

Tumbling Over the Edge. A Rant for Children's Play. Bev Boss and Jenny Chapman. Turn the Page, California, 1995.

Nov. 27/67

Purple paper

permission company

305.23 Elk

Foundations in Early Childhood Education

General Books Suitable for Read & Review Assignments

Raising Your Spirited Child. Mary Sheedy Kurcinka, Harper Perennial, 1998.

Constructing the Child: A History of Canadian Day Care. Donna Varga, James Lorimer & Co., Ltd: Toronto, 1997.

Families: Crisis and Caring. T. Barry Brazelton, M.D., Ballentine Books: New York, 1989.

The Youngest Minds. Ann B. Barnet, and Richard J. Barnet. Simon & Shuster: New York, 1998.

What's Going On In There? How the Brain & Mind Develop in the First Five Years of Life. Lise Eliot, Bantam Books: New York, 1999.

The Canadian Family in Crisis: Johan F. Conway. James Lorimer & Co. Toronto, 1987.

The Hurried Child: Growing Up Too Fast Too Soon. David Elkind, Addison Wesley Publishing Co.: Reading, Mass., 1981.

The Read-Aloud Handbook (Fourth Edition). Jim Trelease, Penguin Books: Toronto, 1995.

The Disappearance of Childhood: Neil Postman. Vintage Books (Random House): New York, 1994.

Stress and Your Child. Archibald D. Hart, Word Publishing: Dallas, 1992.

Any book by Vivian Paley. *including A Child's Work. The Importance of fantasy play*

Bringing Reggio Home. Louise Cadwell. Teacher's College Press: New York, 1997.

Anti-Bias Curriculum. Louise Derman Sparks, NAEYC: Washington, D.C.

Multicultural Issues in Child Care. Janet Gonzalez-Mena, Mayfield: California, 1993.

wrong school entry decisions, whether on the basis of test scores or not, and the increasing practice of voluntary retention by overzealous parents, would be greatly reduced if, at the established age, all children entered school, "ready" or not. As Meisels says, "If you're alive, you're ready to learn, no matter what the tests say."[10]

The next step of assessment reform should be to reach consensus on the expectations we have for young children. We need to know what we want to "ready" children and teachers *for*. That means defining the skills, behaviors, and attitudes children should learn and teachers should teach in the 1st grade of school. Perhaps some of our nation's best minds, most experienced teachers, and most knowledgeable parents—those who understand child development and its many dimensions, its wide variations and its spurts and starts—could reach consensus.[11] Perhaps the encroachment of increasingly higher levels of academic demands into the preschool and kindergarten could be reversed by publicly stating just what we expect *and do not expect* of 1st graders. The precursors to these expectations then could become our readiness indicators.

A Kinder, Gentler Way
We need to develop better means of assessing children's readiness than group-administered readiness tests. The governors, in fact, suggested several strategies for states to use to improve assessments:

"Develop assessment systems for young children that reflect the ultimate goals of producing independent, creative, and critical thinkers. Train teachers to observe and assess children's work in different content areas, using methods such as portfolio systems, observational checklists, and cumulative sampling of children's work. Develop models to use teacher assessments of student proficiencies for reporting to parents and the public . . ."[12]

We know a good deal about assessing readiness from work already begun (Anderson 1987, NAEYC 1988, Meisels 1989, Meisels et al. 1989). This work tells us that, ideally, readiness assessments should:
- encompass the multiple dimensions of readiness, including cognitive, social/emotional, attitudinal, and physical/motor behaviors;
- be an ongoing process of observing a child, rather than a one-time snapshot;

- gather information on behaviors that children have had an opportunity to develop;
- provide data useful for instructional improvement—to help the teacher get ready for the child;
- be indirect measures of children—that is, recorded by an adult, rather than directly by a child on an answer sheet;
- be conducted in a natural setting that is comfortable, familiar, and nonthreatening to the child;
- be administered to individuals, one-on-one, or to very small clusters of children, but not to large groups;
- be designed so that children can respond by pointing, acting, doing, or manipulating;
- be conducted by someone who is properly trained and who can relate well to children;
- be scored to yield a profile along the various readiness dimensions;
- be used in a nonpunitive way—that is, not for sorting, tracking, or denial of school entry. This last point is most important.

Promising Prospects
In this section, I want to highlight three examples of developmental work in progress that appear to offer particular promise: one is from the State of Georgia, one from a test publisher (CTB Macmillan/McGraw-Hill), and one from research scientist Samuel Meisels.

The State of Georgia has now produced a developmentally appropriate method for evaluating readiness called the Georgia Kindergarten Assessment Program (GKAP). This program represents a positive directional change from Georgia's 1988 group-administered, machine-scored, norm-referenced test used for making school entry decisions (which probably did more to advance readiness assessment reform in this country than all other causes combined).

GKAP is a homegrown individually-administered readiness assessment on which three times a year, teachers record children's behavior across five capability areas. A series of "structured assessment activities" involving children's use of manipulatives gives additional information on two of the dimensions. A videotape illustrates the expected behavior for standardization of teacher ratings. The process relies heavily on teacher judgment and

yields good diagnostic information; however, its value for accountability purposes is not yet clear. A mechanism has been designed, but not totally implemented, for aggregating data from classrooms, to schools, to districts, to the state. Teachers record *yes/no* data, but not a total score, for each child on each of the five capabilities, on scannable forms for automatic generation of totals. The new system has been very costly, and the price of maintaining it is not yet known. Further refinements need to be made and analyses conducted.

CTB Macmillan/McGraw-Hill has recently produced a "Developing Skills Checklist" for children aged 4 to 6, which is individually administered and is packaged in a kit with attractive manipulatives. For each child, teachers can generate a criterion-referenced diagnostic profile of performance in eight areas. These checklists produce normative scores on mathematical concepts and operations, language, memory, auditory skills, print concepts, and a prereading composite. National percentiles, stanines, and normal curve equivalents are provided for each scale for four time periods (spring of pre-K and fall, winter, and spring of kindergarten). Included in the process are a method for recording multiple observations throughout the year on seven clusters of social/emotional behavior and a mechanism for compiling group data. So far, researchers have found high internal consistency reliability, and a two-year predictive validity study is now under way.

Samuel Meisels, Professor of Education and Research Scientist at the University of Michigan, is currently developing and piloting in nine school districts a new three-part readiness assessment process consisting of (1) a comprehensive criterion-referenced checklist of developmentally-based classroom learning, completed by the kindergarten teacher for each child on three different occasions throughout the school year; (2) the compilation of a portfolio of samples of the progression of each child's work; and (3) a summative teacher report form for providing year-end comparative, and possibly scaled and aggregate, data.

These three efforts suggest that supportive, child-friendly, and learning-enhancing measures can also produce aggregate data for accountability to the public. Since the governors recommended that a readiness assessment *not* be developed to measure progress toward the national goal, the government will presumably seek methods for indirectly compiling information gathered by others, such as teachers or parents, who have observed the behavior of children. The efforts I have described suggest the kinds of data that might be compiled.

Educators need more information, however, to ensure that the data compiled are valid, reliable, and useful and that they are collected in a uniform and equitable manner. It is essential to assure that observation criteria are clearly specified, that representative samples of all categories of behaviors are observed, and that raters are consistent. Test developers must create effective methods for recording, compiling, analyzing, scaling, and reporting data. They must conduct field tests and validity studies to determine whether performance on a readiness assessment predicts success in school, and evaluate the usefulness of aggregate scores reported to policymakers.

Any new assessment method must be monitored for possible inappropriate uses, such as retaining preschoolers, tracking, narrowing, further academic loading of the curriculum, or "teaching to the test," and evaluated for practical considerations such as costs and time. Finally, test users should compare the overall value of a new assessment method with existing practices.

Having been instructed by the White House to develop "other" readiness measures, OERI should lead the way toward better school readiness assessment by underwriting the consensus-building process and sponsoring

needed research and development. Whether or not a method better than proxies is ever created for national monitoring, readiness assessment in this country needs to be reformed. We need a kinder, gentler way to measure.

---

[1]National Governors' Association, *National Education Goals*. A statement adopted by the members of the NGA in Charlottesville, Virginia, on February 25, 1990, p. 3.

[2]The White House, *National Education Goals*. Press release from the Office of the Press Secretary, January 31, 1990, p. 3.

[3]National Governors' Association, *Educating America: State Strategies for Achieving the National Goals*. Report of the Task Force on Education. (Washington, D.C.: NGA, 1990), p. 15.

[4]See B.J. Turnbull, (April 1990), "Readiness for School—Issue Brief." Washington, D.C.: Policy Studies Associates, and Office of Educational Research and Improvement (OERI), "Education Summit Follow-up, Special Set, 6/1/90," internal document, for a more complete delineation of all the proxy data sources mentioned here.

[5]OERI, Ibid., p. 4.

[6]J. D. Creech, (1990), *Educational Benchmarks 1990*. (Atlanta: Southern Regional Education Board), p. 6.

[7]Southern Regional Education Board, (1989), *Reaching the Goal of Readiness for School* (Atlanta: SREB), pp. 11–12.

[8]S.3095, The National Academic Report Card Act of 1990, introduced by Senator Jeff Bingaman on September 24, 1990.

[9]S. L. Kagan, (July 13, 1990), personal communication, The Bush Center in Child Development and Social Policy, Yale University.

[10]S. Meisels, (July 5, 1990), personal communication, Center for Human Growth and Development, University of Michigan.

[11]See National Association for the Education of Young Children, (1990), "Position Statement on Readiness," for a good discussion of what is meant by readiness.

[12]National Governors' Association, *Educating America: State Strategies for Achieving the National Education Goals*, Ibid.

References

Anderson, L. W. (1987). "Comments on a National Assessment of School Readiness." In *The Assessment of Readiness for School: Implications for a Statistical Program—Report of a Planning Conference*. Washington, D. C.: Center for Education Statistics, pp. 27–36.

Bredekamp, S., and L. Shepard. (1989). "How Best to Protect Children from Inappropriate School Expectations, Practices, and Policies." *Young Children* 44, 3: 14–24.

Meisels, S. J. (1989). "High-Stakes Testing in Kindergarten." *Educational Leadership* 46, 7: 16–22.

Meisels, S. J., D. Steele, and K. Quinn. (1989). "Testing, Tracking, and Retaining Young Children: An Analysis of Research and Social Policy." A commissioned paper prepared for the National Center for Education Statistics, December 1989.

National Association for the Education of Young Children. (1988). "Position Statement on Standardized Testing of Young Children 3 through 8 years of age." *Young Children* 43: 42–47.

Shepard, L. A., and M. L. Smith. (1988). "Escalating Academic Demand in Kindergarten: Counterproductive Policies." *The Elementary School Journal* 89: 135–145.

Shepard, L. A., and M. L. Smith. (1989). "Academic and Emotional Effects of Kindergarten Retention." In *Flunking Grades: Research and Policies on Retention*, edited by L.A. Shepard and M.L. Smith. Philadelphia: The Falmer Press, pp. 79–107.

BEATING
THE
HANDICAP
RAP

J A M E S   N .   B A K E R

Therapists try to develop programs to help the whole family, not just the disabled child
—

All along, it had been a troubled pregnancy. Then, in the summer of 1986, when Claudia Sofield was in her sixth month, her water broke. A 2-pound 5-ounce daughter was delivered by Caesarean section. With the help of medical technology, Farrin survived. When she was ready to go home to Newfane, Vt., the doctors said that she would probably develop more slowly than other children, but would eventually catch up. The next year the Sofields became concerned that she wasn't crawling. "Her legs were hard as rocks," says Claudia. "We thought she was strong." They took 13-month-old Farrin to a specialist, who commented on the hard "tone" of her legs and lower torso. "Is there a name for this pattern?" Claudia asked. "Well, yes," said the doctor, surprised at the question. "Cerebral palsy."

Nowhere is the early tackling of a problem more poignantly critical than in diagnosing and treating children with physical and mental handicaps. The number of children with disabilities is growing in this country, by some estimates from 2 to 4 percent over the last 30 years; as many as 140,000 children are born every year with disorders from minor to life-threatening. Some causes are discouraging: the increase of children born to mothers who have AIDS, substance-abuse histories or who were exposed to toxic substances. Others are heartening: medical advances make it possible to save children who may have otherwise died. Now, tiny premature babies survive. Surgeons can perform lifesaving surgery on infants with spina bifida, a disease of the central nervous system, in the first 24 hours of life. During pregnancy, doctors can identify Down syndrome and a variety of other conditions more quickly than in the past. And with the new techniques of fetal surgery, doctors can correct serious defects as early as the 24th week of pregnancy.

Early intervention began as a trend but has become a mandate. In the 1970s, child-development specialists emphasized how crucial the early years are in a youngster's physical and intellectual development. Therapists for disabled children realized that this focus was monumentally important for their constituencies, since its purpose would be to train the whole family to help the child and prevent institutionalization. Through a network of professionals, a movement grew, and now early intervention is law. In 1986, Congress passed legislation to make funds available to state, local and private agencies to develop free diagnostic and therapeutic services for children under 2, and to improve special-education preschool programs for 3- to 5-year-olds. States enacted similar legislation, but some hard-pressed ones are now cutting programs for disabled children—to the alarm of professionals. Says Dr. Gloria Harbin, formerly an official at the Department of Education and a key player in the early-intervention movement, "We need a comprehensive, coordinated system—medical and educational, birth to age 5—in every state."

Early intervention usually begins with a medical procedure, sometimes something as simple as a hearing test for an infant. But some handicapped children start life with more frightening prospects. Shortly after birth, Hilary Morris nearly

From *Newsweek*, Special Issue, Summer 1991, pp. 36-37, 40-41. Copyright © 1991 by Newsweek, Inc. Reprinted by permission.

died from pneumonia and was put onto a ventilator; she now has bronchopulmonary dysplasia (BPD). "They save their lives," says Melody Morris, Hilary's mother, "but leave them with a chronic lung condition." At 2, Hilary is hooked up to an air compressor during the day, and a ventilator at night. In the past, children with BPD lived in hospitals, but the Morrises took advantage of an early-intervention home-care program in Chicago. Hilary roams free at home, wearing a trach collar attached by a long tube to the compressor; doctors believe she will be breathing on her own by the end of the year. Melody, who says Hilary will "never have the lung stamina of an opera singer," believes home care speeded her daughter's progress. "It's very difficult to parent in a hospital," she says.

Hilary's doctors were able to chart a definite course, but many children are mysteries. Most birth defects, from cerebral palsy to Down syndrome, have degrees of severity, and sometimes doctors cannot positively diagnose the disorder. The extent of the damage becomes apparent only over time; frequently parents don't even realize a disability exists until children reach an age when certain milestones should happen and don't, such as Farrin's failure to crawl. And when a child has a motor disability, he's also likely to have cognitive and speech problems.

Therapists in all three areas—speech, occupational and physical—patiently aim for small gains. "Marginal behavior feels dramatic!" says Mimi Siegel, director of the Merrywood School, a special-education school in Bellevue, Wash. The state-of-the-art therapy is a combination of traditional and experimental methods. Children still work with blocks and have hydrotherapy. Teachers urge them to communicate by speech, hands or their eyes. But handicapped children also live in the age of technology. In Los Angeles, toddlers as young as 18 months work with computers at UCLA's Intervention Program for Handicapped Children. Software programs operated by a switch, a touch window or a power pad let children perform complicated tasks on a computer screen. "Many kids are more cognitively advanced than they can physically show," says IP microcomputer-project executive director Kit Kehr. "Using a computer switch, a child can tell you that he really does know the color blue."

The rate of progress is impossible to predict. What is clear is that a combination of the three therapies, provided on a steady basis, usually shows results. Everett Hillsman, 2½, who has cerebral palsy, was not expected to walk until he was 3. But at 20 months, after only eight weeks at the Crippled Children's Society center in Inglewood, Calif., he was walking. He can feed himself and even walk backward. Says his teacher Diana White, "This is a big improvement over zero."

Therapists relish a triumph, but brace themselves for setbacks. Caitlyn Reed is epileptic and may have mitochondria defect, a metabolic muscular disorder that afflicts one in 300,000 children. When Caitlyn came to Merrywood last August, she was 13 months old, but functioned at the level of a 4-month-old. After three months of therapy, she advanced to an 8-month level, able to crawl. Then, Caitlyn suffered a battery of epileptic seizures, up to 20 a day. She regressed—and is back to a 4-month level. "Her brain isn't equipped to control movement," says her mother.

Advocates of early intervention believe parents are a therapist's most valuable colleagues. "It's not like going to ballet where you get to read your book while your child is at the barre," says Dr. Deborah Gaebler-Spira, medical director of early intervention at The Rehabilitation Institute of Chicago. Schools and day-care centers encourage parents to learn sign language and physical-therapy methods. Many programs offer home visits in which therapists work with parent and child together and give the family assignments. Dr. Susan Landry, head of early assessment at Hermann Hospital in Houston, videotapes parent and child to determine which behaviors are most effective. Professionals have to make sure parents are not allowing unproductive behavior. Alison Schantz, speech therapist at the Winston L. Prouty Center for Child Development in Brattleboro, Vt., says a mother might report enthusiastically that her daughter spends time staring into the mirror. "She doesn't realize that this may be obsessive behavior, and not desirable."

Because the pressure of trying to raise a handicapped child can be disastrous to home life, therapists are trying to develop programs to help the whole family. "People go through the stages of grief," says Merrywood's Siegel. "You are literally burying the child you had hoped for and coming to grips with the child that is." Parents often blame themselves, sometimes illogically: when Anita Whitney of Bellevue, Wash., learned that her son Michael was a special-needs child, she said, "I thought I maybe left him alone too much." Sometimes what looks like a bleak episode turns out to be a blessing. For example, when therapists realize a child is never going to walk and recommend a wheelchair, it's painful for parents to accept. But once they realize the wheelchair gives the child mobility, says Prouty's physical therapist Diana Lange, "it becomes the family's best friend."

Having a handicapped child at home can take a rough toll on fathers and siblings. Frequently, mothers become involved, sometimes to an obsessive degree, with the youngster, causing the rest of the family to feel left out. James May, who was a special-needs child himself, started a father's group, now associated with Merrywood. More than 100 men participate in group therapy twice a month and have been drawn into school activities. Most programs have sibling days, and at the Center for Family Studies in Morganton, N.C., brothers and sisters take part in handicap-awareness exercises, spending the day blindfolded or with slats on their legs to simulate braces.

What parents sometimes need most is a break. Professionals might find foster families to share part-time responsibilities, especially if the mother has to work or the parents want to take a vacation. Other services are less wrenching: Hermann's Children's Hospital opened The Respite House in Houston last year to give mothers a place to kick off their shoes, read a book or even take a bubble bath while the staff looks after the children. "It's wonderful," says Tina Demmon, mother of a brain-damaged boy. "Sometimes I just sit and rest. He's a full-time job."

ome disabled children may never leave hospital care because they have no one to take them home. An alarming byproduct of the nation's drug crisis is the growing phenomenon of hospital "boarder babies," children born to mothers who have died of AIDS or are unable to take care of their babies. Some are brought in critically ill. Zachary, 2, suffered from neurological damage and was curled into a fetal position when he came to New York's Incarnation Children's Center a year ago. Now he takes AZT, which slows the progress of AIDS, and Dr. Steven Nicholas says, "He just unfolded. He has a personality." Hospitals try to find foster care, though often volunteer parents bring the children back. For children with AIDS who have homes, the Bronx Municipal Hospital runs a day-care center where the youngsters can play together with no fear of discrimination that they can encounter in other centers and schools.

Professionals believe the company of children without disabilities gives handicapped youngsters a boost. In 1975, the Education for All Handicapped Children Act called for an end to segregation for disabled students from kindergarten through high school. Now, schools in all 50 states "mainstream" these older children as much as possible because being around nondisabled role models stimulates them. The policy has filtered down to preschools and day-care centers, where handicapped children participate in classroom activities working at their own rate.

In recent years professionals have turned mainstreaming upside down. Centers and schools established to serve handicapped children recruit nondisabled students. These youngsters are taught sign language and encouraged to help their handicapped classmates. Why do families send their kids there? Often the schools have

good reputations. But The Center for Family Services, serving predominantly rural, blue-collar western North Carolina, found there was another reason. "Parents told us, 'I want my child to have that experience of being with kids who are different'," says Angela Deal, head of the center's family, infant and preschool program.

Under the circumstances, a rosy picture overall, no? Well, no. Parents still split up because they have a handicapped child, or decide to give the youngster up for adoption. Tens of thousands of disabled children are still in institutions. There is also a potentially divisive debate over the real value of mainstreaming in school, since it places the disabled child in the care of an untrained teacher; therapists wind up playing a secondary role or acting as consultants, sometimes unpaid. At the same time, there is a shortage of therapists trained to work with preschoolers. And finally, Congress will vote this summer on whether to renew the 1986 legislation. Still, Harbin, now with the Carolina Policy Studies Program, believes that by the end of the century, 50 statewide early-intervention programs will be in place. "We've already done things against all odds," she says. "With young children there is always hope."

"Without early intervention Farrin would have been in a wheelchair," says her mother. Claudia enrolled Farrin in the Prouty Center program where she has learned to speak more clearly, draw a little and write her name. Last year doctors removed part of Farrin's spine and severed the nerves that caused the spasticity in her legs. "She's loose now, no more spasticity," says Claudia. With continual therapy, Farrin progressed to crutches, and is now developing calf muscles. "Our goal is that she will walk with only her braces," says Claudia. When? A year from now? "Oh no," laughs her mother. "By summer."

With Linda Buckley in Bellevue, Wash., Karen Springen in Chicago, David D. Medina in Houston and Larry Wilson in New York

For Many, New Leases on Life

In the past, most children born with spina bifida died by age 10.
Now, average life expectancy is up to 50.

Down syndrome children often have heart defects.
With surgery and other treatments, now they can make it to their 60s.

500,000 Americans have cerebral palsy.
And most can plan to live normal life spans.

Early childhood professionals need to work together to establish safe learning environments and promote growth, development, and appropriate behaviors in the children they serve.

Collaborative Training in the Education of Early Childhood Educators

Barbara Lowenthal

Barbara Lowenthal *(CEC Chapter #302) is an Associate Professor, Department of Special Education, Northeastern Illinois University, Chicago.*

Recent legislation and governmental policy have made it necessary to ensure collaboration in the training of early childhood and special educators. Both Public Law 99-457 (The Education of the Handicapped Amendments of 1986) and the regular education initiative proposed by the federal government have provided a rationale for this cooperation (Guralnick, 1981, 1982; Hanson & Hanline, 1989; Lilly, 1986; Strain & Kerr, 1981; Will, 1986). Early childhood special educators will need to be taught how to practice collaboration, which is defined by Weaver (1979) as "not mere cooperation or a matter of good will, but an agreed-upon distribution of power, status, and authority" (p. 24).

P.L. 99-457 mandates that preschoolers with special needs be placed in the least restrictive environment (Wang, 1989). For quite a few of these children, this mandate means that they will participate in typical preschool settings. One of the difficulties with this requirement is that, historically, many preschoolers with disabilities have been served by public and private agencies

From *Teaching Exceptional Children*, Summer 1992, pp. 25-29. Copyright © 1992 by The Council for Exceptional Children. Reprinted with permission of The Council for Exceptional Children.

other than the schools. These agencies have a great deal of practical experience with and information about these children that schools may lack.

Another difficulty in fulfilling the mandates of P.L. 99-457 is that many public schools will need to establish additional preschool classes, which will require new teachers. Besides the school settings, integrated placement for these young children could be in other sites such as day care centers and day care homes. Therefore, early childhood personnel will need preparation in intervening in these settings as well.

Research clearly indicates that personnel who are well trained are more effective than those who are not (Tingey-Michaelis, 1985). The question then becomes how best to train early childhood personnel, both regular and special, to meet the challenges of teaching in integrated settings (Guralnick, 1981; Hanson & Hanline, 1989). The competencies expected of regular early childhood teachers and those required of special educators are discussed in this article, and possible commonalities and differences between the two roles are elucidated.

Early Childhood Teacher Competencies

Competencies expected of regular early childhood educators can be described in terms of the requirements for the Child Development Associate (CDA) credentials that were initiated in 1972 to alleviate staff shortages and provide training for Head Start and other child care staff (Trickett, 1979). The competencies are summarized in the following list (Jones & Hamby, 1981; Peters, 1981):

1. To establish a safe, healthy environment.
2. To advance physical and intellectual competence.
3. To ensure a well-run program responsive to participant needs.
4. To maintain a commitment to professionalism.

In reviewing these competencies, it is clear that the regular early childhood teacher must be able to accommodate a wide range of abilities, developmental levels, and social-emotional needs of children in the preschool classroom (Bredekamp, 1987; Moyer, Egertson, & Isenberg, 1987). The special educator also will need to do this, but will require extra training in alternative approaches

to intervention, methods and strategies, best practices in consultation and collaboration, available resources, and skills in the processes of referral and transition.

The competencies of the special educator will both overlap and differ somewhat from those required of the regular preschool teacher. These competencies can include knowledge of curricula, class management, professional consultation and communications, teacher-family relationships, child-child interactions, exceptional children, referral, assessment and individualized teaching, and professional values (Guralnick, 1982; Hanson & Hanline, 1989; Hurley, 1989; Zeitlin, du Verglas, & Windhover, 1982). A summary of each of these competencies follows.

Curricula

The term is used here to include the ability to identify curricular goals for teaching each child functional skills for daily living (Hanson, 1984). This ability will be helpful in the development of individualized education programs. Functional skills can be taught effectively through classroom routines and through the use of a curriculum built on a framework of play.

Class Management

This refers to the efficient management of schedules, instruction, materials, and child behaviors within the classroom ecology. Time schedules should be set but be sufficiently flexible to allow for differences in time requirements of individual children. Transitions can be smoothly structured so that children can move from one activity to another as their individual needs dictate. For effective behavior management, the special educator needs training in the following skills: identification of potential reinforcers for each child, positive behavior reinforcement through the use of these reinforcers, provision of sufficient materials to promote cooperation, use of class activities that require cooperation, and reinforcement of appropriate behavior through peer modeling (Cook, Tessier, & Armbruster, 1987).

Professional Consultation and Collaboration

Early childhood special educators need to be able to communicate with regular early childhood teachers to develop common goals for children, methods, materials, assessment, instruction, and evaluation. Personal characteristics that

Early childhood teachers need to work together to make transition for students a positive experience.

can assist in developing good communication include being empathic and open, being able to establish good rapport, respecting different points of view, and being positive and enthusiastic (West & Cannon, 1987).

Teacher-Family Relationships

As a result of P.L. 99-457, early childhood special educators need training in a broad-based, family-focused approach. Some components of this approach include (a) promoting positive child and family functioning through assistance based on the family's identified needs and goals; (b) using family strengths and informal support systems as a basis for empowering the family to make use of existing resources to meet their needs; and (c) allowing families to exercise control over the extent to which they want to be involved in the preschool program (Dunst, 1985; Dunst, Trivette, & Deal, 1988; Hanson, 1984; Hanson & Krentz, 1986; Turnbull, Summers, & Brotherson, 1984).

Child-Child Interactions

Special educators have a responsibility to assist the children in their classes to learn how to interact with one another in appropriate ways and to cooperate in working toward common goals.

Exceptional Children

Special educators need to have both a practical and a theoretical understanding of the characteristics of young exceptional children in all domains of development. This knowledge should be combined with information about how to further children's feelings of independence and task mastery. Preschool children with special needs should be allowed to assume as much control over their environment as possible. The gradual shift of balance of power from teachers to children will facilitate their task engagement and enhance motivation (Dunst, 1985).

Referral

An important skill for early childhood special educators is to know when and where to refer a child with disabilities and his or her family if they require related services such as speech, occupational, and physical therapy; child and family counseling; and health services.

Both special education teachers and regular education teachers need to be able to discuss time schedules of the children.

Assessment and Individualized Teaching

Early childhood special educators need to learn a variety of assessment techniques in order to best determine the strengths and weaknesses of every child. An ecological approach should be stressed that incorporates an understanding of both the child's unique characteristics and environmental influences affecting his or her development. Assessment information can be obtained through observation, case history, tests, and interviews. After assessment, individualized teaching should be stressed using a broad array of teaching methods. Both special educators and regular teachers need training in these techniques, which should emphasize the generalization of skills from one developmental area to another. Teaching techniques that use basic classroom routines as their framework can best develop this generalization of skills. Teaching methods should be as unintrusive as possible so that children are encouraged to explore, play, and experiment as ways of learning (Safford, 1989).

Professional Values

Preschool educators, both regular and special, must incorporate into their personal value systems a respect and consideration for the rights of every child and his or her family.

Special Educator as Resource

Special educators must also recognize another important aspect of their role: that of resource to the regular preschool teacher, especially with regard to mainstreaming needs. A special education teacher's positive and helpful approach toward integration of children with disabilities in the regular preschool class can affect the attitude of the classroom teacher not only about integrating a particular child but also toward the principle of mainstreaming itself (Salend & Johns, 1983).

A related aspect of this resource role is knowledge of successful transition practices when transferring the child with disabilities from a segregated to an integrated preschool setting. To accomplish this transition, the special education teacher must be familiar with the environment of the regular class, the curriculum and behavioral expectations for the children, class schedules, and routines. This will require the special educator to visit the regular class and observe its ecology so that he or she can teach the skills the exceptional child needs to function in the mainstream setting. Another essential transition practice is to be sensitive to the family regarding mainstreaming. This will promote the family's independence and feelings of control (Dunst, Trivette, & Deal, 1988).

Similarities

There are many similarities between the required competencies for regular and special early childhood educators. One of the most significant is that both types of teachers work with preschool children who are at different developmental levels and have varying cognitive and personal-social characteristics within a group program. What is good early childhood practice for typical children in most cases appears to be good for those who have special needs. The presence of children with disabilities does not require a different style of teaching from that which is appropriate for most other youngsters (Bailey, Clifford, & Harms, 1982).

Another significant competency that both kinds of educators should possess is the ability to establish positive and respectful relationships with families. Empathy, responsiveness to family needs, and promotion of family independence and empowerment are essential abilities for both special and mainstream early childhood personnel (Dunst, Trivette, & Deal, 1988; Turnbull, Summers, & Brotherson, 1984; Turnbull & Turnbull, 1986).

Early childhood professionals need to work together to establish safe learning environments and promote growth, development, and appropriate behaviors in the children they serve. Both special educators and regular preschool teachers must be committed to professionalism and ethical values and have a functional knowledge of child development, class management, and record-keeping. However, special educators

have a greater need for alternative approaches in intervention, curricula, and techniques of behavior management, and they need a deeper understanding of atypical development in children. Knowledge of referral sources; related services; best practices in consultation, collaboration, and transition; and family advocacy is useful as well.

A Proposal for Promoting Collaboration

Because of the regular education initiative and the mandates of P.L. 99-457, special and regular preschool teachers need to cooperate more with one another and in some cases even work together in the same classrooms. One way to ensure this collaboration and cooperation might be to train all future preschool teachers in both regular and special early childhood education. Since the required competencies are similar for both kinds of teachers, it might be best to issue a joint certification. Then all preschool teachers would take core courses in normal and atypical development of young children, child psychology, assessment, curriculum and teaching methods, evaluation, classroom management, teaming, and working with families. More detailed coursework could then be required in alternative methods for intervention, techniques for integration, technology for children with special needs, transition, referral and consultation, and knowledge of available resources.

The program could be field based, with practica in integrated settings. Some practicum hours could be credited for doing respite care for interested families, since this work could assist preservice teachers in gaining a better understanding of family needs, strengths, and support systems. Since the training would be intensive and take longer than the customary bachelor's degree requirements, it could lead to a master's degree in the areas of regular and early childhood education. This joint certification would then follow the guidelines of P.L. 99-457, help integration to succeed in mainstreamed settings, and ensure collaboration in the training of early childhood special and regular educators.

References

Hanson, M. J., & Hanline, M. F. (1989). Integration options for the very young child. In R. Gaylord-Ross (Ed.), *Integration strategies for persons with handicaps* (pp. 177-193). Baltimore: Paul H. Brookes.

Hanson, M. J., & Krentz, M. K. (1986). *Supporting parent-child interactions: A guide for early intervention program personnel.* San Francisco: Department of Special Education, San Francisco State University.

Hurley, O. (1989). Implications of P.L. 99-457 for preparation of preschool personnel. In J. Gallagher, P. Trohanis, & R. Clifford (Eds.), *Policy implementation and P.L. 99-457* (pp. 133-146). Baltimore: Paul H. Brookes.

Jones, L., & Hamby, T. M. (1981). Comments on "A review of the Child Development Associate Credential." *Child Care Quarterly, 10,* 74-83.

Lilly, S. (1986). The relationship between general and special education: A new face on an old issue. *Counterpoint, 6,* 10.

Moyer, J., Egertson, H., & Isenberg, J. (1987). The child-centered kindergarten. *Childhood Education, 63,* 235-242.

Peters, D. L. (1981). New methods for educating and credentialing professionals in child care. *Child Care Quarterly, 10,* 3-8.

Safford, P. L. (1989). *Integrated teaching in early childhood.* White Plains, NY: Longman.

Salend, S., & Johns, J. (1983). A tale of two teachers: Teacher commitment to mainstreaming. *TEACHING Exceptional Children, 15,* 82-85.

Strain, P. S., & Kerr, M. M. (1981). *Mainstreaming of children in schools: Research and programmatic issues.* New York: Academic Press.

Tingey-Michaelis, C. (1985). Early intervention: Is certification necessary? *Teacher Education and Special Education, 8,* 91-97.

Trickett, P. (1979). Career development in Head Start. In E. Zigler & J. Valentine (Eds.), *Project Head Start* (pp. 315-338). New York: Free Press.

Turnbull, A. P., Summers, J. A., & Brotherson, M. J. (1984). *Working with families with disabled members: A family systems approach.* Lawrence: University of Kansas, Kansas University Affiliated Facility.

Turnbull, A. P., & Turnbull, H. R. (1986). *Families, professionals, and exceptionality: A special partnership.* Columbus, OH: Merrill.

Wang, M. (1989). Implementing the state of the art and integration mandates of P.L. 94-142. In J. Gallagher, P. Trohanis, & R. Clifford (Eds.), *Policy implementation and P.L. 99-457* (pp. 33-58). Baltimore: Paul H. Brookes.

Weaver, J. F. (1979). Collaboration: Why is sharing the turf so difficult? *Journal of Teacher Education, 30,* 24-25.

West, J. F., & Cannon, G. (1987). Essential collaborative consultation competencies for regular and special educators. *Journal of Learning Disabilities, 21,* 56-63.

Will, M. (1986). Educating children with learning problems: A shared responsibility. *Exceptional Children, 52,* 411-416.

Zeitlin, S., du Verglas, G., & Windhover, R. (Eds.). (1982). *Basic competencies for personnel in early intervention programs.* Monmouth, OR: Western Technical Assistance Resources.

Bailey, D. B., Clifford, R. M., & Harms, T. (1982). Comparison of preschool environments for handicapped and nonhandicapped children. *Topics in Early Childhood Special Education, 2,* 9-20.

Bredekamp, S. (1987). *Developmentally appropriate practice in early childhood programs serving children from birth through age 8.* (expanded edition). Washington, DC: National Association for the Education of Young Children.

Cook, R., Tessier, A., & Armbruster, V. (1987). *Adapting early childhood curricula for children with special needs.* Columbus, OH: Merrill.

Dunst, C. J. (1985). Rethinking early intervention. *Analysis and Intervention in Developmental Disabilities, 5,* 165-201.

Dunst, C. J., Trivette, C. M., & Deal, A. G. (1988). *Enabling and empowering families.* Cambridge, MA: Brookline Books.

Guralnick, M. J. (1981). The efficacy of integrating handicapped children in early childhood settings: Research implications. *Topics in Early Childhood Special Education, 1,* 57-71.

Guralnick, M. J. (1982). Programmatic factors affecting child-child social interactions in mainstreamed preschool programs. In P. S. Strain (Ed.), *Social development of exceptional children* (pp. 71-92). Rockville, MD: Aspen.

Hanson, M. J. (1984). Early intervention: Models and practices. In M. J. Hanson (Ed.), *Atypical infant development* (pp. 361-384). Austin, TX: PRO-Ed.

Preschool Classroom Environments That Promote Communication

Michaelene M. Ostrosky

Ann P. Kaiser

Michaelene M. Ostrosky *(CEC Chapter #46) is a Doctoral Student and* **Ann P. Kaiser** *(CEC Chapter #69) is Professor, Department of Special Education, Peabody College of Vanderbilt University, Nashville, Tennessee.*

hildren learn what language *is* by learning what language can *do* (Bates, 1976; Hart, 1985). The function of language depends upon it's effects on the environment. An environment that contains few reinforcers and few objects of interest or meets children's needs without requiring language is *not* a functional environment for learning or teaching language.

Recent research suggests that environmental arrangement is an important strategy for teachers who want to promote communication in classrooms (Alpert, Kaiser, Ostrosky, & Hemmeter, 1987; Haring, Neetz, Lovinger, Peck, & Semmell, 1987). To encourage use of language, classrooms should be arranged so that there are materials and activities of interest to the children. In addition, teachers must mediate the environment by presenting materials in response to children's requests and other uses of language (Hart & Rogers-Warren, 1978). Creating such opportunities and consequences for language use through environmental arrangement can play a critical role in a child's language acquisition (Hart, 1985).

Both social and physical aspects of the environment set the occasion for communication (Rogers-Warren, Warren, & Baer, 1983). The physical environment includes the selection and arrangement of materials, the arrangement of the setting to encourage children's engagement, and scheduling of activities to enhance children's participation and appropriate behavior. The social environment includes the presence of responsive adults and children and the verbal and nonverbal social interactions that occur among the people in the environment. In addition, contingencies for language use, the availability of a communication partner, the degree to which adults preempt children's communicative attempts, and the affective style of the listener have an impact on children's language acquisition and production (Hemmeter, 1988).

As shown in Figure 1, the social and physical aspects of the environment are linked to communication when an adult mediates the physical environment in response to children's use of language. The adult links the child's language to the environment by ensuring that the child's communication attempts are functional and reinforced. As a mediator, the adult can use an incidental teaching process to model and prompt elaborated language in order to expand the child's current skills (Hart, 1985).

Environmental arrangement can encourage children to initiate language as a means of gaining access to materials and getting help. By providing the materials requested by a child, the adult serves the important function of specifically reinforcing that child's use of language. In addition, the environmental arrangement supports the adult in attending to the child's interest and communication attempts, thereby increasing the likelihood that the adult will respond to the child's interest and provide materials contingently (Haring et al., 1987).

Seven Strategies for Arranging the Environment

The basic goal of environmental arrangement is to increase children's interest in the environment as an occasion for communication. The environment is managed and arranged to promote requests and comments by children and to support language teaching efforts by adults. Using the environment to prompt language includes the following steps:

1. Focusing on making language a part of children's routines.
2. Providing access to interesting materials and activities.
3. Providing adult and peer models who will encourage children to use

From *Teaching Exceptional Children*, Summer 1991, pp. 6-10. Copyright © 1991 by The Council for Exceptional Children. Reprinted with permission of The Council for Exceptional Children.

language and respond to their attempts to do so.

4. Establishing a contingent relationship between access to materials or assistance and use of language.

The seven environmental strategies described here are designed to (a) increase the likelihood that children will show an interest in the environment and make communicative attempts and (b) increase the likelihood that the adult will prompt the use of language about things of interest to the children by providing clear and obvious *nonverbal* prompts for them to communicate. When the environment is arranged in this way, attractive materials and activities function as both discriminative stimuli and reinforcers for language use.

Interesting Materials

Materials and activities that children enjoy should be available in the environment. Young children are most likely to initiate communication about the things that interest them. Thus, increasing the likelihood of children's interest in the environment increases the opportunities for language use and teaching. Teachers usually know which toys and materials individual children prefer. However, a simple inventory of preferences can be taken at staff meetings or by systematically observing children's choices during free play. Parents often can provide information regarding their children's preferred toys and activities. Once toy preference has been determined, teachers can enhance interest in the environment by making such toys or materials available. For example, if a child enjoys bead stringing, various shaped and colored beads, noodles, and sewing spools could be made available. Identifying preferred activities and materials is especially important for a young child with severe disabilities. Variations in activities and materials must be carefully monitored to ensure that the child remains interested. For example, a child with severe disabilities who likes squeak toys may enjoy a variety of these toys but not like a Jack-in-the-box that makes a similar sound. Rotating the toys available at any given time is also a good way to make old toys more interesting; when they reappear they seem brand new!

Out of Reach

Placing *some* desirable materials within view but out of reach will prompt children to make requests in order to secure the materials. Materials may be placed on the shelves, in clear plastic bins, or simply across the table during a group activity to increase the likelihood that the children will request access to them either verbally or nonverbally. These requests create opportunities for language teaching, since when children request a specific material they are also specifying their reinforcers (Hart & Rogers-Warren, 1978). Thus, a teacher who prompts language and provides the requested material contingent on the child's response effectively reinforces that response. The effectiveness of this strategy can be enhanced by showing the children materials, naming the materials, and then waiting attentively for the children to make requests. During snack time or before a cooking activity, a teacher can prompt children to make requests by placing the cooking materials across the table from them. Children with severe disabilities might gain access to these materials by point-

Figure 1. Social and physical aspects of the environment set the occasion for communication as the adult serves as the mediator in response to children's use of language.

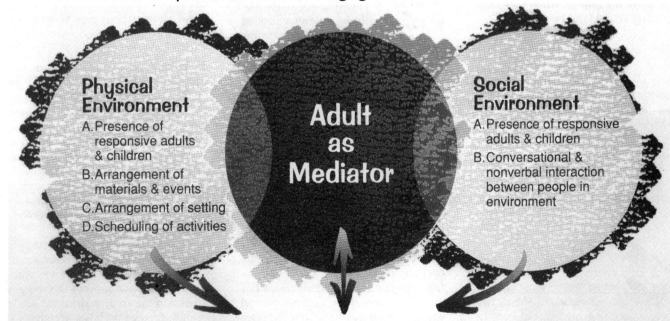

ing or eye gazing, whereas more skilled children might be encouraged to use signs, words, or even complete sentences. Teachers must be careful not to frustrate students by placing too many communicative demands on them. A balance of requesting materials and playing independently is important in every activity.

Inadequate Portions

Providing small or inadequate portions of preferred materials such as blocks, crayons, or crackers is another way to arrange the environment to promote communication. During an activity the children enjoy, an adult can control the amount of materials available so that the children have only some of the parts that are needed to complete the activity. When the children use the materials initially provided, they are likely to request more. Providing inadequate portions of an interesting and desirable material creates a situation in which children are encouraged by the arrangement of the physical environment to communicate their needs for additional materials. For example, during snack time, an adult can encourage requests by presenting small servings of juice or pieces of a cookie rather than a whole cookie. A child who enjoys watching the teacher blow bubbles can be encouraged to make requests if the teacher blows one or two bubbles and then waits for the child to request more.

When children initiate language with requests for more, the teacher has the opportunity to model and prompt more elaborate language as well as to provide functional consequences for the children's communicative attempts. For example:

Teacher: (Blows two bubbles and stops.)
Child: "More"
Teacher: "Blow more bubbles?"
Child: "Blow more."
Teacher: (Blows more bubbles)

Choice Making

There are many occasions when two or more options for activities or materials can be presented to children. In order to encourage children to initiate language, the choice should be presented nonverbally. Children may be most encouraged to make a choice when one of the items is preferred and the other is disliked. For example, the adult may hold two different toys (e.g., a big yellow dump truck and a small red block) and wait for the child to make a verbal or nonverbal request. If the child requests nonverbally, the adult has the option of prompting the child to verbalize ("Tell me what you want") or simply modeling a response for the child ("Yellow truck"). Children's verbal requests can be followed with expansions of their language ("You wanted the yellow truck") or models of alternative forms for requesting ("Yellow truck, please").

Assistance

Creating a situation in which children are likely to need assistance increases the likelihood that they will communicate about that need. The presence of attractive materials that require assistance to operate may encourage children to request help from adults or peers. A wind-up toy, a swing that a child needs help getting into, or an unopened bottle of bubbles are all examples of materials that can provide a nonverbal prompt to ask for help.

Sabotage

Setting up a "sabotage" by not providing all of the materials the children will need to complete a task (e.g., paints and water but no paintbrush following an instruction to paint), or by otherwise preventing them from carrying out an instruction, also will encourage them to make requests. This environmental strategy requires children o problem solve and indicate that something is wrong or missing. They must first determine what is needed, and this initial discovery may require prompts from an adult. The missing materials are cues for the children to communicate that something is not right or that additional materials are needed. Sabotage is an effective prompt for language when the cues are obvious and children's cognitive skills are sufficiently developed to make detection of the missing material easy and rapid. Sabotage should be carried out in a warm, engaging manner by the teacher; the episode should be brief and never frustrating to the child.

Silly Situations

The final environmental strategy is to create a need for children to communicate by setting up absurd or silly situations that violate their expectations. For example, an adult who playfully attempts to put a child's shoes on the adult's feet may encourage the child to comment on the absurd situation. During snack time, an adult can set up an absurd situation by placing a large piece of modeling clay or a colored block on a child's plate instead of a cracker, then waiting expectantly for the child to initiate a verbal or nonverbal request.

Children develop expectations for the ways things should be in everyday environments. They learn routines and expect that things will happen in a particular order. When something unexpected happens, they may be prompted to communicate. Of course, children must *have* expectations before the expectations can be violated. Thus, use of this strategy must be tailored to the individual skills of the children and to their familiar routines. For example, a child who always stores articles of clothing and materials in a specific "cubbie" will probably notice when an adult places a silly picture over it; a child who does not consistently use a specified "cubbie" would be unlikely to notice and respond to such a change in the environment.

Making the Strategies Effective

To make these seven environmental strategies work, the teacher must follow the student's lead. The teacher must notice what the child is interested in, establish joint attention on the topic of interest, and encourage the child to make communicative attempts. By monitoring the child's interest and identifying which materials and activities the child enjoys, an adult can select the ones that will best serve as reinforcers for language.

The nonverbal cues that accompany the environmental arrangement strategies should be faded over time so the child is responding more to things of interest in the environment and less to the adult's cues (Halle, Marshall, & Spradlin, 1979). For example, it may be necessary at first for teachers to shrug their shoulders, raise their eyebrows, and tilt their heads, while extending their hands containing different toys, in order to direct children's attention to the environment and to the opportunity for choice making. As children become more skilled at initiating requests, fewer and less obvious nonverbal prompts should be given.

The use of environmental strategies must be tailored to each child's cognitive level and responsiveness to the environment. For example, putting a coat on a child backward and waiting for the child to communicate that something is wrong may require additional prompts if the child is unable to problem solve at this level. For environmental strategies to be effective, they must be geared to each child's level and they must cue communicative responses that are emergent in the child's repertoire.

Conclusion

How adults respond to children's communication attempts when they are elicited by environmental arrangement is extremely important. Immediate feedback and access to the desired material or requested assistance, as well as a positive affective response, are essential consequences for communication attempts. As in all applications of naturalistic teaching processes, these episodes should be brief, positive, successful for the children, and designed to reinforce the children's use of language and their social engagement with adults (Hart & Rogers-Warren, 1978).

References

Alpert, C. L., Kaiser, A. P., Ostrosky, M. M., & Hemmeter, M. L. (1987, November). *Using environmental arrangement and milieu language teaching as interventions for improving the communication skills of nonvocal preschool children.* Paper presented at the National Early Childhood Conference on Children with Special Needs, Denver, CO.

Bates, E. (1976). Pragmatics and sociolinguistics in child language. In O. M. Moorehead & A. E. Moorehead (Eds.), *Normal and deficient child language* (pp. 411–463). Baltimore: University Park Press.

Halle, J., Marshall, A., & Spradlin, J. (1979). Time delay: A technique to increase language use and facilitate generalization in retarded children. *Journal of Applied Behavior Analysis, 12,* 431–439.

Haring, T. G., Neetz, J. A., Lovinger, L., Peck, C., & Semmel, M. I. (1987). Effects of four modified incidental teaching procedures to create opportunities for communication. *The Journal of the Association for Persons with Severe Handicaps, 12,*(3), 218–226.

Hart, B. M. (1985). Naturalistic language training strategies. In S. F. Warren & A. Rogers-Warren (Eds.), *Teaching functional language.* Baltimore: University Park Press.

Hart, B. M., & Rogers-Warren, A. K. (1978). Milieu language training. In R. L. Schiefelbusch (Ed.), *Language intervention strategies* (Vol. 2, pp. 193–235). Baltimore: University Park Press.

Hemmeter, M. L. (1988). *The effect of environmental arrangement on parent-child language interactions.* Unpublished master's thesis, Vanderbilt University, Nashville, TN.

Rogers-Warren, A. K., Warren, S. F., & Baer, D. M. (1983). Interactional bases of language learning. In K. Kernan, M. Begab, & R. Edgarton (Eds.), *Environments and behavior: The adaptation of mentally retarded persons.* Baltimore: University Park Press.

The development and dissemination of this paper were partially supported by Grant No. G008400663 from the Office of Special Education and Grant No. G008720107 from the National Institute for Disability and Rehabilitation Research. The authors are grateful to Cathy Alpert and Mary Louise Hemmeter for their contributions in the development of these environmental arrangement strategies.

Implementing Individualized Family Service Planning in Urban, Culturally Diverse Early Intervention Settings

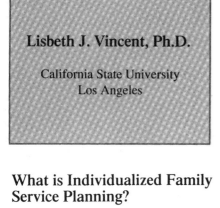

Lisbeth J. Vincent, Ph.D.

California State University
Los Angeles

What is Individualized Family Service Planning?

P.L. 99–457, the Individuals with Disabilities Education Act, formerly the Education of the Handicapped Act, modified the requirements of P.L. 94–142, the Education For All Handicapped Children Act, in such a way as to create new services for children with disabilities between three and six years of age and new incentives for states to develop a comprehensive system of services for children birth to three years of age and their families. Specifically the law directed states "to develop and implement a statewide, comprehensive, coordinated, multidisciplinary, interagency program of early intervention services for handicapped infants and toddlers and their families" (Section 671(b)). This section of the law is referred to as Part H and includes:

1. services must be provided under public supervision;

Photo by J. Brown/G. Simon

   Reprinted by permission from *Osers News in Print*, Summer 1992, pp. 29-33.

2. services must be provided at no cost, except where federal or state law allows;

3. services must meet the developmental needs of children across language, psychosocial, cognitive, self-help, and physical areas;

4. services must meet state as well as federal standards;

5. services must include family training and counseling speech pathology, occupational therapy, physical therapy, case management, medical evaluation and diagnosis, special education, and screening;

6. services must be provided by qualified personnel; and

7. services must be delivered in conformity with the goals and services outlined in the Individualized Family Service Plan (IFSP) (Trohanis, 1989).

No requirement of Part H has generated more discussion than the requirement that each child and family have an Individualized Family Service Plan (IFSP) in place. Developing the IFSP requires a family centered, family focused, family driven approach to service delivery. It obviates the requirement for the Individualized Educational Plan (IEP) which exists for preschool and school age children under Part B. The IFSP differs considerably in both spirit and intent from the IEP, which is solely child focused.

Two of the primary purposes seen by the developers of Part H were to "enhance the capacity of families to meet the needs of their infants and toddlers with handicaps" in addition to enhancing "the development of handicapped infants and toddlers and minimizing their potential for developmental delay." (Education of the Handicapped Act Amendments of 1986, Sec. 101(a)). As Johnson, McGonigel, and Kaufmann (1989) stated so clearly "the IFSP is a promise to children and **families**—a promise that their strengths will be recognized and built on, that their needs will be met in a way that is respectful of their beliefs and values, and that their hopes and aspirations will be encour-

aged and enabled (p.1)." Families would be truly equals in a partnership designed to maximize the development of the child and the functioning of the family (Vincent, 1985).

Translating Philosophy to Reality

Translating the spirit of Part H, as it relates to IFSP, into reality in early intervention programs all around the country is a major task. In the past five years, professionals and family members have realized that the task is to define the process that will underlie the implementation of IFSPs. IFSP is not a set of forms, but a process. The most important part of the process is the relationship that is developed between the family and the early intervention service provider. As one early intervention provider explained:

"As you begin this early intervention program, you will be asked to form a partnership with the professionals who will be working with your child and family. As with all good relationships, it takes time to build the trust, respect, and sharing that is the foundation of a successful partnership. To this end the Individualized Family Service Plan (IFSP) is not just paperwork or evaluations that must be done so that your child can be enrolled in a program, it is a partnership that will last the entire time your child and family are with the early intervention program" (Parents as Partners Project, 1988, p.1).

Trohanis (1989), Johnson, McGonigel and Kaufmann (1989) and Turnbull, R. (1989) have all summarized the required components of an IFSP as follows:

- family concerns, priorities, and resources assessment, along with a summary statement of a family's unique resources and

coping styles related to enhancing the development of the child;

- multidisciplinary child assessment along with a statement of a child's present level of functioning in psychosocial, cognitive, speech and language, and physical development;

- a statement of the major outcomes expected to be achieved for the child and the family;

- the criteria which will be used to evaluate whether the stated goals and objectives have been reached, along with a timeline for achieving goals and monitoring progress;

- a statement of the specific early intervention services to meet the identified and prioritized needs of the child and family as related to enhancing the child's development with the frequency, intensity, and method of service delivery;

- the expected dates for the initiation of services and their anticipated duration;

- when appropriate, a statement of medical and other services to which a child and family will be referred;

- the service coordinator/case manager from the most appropriate discipline who will be responsible for monitoring the ongoing process of delivering and evaluating services and coordinating with other agencies; and,

- the plans and steps which will be taken to prepare the child and family for transition to mandated public school funded services at three years of age, if such a referral is appropriate.

As can be seen by inspecting this list, the requirements of the IFSP process are extensive and require substantial training of existing early intervention program staffs as well as modifications in the preservice training of professionals from a wide variety of disciplines.

A review of preservice programs conducted by the North Carolina Research Institute on Personnel Preparation (Bailey, 1989) indicated that most training programs did not have an emphasis on infancy and had even less coursework devoted to a family focused approach to intervention. Whether the discipline surveyed was nursing, occupational therapy, speech and language therapy, special education, nutrition, medicine, social work, psychology, or physical therapy, the amount of academic coursework and practicum experience devoted to young children with risk factors or disabilities and their families was extremely limited, often encompassing less than twelve hours of coverage. Thus, there is a continuing need for inservice and continuing education activities in order to bring the skills of the early intervention practitioner into line with the stated requirements of P.L. 99–457 as it pertains to developing IFSPs in conjunction with the child's family.

Photo provided by L. Vincent

Families as Experts

Particularly as it relates to working with families who come from different cultures, speak different languages, and have different values than that of the early intervention professional, inservice training and monitoring is a necessity. The likelihood that early intervention professionals will be representative of diverse/minority cultures is **not** very high. The enrollment of ethnolinguistically diverse minority students in the departments or schools associated with the "helping professions" has been declining; the percentage of professional staff members who are from diverse or minority backgrounds is often less than five percent (Federal Bureau of Labor Statistics, 1987). Thus, in addition to learning about the requirements inherent in P.L. 99–457, early intervention program staffs often need to learn about different cultures and child rearing practices. Thus, training materials are needed that will help to ensure that the IFSP

process is implemented as *respectfully* and *effectively* with ethnolinguistically diverse/minority families as possible.

One purpose of the model demonstration project operated through the SHARE Center for Excellence in Early Intervention, Division of Special Education, California State University-Los Angeles is the development of these materials in conjunction with families and early intervention programs and staff who serve ethnolinguistically diverse/minority children and families. While sequences of activities and steps have been proposed to help guide the development of IFSPs, the use of these procedures with many different types of families has not yet been documented. Thus, although we have been able to describe the process to be followed, we have not established the parameters of its successful use with real families in real early intervention projects.

Johnson, McGonigel and Kaufmann (1989), in summarizing the work of the expert team, presented ten principles which underlie the IFSP process:

1. infants and toddlers are uniquely dependent on families for their survival and nurturance. This dependence neces-

sitates a family-centered approach to early intervention;

2. states and programs should define "family" in a way that reflects the diversity of family patterns and structures;

3. each family has its own structure, roles, values, beliefs, and coping styles, and respect for and acceptance of this diversity is the corner-stone of family-centered early intervention;

4. early intervention systems and strategies must reflect a respect for the racial, ethnic, and cultural diversity of families;

5. respect for family autonomy, independence, and decision making means that families must be able to choose the level and nature of their involvement with early intervention;

6. family/professional collaboration and partnerships are the keys to family-centered early intervention and to successful implementation of the IFSP process;

7. an enabling approach to working with families requires that professionals re-examine their traditional roles and practices and develop new practices when necessary—practices that

promote mutual respect and partnerships;

8. early intervention services should be flexible, accessible, and responsive to family needs;

9. early intervention services should be provided according to the normalization principle—that is, families should have access to services in as normal a fashion and environment as possible and that promote the integration of the child and family within the community; and,

10. no one agency or discipline can meet the diverse and complex needs of infants and toddlers with special needs and their families, therefore, a team approach to planning and implementing the IFSP is necessary (p.6).

Families are capable and competent decision-makers. Professionals provide assistance and support to families, rather than directions and solutions. The idea of using a family systems perspective in developing early intervention services is not a new one. As early as 1981, Foster, Berger, and McLean wrote about rethinking parent involvement activities from the perspective of the family, not that of the early intervention service provider. This family-centered approach is essential in our model project as we implement the IFSP process with ethnolinguistically diverse/minority families and their infants and toddlers with special needs.

As Vincent and Salisbury (1988), Fradd, Figueroa and Correa (1989), Vincent, Salisbury, Strain, McCormick and Tessier (1990), and Hanson, Lynch and Wayman (1990) have indicated, the face of the American family is changing rapidly. The majority of children entering public schools by the year 2010 will be of minority status. This change has already taken place in California. As of the 1989–90 school year, the state's students are 48.8 percent Anglo, 31.4 percent Hispanic, 8.9 percent African American, 7.5 percent Asian, 2.2 percent Philipino, .5 percent Pacific Islander, and .8 percent American Indi-

an or native Alaskan (Daily Breeze, 11/12/89). This cultural, racial, ethnic, and language diversity necessitates that professionals do not make assumptions about family structures or roles. Sensitivity to differences in values, priorities, and experiences is essential.

The approach to family service delivery must value family differences while working to empower the family. Overall, current wisdom and accepted practice in the field of early intervention is to use a family systems perspective to empower and strengthen families as they work to meet the needs of their infants and toddlers with special needs. Sensitivity to the impact of culture, language, and race is essential. Hanson, Lynch and Wayman (1990) pointed out that early intervention and cultural values interact in the following areas: views of children and childrearing, views of disability and its causation, views of change and intervention, views of medicine and healing, views of family and family roles, and language and communication styles.

One task in our model project is to examine processes, procedures, and forms which currently exist to plan, implement, and record the IFSP. Family members from diverse backgrounds have been hired as experts to assist and guide us in this process. We have seen that particularly the initial steps in the IFSP process must receive careful systematic attention. The development of rapport and a relationship with the family is dramatically affected by cultural experiences and expectations, including previous experiences with the early intervention service delivery system. In our community, the average family of a child with a disability who is between two and three years of age is working with five different agencies to meet the needs of the child and family. This necessitates many visits and contacts with multiple professionals. Often these visits are not coordinated and families are asked to provide the same information over and over again. Eligibility is not the same across agen-

cies and families often find themselves denied services which they believe their children need. In our community, a survey conducted by the Los Angeles Early Intervention Project (a county-wide project responsible for planning for the implementation of Part H), found that one third of parents were not able to obtain the services they believed their children need. The required identification of family concerns and priorities is often overlooked. Instead, families told us that agencies and professionals decided what was right for them and their children. Documenting the concerns and priorities of Hispanic families has been a major focus of the model project.

The model proposed for our project involved providing families with choices on how to participate in the family identification of concerns, priorities, and resources (CPR) as required by Part H. The CPR assessment model was based on the premise that families can identify their concerns, priorities, and resources using a variety of techniques, from structured interviews and questionnaires to story telling techniques. Families should be given the choice of method.

We have also seen the need to explore techniques that do not involve professionals as the center of the information gathering process. We are utilizing parents as experts in the area of identification of concerns, priorities, and transition planning. We also have come to realize the vital role that paraprofessionals play in the early intervention service delivery system. Often, the paraprofessional has built a strong relationship based on trust with the family. The IFSP process should recognize, respect, and capitalize on this relationship.

Finally, we are coming to accept the IFSP form as a valuable tool. While true that the purpose of the form is to record the process, it communicates a set of beliefs about families and systems based on how it is structured and implemented. We have a small group of parents, professionals, and paraprofessionals working on a culturally sensitive, family friendly form. Piloting and refining the form and the training package will be a major focus of our third year of the model project.

Summary

Overall, we have learned a great deal. We believe even more strongly in the need for family-centered early intervention services and in the ability of families to be decision makers in theirs and their children's lives. We see a strong need for family members to be in leadership roles in policy and program implementation. We see a continuing need for personnel training related to cultural diversity, particularly in the area of building relationships. We believe that families and paraprofessionals as well as professionals must be included as partners in these training efforts.

References

Bailey, D.B. (1989). Issues and directions in preparing professionals to work with young handicapped children and their families. In J.J. Gallagher, P.L. Trohanis & R.M. Clifford (Eds.), *Policy Implementation and PL 99–457* (pp. 97-113). Baltimore, MD: Paul H. Brookes.

Bailey, D.B., Winton, P.J., Rouse, L. & Turnbull, A.P. (1990). Family goals in infant intervention: Analysis and issues. *Journal of Early Intervention.*

Daily Breeze (11–12–89). Copley Newspapers, Inc. Los Angeles, CA.

Dunst, C.J., Trivette, C. & Deal, A. (1988). *Enabling and empowering families: Principles and guidelines for practice.* Cambridge, MA: Brookline Books.

Federal Bureau of Labor Statistics (1988). Reported in *Occupational Outlook Handbook.* Washington, D.C.: U.S. Government Printing Office.

Foster, M., Berger, M. & McLean, M. (1981). Rethinking a good idea: A reassessment of parent involvement. *Topics in Early Childhood Special Education, 1(3),* 55–56.

Fradd, S.H., Figueroa, R.A. & Correa, V.I. (1989). Meeting the multi-cultural needs of Hispanic students in special education. *Exceptional Children,* 56(2), 102–05.

Hanson, M.J., Lynch, E.W. & Wayman, K.I. (1990). Honoring the cultural diversity of families when gathering data. *Topics in Early-Childhood Special Education,* 10(1), 112–131.

Johnson, B.H., McGonigel, M.J. & Kaufmann, R.K. (1989). *Guidelines and recommended practices for the individualized family service plan.* NEC*TAS & ACCH.

Klein, M.D., Briggs, M.H. & Huffman, R.N. (1985). Facilitating caregiver infant communication. California State University-Los Angeles.

Parents as Partners Project (1988). Preparing for the individualized family service plan. Albuquerque, New Mexico, Alta Mira Specialized Family Services.

Salisbury, C. & Vincent, L.J. (1991). Criteria of the next environment and integration: Best educational practice. *Topics in Early Childhood Special Education.*

Trohanis, P.L. (1989) An introduction to PL 99–457and the national policy agenda for serving young children with special needs and their families. In Gallagher, J.J., Trohanis, P.L. &. Clifford, R.M (Eds.) *Policy implementation and PL 99–457* (pp. 1–19). Baltimore, MD: Paul H. Brookes.

Turnbull, A.P. & Turnbull, H.R. (1986). *Families, professionals, and exceptionalities: A special partnership.*Columbus, OH: Charles E. Merrill.

Turnbull, H.R. (1989). Summary of the federal regulations regarding the individualized family service plan. Beach Center on Families, University of Kansas, Lawrence.

Vincent, L.J. (1985). Family relationships. In *Equals in the Partnership.* Washington, D.C.: National Center for Clinical Infant Programs.

Vincent, L.J. & Salisbury, C. (1988). Changing economic and social influences on family involvement. *Topics in Early Childhood Special Education,* 8(1), 48–59.

Vincent, L.J., Salisbury, C., Strain, P., McCormick, C. & Tessier, A. (in press). An ecological-behavioral approach to early intervention. In S. Meisels & J. Shonkoff (Eds.), *Handbook of early intervention.* Cambridge: University Press.

Parental Feelings

*The Forgotten Component When Working
with Parents of Handicapped Preschool Children*

**Richard M. Gargiulo
and Stephen B. Graves**

*Richard M. Gargiulo is Professor,
Department of Special Education, The
University of Alabama at Birmingham.
Stephen B. Graves is Assistant Pro-
fessor, Department of Curriculum and
Instruction.*

E ducators are becoming increasingly aware of the importance of parental participation
in the education of young handicapped children. The idea of involving parents in the educational
decision-making process is experiencing a rebirth due to the recent
enactment of the preschool mandate P.L. 99-457, the Education of
the Handicapped Act Amendments of 1986. This federal initiative directs local education agencies
to serve children, ages 3 to 5, who
are developmentally delayed or
"at-risk" for future problems.
Youngsters who, for instance, were
born premature, manifest Down
syndrome, suffer from fetal alcohol
syndrome or have parents who are
mentally retarded will be provided
early educational experiences.

Like its predecessor P.L. 94-142,
parental involvement constitutes a
significant element of this new
legislation. Although both of these
enactments recognize parents'
rights to be involved and actively
participate, schools by and large
have exhibited little sustained effort
in working with parents or solicit-
ing their assistance in the instructional process (Schulz, 1987). This

is truly unfortunate, for research
suggests that parent participation
can oftentimes be the difference
between program success and
failure (Mandell & Fiscus, 1981;
Swick, 1987).

An Arena for Conflict
The education of the preschool
child with special needs does not
fall within the exclusive jurisdiction
of the early childhood professional;
parents are an important and necessary part of the team (Graves &
Gargiulo, 1989). Yet, according to
Gallagher and his colleagues
(Gallagher, Beckman, & Cross,
1983), the history of parent-professional relationships is gloomy
and counterproductive. Barriers
frequently exist between parents
and educators. These obstacles to
partnerships may result from actions on the part of professionals.
Some workers consider parents
more of a nuisance than a resource
(Seligman & Seligman, 1980).
Teachers have occasionally blamed
parents for causing, or at least not
preventing, their child's disability
(Seligman, 1979). Gargiulo (1985)
observed that some professionals
are opposed to parent involvement

From *Childhood Education*, Spring 1991, pp. 176-178. Reprinted by permission of Richard M. Gargiulp and Stephen B.
Graves and the Association for Childhood Education International, 11141 Georgia Avenue, Suite 200, Wheaton, MD.
Copyright © 1991 by the Association.

and, therefore, are reluctant to share responsibilities and allow meaningful participation.

Parents frequently view their interactions with professionals as adversarial. Roos (1978) asserted that professionals have mishandled parents. Perhaps the most demeaning and devastating trait of professional people, according to Schulz, is the tendency to deny parents' expertise and knowledge about their own child (1987, pp. 117-118).

In all fairness, impediments to collaboration can be a product of the parents' behavior. Professionals do not have a monopoly on negative attitudes (Schulz, 1987). Parents, on occasion, can be demanding, uncooperative, overly dependent, defensive and hostile. Some parents criticize professionals for not recognizing their child's disability earlier, while others have even accused the professional of causing the handicap (Gargiulo, 1985). Kraft and Snell (1980) identified four types of parents frequently encountered by school personnel: the blame-oriented parent who regularly calls attention to shortcomings in the school; the invisible parent who takes no initiative and fails to respond to messages; the supercooperative parent who continually abuses the teacher's time; and finally, the pseudoexpert parent who knows more about education than the teacher.

Given this arena of mutual distrust, antagonism and suspicion, it is easy to understand how relationships between professionals and parents fail to develop.

Understanding Parental Reaction to Exceptionality

Fortunately, in many situations, parental status has changed from one of mere recipient of services to that of active participant. In addition, there have been recent appeals for early childhood professionals to view parents as program partners (Graves & Gargiulo, 1989;

Peterson, 1987). Although currently professionals are more sensitive to the contributions of parents, one critical component is frequently absent from discussions on working with parents of exceptional children. Rarely is consideration given to how parents *feel* about being the mother or father of a child with a disability. Parental reaction to exceptionality can significantly influence the parent-professional relationship. Many of the behaviors and actions exhibited by parents, such as those identified herein, are the direct result of the parents' interpretation of what exceptionality means to them and their son or daughter.

> **When professionals are able to demonstrate empathy as well as respect for the parents' perspective of exceptionality, misinterpretation of parental actions diminishes.**

Parental reaction to a handicapping condition is highly individualistic. Each parent will respond in his or her own way. Helping professionals will, therefore, encounter parental conduct that varies along a continuum of emotional responses. Stage models, such as those developed by Opirhory and Peters (1982) and Gargiulo (1985), are useful for explaining parental behavior. Workers, Gargiulo (1985) contends, who view feelings such as denial, anger, grief, guilt and shame as necessary, normal and perfectly legitimate human responses to a crisis are in a good position to understand parents

and effectively interact with them.

When professionals are able to demonstrate empathy as well as respect for the parents' perspective of exceptionality, misinterpretation of parental actions diminishes. Parents who refuse early intervention services, fail to keep appointments or seek second opinions, for example, should not be condemned or criticized. Rather, these behaviors should be seen as natural and an indicator of the parents' degree of acceptance of their preschooler with special needs. The parents' level of involvement and extent of participation is a gauge of their location on the acceptance continuum.

Stage models are beneficial for understanding parental responses to exceptionality. Yet, the needs of the parents reflect not only their ability to cope but also the developmental needs of the child (Schulz, 1987). Professionals must be cognizant of this and customize their interactions with parents to meet these changing needs. For example, the demand placed upon the professional who has the responsibility of informing parents that their son or daughter is handicapped is most likely different from the counsel required of a teacher who is dealing with parental fears and concerns as the youngster makes the transition from a preschool program to public school.

Parents will also recycle their feelings. Stages that were previously navigated will reappear and demand attention. This review of prior feelings is usually in reaction to specific events in the life of the child or the family, such as the beginning of a new school year or the birth of a sibling. Recapitulation is normal. Professionals should be prepared for it. Additionally, both parents may not necessarily be at the same stage of acceptance. As noted previously, exceptionality frequently means different things to mothers and fathers. Individuality of response should be accepted as well as respected. Not only do parents commonly traverse the continuum separately, they do so according to their own timetable.

Suggestions for Working with Parents

The following list of nonprioritized hints is designed to facilitate an effective and meaningful relationship with parents of young children with handicaps.

■ Explain terminology. Many parents have no previous experience with exceptionality. This may be their first exposure to a disability label. The parents' conceptualization of cerebral palsy or mental retardation is most likely different from that of the professional.

■ Parents will frequently exhibit negative feelings when confronted with the news that their son or daughter is handicapped. Workers need to send a message that it is okay to have these feelings. They need to be acknowledged and then understood.

■ Teachers must listen! If one wishes to discover the parents' agenda and wishes concerning their child, active listening is of critical importance. Effective helpers want to know what the parent is thinking as well as feeling.

■ Use a two-step process when initially informing parents that their child requires special educational services. After sharing diagnostic information, it is strongly suggested that professionals allow parents time to comprehend and absorb what they have been told. The parents' affective concerns must be dealt with prior to proceeding with matters such as intervention recommendations, treatment regimens and strategies or duration of services. These issues should be addressed in a follow-up interview as the parents' emotional state permits.

■ Keep parents informed. Use a variety of two-way communication techniques. Be as positive as possible when discussing a child's performance. Demonstrate respect, concern and a sincere desire to cooperate.

■ Be accountable. If you agree to assume certain responsibilities or gather information for the parent, be certain to follow through. Accountability demonstrates to the parents that they can depend on you. Trust, consistency and dependability significantly increase the chances for an effective relationship.

■ Recognize that diverse family structures and parenting styles will influence parent participation. In some circumstances, the responsible or concerned individual may not be the child's biological parent. Therefore, respect the parent's right to choose his or her level of involvement. Turnbull and Turnbull (1982) urge professionals to tolerate a range of parent participation matched to needs and interest.

A Final Thought

Today, parent participation is a right, not a privilege. While professionals may encounter parents with so much emotional and attitudinal baggage that it prohibits real dialogue with them (Gorham, 1975), it is the professional's job to find ways, rather than excuses, of involving parents (DeWert & Helsel, 1985). Successful early intervention efforts require that parents and professionals collaborate as equals. The ultimate beneficiaries of this partnership will be our young children with special needs.

References

DeWert, M., & Helsel, E. (1985). The Helsel family today. In A. Turnbull & H. Turnbull (Eds.), *Parents speak out* (2nd ed.) (pp. 101-106). Columbus, OH: Charles Merrill.

Gallagher, J., Beckman, P., & Cross, A. (1983). Families of handicapped children: Sources of stress and its amelioration. *Exceptional Children, 50,* 10-19.

Gargiulo, R. (1985). *Working with parents of exceptional children.* Boston: Houghton Mifflin.

Gorham, K. (1975). A lost generation of parents. *Exceptional Children, 41,* 521-525.

Graves, S., & Gargiulo, R. (1989). Parents and early childhood professionals as program partners: Meeting the needs of the preschool exceptional child. *Dimensions, 17,* 23-24.

Kraft, S., & Snell, M. (1980). Parent-teacher conflict: Coping with parental stress. *The Pointer, 24,* 29-37.

Mandell, C., & Fiscus, E. (1981). *Understanding exceptional people.* St. Paul, MN: West.

Opirhory, G., & Peters, G. (1982). Counseling intervention strategies for families with less than the perfect newborn. *The Personnel and Guidance Journal, 60,* 451-455.

Peterson, N. (1987). *Early intervention for handicapped and at-risk children.* Denver: Love.

Roos, P. (1978). Parents of mentally retarded children—misunderstood and mistreated. In A. Turnbull & H. Turnbull (Eds.), *Parents speak out* (pp. 13-27). Columbus, OH: Charles Merrill.

Schulz, J. (1987). *Parents and professionals in special education.* Boston: Allyn & Bacon.

Seligman, M. (1979). *Strategies for helping parents of exceptional children.* New York: Free Press.

Seligman, M., & Seligman, P. (1980). The professional's dilemma: Learning to work with parents. *Exceptional Parent, 10,* 11-13.

Swick, K. (1987). *Perspectives on understanding and working with families.* Champaign, IL: Stipes.

Turnbull, A., & Turnbull, H. (1982). Parent involvement in the education of handicapped children: A critique. *Mental Retardation, 20,* 115-122.

Guiding Behavior

Guiding children's behavior actually starts well before teachers and children interact. It begins by preparing the room and scheduling activities before the children have arrived. Teachers who learn the basics of preplanning find that they spend less time resolving conflicts while they are teaching. Careful attention to the details of a daily schedule can help teachers avoid behavior problems.

Preparation is vital to effective guidance, but conflict is inevitable. As children move through a schedule of activities, they are likely to be in conflict with each other. Teachers can facilitate the resolution of conflict by teaching children to settle their problems with each other. Settling problems takes skill on the children's part, skill that must be taught and practiced during the course of the day.

For early childhood educators, discipline means guidance. It involves the following steps: (1) understanding typical child development and examining one's attitudes about children; (2) redirecting and modifying undesirable behavior; (3) modeling and explaining more acceptable, appropriate, or mature behavior; and (4) using reasoning with children and teaching them verbal skills for peer interaction. Discipline, in this connotation, means steadily building self-control so children can develop positive self-esteem, respect for the needs of others, and gradually move toward healthy independence and problems-solving skills that they may draw upon in future situations.

The emphasis of this approach to guiding behavior is positive, since punishment is not the goal. A positive approach allows teachers to avoid two extremes; putting pressure on children or giving in to them. Both of these extremes have negative consequences for everyone involved. Children may react to pressure by challenging the teacher's decision. And when a teacher gives in, the teacher loses the children's respect. By teaching children to take responsibility for their own behavior, teachers are expressing respect and kindness.

Guiding behavior is a two-way process. Not all of the work is done by the teacher. The children have their own work to do in behavior management. They are practicing the skill of self-control. This skill involves cooperating with adults, taking turns, channeling anger, and delaying gratification. This is hard work for young children because it means learning internal standards of conduct. Behavior management is based in the emotions, which go through highs and lows, so loss of control can be a problem for some children. Gaining control is a major task of early childhood.

In devising a plan for guiding behavior, a teacher is concerned with both validating children's feelings and heightening their awareness of the feelings of others. It takes careful communication to guide children in negotiating problems while affirming all parties. When to intervene in a situation or when to allow natural consequences takes thought and skill. If teachers understand the causes of frustration and aggression in children, such as unnecessary waiting, crowding, insufficient play materials, or poor curricular planning, they can make changes so that children's self-esteem and control are supported in healthy ways.

As with all areas of early childhood education, a high-quality, effective plan for guiding behavior does not arrive prepackaged for the teacher's immediate use. Guiding and disciplining is hard work, requiring careful attention to individual children and differing situations. It is largely a mental and verbal process, teaching young children to negotiate problems. Mastery of authentic and humane guidance techniques takes time, reflecting on ethical principles, refining strategies, and seeking the best emotional climate.

Looking Ahead: Challenge Questions

Before school even begins, what arrangements should be made to ease behavior management once the children arrive?

How do teachers enable children to analyze situations before problems occur?

What communication skills are helpful to use in assisting young children to negotiate problems?

During the preschool years, what abilities are involved in developing self-control?

How can teachers promote self-control in early childhood settings?

What are the behaviors that might indicate a young child is under pressure?

Why do teachers often find classroom discipline to be their greatest challenge?

Unit 4

Managing the Early Childhood Classroom

Sandra Crosser

Sandra Crosser taught kindergarten and primary children for 12 years. She has operated a private preschool since 1978 and is an assistant professor of education at Ohio Northern University.

Mrs. Green's kindergarten was a zoo. She planned lessons thoroughly and was creative in her choices of age-appropriate activities. She provided a variety of materials and truly cared for the children. Mrs. Green's kindergarten remained a zoo, however. The teachers gossiped about it, the principal thought it might get better in time, the parents blamed it on Rowdy Ralph, and Mrs. Green contemplated the merits of a career as a mortician.

What was it that confounded Mrs. Green's best efforts? What factor could she have neglected? Was she just not cut out to be a teacher?

Successful teachers know that the arrangement and management of the early childhood classroom have a direct effect on the kinds of behaviors children exhibit as they live and work together. The difference between chaos and an orderly atmosphere that facilitates learning depends in great part on how the teacher prepares the environment. That preparation involves what happens before school begins, when children arrive and depart,

First of all, arrange your room to maximize possibilities for satisfying play, optimal supervision, and a safe, orderly environment.

when schedule transitions occur, when children interact freely with equipment and materials, and when conflicts arise. Taken together, "BASIC" classroom management includes carefully preplanning:

Before school begins
Arrival and departure times
Schedule transitions
Interactions with equipment and materials
Conflict management

The practices recommended in this article have been standard among skilled preschool, kindergarten, and first grade teachers for several generations. If any or many of them are new to you, you may want to implement them to create a more effective setting in which young children can learn through play and projects.

Before school begins

Before children are in the classroom, the successful teacher carefully plans the physical arrangement of the room and the routines for using it. The following considerations are important because they can facilitate movement, inhibit rowdiness, enhance safety, and invite meaningful exploration.

Although learning through self-selected play experiences is the cornerstone of developmentally sound early childhood programs, children may occasionally need to come together for large group meetings. Those meetings should be called sparingly and kept short so children are not required to sit and participate for long periods of time.

1. Is there an open area large enough for the entire group to meet together? Can children sit comfortably without being crowded? Is there enough room for large muscle movements? Are there attractive nuisances located so close to the area that children will be distracted during group meetings? Are there electric outlets close enough for using tape recorders and record players? If children are to sit in a circle or other pattern, are there physical indicators such as tape or carpet squares to show

From *Young Children*, Vol. 47, No. 2, January 1992, pp. 23-29. Reprinted by permission of the publisher, the National Association for the Education of Young Children.

children where to sit? If children are expected to bring chairs to group meetings, will they be shown how to carry a chair safely across the room?

2. Does the physical arrangement of work centers allow for quiet areas to be located away from noisier activities? Puzzles, puppets, books, and other quiet activities need to be set apart from the workbench, block, and dramatic play centers. Hollow wooden blocks and housekeeping/dress-up areas facilitate creative interaction when placed close together.

Some centers, such as art, cooking, painting, and water play require frequent cleanups. Are they located near a sink and sponges or paper towels? If no sink is available, can a baby bathtub or bucket of water be substituted?

3. Are centers arranged within the classroom so that they are defined by low boundaries, such as room dividers, shelves, tables, floor mats, or tape? Can the teacher see over and around equipment so that all children are visible at all times?

Are centers arranged to avoid the "hallway effect"? Long, open spaces and runways invite take-off and flight. Room arrangement should suggest walking, rather than running.

4. Are most materials located where children can reach them wihout asking the teacher for help? Can children obtain their own paint shirts, pencils, crayons, paper, yarn, and tissues?

5. Is there a place for everything? Children need the security of organization. Like things belong together, placed low within reach of the shortest arms. Cleanup is easier to manage and safety is easier to maintain when there is one basket for crayons and another for markers, a file box for records, and a rack for scissors. Sectioned cardboard boxes divide kinds and colors of paper. Things to go home belong in each child's mailbox or school bag. Wastepaper baskets

are strategically located where most often needed. Tools hang on pegboard where shapes of hammers and drills indicate placement. Games belong on the game shelf, and building toys each have their own tubs for small pieces. A box of paper sits by the typewriter. Puzzles have individual trays or racks. Dress-up clothes belong on hooks or in a suitcase. A shoe rack holds high heels, and a jewelry box contains gems. Cupboard shelves hold the tea set, and flatware is sorted in a divider tray. There are no toy boxes for indiscriminate dumping (Schilmoeller & Amundrud, 1987). When the child is helped to organize her world, she learns classification skills and a sense of satisfaction from being independent and self-sufficient. An orderly environment can eliminate potential behavior problems.

6. The busier and more involved the children are, the less likely they are to exhibit behavior problems. Is there enough equipment for everyone, but not so much to choose from that the child becomes overwhelmed? Young children can be overstimulated to the point that they move aimlessly from one center to another without becoming involved in any one activity (Shapiro, 1975); therefore, it seems wise to provide basic equipment at first, adding variety and alternatives on a regular basis. The unexpected challenges the child's imagination as the teacher creates variety throughout the school year. For example, one day the water table may contain bubbles and egg beaters. Another day it may have food color and rubber canning rings. Nuts to crack or Cheerios to "cook" offer new

possibilities for the housekeeping corner, keeping children so involved that discipline needs are minimized. Possibilities for enhancing basic equipment are endless.

7. Are routines set? Do children know how to handle routines? What are children expected to do when they take off their coats? How will attendance be taken; can children do it themselves? Is there a routine for giving the teacher messages from home? Is there a set procedure for using the bathroom? Can more than one child go at one time? Is there a sign on the door indicating whether or not the bathroom is in use? How will thirsty children get a drink? What will be the routine if a snack is served? Is there a typical schedule for the day so that children will generally know what happens next? Do we go outdoors to play after snack, or do we have a story? Establishing policies for routines eliminates many possible conflicts and frustrations (Brophy, 1983).

Arrival and departure times

Arrivals. How children's arrival is managed can, and usually does, set the tone for the entire day. The successful teacher meets and greets children as they arrive, whether singly or in a group. Physical presence of the teacher can prevent excessive silliness, tears, and escalating voices. A routine for handling wraps and boots should involve the children in doing as much for themselves as they can without waiting for the teacher's help.

The children need to know what

Thoughtfully established routines are the vaccination against classroom chaos. Too much waiting begets wiggle, giggle, squirm, and poke.

---

is expected upon entering the classroom. Do they indicate attendance by placing name cards in a basket? Do they hang up school bags? Do they select a free choice activity? Is that choice limited? What should be done with any items brought from home?

Quite frequently young children are expected to wait for everyone to arrive in order for some sort of opening exercise to formally start the day. Perhaps children should not be expected to spend valuable time waiting to start the day's activities. Waiting begets wiggle, giggle, squirm, and poke. If children are encouraged to go right to play upon entering the classroom, many potential discipline problems can simply be avoided.

Departures. Departure, as well as arrival, should follow set routines. Departure routines may begin with a final group meeting to evaluate the day's activities. Plans for making tomorrow even better than today help children see ways to make choices and increase control over their own lives.

The successful teacher remains in control throughout preparation for leave-taking. She plans for quick and easy ways to distribute notices or work to take home. If each child has an individual mailbox or school bag, time waiting for paper-passing can be avoided, along with the disruptive behavior that accompanies that waiting. Thoughtfully established routines are the vaccination against classroom chaos.

Routines might include how many children go to get their coats at one time. When children are moved in herds, stampedes occur.

Early childhood teachers frequently use some sort of good-bye song or poem to end the day pleasantly and calmly when children are all ready to go home. Such practices let children know that the day has officially ended. More important, at the conclusion of the song or poem the teacher is left

with a quiet group of children to whom she can address individual praise, recognition, comments, pats, encouragement, smiles, or winks as they file past and out the door. Kindergarten and first grade children most often end the school day all at the same time with a group dismissal. Day care or preschool dismissals, however, frequently involve individual pickups. In either case, the teacher needs to individually acknowledge the departure of each child. Through thoughtful planning, the teacher can transform the potential hassle of last-minute rush into building one-on-one relationships.

Schedule transitions

Effective classroom managers seem to have a sense of timing very much like a comedian's. They sense when it is time to stop an activity early, when to let things continue longer than usual, and how to move gracefully from one topic to the next. They entice children by subtly capturing their attention, by intriguing them.

Capturing children's attention

Finger plays, rhymes, and action songs can be extremely useful methods of intriguing children who have become inattentive or who need to be brought together for any purpose. For decades, finger plays have been part of the early childhood classroom because they are so useful. Children love the fun and challenge and are curious to see if they can make their fingers do what the teacher's are doing. When the finger play has been completed, children are quiet and ready to listen. The teacher must seize the moment to quickly give directions or move on to the next scheduled activity. The secret is in the timing. If the teacher hesitates for even a moment, attention is once again lost. Short action songs can

be used in the same manner as finger plays. Both can be learned from source books available in libraries or from educational supply houses. The teacher needs to memorize a variety of these transition facilitators in order to have a well-stocked repertoire at her disposal. Children like to repeat rhymes and songs they know, but by adding new ones to the old, teachers keep interest piqued.

Having to stop one activity to move to something else can be very disconcerting for young children. Preparing children for the transition permits them to finish what they are doing, or at least recognize that they will need to stop soon. The teacher might tell children that it is almost cleanup time, or that it will soon be time to stop. Children then are mentally prepared to change gears.

Appropriate signals. Signals can be useful to cue transition times if used sparingly; used too frequently they lose their effectiveness. A designated song played on the piano or record player can signal cleanup time. A bell, a sign, a hand signal, or a flick of the lights can signal time to gather for a story. Signals should be low-key so as not to startle or frighten. A tinkling triangle has the same effect as a loud whistle, without the accompanying shrillness. Shrill or loud noises tend to increase the overall noise level in the classroom, just as an increase in the volume of the teacher's voice tends to increase the volume of the children's voices. Shouting is neither appropriate nor effective. Whispering can be more of an attention-getter than yelling. A low, calm adult voice has a soothing effect, by itself reducing the overall noise level.

Moving groups of children

Frequently, transitions involve moving groups of children some distance. Because small groups tend to move in a more orderly fashion than large groups, the teacher might call for all children with buckle shoes, then tie shoes, then velcro shoes. Eye color, hair color, beginning letters of names, pattern of clothing (plain, striped, solid), color of socks, and other categories are possibilities.

Standing in line and walking in line are regimentations natural to ducks, not children. On occasion, however, children need to move in organized lines for purposes of safety. If children are expected to form a line, they need to know how to do it. Children can line up as a sandwich with two children desig-

---

A teacher can redirect restless energies by stimulating and modeling purposeful play. The teacher's invitation to play "bus" leads to problem-solving: "How can we make seats for the bus?"

---

nated as pieces of bread, and the other children choosing to become good things to eat in between. Pickles, mustard, and bologna must stay in the sandwich. Lining up as a parade or train can also help teach the concept of a line.

Moving the line through hallways can be accomplished by having the first child lead to a stopping place while the remainder of the children pass in front of the teacher. The teacher then designates the next stopping place, and the process is repeated until the group reaches its destination.

When young children walk in strange or potentially dangerous areas, the teacher must exercise a great degree of care to keep them together and away from traffic or other danger. Partners may be chosen for holding hands as they walk, or children may walk holding individual knots on a long rope. Clothesline rope works well, with knots tied at least fifteen to twenty inches apart so children can walk comfortably.

At journey's end. Upon reaching the destination, children must be told what to do *before* they enter the area. Are they to bounce a ball with a partner in the gym, sit at a table in the art room, or run two times around the yellow line on the playground? If children do not know what to do when they enter a new space, they will explore it on their own, making it difficult for the teacher to maintain a controlled situation. Large, open spaces, such as gyms and playgrounds, invite large muscle movements. Children need to know what they are expected to do, therefore, before they enter such spaces.

Interactions with equipment and materials

Most of the young child's day should be invested in purposeful play. The teacher provides for active engagement with materials and equipment that individual children choose for themselves as they explore their world. The free choice play or work time is a vital part of the early childhood program, but it can become a time for horseplay and haphazard activity if not properly managed. The teacher can, and should, shape interactions with equipment and materials to

• stimulate learning possibilities;
• protect children;
• protect equipment; and
• maintain a peaceful learning environment.

Seven things to think about before school begins:

1. Group time area
2. Location of centers
3. Shapes and boundaries of centers
4. Accessibility of materials
5. Orderly organization of materials and equipment
6. Level of stimulation
7. Routines of classroom life

Questioning and commenting

The skillfully placed question or comment can stimulate learning and deter rowdiness. The teacher needs to move around the room, challenging children to look at different ways of using materials to solve problems (Day, 1975) and acknowledging them for constructive efforts (Katz & Chard, 1989).

"How else could you do it?" "Which container holds the most sand? How can you prove it?" "How did you paint the brown color when we have no brown paint?" "Why do you think your block building fell down? How could you change it next time so it won't fall down?" "I see you are working very hard." The moving teacher manages the early childhood environment through physical presence and by being there to ask the challenging question or make the encouraging comment.

Redirecting play

At times the work/play free choice time reveals children moving aimlessly. Some children have difficulty planning a meaningful activity. At those times, the teacher may observe the need to play *with* children to suggest new play ideas and redirect behavior. In playing with children, the teacher stimulates and models purposeful play without dominating the situation. For example, the teacher may invite a group that has become restless to play "bus" or "restaurant." The teacher asks questions such as, "How can we make seats for the bus?" "Do we need tickets?" "Where is the bus going?" The teacher engages in the play long enough to establish purposefulness, then moves on. Positive redirection can, in this way, replace nagging and similar negative teacher behaviors.

Setting limits with equipment and materials

Some controls need to be placed on use of equipment and materials for safety purposes. The early childhood teacher needs to make rules for the safe use of tools, scissors, blocks, sand, and climbing or swinging apparatus. Children should be expected to follow the rules if they choose to use the equipment. When safety rules are broken, the child needs to be reminded that the teacher is worried about his safety and that repeated misuse will mean that he will no longer be allowed to choose that particular piece of equipment.

Because blocks and dramatic play seem to be favorites of many children, teachers frequently see the need to limit the number of children in each of these areas at one time. A kitchen timer may be used to ensure that each child has a chance to participate. Children can choose centers by placing a name card on a hook or a sign that indicates the maximum number of children to use a center at one time.

Conflict resolution

Preventative classroom management can eliminate many potential discipline problems. Conflict is a natural part of living and working together in groups. It is good that conflicts arise in the early childhood classroom because it is only through facing conflicts that children can learn the skills necessary to resolve real-life problems. Problem and conflict resolution skills are not automatically part of the child's repertoire; they are skills that must be taught and practiced, just as counting or reading skills must be taught and practiced before they become automatic (Brophy, 1985).

Teaching conflict resolution

When conflicts arise, the teacher can facilitate resolution by helping children to identify the choices they have and the variety of behavior options they could employ to resolve the problem. When a child has made an inappropriate choice, the teacher needs to help her examine alternative acceptable choices (McNergney & Haberman, 1988). For example, the child who hits to obtain a desired piece of equipment does need to learn that hitting is an unacceptable way to obtain the goal. Too often, however, the child who hits or exhibits other unacceptable behavior is punished or scolded without being offered follow-up discussion of acceptable behaviors that could replace the inappropriate behavior. The teacher can act as a guide to help the child identify and practice new options (Stocking, Arezzo, & Leavitt, 1979). Teacher and child can role-play new behavior as a replacement for the inappropriate behavior. The teacher may need to play the part of the child, at first, in order to model the new behavior.

Puppet skits presented by the teacher can model common problem situations for group analysis and resolution. The puppets dramatize the conflict. Then the children suggest behavior choices the puppets might employ to resolve the conflict. The puppets then act out the children's suggestions. Finally, children evaluate the effec-

tiveness and appropriateness of each scenario. The same effect can be achieved by parent volunteers or older children acting out skits depicting common conflict situations. Whichever method is used, children are being taught skills in conflict resolution. The teacher guides children to think about their own behavior in an effort to teach socialization and self-discipline.

It's BASIC

When the teacher attends to the BASIC classroom management techniques of preparation—

Before school begins
Arrival and departure times
Schedule transitions
Interactions with equipment and materials
Conflict management

—many potential discipline problems can be avoided. By anticipating possible problems and planning routines and methods to minimize problem times, the teacher can create an orderly classroom environment in which children can learn and work in harmony.

For further reading

Doescher, S. M., & Sugawara, A. I. (1989). Encouraging prosocial behavior in young children. *Childhood Education, 65,* 213–216.

Glasser, W. (1985). Discipline has never been the problem and isn't the problem now. *Theory Into Practice, 24,* 241–246.

Kelman, A. (1990). Choices for children. *Young Children, 45*(3), 42–45.

Nash, B. C. (1981). The effects of classroom spatial organisation on four- and five-year-old children's learning. *British Journal of Educational Psychology, 51,* 144–155.

Neill, S. R. St. J. (1982). Preschool

design and child behavior. *Journal of Child Psychology and Psychiatry, 23*, 309–318.

Ryan, W. P. (1974). Workshops about the physical structure of the classroom: An interesting way to work with teachers. *Journal of School Psychology, 12*, 242–246.

Sargent, B. (1972). *The integrated day in an American school.* Cambridge, MA: National Association of Independent Schools.

Spodek, B., Saracho, O., & Davis, M. (1991). *Foundations of early childhood education.* Englewood Cliffs: Prentice-Hall.

Tegano, D., Sawyers, J., & Moran, J. (1989). Problem-finding and solving in play: The teacher's role. *Childhood Education, 66*, 92–97.

References

Brophy, J. (1983). Classroom organization and management. *The Elementary School Journal, 83*, 265–285.

Brophy, J. (1985). Classroom management as instruction: Socializing self-guidance in students. *Theory into Practice, 24*, 233–240.

Day, B. (1975). *Open learning in early childhood.* New York: Macmillan.

Katz, L., & Chard, S. (1989). *Engaging children's minds: The project approach.* Norwood, NJ: Ablex.

McNergney, R., & Haberman, M. (1988). Research on teaching. *Educational Leadership, 45*(4), 96.

Schilmoeller, G. L., & Amundrud, P. A. (1987, Spring). The effect of furniture arrangement on movement, on-task behavior, and sound in an early childhood setting. *Child and Youth Care Quarterly, 16*(1), 5–20.

Shapiro, S. (1975). Some classroom ABC's: Research takes a closer look. *The Elementary School Journal, 75*, 436–441.

Stocking, S. H., Arezzo, D., & Leavitt, S. (1979). *Helping kids make friends.* Allen, TX: Argus Communications.

A Positive Approach to Discipline in an Early Childhood Setting

"Sit Down!" shouts Judy, with more than a trace of frustration in her voice. She is trying to maintain control of a group of preschoolers who are none too interested in the lesson she has worked so hard to prepare. "Jonathan, if you won't join the circle you'll have to sit in the time-out chair," she states with determination.

Marianne Modica

Marianne Modica is Program Coordinator for the Calvary Christian Academy and Happy Day Child Care Center in Wayne, NJ.

Jonathan counters with his usual response to adult commands. "No," he says flatly. He, like most two-year-olds, can't be faulted for verbosity. The next move is up to Judy. If she ignores Jonathan, she risks "losing face" in front of the rest of the children. If she follows through with her threat, she must interrupt her lesson and will probably lose control of the group anyway.

Unfortunately, this exhausting game of clashing wills is too frequently played in the early childhood arena. Equally unfortunate is the fact that in this game, nobody wins. Teachers and children alike become angry and frustrated, and the classroom becomes a battleground rather than a nurturing place of growth and development. Why is it that so often we as teachers find classroom discipline to be our greatest challenge?

Discipline can be defined as teaching that corrects, molds, or perfects, and all would agree that it is an important element in any classroom situation. Without it the classroom is unsafe, the children are insecure, and teachers will quickly lose their sanity. Be that as it may, the goal of discipline is not to make the teacher's life easier. The goal of discipline is to guide the behavior of children in such a way that they will internalize our outward expectations and develop the inner controls they need to function as whole and happy individuals.

These goals can easily become muddled when we confuse discipline with punishment. For example, I recently witnessed the following scene while observing a class of three-year-olds. While most of the children were engaged in typical preschool activities, one small child was sitting off to the side in what I quickly ascertained to be the "time-out chair." She was not facing the class, but was seated directly behind the teacher, who was working at a table with another child. The girl was crying pitifully but was obviously being ignored. The teacher saw my concern and proceeded to describe to me, in a loud voice, the child's disruptive behavior. I'm sure this teacher thought she was disciplining her young charge "for her own good." However, little good will result from the way this situation was handled. If we agree with Webster's definition of punishment ("a penalty imposed for a violation; suffering, pain, or loss that serves as retribution"), there can be no doubt that this child was being punished. Perhaps our first task as teaching professionals should be to commit ourselves firmly to the ideal that we are not in the business of punishing children.

Under the umbrella of classroom discipline, there is much room for flexibility and individual differences in teaching style. Some teachers function best in an atmosphere of "controlled chaos." Others prefer a more orderly environment and stick closely to their predetermined schedules. The danger lies in allowing one's personal preference for a discipline style to move too far left or right on the continuum of healthy practice for preschool children. A strict, authoritarian approach to discipline (what I call the "because-I-said-so method") is both an inappropriate and an unrealistic way to handle a class of young children. This method leads children to behave well only to escape punishment, and they will not develop the inner self-control they need. In fact, children who find themselves under this authoritarian style may actually become more aggressive toward other children as a result (Harms, cited in Leeper, Witherspoon, & Day, 1984, p. 444).

At the other end of the spectrum,

From *Day Care and Early Education,* Summer 1992, pp. 32-34. Copyright © 1992 by Human Science Press, Inc., 72 Fifth Avenue, New York, NY 10011. Reprinted by permission.

and equally inappropriate, is the permissive or "anything-goes" style of discipline. Children neither need nor want to be left to their own devices, and they are not likely to develop inner controls without adult input. Hopefully we will find ourselves somewhere in the middle of these two extremes and will provide developmentally appropriate guidance to the children in our care. Being a teacher means being a model for young children; it is our responsibility to model a reasonable approach to life.

Many discipline problems can be avoided by an awareness of basic classroom management. Things like group size, child-adult ratio, room size, and the availability of materials and equipment are important elements in group interaction and should be considered carefully. More aggressive behavior has been observed in children who are members of larger groups with higher child-adult ratios (McConkie & Hughes, cited in Leeper et al., 1984, p. 446). Likewise, we've all witnessed certain combinations of children that are explosive, and that may need to be gently redirected to more calming activities. Transitional periods between activities are also times of stress for some children. I know a child who needed to be told, "In five minutes I will tell you that in five more minutes it will be cleaning-up time." This may sound elaborate, but with a little extra consideration from a caring teacher, a five-year-old boy was given the tools he needed to cope with an otherwise stressful situation (and I was grateful, since the child is my son!).

Other possible causes of discipline problems in preschoolers are developmentally inappropriate subject matter and unrealistic expectations. Are your children bored during circle time? Is your curriculum uninteresting or too difficult? Have they been sitting still for too long? Expecting children to sit quietly during lessons and activities that they cannot relate to and that do not meet their needs is asking for trouble. Sometimes the fault lies not in the child but in the program itself.

Even the most astute classroom manager and developmentally appropriate teacher sometimes encounters disruptive behavior in preschoolers. Other factors that may affect the children we teach are nutrition, fatigue, and changes in the home life or family structure. A wise teacher will not overlook the obvious when a child's behavior begins to change. Once these influences have been ruled out, we need to take a deeper look into the problem at hand before we can decide how to deal with any discipline concern.

If a child is disruptive and exhibits aggressive or violent behavior consistently, it may be that there is a deeper emotional problem at work, and some type of family counseling may be needed. It is also true that some children develop negative patterns of behavior and learn to draw attention to themselves with this behavior. Often teachers try behavior modification techniques with young children, but, as Lillian Katz warns, it is wise to "Stop, look and listen before you condition" (cited in Leeper, et al., 1984, p. 454). Not every child is an appropriate candidate for this approach, and behavior modification involves more than putting stickers on a chart at the end of the day. If a child has been carefully observed and it is agreed that behavior modification should be attempted, there are many resources available to instruct classroom teachers on the correct way to carry out this plan (see Leeper, et al., 1984; Osborn & Osborn, 1977).

Most disruptive or aggressive behavior in young children can be explained as simply a need to develop skills in social interaction. Teaching young children to relate to others in a positive way is one of our biggest jobs, and if we expect the children who come to us to be already socialized so that we can "teach" them, we are in the wrong profession. There are some basic practices we can follow to help children grow in these important social skills.

First, children need guidance to develop self-expression. When we encourage children to use their words to express anger or frustration, they will be less likely to strike out when these feelings boil over. Say, for instance, Billy knocks down Susie's blocks. Susie can be helped to express her anger in words ("That makes me angry, Billy!") rather than hitting or pushing to show her feelings. By giving children the language they need to express their emotions freely, we are working to build their self-esteem as well, for children will learn that their feelings matter and that they are important enough to be listened to.

Second, teachers can help build self-worth by avoiding the use of labels such as *good* and *bad* when referring to children or their actions. "Great job, Juan" is more desirable than "Good boy, Juan," for Juan will sense that if the teacher thinks he's good today, maybe she will think he's bad tomorrow.

Third, directions and requests can be phrased positively. Rather than "Don't stand on the chair," a child may be told, "Chairs are for sitting on." When we take the time to talk to children and explain our reasoning to them, we are modeling respectful behavior that will go a long way in boosting the self-esteem of our preschoolers.

Perhaps one of the most valuable tools we can give children is the ability to negotiate with their peers. Susanne Wichert explores this idea beautifully in her book *Keeping the Peace*. Wichert believes that children can engage in conflict resolution once we provide them with the tools and practice they need. Suppose two children are fighting over a toy. The first step in the negotiating process is calming the children involved in the conflict and focusing their attention on the problem at hand. This can be done by saying something like "Just a minute, can I help you with this problem?" Then each party involved is given an opportunity to tell his or her side of the story uninterrupted. The next step is to clarify the problem by restating what the children have explained ("So the problem is...right?"). The adult continues to encourage the children to talk to each other as they bargain and ultimately come to a resolution ("I'll let you use the puzzle when I'm done"). How much adult input is actually needed depends on the level of maturity of the children involved. Once resolution has been reached and the children have reconciled, the adult says a few words to the offending party to prevent a recurrence of the behavior ("It's a good idea to ask when you want to use something and someone else is using it"). Finally, the adult affirms the children for the good job they've done in finding a solution. These children have learned to take a reasonable approach to their problem, and they have successfully negotiated a resolution. Can you think of some adults who would benefit from learning this lesson as well?

So, are your preschoolers driving you to the brink of professional burnout? Remember that they basically want to please us, and they will model our behavior, for better or worse. If we control them by harsh demands and criticism, they will learn to be demanding and critical and will think little of themselves and others. If we raise our voices to them, they will do the same to us and to each other. But if we provide the consistent, caring guidance that young children need and deserve, they will gradually develop the inner discipline and controls that will guide them well in future years.

References

Greenberg, P. (1990, Jan.). Why not academic preschool? (Ideas that work with young children). *Young Children*, 70-80.

Leeper, S. H., Witherspoon, R. L., & Day, B. (1984). *Good schools for young children* (5th ed.). New York: Macmillan.

Osborn, D. K., & Osborn, J. D. (1977). *Discipline and classroom management*. Athens, GA: Education Associates.

Wichert, S. (1989). *Keeping the peace*. Philadelphia: New Society Publishers.

Children's Self-Esteem
The Verbal Environment

Marjorie J. Kostelnik, Laura C. Stein and Alice P. Whiren

Marjorie J. Kostelnik, Laura C. Stein and Alice P. Whiren are faculty members in the Department of Family and Child Ecology, Michigan State University, East Lansing.

Young children continually gather information about their value as persons through interactions with the significant adults in their lives (Coopersmith, 1967; Swayze, 1980). This process begins in the home but very quickly extends to the educational settings in which children participate. Thus family members, caregivers and teachers serve as the mirror through which children see themselves and then judge what they see (Maccoby, 1980). If what is reflected is good, children will make a positive evaluation of self. If the image is negative, children will deduce that they have little worth; they are sensitive to the opinions adults have of them and often adopt these as their own.

In the classroom, teachers convey either enhancing or damaging attitudes that frequently are manifested in what they say to children and how they say it. Such manifestations may or may not be the result of conscious decisions on their part. Yet teacher verbalizations are a key factor in the degree to which children perceive themselves as worthy and competent or the opposite (Kostelnik, Stein, Whiren & Soderman, 1988). Consider the following scenario:

Imagine that you are invited to visit an early childhood program in your community. You arrive early and are asked to wait in the classroom until the youngsters return from a field trip. Surveying your surroundings, you notice brightly colored furniture comfortably arranged, sunlight softly streaming through the windows, children's art work pleasingly displayed and a large, well-stocked aquarium bubbling in a corner. You think to yourself, "What a pleasant environment for children."

Just then, a child bursts into the room sobbing. She is followed by an adult who scolds, "Maria, stop that bawling." As the other youngsters file in, you hear another child exclaim, "When do we get to take our projects home?" An adult snaps, "Why can't you listen. I just said they stay here until tomorrow."

Your favorable impression is ruined. Despite the lovely physical surroundings, the way in which adults are talking to children has made the setting uninviting. You wonder whether children could ever feel good about themselves under such circumstances. What you have overheard has made you privy to an invisible but keenly felt component of every program—the verbal environment.

THE VERBAL ENVIRONMENT

Adult participants in the early childhood setting create the verbal environment. Its components include words and silence—how much adults say, what they say, how they speak, to whom they talk and how well they listen. The manner in which these elements are enacted dictates children's estimations of self-worth. Thus verbal environments can be characterized as either positive or negative.

From *Childhood Education*, Fall 1988, pp. 29-32. Reprinted by permission of Marjorie J. Kostelnick, Laura C. Stein, Alice P. Whiren and the Association for Childhood Education International, 1141 Georgia Avenue, Suite 200, Wheaton, MD. Copyright © 1988 by the Association.

4. GUIDING BEHAVIOR

Characteristics of the Negative Verbal Environment

Negative verbal environments are ones in which children are made to feel unworthy, incompetent, unlovable or insignificant as a result of what adults say or do not say to them. Most practitioners can readily identify the most extreme illustrations: adults screaming at children, making fun of them, swearing at them or making them the target of ethnic slurs. Yet there are less obvious, more common adult behaviors that also contribute to negative verbal environments:

1) *Adults show little or no interest in children's activities because they are in a hurry, busy, engrossed in their own thoughts and endeavors, or tired.* Whatever the reason, they walk by children without comment and fail to acknowledge their presence. When standing near children, they do not talk with them and respond only grudgingly to children's attempts to initiate an interaction. In addition, grownups misuse time designated for interaction with children by talking more with their colleagues than the youngsters. Rather than paying attention to children, most of the adult's time is spent chatting with other adults. Children interpret these behaviors as obvious signs of disinterest.

2) *Teachers pay superficial attention to what children have to say.* Instead of listening attentively, they ask irrelevant questions, respond inappropriately, fail to maintain eye contact or cut children off. Occasionally they simply ignore the communication altogether, saying nothing, thus treating the children as if they were not present.

3) *Adults speak discourteously to children.* They interrupt children who are speaking to them, as well as youngsters who are talking to one another. They expect children to respond to their own requests immediately, not allowing them to finish what they are doing or saying. Their voice tone is demanding, impatient or belligerent; they

neglect such social courtesies as "Excuse me," "Please" and "Thank you." In addition, their remarks often make children the butt of a group joke. Young children attend as much to the sarcastic tone of voice as to the meaning of words and are not able to appreciate the intended humor.

4) *Teachers use judgmental vocabulary in describing children to themselves and others.* Typical demeaning labels include "hyper," "selfish," "greedy," "uncooperative," "motor mouth," "stubborn," "grabby" and "klutsy." Adults say these words directly to children or to another person within the child's hearing. In either case, youngsters are treated as though they have no feelings or are invisible or deaf.

5) *Staff members actively discourage children from talking to them.* They tell children that what they are doing or saying is uninteresting or unimportant and that they should be doing or talking about something else. Thus youngsters hear admonishments like: "All right, already! I'm sick of hearing about your troubles with Rhonda; find something else to talk about." Or, "I don't want to hear one more word about it. Not one peep!" Sometimes adults put children off by saying, "Hush," "Not now" or "Tell me about it later." The "later" seldom comes.

6) *Grownups rely on giving orders and making demands as their number-one means of relating to children.* Their verbalizations consist of directions ("Sit in your chair") and admonishments ("No fighting," "Everybody get your coats off and settle down for lunch," "Stop fooling around"). Other comments that are positive in tone or content are relatively scarce.

7) *Adults ask questions for which no real answer is expected or desired.* Typical queries might include: "What do you think you're doing?" "Didn't I tell you not to stomp in the mud?" "When will you ever learn?" Regardless of how chil-

dren respond, their answers are viewed as disrespectful or unwelcome. Children soon learn that these remarks are not a real invitation to relate to the adult.

8) *Caregivers use children's names as synonyms for the words "no," "stop" or "don't."* By barking out "Tony" or "Allison" as a reprimand, adults attack the essence of the child's being, thereby causing children to associate the most personal part of themselves with disapproval and rejection. When using this tactic adults fail to describe the objectionable behavior or to clarify the reason for the negative tone of voice, thus leaving children with the notion that something is inherently wrong with them as persons.

9) *Teachers use baby talk in giving information or directions.* Instead of clearly stating, "Ruth and Toby, please put the puzzles in the puzzle rack," adults confuse and demean children by saying, "We need to put the puzzles in the puzzle rack," when they have no intention of assisting. Other kinds of baby talk involve using the diminutive form of a name (*Jackie* instead of *Jack*), even though the child and the parents prefer the other. These may be combined in particularly exaggerated ways, as when one caregiver pursed her lips and squealed in a high pitch, "How are we today, Jackie? Shall we quit crying and ride the horsie?" Such messages define children as powerless and subservient; these statements are never used between persons of equal status.

10) *Adults dominate the verbal exchanges that take place each day.* They do all the talking and allow children little time to respond either to them or their peers. Feeling compelled constantly to query, inform or instruct, they bombard children with so much talk that youngsters have few opportunities to initiate conversations on topics of their own choosing. This leaves children feeling rushed and unsatisfied.

All of the preceding verbal behaviors convey to children adult attitudes of aloofness, disrespect, lack of acceptance and insensitivity. Such encounters tend to make children feel inadequate, confused or angry (Hoffman, 1963). A different set of circumstances exists in programs characterized by a positive verbal environment.

Characteristics of the Positive Verbal Environment

In a positive verbal environment, adult words are aimed at satisfying children's needs and making children feel valued. When speaking to children, adults focus not only on content but also on the affective impact their words will have. Adults create a positive verbal environment when their verbal exchanges with children have the following attributes:

1) *Adults use words to show affection for children and sincere interest in them.* They greet children when they arrive, take the time to become engaged in children's activities and also respond to their queries. In addition, they make remarks showing children they care about them and are aware of what they are doing: "You've been really working hard to get the dinosaur puzzle together." "You seem to be enjoying that game." They laugh with children, respond to their humor and tell children they enjoy being with them.

2) *Adults send congruent verbal and nonverbal messages.* When they are showing interest verbally, they position themselves near the child at a similar height from the floor, maintain eye contact and thoroughly pay attention. Other actions, such as smiling or giving a pat, reinforce praise and words of positive regard. Incongruent messages, such as following through on a limit while smiling or pinching a child's cheek hard while giving praise, are avoided.

3) *Adults extend invitations to children to interact with them.* They may say, "Here's a place for you right next to Sylvia" or "Let's take a minute to talk. I want to find out more about your day." When children seek them out, grownups accept the invitation enthusiastically: "That sounds like fun." "Oh good, now I'll have a chance to work with you."

4) *Teachers listen attentively to what children have to say.* They show their interest through eye contact, smiling and nodding. They encourage children to elaborate on what they are saying by using such statements as "Tell me more about that" or "Then what happened?" Moreover, adults pause long enough after making a comment or asking a question for children to reply, giving them time to gather their thoughts before responding. Such reactions make children feel valued and interesting.

5) *Adults speak courteously to children.* They refrain from interrupting children and allow them to finish what they are saying, either to the adult or another child. The voice tone used by adults is patient and friendly, and social amenities such as "Please," "Thank you" and "Excuse me" are part of the verbal interchange.

6) *Adults use children's interests as a basis for conversation.* They speak with them about the things youngsters want to talk about. This is manifested in two ways. First, they follow the child's lead in conversations. Second, they bring up subjects known to be of interest to a particular child based on past experience.

7) *Adults plan or take advantage of spontaneous opportunities to talk with each child informally.* In the course of a day, children have many chances to talk with adults about matters that interest or concern them. Eating, toileting, dressing, waiting for the bus, settling down for a nap and just waiting until the group is called to order are treated as occasions for adult-child conversation. Adults do not wait for special, planned time to talk with youngsters.

8) *Teachers avoid making judgmental comments about children either to them or within their hearing.* Children are treated as sensitive, aware human beings whose feelings are respected. Discussions about children's problems or family situations are held in private between the appropriate parties.

9) *Adults refrain from speaking when talk would destroy the mood of the interaction.* When they see children deeply absorbed in activity or engrossed in conversation with one another, staff members allow the natural course of the interaction to continue. In these situations they treat silence as a sign of warmth and respect and refrain from too much talk at the wrong time.

10) *Grownups focus their attention on children when they professionally engage with them.* They put off housekeeping tasks and personal socializing so that they are fully available for interaction with children. When possible, adults involve children in maintenance tasks and interact with them. In a positive environment, adults are available, alert and prepared to respond to children.

Importance of a Positive Verbal Environment

Positive verbal environments are beneficial both to the children and the adults who participate in them. In such an atmosphere, children get the message that they are important. This enhances their self-perceptions of competence and worth (Openshaw, 1978). Additionally, children's self-awareness increases as they have opportunities to express themselves, explore ideas and interact spontaneously with other children and adults (Kostelnik et al., 1988). These conditions also increase the likelihood that youngsters will view the adults in the program as sources of comfort and support. As a result, adults find it easier to establish and maintain rapport with the children. This in turn makes youngsters more receptive to the social learnings adults wish to impart to them (Baumrind, 1977; Katz, 1977). These include rules, customs and how to get along with other people.

In sum, adult behaviors that characterize a positive verbal environment are synonymous with those commonly cited as representing warmth, acceptance, respect and empathy (Coletta, 1977; Gazda, 1977; Rogers, 1961). All four of these components contribute to the relationship-building process and provide the foundation for constructive child growth and development.

Establishing a Positive Verbal Environment

Few helping professionals would knowingly act in ways that damage children's self-esteem. Observations of early childhood settings, however, show that frequently adults unintentionally slip into verbal patterns that produce the negative verbal environment described here (Kostelnik, 1978, 1987). Recent interviews with day care, Head Start, preprimary and elementary school teachers point to three common reasons why this occurs (Kostelnik, 1987):

• Adults fail to consciously consider the impact their words have on children.

• Adults get caught up in the hurried pace of the job and think they cannot take the time to have more positive verbal interactions with the children.

• Adults are not used to thinking before speaking and, as a result, say things they do not really mean and talk in ways they do not intend.

Over the years it has become increasingly clear that positive verbal environments do not happen by chance. Rather, their creation is the result of purposeful planning and implementation. Those who are successful in their efforts first recognize the characteristics of the positive verbal environment and then incorporate the corresponding behaviors into their interactions with children. The steps for achieving these results are listed below:

1) *Familiarize yourself with the features of both positive and negative verbal environments.* Reread the guidelines presented here. Think about situations from your experience that illustrate each one.

2) *Listen carefully to what you say and how you say it.* Consider how children may interpret your message. If you catch yourself using habits that are poor, correct them on the spot. Ask colleagues to give you feedback about how you sound, or carry a tape recorder with you for a short period of time as a means of self-observation.

3) *Make a deliberate decision to create a positive verbal environment.* Select one characteristic and think of how to integrate it into your daily routine. Practice such simple strategies as using children's names in positive situations, showing your pleasure in their company or inviting children to elaborate on what they say. Try these techniques one at a time, until they become second nature to you. As you become more proficient, gradually increase the number of techniques you use.

4) *Keep track of the positive verbal behaviors that you use.* Ask a colleague to help you identify positive verbal characteristics and determine how often you use them. As you substitute more positive approaches to verbal interaction for the negative ones, you will have a record of your success. Self-improvement is easier to recognize when short evaluations are carried out periodically.

5) *Give recognition to other staff members who are attempting to improve the verbal environment for children.* Words of approval and encouragement are as important to adults as they are to children. Progress toward any goal is made easier when others recognize both effort and achievement.

What adults say to children conveys to them messages of competence or inadequacy. Through their verbalizations teachers create a climate in their classroom that is called the verbal environment, a key factor in the degree to which children develop high or low self-esteem. Such environments are characterized as either positive or negative. Continual exposure to a negative verbal environment diminishes children's self-esteem, whereas exposure to a positive verbal environment enhances children's self-awareness and perceptions of self-worth. To ensure that the verbal environment is a positive one, teachers should consider carefully what they say to children and make purposeful attempts to follow the guidelines cited in this article. The outcome of these efforts is a classroom in which children feel good about themselves and see the teacher as a positive presence in their lives.

References

Baumrind, D. (1977). Some thoughts about childrearing. In S. Cohen & T. J. Comiskey (Eds.), *Child Development: Contemporary Perspectives.* Itasca, IL: F. E. Peacock.

Coletta, A. J. (1977). *Working together: A guide to parent involvement.* Atlanta: Humanics.

Coopersmith, S. (1967). *The antecedents of self-esteem.* Princeton, NJ: Princeton University Press.

Gazda, G. M. (1977). *Human relations development: A manual for educators* (2nd ed.). Boston: Allyn & Bacon.

Hoffman, M. L. (1963). Parent discipline and the child's consideration of others. *Child Development 34*, 573-595.

Katz, L. G. (1977). What is basic for young children? *Childhood Education 54*(1), 16-19.

Kostelnik, M. J. (1978). *Evaluation of a communication and group management skills training program for child development personnel.* Unpublished doctoral dissertation, The Pennsylvania State University.

Kostelnik, M. J. (1987). *Development practices in early childhood programs.* Keynote Address, National Home Start Day, New Orleans, LA.

Kostelnik, M. J., Stein, L. C., Whiren, A. P., & Soderman, A. K. (1988). *Guiding children's social development.* Cincinnati, OH: Southwestern.

Maccoby, E. E. (1980). *Social development—Psychological growth and the parent-child relationship.* New York: Harcourt Brace Jovanovich.

Openshaw, D. K. (1978). *The development of self-esteem in the child: Model interaction.* Unpublished doctoral dissertation, Brigham Young University, Provo, UT.

Rogers, C. R. (1961). *On becoming a person.* Boston: Houghton Mifflin.

Swayze, M. C. (1980). Self-concept development in young children. In T. D. Yawkey (Ed.), *The self-concept of the young child.* Provo, UT: Brigham Young University Press.

SOLVING PROBLEMS TOGETHER!

ADAPTED FROM *KEEPING THE PEACE* BY SUSANNE WICHERT

"My tower won't stay up!" "It's my turn to use the blocks!" "I don't have anywhere to play!" Whether a child experiences frustration with a situation or with another child, resolving a dilemma nonaggressively incorporates problem-solving skills. Whether this process involves children working things out on their own or the skillful intervention of an understanding adult, the components of nonaggressive conflict resolution—cooperation, communication, and empathy—do much more than enhance children's self-esteem. They form the basis of important coping skills that encourage the participants to want to cooperate more fully and enable them to do so. These are skills on which children can build for a lifetime.

YOUR PHYSICAL ENVIRONMENT

The amount of unresolved conflict in any setting can be reduced by creating an environment where people feel comfortable, valued, free to express their feelings, and assured of getting what they need. Your setting can also help children engage repeatedly in the communication and problem-solving skills that foster cooperative conflict resolution. Take a look at your environment. Make sure your setting allows children to:

● **Function with the maximum degree of independence.** When children are able to do many things for themselves, alone or with the help of another child, their self-esteem is enhanced, and you can spend time observing, supporting, and guiding.

● **Function at low stress levels.** Physical factors such as noise level, visual clutter, use of color, and space/child ratio influence stress levels. (This includes stress on adults as well.)

● **Be as comfortable as possible.** Does your setting help to establish a strong link between family members and your program with places where a parent or other family member and child can be together comfortably for a while? Does your setting have "retreat" spaces for children and adults who need time to be alone during the day?

SUPPORTIVE INTERACTION

The daily role adults play can help children develop the wide array of attitudes and skills necessary for cooperative conflict resolution, and, in turn, reinforce children's self-confidence so they can handle even more difficult situations. Here's an example:

On a bright, sunny morning after three days of rain, the

Reprinted from *Scholastic Pre-K Today*, March 1991, pp. 46-52. Adapted from *Keeping The Peace: Practicing Cooperation and Conflict Resolution with Preschoolers* by Susanne Wichert. Copyright © 1991 by Susanne Wichert.

preschoolers were glad to be playing outside again. Kudra was carefully scooping up a pile of wood chips and carrying them to his "mountain." Andy and Joan were so involved in their game they barely noticed when Joan ran right through Kudra's mountain, or that Kudra called angrily after them.

Their teacher, who had seen what happened, called Andy and Joan to her: "I think Kudra has something he needs to tell you." She walked with them over to Kudra, who was restoring his pile, and said, "Kudra, I think you had something you wanted to tell Joan."

"You ran right through my mountain and wrecked it!"

"Sorry!" Joan yelled as she hurried back to the game.

The teacher asked them to wait, saying, "I think we have a little problem," and gathered them into a huddle. "Kudra, can you tell Joan and Andy how you felt?"

"I didn't like it."

Then she turned to Joan and Andy. "Let's go over here and see if we can think of a way you can keep from running into Kudra again." They went a small distance away from Kudra, who continued his play, and the teacher asked, "What do you think the problem was?"

Andy responded, "Joan wrecked Kudra's pile and he didn't like it."

Joan interjected, "Well, it wasn't all my fault. Andy was chasing me!"

"Tell Andy that, and then maybe the two of you can figure out what you need to change about your game to keep it from happening again." The teacher waited while the two children worked through some ideas. When they turned back to her they suggested that they could run in an area where there were no other children.

"That's a good idea! It's great that you worked the problem out."

The process illustrated in the scenario achieves a number of things. Kudra was given an opportunity to state the problem to Andy and Joan in a setting where his right to express his feelings was validated. Andy and Joan got a very clear message that what another child has to say is important and they have an obligation to listen. In the process of finding a solution, their teacher asked Joan and Andy to define the problem and made sure they understood that Kudra's feelings were the result of their actions. In this case, she allowed them to try out their solution. If there was still a problem, she could then go to them and say, "Your idea was a good one, but it doesn't seem to be working," and engage the children in continued discussion.

Considering Feelings and Predicting Consequences

Like curiosity, empathy occurs naturally in children. However, it varies from child to child, often influenced by the responses of adults who are important in their lives. A child's curiosity is enlivened when we respond patiently to questions and when we ask questions intended to make that child think about why something might be. In much the same way, we can strengthen a child's ability to respond empathetically.

"Empathy training" involves enabling children to begin to make decisions about their behavior on the basis of understanding its consequences. Learning about consequences requires that we talk with children about them and

give children opportunities to predict them. Look again at the story of Kudra, Andy, and Joan and how the teacher might have handled it had she decided to intervene at an earlier point:

Realizing that Andy and Joan were so intent on their game that they probably wouldn't notice Kudra building a mountain nearby, the teacher stopped them to explain: "Your game looks like a lot of fun, but it doesn't seem like you're looking where you're running. That might cause a problem. What do you think?"

The children weren't sure, so the teacher continued: "The last time you went around the climber, I noticed that you came pretty close to Kudra. How do you think he feels when you come by him fast and close?"

"It might be kind of scary," Andy volunteered, and Joan added, "Yeah, he might be afraid we'll bump him."

"Mmmm... what do you think he would tell you about how it makes him feel?" asked the teacher.

"Bad," came the answer from both the children.

"He looked kind of sad before," said Andy.

The teacher responded, "I think so, too. You can tell a lot about how people feel by what their faces look like, can't you? I'm glad you noticed. Now, how do you think you can change your game so that Kudra will feel comfortable, too?"

In this case, the teacher didn't wait for the consequence but chose to give the children an opportunity to try to predict what might happen. This strategy is very useful because even though we acknowledge that people can learn from mistakes, they can also learn without having to make them. Predicting consequences gives children practice in analyzing situations before problems occur.

Understanding Responses

It is also important to give children opportunities to understand situations from the point of view of others. Children can learn tolerance and understanding of individual responses through discussions and from the kind of behaviors adults model. Here is an example:

Three-year-olds Jon and Lena were very close friends, often inseparable during the day. One morning Jon arrived earlier and waited eagerly for Lena. When she came in the door with her father, he ran to her, grabbed her, and hugged her with a great amount of energy. Lena clung to her father's leg, frowning. After a few days, with no sign of change in this routine, the teacher decided to approach Jon about it. Rather that tell him not to run to Lena, she decided to help him figure out the problem. The next morning, after he made his usual run, she took him aside. "You like Lena a lot, don't you?" she asked.

Jon nodded.

"It's pretty hard for you to wait for her to come to school, isn't it?"

Jon nodded again.

"When she finally comes, it seems like you want to run right over to her and give her a big hug..."

"Yeah, and I want her to come play with me."

"Have you noticed what she does when you do that?"

"Yeah, she holds on to her dad. Sometimes she says mean things to me."

"Why do you think that is?"

"Maybe she doesn't want me to hug her?"

4. GUIDING BEHAVIOR

"I think you're right. Why do you think that is? She likes to give you lots of hugs other times."

"I don't know."

The teacher decided that she should help explain. "Well, you know how when you first come in the morning, sometimes you like to be alone with your mom for a little while? You like to take your time to say goodbye, and you want time to get a hug from her?"

Jon nodded.

"I think maybe Lena wants to take some time like that with her father. When you run over to her she may feel like you aren't giving her that time. I know that you're excited to see her, but do you think you could give her that time? If you keep playing when she comes in, she'll probably come over to you when she's ready. Do you think you might like to try that tomorrow? I could help you if you want."

In this situation, the teacher helped Jon understand what Lena's response meant and also validated his feelings in a way that related to an experience he'd had. Then she explained to Lena (when Jon was there) what Jon would be doing. The next day she helped Jon remember, and after Lena said goodbye to her father, engaged both of them in a conversation encouraging Lena to tell Jon how she felt, and asking Jon to share his feelings, too.

Applied consistently, this process of validating children's feelings and helping them understand the feelings of others ultimately enables children to work out situations by themselves. Self-esteem is enhanced as children begin to feel more in control of their lives. However, in order for the process to work, the adults involved need to help one another — if one is engaged in a discussion with children, another covers the group. This cooperation is a type of modeling; and modeling concern, honesty, respect, and thoughtfulness for one another makes it possible for these attitudes and qualities to grow.

COMMUNICATION SKILLS

Negotiation means communication, and clear communication involves a number of skills. The common element running through all of these skills is a person's ability to focus on what's going on for the other person involved, and to respond to it. As you work with children, remember that this is a process — a developing skill.

Focusing Attention

When you encourage children to talk to one another, help them make sure the other person is listening. Model appropriate behaviors by getting down to children's level, using their names to make sure you have their attention, and remaining focused on them while you speak.

Children may also have difficulties focusing on the person who is talking *to* them, so move everyone to a place where there will be few distractions. Let children know that you will help if they have trouble getting someone's attention. (You can simply go with the child and say, "Ellen has something she needs to tell you.") Then let the children take it from there.

Children have to be guided through the process of negotiation as they address interpersonal problems. Establishing effective communication between children is key to their being able to handle problems. (photo credit Elaine M. Ward)

Hearing and Being Heard

You may need to help children put their problems into words — stating why they are upset *and* what they want the other person to do. Here are some familiar examples with possible clarifications. A child might say:

"I won't be your friend anymore!" which could translate into, "I don't like it when you grab things from me. Please give it back."

"I never get to go on the swing!" might be, "Can I have a turn next?"

"You're mean!" might translate to, "I don't want you to chase me."

One sentence you can use frequently is, "Tell me (him/her) what it is that you want (need)." With smaller children you might say, "Use words to tell me (him/her) what you want (need)." Once the problem is stated in these terms, the solution is usually close at hand. Your involvement helps get children into the habit of saying what they mean.

Understanding Body Language and Facial Expressions

During the normal course of a day there are many opportunities to comment on facial expressions or body language. Observations such as, "He certainly looks angry, doesn't he?" and "Her face looks very sad. What do you think might be making her feel that way?" help children to understand some of the nonverbal ways people communicate. If a child responds with, "I don't know," encourage her to ask how the other person is feeling.

NEGOTIATING PROBLEMS

As you guide children through negotiating problems, remember that your primary purpose is to encourage communication and keep them focused on coming to a resolution. Help the problem-solving proceed with the following steps: 1. focusing and calming; 2. giving attention to everyone involved; 3. helping children clarify and state the problem; 4. involving them in bargaining, resolving, and/or reconciling; 5. looking for a way to prevent the problem from continuing; and 6. affirming the process.

Children's abilities can be broken down into three skill levels — high adult intervention, minimal adult intervention, and letting children take charge. The following are examples to illustrate the particular kind of adult involvement required for each one.

High Adult Intervention

At this level, the adult helps define the problem and models language:

Maria was busy doing a puzzle when Sean came over and took a piece from the table. He had to reach over Maria's arm to try to make it fit. Their teacher was alerted when each child was trying to take the piece from the other. Sensing that they wouldn't be able to resolve the problem without help, she moved closer and knelt down, saying quietly, "Excuse me. Will you please hand me the puzzle piece?"

*The children let go, both talking at once, upset and in loud voices. She gently touched both of them, saying, "You'll both have a turn to talk. Let's all take a deep breath and be quiet for a minute." (**focusing and calming**)*

She turned to Sean. "I'm going to ask Maria to talk first, but you'll have a turn, too. It will help a lot if you
don't interrupt her." Then she turned to Maria and asked, "Would you tell me what the problem is?"*

*Maria explained, with Sean interrupting on several occasions. The teacher assured him that he would have a turn to talk and went back to listening to Maria. Then Sean was given an opportunity to explain the problem. (During this kind of exchange, the child "placed on hold" inadvertently hears the other child's perspective.) (**attention to all children concerned**)*

*After the teacher heard both sides, she stated the problem in clear and simple terms: "So the problem is that Maria didn't like it when Sean took the puzzle piece from the puzzle she was working. And Sean wanted to help Maria work the puzzle. Is that right?" (**clarification**)*

*Then she turned to Sean and said, "Tell Maria what you wanted when you took the puzzle piece." (If a child isn't able to come up with the language, the teacher could model it. She might say, "Do you want to tell her that you want to help her with the puzzle?" or "Why don't you ask her if she would like some help with the puzzle?" If the other child doesn't want any help, making a face at the prospect and saying nothing, the teacher can model the language: "Tell him that you don't want any help right now.") In this case, Maria turned to Sean and said, "I don't want any help right now," and he responded, "Okay, I'll get my own puzzle." (**resolution**)*

*If Sean didn't come to his own resolution, the teacher could still support Maria in her decision to work alone, and help Sean find an alternative choice of play. After going through a discussion like this, the most the adult usually needs to say about the initial grabbing might be a comment such as, "It's a good idea to ask people if they want help." (**prevention**)*

*The teacher closed this interaction by acknowledging the part the children played in resolving the problem. "You did a great job talking to each other (not interrupting each other, listening to each other, etc.). (**affirmation**)*

Minimal Adult Role

This is the same situation but at this level the children are able to use their own language to define the problem. However, they still need an adult to help clarify and model.

Maria is doing the puzzle when Sean comes over and takes a piece. She turns to him and says, "I'm doing this puzzle."

He answers, "But I know where this one goes!"

*"No!" she says as she pushes his hand away. He continues to try to fit the piece in and the teacher comes over. "It looks like you have a problem. Would you like some help?" (Because the children are not really agitated, her statement is sufficient for **calming**.)*

Maria looks at the teacher and says, "He won't give me back my puzzle piece."

*"Tell him what you want." (**attention**)*

"I want you to give me back the puzzle piece."

*(The teacher makes sure Maria has Sean's attention and is speaking so he can hear.) (**clarification**)*

"But I just wanted to help her do the puzzle."

*"Then you need to tell Maria what you wanted and ask her if she would like some help." He does, and Maria answers, "I don't want any help. You can do the puzzle when I'm done." (**resolution**)*

4. GUIDING BEHAVIOR

Children Taking Charge

At this level, children are able to go off by themselves to solve the problem. Encourage the transition to this level by suggesting they go to a specific area, assuring them that their play spot will be saved, and letting them know you're available to help. Be sure to ask the children to come tell you their solution (so you can make sure it's mutually satisfying and affirm their process). Back to Maria and Sean...

As before, Sean has taken a puzzle piece, reached over Maria's arm, and tried to fit it in the puzzle. Maria tells him that she is doing the puzzle herself, and he responds that he knows where this piece goes. Maria says, "No!"

The teacher judges that the children will probably not take the initiative to remove themselves from the table to work out the problem, so she goes over and suggests, "It looks like you two are having a problem. Would you like me to save your places while you go to the couch to work it out?"

The children decide they would and proceed to the couch. They return shortly, and Maria tells the teacher, "We've decided that I'm going to do the puzzle alone, and then we're going to do one together."

The teacher asks Sean, "Is that okay with you?"

He nods and she tells them, "I'll bet it felt good to work that out all by yourselves. Great job!"

Obviously the process of resolving a situation will not always go as smoothly as illustrated in these examples. Sometimes children need more practice, are moving from one skill level to another, or are having a stressful day. As you assist, remember that the most difficult part of helping children negotiate can be resisting jumping in. Keep in mind that even though a solution may seem perfect to you — it is still *your* solution.

Cooperative conflict resolution is a process that reflects the intertwined relationship between self-esteem, tolerance of differences, understanding feelings, creative problem-solving skills, and the ability to interact nonaggressively. When you join in this process, you provide children with opportunities to develop positive self-concepts, encourage the development of caring behaviors, teach children to express and value their own feelings and the feelings of others, and show children how to resolve conflicts in non-violent ways. What could be more important? . . .

We all want children to grow up with a strong sense of values that will enable them to be fair and kind. Part of this growth is learning to understand feelings—their own, and those of others—and being able to express those feelings. This ability, just like the ability to solve problems and cooperate, can be learned through practice and experience. You'll find additional activities and important information in *Keeping the Peace: Practicing Cooperation and Conflict Resolution with Preschoolers* by Susanne Wichert.

The Role of the Child Care Professional in Caring for Infants, Toddlers, and Their Families

Nancy Balaban

Nancy Balaban, Ed.D., is director of the Infant and Parent Development Program at Bank Street Graduate School of Education. For the past 20 years, Nancy has worked as a teacher educator. Most recently her work has focused on the preparation of those who wish to work with children younger than age three and their families.

I reflect on the number of times my students complain to me that well-meaning friends and relations look astonished when told that they—the students—are studying on the graduate level to work with children under age three and their families. "You mean you're getting a master's degree to be a baby-sitter?" is the frequent reaction. It seems that many people, parents or not, are totally ignorant of what it means to work with young children. If nothing else, we certainly don't sit on babies—indeed, we need to discard this term. Furthermore, just because former President Reagan stated that "mothers and grandmothers have been caring for children for thousands of years" doesn't mean that *anyone* can be entrusted with someone else's baby. Being a child care professional means being an exceptional person, one with experience, knowledge, and special personal qualities—three characteristics that come in varying forms.

WHAT'S SO SPECIAL ABOUT CHILD CARE PROFESSIONALS?

Let's look at these characteristics—experience, knowledge, and personal qualities—one by one.

First on our list—experience

Some of us may have entered this profession because of the satisfaction derived from our role as parents or from positive experiences with nieces, nephews, or the children in our neighborhood. Others may have worked with preschoolers or older children, become intrigued with very early development, and decided that we could have the most impact working with infants and toddlers and their parents. I wonder how many of us have come from other professions or occupations such as retailing or accounting and have found more meaning in working with young children than in our former jobs. Each of us brings something from our own background to our work with children under age three and their families. We bring different ideas about childrearing that spring from our childhood, our culture, our neighborhoods, our parents, and our values as adults. This background experience influences us as we interact day by day with infants and toddlers and their parents.

Experience not only influences our behavior; experience teaches us, as well. It teaches us, for example, about the dramatic variety that characterizes little children. I refer to variety in temperament (Alice, who falls, brushes herself off and toddles away; Jeremy, who falls, screams, goes limp on the floor, and continues to wail even while being held and consoled); variety in physical ability (at 10 months, Zeke is beginning to walk unaided, while Molly, at the same age, does a hitch crawl, but would just as soon sit and watch the world go by); variety in interests (at 14 months, Juan thinks pots and pans are the best inventions ever made, while Ellen finds examining the smallest threads and specks fascinating).

Experience alone can't be the teacher. There is another very important part of the equation—*us* and how we think and feel about our work with young children. What we learn from our experience with children is very much dependent on how we view ourselves as child care professionals. If we enjoy our day with children—that means being tired, of course, but satisfied; if we take pleasure in changes—both large and small—that occur in children; if we feel great when our actions help a child give up a negative behavior for a positive one; if we regard our responsibility to parents as equal to our responsibility to children; if we see ourselves as learners as well as teachers, then professional experience becomes meaningful and growth producing and contributes to the development of the youngest children who are in our care and their families. Our attitude about our work makes the difference.

Second on our list—knowledge

While it's clearly important to love babies, love is not enough. We need knowledge. Knowledge about babies is

From *Young Children*, July 1992, pp. 66-71. Reprinted by permission of the publisher, the National Association for the Education of Young Children.

different from loving them. Knowing babies helps us love them even more because we look at them with fascination and with respect for their personhood. When we possess knowledge we see the two-year-old who refuses to go to the potty, not as stubborn, but as self-assertive. When we possess knowledge we see the baby reaching for our earrings or eyeglasses, not as pesky, but as explorative. We see the toddler eating off someone else's plate, not as greedy, but as curious. When we possess knowledge we understand why we need to think "parents" whenever we think "babies," in the context of "family." Knowledge of child development and of the needs of children under age three shapes our perceptions and influences our behavior. Such knowledge places our responses in a broader context, backed by theory, so that we do not behave only in a subjective manner.

We are comforters who soothe distressed children.

We construct such knowledge through various forms of education. There is formal education—courses taken at a university or at a community college or through the Child Development Association (CDA). There is the less formal education of workshops and conferences. There is the education contained in books and journals and in media such as films and videos. There is education in regularly held staff development meetings that encourage person-to-person exchange. There is the education that comes from working directly with another more experienced, admired professional, which produces knowledge of children's development and the ways of working with children. To this day I shall never forget the teacher I worked with so long ago as a student; she became a model for the kind of teacher I wanted to be. Working with her was an important part of my education. I gained knowledge of what a good teacher is. One of my students had a similar experience working with a teacher named Molly—"I carry a little Molly within me," she told me.

It is through our interaction with both formal and informal education with other professionals as well as with children and their families that we acquire knowledge about the needs and development of the child from birth to age three. It is this knowledge that enables us to possess *appropriate expectations* of these little ones—to understand, for example, that two-year-olds need to concentrate on their budding abilities to jump, climb, talk, and listen to stories, and not on learning to read. It is our knowledge of development that leads us to understand that seven- to nine-month-olds often resist leaving their parents' arms for the arms of the caregiver. It is our knowledge of development that helps us understand the toddler's need to say "no" and leads us to find an alternative to the request we have made of that child.

Last, but not least on our list—special personal qualities

I have mentioned experience and knowledge as two distinguishing characteristics of the child care professional. The third comes under the heading of "special personal qualities." In enumerating those qualities I thought about how we are with children under three. In their book *Who Am I In the Lives of Children?*, Feeney and Christensen write that

> . . . the most important characteristic of a good teacher is her ability to be *with* children and not what she does to or for children. Being with children means *really being there*, aware of the child and yourself in relation to the child. (1979, p. 22)

I would like to describe what I think must be our *special qualities* as professional caregivers.

1. *We are anticipators and planners.* Here's an example. Because her caregiver anticipates that Melissa is about to get the 4:30 blues, the caregiver sets Melissa up at the sink with some bubbles in a pot and a big stirring spoon. The caregiver's plan helped Melissa cope with the long day.

Here's another example. After the morning snack, Sandy, the caregiver, tapes a few pieces of brightly colored paper to the table and places a basket of fat, chunky chalk in the center. Four two-year-olds who were at loose ends make a beeline for the table. The caregiver's anticipation made it possible for her to plan for a smooth transition.

2. *We are providers of an interesting environment.* Twenty-month-old Charlie stands next to a large basket of dress-up clothes. A hat, a vest, two lengths of cloth, a skirt, and a shawl are in the basket. He takes them out one by one, looks at each one, and then throws it over his shoulder onto the floor—a perfect toddler activity. The caregiver sits on the floor next to him and says, "That was fun, Charlie; now let's drop them back in the basket," and she hands him the hat for starters. He puts the hat on his head before he drops it in the basket. Then he drops the other items in, one by one.

3. *We are elicitors of language, of problem solving, and of playing.* In *Observing Intelligence in Young Children: Eight Case Studies*, Carew, Chan, and Halfar described a study of 46 children, ages 12 to 33 months, who came from a variety of cultural backgrounds and social classes. The authors' research revealed that certain experiences for these children with their mothers seemed to provide opportunities to learn four types of skills. I describe them here because I think they have important implications for our work as professional caregivers. "The *first* type involves experiences that enable children to learn new words, symbols, or information" (p.7). We do this when we label objects for children—"Oh, thank you for bringing me this beautiful pointed leaf that you found"—or when we read stories or describe events in the environment—"I'm cleaning out the rabbit cage and putting in this fresh newspaper and covering it with these cedar chips so it will be nice and clean."

"The *second* type of experience provides an opportunity for children to master perceptual, spatial, and fine motor skills." We offer this when we provide appropriate puzzles, stacking and nesting cups, or unit blocks that are arranged by shape and size.

"The *third* type of experience gives the child the opportunity to learn basic reasoning skills." We do this in many ways, for instance, when we provide different objects for water play—sieves, which allow the water to run out; cups that keep the water in unless the water flows over the top. "Oh, look, you poured the water in and it came out the holes" or "You put your finger into the play dough and you made this mark" or "What will happen if you put these pebbles in the basin of water?"

Good caregivers provide an interesting environment that includes conversation and opportunities to master perceptual, spatial, fine motor, basic reasoning, and expressive skills, such as those involved in simple art activities and dramatic play.

"The *fourth* category of intellectually valuable experiences provides the child with the opportunity to learn expressive or artistic skills." We do this when we provide space and time for make-believe play or for pretending to be someone else, such as a mommy, a daddy, a dog, a plane, or a baby. We do this when we provide materials like paint, crayons, felt-tipped markers, clay, dough, and blocks, with which children are able to represent their ideas and thoughts. We do this when we value their process rather than their product—"Wow, you went 'round and 'round with that red crayon!"

These authors stress that "any situation, no matter how mundane, can become an intellectually profitable experience for the child depending on what is put into it" (p. 11). What we need to look for is the child's involvement, the child's struggle to understand, the purposefulness of the child's activity—not just the passive reception of information. Dombro and Wallach have written a wonderful book—*The Ordinary is Extraordinary: How Children Under Three Learn.* They help us understand how everyday circumstances like dressing, eating, and doing the laundry are important and learning experiences for babies and toddlers. You don't need a lot of fancy stuff; you need your observant self and attention to the possibilities in the ordinary life around you.

4. *We are protectors.* When Kim tries to take Sabrina's play dough, Sabrina bites Kim's arm before the caregiver can

reach her. Kim lets out a shattering shriek. The caregiver cradles Kim with one arm, checks for broken skin, and strokes Sabrina with the other arm. "No biting," she says firmly. "Tell her 'No, don't take my play dough'—and no biting."

It's hard to be the protector. We need to protect the biter as well as the one who has been bitten because the biter has lost control and needs our help. And let's face it, it's hard to help a biter when you are angry with her for biting. No one ever said child care was easy.

5. *We are listeners and watchers.* Three toddlers are at the snack table eating Cheerios and drinking milk. One toddler decides to pour his milk over the cereal, which is also in a cup. He asks for a spoon. Then the other toddlers, of course, do the same thing. They all want spoons. A lot of Cheerios end up on the table, some on the floor. The caregiver talks with the children about how hard it is to keep those Cheerios on the spoon. There is a lot of giggling as the children imitate one another. Because the caregiver was watching so closely, she could tell when the activity had run its course—"Looks like you're finished, Jessica. Put your cups in this garbage pail," which Jessica does. The caregiver hands her a small sponge and they both wipe up. The other two toddlers join in. It is by listening and observing that we are able to go with the child's rhythm and, by not intruding, become part of the child's process. For example, Andrea watched 12-month-old Gina stand at the plastic garbage pail and swing the top 'round and 'round with her hand. Andrea's observation of Gina's satisfaction with her discovery of how the top of the garbage pail worked kept her from telling Gina "don't play in the garbage"—because she wasn't.

6. *We are smoothers of jangled feelings.* It's Evan's second day in the family day care home, and he's leaving before lunch as part of the gradual entry plan—but he doesn't want to stop playing to leave. His mom tells him, "We'll be back tomorrow and you can play for a longer time." He stamps his feet and begins to whine. The caregiver, smoothing his feelings, says, "Look, Evan, here's a cement mixer. You can take it home and then bring it back tomorrow." He hugs the toy cement mixer to his chest, takes his mother's hand, cheerfully waves goodbye, and leaves.

Good caregivers anticipate trouble and plan so it won't happen.

---

7. *We are comforters.* Jamila's mother just left, but Jamila isn't really happy. She sucks her thumb, whimpers, and has a downcast look on her face. The caregiver holds her. "You miss your mom. She's gone to work, but she'll be

back. She always comes back." She guides Jamila to the wall where the family photographs are displayed, and together they look at the picture of Jamila's mom for a few moments. "You can make a painting for your mom. You can give it to her when she comes back." They go to the easel. Jamila says, "Mommy come back, Mommy come back," and she begins to paint.

8. *We are wizards at coping.* Kathy Modigliani of Wheelock College interviewed caregivers about their satisfaction with their work. She asked, "What makes you happy?" This is what one head teacher of an infant group told her:

> I had one little guy who had a hard time taking to the bottle. He was a breast-fed child. We tried everything. There was no way he would take the bottle. The mom worked well with us. At first she worked half-time. She would come in at noon and nurse him. We kept trying, with breast milk, water, formula, different nipples, everything. One day we were about to give up, when I decided to try putting his blanket over his head so he couldn't see me. He took the milk! It must have been the smell of his blanket, or the fact that he couldn't see my face. It's very encouraging to be able to come upon a problem like that, and solve it. The mom only had a few days before she had to go back to full-time, so that made her happy, and now the child is happy as a clam. So of course that makes me happy.

9. *We help children with social interaction.* The following vignette is from *1, 2, 3, . . . The Toddler Years*, a book written by the staff of the Santa Cruz Toddler Center. It describes children in a sandbox.

> When Sally and Nick grabbed the same bucket they began to yell, "Mine! Mine!" Their caregiver, Carol, knelt down next to the two yelling children and said "You're both pulling on that bucket. You both want it." Sally and Nick kept trying to pull the bucket away from each other, yelling louder and louder. Carol added in a calm, loud voice, "I see you're both mad. You both want that bucket. There are more buckets over there." She pointed to the other buckets lying in the sandbox. Sally stopped yelling and looked to where Carol was still pointing. She ran to the sandbox and grabbed a bucket. Then she looked up at Carol with a big grin on her face, shouting "Bucket!" Carol smile, "That's great, Sally. You found another bucket!" (Van der Zande with Santa Cruz Toddler Care Center Staff, 1986 pp. 62–64)

10. *We are facilitators of parent-child separations.* Two-and-a-half-year-old Alex screamed for quite a long time each morning when his father left. It took three caregivers, working together, more than an hour to calm Alex down. Even then, for a long time after, he still sat in the window where he had watched his dad leave. Maria, the caregiver, observed Alex's face—his furrowed brow, his puckered lips—and realized that he was angry with his dad for leaving. Because she knew how important it is for children to express their feelings, she thought of a way to help Alex. She helped him "write" an angry letter to his father for the next few mornings, after which he was able to get involved in playing. After a few days he no longer needed to write the letter.

11. *We care for the whole family, not only the child.* In one center the cook makes up suppers that parents can buy on their way home. The cook makes some extra money, and *parents* feel cared for. In another setting the provider makes some coffee for herself at the end of the day and shares it with any parent who has a few minutes to spare before going home.

* * *

This list of attributes of the child care professionals is indeed impressive. We may not always realize how many-faceted our work is because we're often too busy doing it. In 1921 Jessie Stanton, a pioneer in early childhood education, set down her tongue-in-cheek notion of the ideal teacher. Among her ideas were that the teacher should have

> . . . a strong physique and a strong well-balanced nervous system. . . . She should be gentle but not sloppy; strong but not impetuous when bitten or scratched. She should have a fair education. By this I mean she should take a doctor's degree in psychology and medicine. . . . She should be an experienced carpenter, mason and plumber and a thoroughly trained musician and poet. . . . She should be able to hypnotize the parents of her young pupils and to cause them to change life-long habits of thinking in two mothers' meetings. (Stanton, 1988)

I am certain that we, too, often feel that to work with young children we truly need all of those characteristics. Yet despite the difficult nature and the public's lack of understanding of our job, research reveals that most

---

Good caregivers are wizards at coping. We sometimes come up with very creative solutions to problems!

---

people who work with young children feel a sense of commitment, satisfaction, and challenge. At the same time, however, the low wages and lack of benefits are driving good people out of the field. As a society we cannot afford this jeopardy to the future of our children and their families.

WE ARE NOT ALONE IN OUR CONCERN

We are beginning to see some coalition building on behalf of the needs of families and children, such as the recent push for federal legislation, candidates addressing child care issues, and the interest of the business community through sponsorship of conferences that address child care and families. Modigliani writes,

> Now parents, community organizations, policy makers, corporations, and foundations are joining us in coalitions to seek solutions. Our problems are being identified and they are beginning to be heard. That is the first step toward solutions. (1986, p. 61)

Passage of the first federal child care legislation, the Child Care and Development Block Grant, is a major accomplishment. Not only does this law assist low-income families in purchasing child care but it give parents a choice in locating their own child care and is designed to help parents determine the characteristics of quality care.

These are important steps toward solutions; however, child care is only as good as the caregivers. We are professionals by the strength of our experience that teaches us to care about children and families; we are professionals by the strength of our knowledge of child development and behavior and the important role of families in children's growth; we are professionals by the strength of our special qualities that enable us to guide children through our understanding, respect, interest, enjoyment, and ability to make supportive relations with them, and their families—to see the child and her family as one unit and the care of the whole family as our goal.

Let us continue to work together toward these common goals—a better life for children and families as well as a better life and much-improved professional status for caregivers.

FOR FURTHER READING

Dittmann, L. (Ed.). (1984). *The infants we care for.* Washington, DC: NAEYC.

Ford, S. (1991). "Real" careers. *Young Children, (46)5*, 56–57.
Goodwin, A., & Schrag, L. (1988). *Setting up for infant care: Guidelines for centers and family day care homes.* Washington, DC: NAEYC.
Greenberg, P. (1991). *Character development: Encouraging self-esteem & self-discipline in infants, toddlers, & two-year-olds.* Washington, DC: NAEYC.
Hendrick, J. (1987). *Why teach?* Washington, DC: NAEYC.
Howes, C. (1989). Infant child care. *Young Children, (44)6*, 24–28.
Weissbourd, B., & Musick, J. (Eds.). (1981). *Infants: Their social environments.* Washington, DC: NAEYC.

REFERENCES

Carew, J.V., Chan, I., & Halfar, C. (1976). *Observing intelligence in young children: Eight case studies.* Englewood Cliffs, NJ: Prentice-Hall, Inc.
Dombro, A., & Wallach, L. (1988). *The ordinary is extraordinary: How children under three learn.* New York: Simon & Schuster.
Feeney, S., & Christensen, D. (1979). *Who am I in the lives of children?* Columbus, OH: Charles E. Merrill Publishing Co.
Modigliani, K. (1986). But who will take care of the children? Childcare, women and devalued labor. *Journal of Education, 168(3)*, 46–69.
Modigliani, K. (1987, November). *The satisfactions and dissatisfactions of early childhood professionals.* Presentation given at NAEYC Annual Conference, Chicago, IL.
Stanton, J. (1988, Fall). The "ideal teacher"—and how she grows. *NY Early Education Reporter,* 5 (originally published in NY Nursery Education News, Winter 1954).
Van der Zande, I., with Santa Cruz Toddler Care Center Staff. (1986). *1, 2, 3 . . . The Toddler Years* Santa Cruz, CA: Santa Cruz Toddler Center.

The Tasks of Early Childhood:
The Development of Self-Control —
Part II

Four-year-old Tommy felt mad that Jonah was hogging the big building blocks. He stood nearby, feeling more and more disgruntled. Just a week ago, his teachers had carried out a group discussion about hitting and hurting. No one was supposed to hit, even if you were mad. The group had discussed other ways to express their feelings. They had talked about telling a child what you wanted, or getting a teacher to help you out.

Alice Sterling Honig
and Therese Lansburgh

Alice Sterling Honig teaches at Syracuse University in the Department of Child and Family Studies, College for Human Development, in Syracuse, NY. She is an editorial board member of Day Care & Early Education. *Therese Lansburgh is Chair of the Maryland Committee for Children and an advocate for families and children at the state and national levels.*

But Tommy got so frustrated. Impulsively, he clenched his fist and raised his arm above his head. Ms. Ida glanced over and looked straight at him with a reminding look. "I wasn't going to hit him. I was only just raising my arm, Ms. Ida," Tommy protested. She smiled encouragingly and helped Tommy find another activity to interest him.

Nine-month-old Natalie was restless and whimpering, feeling so hungry she was ready to start hard crying. She needed her bottle and she needed it right away. But Ms. Mollie was not quite ready. She was just finishing a diaper clean-up and was washing her hands. She called softly over to reassure Natalie. Hearing her caregiver's reassuring tones, Natalie brought her fist up to her mouth. She managed to get some fingers into her mouth and suck vigorously. She was able to calm herself and keep in control for a few minutes until her caregiver came over with a bottle of milk and a lap to snuggle Natalie while feeding her.

Three-and-one-half-year-old Deanna was in a crowded shopping mall with her parents. They needed to buy many more items than those on their list, and the shopping trip was growing very long and tiring for their little girl. Papa said, "Deanna, we did not realize that we would need to buy so many extra things, and that our

From Day Care & Early Education, Summer 1991, pp. 21-26. Published by Human Sciences Press, 72 Fifth Avenue, New York, NY 10011.

shopping trip would take this long. We're sorry. Thank you for being so patient." The little girl acknowledged her father's courteous explanation and apology and sighed, *"Well, I guess it was necessary."* Her father smiled with pride — at her forbearance and her big vocabulary for such a little girl.

The children described above were practicing a precious skill — the skill of *self-control.* In a time when crime levels are soaring, and many persons heedlessly hurt others horribly with assault, rape, and murder, the personal attributes of self-control are particularly important. The sophisticated conscience of an adult may take years a-building. But the building blocks begin in early childhood. Self-control is a good signpost that moral development is proceeding well for young children.

What Is Self-Control?

Self control in the preschool years is expressed in the ability to:

Trust and cooperate with adults.

Delay the gratification of immediate needs or wants for a little while.

Find internal ways to be more patient without blaming or hurting others.

Channel angry impulses so that words instead of fists are used.

Think about and empathize with upset feelings of others.

Balance rights with responsibilities.

Find ways to cheer up even when things go wrong.

Take turns.

Recognize other's rights as well as one's own.

Find inner ways to keep from whining or falling apart into temper tantrums despite frustrations.

Modify the frequency and intensity of unacceptable actions according to situational needs, even when teachers or parents are not present.

All societies have rules regarding acceptable or unacceptable behavior for children beyond infancy. Parents and other caregivers in the culture teach children what is permitted (toileting on a potty; blowing your nose in a hanky; asking for a turn with a toy) and what is disapproved (wiping one's nose on one's hand; whacking a peer so you can grab a toy).

When children are very young, adults often maintain strong *external* controls over child behavior. Adults scoop up a toddler who may be ready to bop another baby over the head with a toy. They use scolds, or they distract and refocus the little one. They repeat simple rules over and over. Sometimes they arrange environments to *prevent* conflicts of interest or will when a toddler will get too frustrated and then burst into a temper tantrum or act out angrily. Often *proactive* discipline techniques are used to prevent loss of self-control. For example, a wise parent (knowing that sitting a child in the grocery cart while Papa shops in a crowded store may well end up in a cranky scene, with the child demanding sweets at the checkout counter) often brings along an apple or a few crackers to head off the child's loss of emotional control.

As a preschooler grows, her or his behavior seems to be more and more maintained by *internalized* standards of conduct, particularly when authority figures are not around to say, "No!" Consider the young toddler who moves with fascination toward the wall plug into which a tempting lamp cord is plugged. As she approaches and wants to reach to pull out the cord or poke a finger into the plug, she says to herself, "No, no, no plug" and toddles sadly away. She is well along in the process of developing self-control.

Such behavior begins very early with the help of skilled caregivers who understand the individual differences in children and the seesawing that a child will go through while learning more mature emotional behavior.

Flexibility of Control: Our Goal for Children

Self-control is not easy to learn. Young children have strong needs and few cognitive skills for understanding why they have to wait for a turn or to take others' needs into account.

Sometimes caregivers are so anxious to "civilize" young children that they teach a rote technique like saying, "I'm sorry," without helping a youngster to develop more awareness of others' rights or awareness of the effects of hurtful actions.

Four-year-old Vern had hit a child just a few minutes ago. The teacher had quietly and firmly restated classroom rules about hitting. Now he again raised his fist angrily, about to hit another child. The teacher swiftly moved over and kneeled in front of him, looking him directly in the eye. "Vern, what are you going to do with your hands?" she asked. He was silent. "You were about to hit someone," the teacher said. "That makes me feel angry. We just talked about what hands are for. And hands are not for hitting or hurting someone. Now, you tell me, Vern, what are hands for?" "For hugging ... for playing with toys," Vern answered tentatively. "OK, then, when you feel angry, Vern, what could you do?" the teacher inquired. "I could hug somebody," Vern rejoined. The teacher looked at him. "Vern, I was feeling so angry with you when you went to hit someone that I didn't want to hug you. When you are feeling angry, do you really want to hug someone?" Vern shook his head no. The teacher continued, "When I am angry with you, do I hit you?" Vern said, "No, never." The teacher pursued, "Vern, what *am* I doing with you?" Vern replied, "Talking." "Yes," agreed the teacher, "And what could *you* do when you are feeling angry?" "I could talk," suggested Vern.

Some adults place very high demands for obedience, polite behavior, and neatness on young children, so that the children feel anxious and overcontrolled. Such children may be fearful of using finger paint or playdough because they have been taught that getting messy is something strongly disapproved of by their special adults. Some preschool children have difficulties with constipation because they have been made too fearful about a possible mess in their pants.

On the other hand, some adults bring up little children without the firm guidance, clear rules, and social expectations necessary to assist young children into more socially acceptable interactions. Such children may act rudely, gallop wildly, kick or hit others, and be heedless of other children's or the teacher's needs and rules in the preschool classroom. Neither *overcontrol* nor *undercontrol* is a desirable outcome. Overcontrolled children often act rigid and joyless, not spontaneous. They may be highly anxious, or critical of other children's misbehavior. Undercontrolled children may lash out aggressively or crumple into temper tantrums and whining at the slightest frustration, or they may be easily led into mischief by more dominant peers. *Ego resiliency* refers to flexibility of controls (Honig, 1985), a highly desirable goal for children.

Factors That Influence Self-Control

What factors influence the development of *knowledge* of what is permissible and what is prohibited, of what situations require patience and a willingness to wait? What factors influence children's *ability* to wait, to use words instead of fists, to take others' feelings into consideration, to cooperate instead of defy or cry? Parental child-rearing techniques and the child's cognitive level are probably the most important influences, but other factors come into play, too. Inherited capacities, cultural and religious norms and practices, child-care-setting characteristics, peer interactions (such as bullying or friendliness), and teacher support for prosocial learnings in the classroom are also important influences in shaping children's development of self-control (Honig, 1982).

Babies learn only gradually *what* they must control about their strong emotional responses and *when* and *how* they are expected to control them. Learning self-control begins early. By four months, a baby picked up for nursing may strain and fuss a bit, but she can wait for a few minutes until her caregiver is ready to begin the feeding. She no longer yowls immediately or loudly in response to pangs of hunger when her caregiver has picked her up. She has begun already to learn self-control.

Differences in Temperament

Some children are born more easygoing. Some have a more cheerful mood, and some are more cautious (Thomas and Chess, 1981). Helping easygoing children develop self-control can be easier than working with children whose temperaments are more triggery or impulsive, or who have a low tolerance of any sort of frustration.

Some toddlers have a predisposition to shyness. They stay close to an adult when taking a walk in the neighborhood around the child care center. Others may try to dash madly off down the street. Some are frightened by new experiences, tend to comply with adults, and seem more obedient. Thus, some children may appear self-controlled, but their temperamental fearfulness is what impels their "good" behavior.

Age and Maturity

Just as they differ in the timing and skill with which they develop motoric competence in walking, running, and climbing, children differ in their ability to learn the task of self-control. Some adults have inappropriate expectations about when a child will be able to handle disappointment, anger, frustration, or jealousy more maturely. Children who are expected to develop adult-desired self-control in too many areas too soon, before they are ready, may become overly solemn, sullen, and sneaky, or defiant and noncooperative.

Mastery of Other Emotional Tasks

Children who have developed a basically trusting and secure relationship with their caregivers, who feel that their actions bring results and that they are *willing to try* (Honig and Lansburgh, 1990) are more likely also to develop a sense of personal responsibility for their own actions. Such children learn to influence others in positive ways as friends. They also feel confident enough so that they can have influence over their own internal impulses. Those with little basic trust

in the positive regard of their caregivers or those in whom severe threats and punishments have damaged the will to try may be too discouraged to tackle the work of controlling their impulsive, disapproved behaviors toward others. Grown-ups have dominated them, and they do not see that their own internal efforts at control can be successful.

Parental Methods of Teaching Self-Discipline and Control

Parents and caregivers differ in their ways of socializing and disciplining children. They vary in their ability to "read" a baby's signals. Caregiver beliefs and skills in socializing children are crucial determinants of how successful a young child will be in developing self-control. *Socialization* means learning how to behave in ways approved by your family and culture. For example, during the first year of life, infants gradually learn to obey an adult's firm "no-no" for touching dangerous objects, such as a sharp pair of scissors or an unprotected electrical plug.

Some adults have unrealistic expectations too early that a baby can understand the meaning of "No" or "Quit that!" Often, a baby is bewildered and frightened by the sharp tone and the anger and threat in the adult's voice. Suppose a baby in a high chair is curious about what has happened to the toy he just pushed off the edge of the table top. Where could it be? Curiously the ten-month-old lifts his body to peer over the edge. "Cut that out!" says the caregiver sharply. Startled, the baby bursts into tears. His behavior was interpreted by the adult (unaware of how the baby is figuring this situation out) as deliberate and willful disobedience of the rules for staying in one's seat.

When teachers and parents understand developmentally what task a very young child is trying to accomplish, they may not be so overcontrolling. Finding a positive way to say, "Sit down, honey. Your toy fell down on the floor and I will get it for you. Sit down nice and safe, please!" will be more helpful than undecipherable warnings and prohibitions that cause a baby to freeze but do not lead to either understanding or inner controls.

Some discipline techniques work better than others at helping children develop self-control. Researches have shown that *power-assertive* discipline that involves physical punishment or threats of physical punishment, in particular, leads to defiance and lack of mastery of aggressive actions. Even though they may temporarily stop "misbehaving," these children have been given a strong example of *how* to lose self-control and to use external power to get others to do what they want!

Some types of discipline have been found far more likely to lead to compliance and self-control. Where *inductive discipline* is used by parents, toddlers begin early to self-monitor and to avoid actions for which they have internalized the rules (Hoffman, 1977). What are inductive methods? They include *reasoning with children* and *explaining the reasons for rules*, rather than using forceful commands, punishments, or threats. Children who have been brought up with parents who use firm rules, give explanations, have high expectations of approved behavior, and are positively and genuinely committed to their child's welfare are more likely to internalize controls. Baumrind (1977) has called this kind of parenting "authoritative" in contrast to either "permissive" or "authoritarian" (dictatorial) disciplining.

Authoritative caregivers are *for* their children. They are warm and nurturant, yet they have high expectations of their children. They are firm in not accepting unacceptable behavior, are effective in disciplining, and explain clearly the reasons why they discipline as they do. Permissive caregivers act in a nonpunitive way, but they let unacceptable behavior go on without dealing with it, and they do not require the child to learn to behave more responsibly and maturely.

Lara came home from the day care and told her mother, "It's OK to hit. You just don't know. It's OK to hit, 'cause when we hit in the day care, Miss Kathy doesn't do anything to anybody."

When adults do not firmly stop bullying or do not notice scapegoating, then they are supporting the continuation of social patterns that do not promote self-control, positive socialization, or optimal peer interactions. Authoritarian patterns are also nonproductive. If a child is required to accept forceful discipline and an adult's authority as absolute, that child can become more nervous, more stressed, and more likely to act out insecurity and resentment by aggressive or aggrieved actions toward others.

Research on Self-Control

Toddlers who have had secure attachments to a nurturant, responsive parent do not fall apart or give up when faced with a difficult tool-using task. Sroufe (1979) found that such toddlers, when faced with challenging tasks, were more able to maintain self-control; they persisted longer without temper tantrums and were more likely to enlist their parents' support in struggling to solve the tool-using tasks which were too hard for them to solve on their own. In contrast, other mothers gave orders but not helpful assistance to their toddlers. They had been insensitive to their children in infancy. These children gave up easily, were unable to maintain self-control, became oppositional, and had more temper tantrums.

The securely attached infants who had exhibited more self-control in the tool-using tasks as toddlers were rated at five years of age, by their preschool teachers as highly ego-resilient, self-reliant, and moderate in self-control. The children who had been insecurely attached in early infancy, and who had had been poor at self-control as toddlers under the stressful task conditions in the laboratory, were rated either as much more undercontrolled or overcontrolled. Thus, research has significantly linked self-control to early patterns of infant-parent attachment.

Longitudinal studies follow children over several years. In one such study at the University of Minnesota, 120 children aged three to seven years were given an attractive toy for a short period of time and were then told to stop playing with it (Masters and Binger, 1976). Almost half of the two-year-olds were able to inhibit their impulses when their parents asked them to stop playing with the attractive toy. The percentages of self-control rose dramatically with age, most sharply between two and three years of age. When the children were followed over time, self-control proved to be quite a stable individual characteristic. That is, the children who had good control at age two made greater progress later in self-control.

A talking-clown box was used with 70 four-year-old boys and girls by Patterson and Mischel (1976) to tempt children off-task. The preschoolers were warned that the clown box might tempt them to stop working at their pegboard task, and in that case they would lose an opportunity to play with attractive toys after the pegboard work and would be allowed to play only with broken toys.

Groups of children were taught verbalizations that they could repeat to the clown box in order to help them control the temptation to give up working and thus forfeit the reward they desired. The first group were helped to resist temptation by concentrating on the promised reward. The researcher suggested that they say to themselves, "I want to play with the fun toys and Mr. Clown Box *later*." In the second group the children were to say to themselves, "I'm going to look at my work." Children in a third group were told they could say anything they wanted to themselves to help them avoid looking at the clown box. A nursery rhyme or something else irrelevant was suggested to the fourth group, and the fifth group received no instructions. Children in the first and second groups — those for whom the later reward was emphasized and those who were helped to plan in detail how to ignore Mr. Clown — worked longer at the pegboard task than those children who has less specific plans or no plan. Thus, some self-instructional plans of what to say to yourself are more helpful than others in boosting children's ability to resist temptations that can distract them from their tasks.

At what point, while a child is misbehaving, does a caregiver need to intervene? Some boys in one research study were stopped just before they reached for a forbidden toy. Others were not stopped until after they had touched the toy (Walters, Parke, and Cane, 1965). Adult prevention *prior* to the unacceptable behavior was more effective: The boys in that group demonstrated greater self-control in resisting temptation later when they were left alone with the forbidden toy.

In stress research, self-control has proved to be a factor, along with high self-esteem, problem-solving skills, and higher empathy, that allows children to cope when they live highly stressed lives. Fourth- to sixth-grade urban children who proved resilient despite many stresses were found to have more internalized controls and more realistic expectations for self-control in mastering stressful life conditions (Parker et al., 1990).

Teacher Techniques for Promoting Self-Control

What can caregivers do to promote self-control in early-childhood educational settings? Researches suggest first that a warm, personally attentive, genuinely focused relationship with a child will increase that child's self-esteem and chances of trying harder to control impulses toward disorganization or hurtfulness toward others.

The *teacher is a powerful role model.* If a caregiver shouts, acts very irritated, or blows up at naughtiness, then children are being given a message that it is OK to have a short fuse and lose control.

Teachers can stay near a child who has difficulty in mastering forbidden actions. If an adult is nearby and caring and supportive, the child who may have a strong urge to act out aggressively by sweeping the frustrating puzzle pieces off the table or hitting a peer will get prompt signals from the teacher. The teacher will keep the classroom and the children safe and secure. The child does not have to explode or act out in anger and fright. A calm, supportive, and alert teacher nearby serves as a beacon of security (Wolfgang, 1977).

Prevention Helps

When children are overtired or teased or feel that others have unfairly received more than their share, they may more easily act out. Teachers need to make sure that fair access to toys and materials is provided. Overcrowding, as when too many children are in a small block corner, can trigger out-of-control use of blocks as pretend guns or throwing toys, which results in hurt children and hurt feelings. Thoughtful planning and judicious use of space as well as resources both help children maintain good self-control in play.

Reasoning with children, as well as providing understandable explanations of regulations, promotes children's development of notions of what is acceptable and what is expected. Such *inductive techniques* promote self-control far more than overcontrolling, critical, or overly permissive methods.

Bibliotherapy is a helpful aid. Teachers need to choose books that tell stories about animals or children who are in difficult, stressful, scary, or frustrating situations where the characters try hard not to use mad feelings or angry outbursts and do try to use more reasonable ways to solve their problems. Children identify with such story characters.

Good plans to remember rules and reasons boost self-control. Teachers can help children think of good plans to help themselves remember rules against hitting. Caregivers can give children words to say that will aid them in controlling impulsivity. One preschooler ran and ran in the long hallways of his center located in a church basement. He would yell out, "Yo-yo, come and play with me," to a four-year-old girl he liked very much. The teacher explained to Yolanda that she could keep working on her puzzle, and tell her friend, "I'm busy working on my puzzle. You come here and do puzzles with me." This verbal scaffolding helped Yolanda not to dash off and run aimlessly as well as helped lure her playmate into a more constructive activity.

Refocus children on appropriate interactions and activities. If children's play seems to be veering toward a loss of self-control, the caregivers need to step in judiciously and redirect the children. Adults can use firm suggestions. With toddlers, distraction and luring the toddler into more appropriate activities help support positive play while preventing inappropriate behaviors.

If a child has totally lost self-control and is kicking and yelling, a caregiver may need to hold that child firmly so that the child cannot pose a danger to others. The teacher can reassure the child, "I will not let you hurt others or yourself. You can get back into control. I will help you. You are feeling very upset. I will hold you so you feel safe until you can get calm again and get back into control."

Use encouragement and admiration when children are showing good self-control. Specific praise helps. Admire a child who has struggled to use words instead of fists. In the child care setting, express appreciation when children have been patient even though the lunch delivery was delayed. Children need to know that their special persons, their teachers, value their struggles to work toward self-control, an important foundation for classroom cooperation and compliance.

References

Baumrind, D. (1977). Some thoughts about childrearing. In S. Cohen and T. J. Comiskey (eds.), *Child Development: Contemporary perspectives.* Itasca, IL: Peacock.

Hoffman, M. L. (1977). Moral internalization: Current theory and research. In L. Berkowitz (ed.), *Advances in experimental social psychology,* Vol. 10. New York: Academic Press.

Honig, A. S. (1982). Prosocial development in children. *Young Children, 37*(5), 51-62.

Honig, A. S. (1985). Research in review: Compliance, control, and discipline. *Young Children*, Part 1, *40*(2), 50-58; Part 2, *40*(3), 47-52.

Honig, A. S., and Lansburgh, T. (1990). The tasks of early childhood: Part I. The will to try. *Day Care and Early Education, 18*(2), 4-10.

Masters, J.C., and Binger, C.C. (1976, Sept.). *Inhibitive capacity in young children: stability and development.* Paper presented at the annual meeting of the American Psychological Association, New York.

Parker, G. R., Cowen, E. L., Work, W. C., and Wyman, P. A. (1990). Test correlates of stress affected and stress resilient outcomes among urban children. *Journal of Primary Prevention, 11,* 19-35.

Patterson, C. J., and Mischel, W. (1976). *Self-instructional plans and children's resistance to temptation.* (ERIC Document Reproduction Service No ED 141-679).

Spaner, S. D., and Jordon, T. E. (1973). *Analysis of maternal antecedents to locus of control at age 60 months.* (ERIC Document Reproduction Service No. 087 555).

Sroufe, L. A. (1979). The coherence of individual development. *American Psychologist, 34* 834-841.

Thomas, A., and Chess, S. (1981). The role of temperament in the contribution of children to their own development. In R. M. Lerner and N. A. Busch-Rossnagel (eds.). *Individuals as producers of their own development.* New York: Academic Press.

Walters, R. H., Parke, R. D., and Cane, V. A. (1965). Timing of punishment and the observation of consequences to others as determinants of response inhibition. *Journal of Experimental Child Psychology, 2,* 10-30.

Wolfgang, C. H. (1977). *Helping aggressive and passive preschoolers through play.* Columbus, OH: Merrill.

A is for Apple, P is for Pressure—
Preschool Stress Management

JANAI LOWENSTEIN

Janai Lowenstein is codirector of the Conscious Living Foundation in Drain, OR 97435.

"Why, preschoolers don't need stress management. They don't have stress! All they have to do is play and grow up." The person responsible for this statement had no daily contact with or knowledge of the dynamics involved in a child's reality. While the sources of stress may differ—for example, a child may be stressed from learning how to share toys while mom and dad are plagued with financial concerns—all individuals, whether adults or children, experience stress. We develop our patterns of stress response when we being life and interact with the environment around us.

Although children learn about stress in much the same way that adults do, the physical aspects are more important to them. From the onset, their learning has to be tactile; they need to see, touch, hear, and feel their way through stress signs in order to fully understand the concepts of stress management. They are accustomed to learning about themselves in relationship to their environment outside their bodies: tie shoes to prevent tripping; wear a raincoat when it is raining, and so on. Therefore, a structure must be built to bridge a child's internal experience with the external environment for greater understanding of self.

By teaching preschoolers how to make healthy choices for themselves regarding their own behavior, teachers and parents give children a foundation for building self-care and self-confidence. Helping children develop an internal frame of reference will increase their self-control in dealing with life's ongoing stressors rather than allow them to feel victimized by blaming those stressors for how they think, feel, and act. Children can polish their skills by practicing during stressful events and as a result, gain self-esteem. Without skills for handling stress, they are more apt to wallow in confusion, self-doubt, and self-pity, and depend on external stimuli for temporary gratification.

Two basic concepts must be established through teaching modalities to firmly set the groundwork for teaching stress management skills:

1. Understanding how the mind, body, and emotions work together; and
2. Realizing that there are appropriate and inappropriate levels of relaxation and tension.

Since learning, adaptability, curiosity, and implementing new skills with self and the environment are at a premium for readiness in the preschool years, children in this age range can easily be taught stress management skills. However, applying and reinforcing these skills in daily occurrences creates the real potential for practical use over the life span. To teach stress management skills and to apply stress management techniques, teachers must recognize stress signs. As children become aware of their own stress signs, they can prevent unnecessary tension and assume more responsibility for their own psychophysiological health.

Recognizing Stress

In most instances, stress signs are easily monitored in children. By knowing a child's normal state of being (body language, ways of expression, eye sheen, eating and sleeping habits, ways of interacting with others, and playing behaviors) it is easier to notice changes. For example, withdrawal or frequent acting out, restlessness during the day or night, destruction of objects, nightmares, biting nails, jiggling hands and feet, abrupt body movements, changes in vocal tones and energy levels, cold hands/feet, irritability, lack of concentration, extra body tension (e.g., twitching, stiff shoulders) can all be signals that something is not right. However, deviations in a child's normal range

This article is reprinted with permission from the *JOPERD* (Journal of Physical Education, Recreation & Dance), February 1991, pp. 55-58. *JOPERD* is a publication of the American Alliance for Health, Physical Education, Recreation and Dance, 1900 Association Drive, Reston, VA 22091-1599.

of behaviors can also mean there is a new stage of growth or an illness setting in. Such deviations also could be indicative of nutritional deficiency, allergy or physical ailment, all of which are stressors themselves. One of the benefits gained in the analysis of this unknown sea of stressors and signals is the fact that as children learn to recognize their own stress signs, they learn more about themselves.

Another point to remember is that if there is stress in the lives of

> **If there is stress in the lives of the adults who care for the child, there will undoubtedly be stress signs in the child.**

the adults who care for the child, there will undoubtedly be stress signs in the child because he or she is an integral part of the system, whether at home, school, or elsewhere.

Beyond normal stress, "superstress" is sweeping the land and children are not forgotten in its wake. Our culture is filled with cancer producing food additives, water-air-land-sun polluting toxins, disintegration of the family system, soaring economic pressures upon the working classes, lack of reality in television programming, and rampant drug use. Consequently, what were once considered stress-related illnesses for adults are now infiltrating very young bodies. Professionals in the medical field agree that an increasing number of young children are suffering from tension migraine headaches, ulcers, eating and sleeping disorders, hyperactivity, nervous disorders, blood sugar imbalances,

violence and suicides, and depression and apathy.

What Teachers Can Do

Teachers at all levels must teach and use basic stress management skills in the classroom. Demonstrate the difference between appropriate and inappropriate levels of tension and relaxation. For example, show children which groups of muscles it is necessary to tighten while carrying a chair or heavy object across the room. Let them do it, then discuss the experience. Next, demonstrate how you would look if you tensed those same muscles while talking with a friend. Again, let the children experience it to feel and know for themselves. Assign partners and let the children role-play with each other.

Between activities requiring focused attention, choose one emotion at a time to explore. For example, suggest everyone (including you) make an angry, tense face and body; make angry sounds, stomp around with angry movements, even dance an angry dance. Point out that the mind, body, and emotional feelings always work together. To do a thorough job, the children should notice how their angry thoughts and emotions create body tension. Next, have children do the same for a totally different emotion such as happiness, noticing again how the mind, body, and emotions work together. Let the children understand that it is impossible to have angry thoughts and a happy body or feelings. They should also pay attention to the fact that they are in control of changing everything inside them! By playing with the spectrum of emotions in this way, children can become aware of their internal body signals, telling them which emotion is in place at any given time. It is much harder to lose control when an internal reference point is in place.

Exploring Stress through Role-Playing

Nonverbal role-plays can be used to help children exaggerate a situation

with their bodies. This type of activity facilitates an increased awareness internally for personal stress signs. Begin by first role-playing an emotion. Show facial tension, body tension and movement. Let the children guess what emotion you are depicting and which of your body parts are tense. Ask them what kinds of thoughts you were having, too. It is important to reinforce the mind/body/emotional connection frequently.

An energizing way to reinforce the concepts of tension/relaxation, emotional awareness and mind/body coordination is to explore a jungle with the children right in your own living room, backyard, or school gymnasium. Simply ask children to join you in becoming an angry ape, sad snake, tense tiger, happy hyena, cowardly kitten who can turn into a courageous cat, or any combination of tense and relaxed animals. Act out each animal, making appropriate noises and body motions. Children are enthusiastically creative when they can learn through their own fun experiences.

Find other modes of reinforcement that can meld into the stream of activities already established. If children already stretch occasionally, vary the stretching pace through emotional awareness (e.g., excited stretch, slow and sad stretch, etc.). If it is rainy outside and there's a need for stress-relief from lack of exercise, children can do some jealous jumping in place, some happy arm swinging, and nervous body jitters.

When eyes are dazed, attention span is scattered, and yawns dot the classroom, allow the children to drift into right brain activity with a relaxation exercise emphasizing health, history, or science fiction exploration. The quickest way for children to enter a deep state of relaxation and simultaneously release some tension, is to tell them to put lots of hard, tight, tense spots all over their bodies. Tell them to hold tension everywhere while you count to five. Look for scrunched up faces, contorted torsos, tightened toes, and shallow breathing movement. Demonstrate how to do it first. While they are all tense, have them pay attention to the fact that they are holding their breath. Then instruct them to release all the tension at once, letting out deep sighs of relief. If time allows, use imagery by having the children close their eyes while you guide them on a fun, relaxing journey to a rainbow planet, another time in history, or to magical woods where you can encourage them to feel good about themselves. When children are relaxed, with eyes closed, it is easy to reinforce the lessons of the day by reviewing them briefly.

In everyday interaction with children, it is important to integrate stress management concepts into normal activities. First, develop a language system to fit your needs and the activities you are already engaged in with the children. Speak more about emotions, where you feel tense inside, what your thoughts are like, and the fact that you need to take a deep breath when you are upset.

Help children become more aware of stressful situations and make healthier choices by saying, "Gee, Bobby, your shoulders look pretty tight and tense. And your forehead looks wrinkled like something is bothering you. What are you feeling and thinking right now?" As the role model, you may need to share how you feel when you tense similar areas. Provide a body outline for the child to use, coloring body parts that feel hard and tense or simply marking them with an "X." This provides a tactile mode of expression and reinforcement in the child's internal awareness as well as improved ability to communicate clearly about his or her internal world.

In addition, create space on the agenda for children to personally share what causes stress or tension in their lives. Lists (words or pictures) can be made and group discussions can be facilitated. Role-

plays can be generated for awareness, expression, and creative problem-solving once children understand the basic concepts of stress management.

When a few minutes are available, children can close their eyes and slowly, deeply, breathe rainbow colors into their bodies. (They can color this later to show you what they look like when they help themselves feel good by filling themselves with different colors or rainbows.) Also, if difficulties arise helping a child discover which emotion he or she feels, choosing a color that rep-

> *Create space on the agenda for children to personally share what causes stress or tension in their lives.*

resents the feeling inside his or her body can help. Follow through with artwork if appropriate. Help children to breathe fun colors into the body parts that were tense after processing uncomfortable situations.

What Parents Can Do
Parents can teach and role-model basic stress management skills easily in the home. They can also reinforce skills being taught in preschool or day-care, or suggest to their child-care administrators that these concepts be taught if they are not presently utilized.

All the aforementioned techniques can be introduced in the home setting with one or more children. If only one child is present, puppets can be used to enhance group discussions. Puppets are also handy in any young children's group to prompt discussions and

understanding as well as to reinforce concepts. A fun, tactile exercise for teaching the difference between tension and relaxation is easily facilitated if a rock and sock are available. Place a rock in one of the child's hands, a soft sock in the other. Model the exercise yourself as you explain how to tighten body parts to make them hard like the rock, then take a deep breath and relax individual body parts to make them soft like the sock. Start with the face, tensing and then relaxing, and progress all the way down to the feet, one body part at a time. Be sure to use the words "tight, hard and tense," referring to the rock and "soft, calm and relaxed," referring to the sock.

Children frequently are so subjectively caught in their emotional turmoil that they have little or no understanding of what they are projecting into the world around them, let alone what their appearance is to others. A portable mirror is an unpopular tool (from the child's point of view) to use during outbursts of emotion caused by anger, jealousy, frustration or the like. Have this self-reflector easy to reach, but out of the child's sight, then raise it up to meet the child's eyes right in the middle of the tantrum or experience you want the child to see. This reflection can teach children more about themselves than any number of words. However, it will be important to explain why this is being done and ask children at the appropriate moment what they have seen and learned about themselves. Another dynamic tool is to role-play a child's emotional outburst. After this, ask the child to display the way he or she sees you expressing yourself when upset. Stress management reinforcement is a two-way street!

The Breath of Life
Whether working with children at home, school, the playground, in the grocery store or in a car, there is one central key that can provide magic in this process for all parties concerned…the breath of life! All

relaxation skills have one true core: deep, even, slow breathing. Just as tension can create more tension in any situation, deep breathing can render speedy healing to an ailing body, mind, or emotions, as well as provide self-control in the midst of anxiety and chaos. Make a game of checking heart rates by placing hands on chests to feel fast or slow heartbeats.

Take deep breaths every time the cuckoo clock strikes or a telephone rings. Make it fun and easy to integrate! Have hand-check games: touch each others' hands to see if they are warm, which generally indicates relaxation, or cool, indicative of internal arousal.

Educating children about life has always been a major responsibility of a society in any given time. If we want our most precious resource, children, to survive whatever is ahead in our super-stressed world, they must have the tools made available to them to cope with daily stressors. Their own internal resources are waiting to be tapped, the resources they will have with them through every step in life's journey. Without these basic life skills, they will have difficulty making healthy choices for their own well-being. By knowing themselves, they can choose right actions over wrong actions, feel good enough about themselves to be content without substance abuse, and know how to prevent stress-related illnesses. They will also be able to communicate clearly, to respect others because they respect themselves, and be able to nurture healthy relationships. Most of all, they will care. It is easy to incorporate stress management skills into children's lives, as easy as remembering that A is for Apple, P is for Pressure.

The Role of Art in Stress Management

In both home and school settings, artwork can prove to be an invaluable tool for awareness, expression, and reinforcement. Preschoolers who can understand the spoken word and hold a crayon can use colors on paper to express their feelings if given instructions and opportunities to do so. The artwork of an angry child will present quite a contrast to that of a child who is feeling content. Use the artwork as a media to help young children learn to label, understand, and talk about their emotions. Place a variety of colored sheets done by children on the refrigerator or a wall and ask them what feeling each sheet has.

Once again, create every opportunity that can possibly be woven into life's scheme. Have body outlines available for children to color regarding their internal experiences, thus providing a steady stream of tactile bridging between their inner and external worlds. The body outlines become a self-made mirror for the children, and provide adults with a means of helping the children to help themselves.

A note of caution regarding use of the body outlines: When children first begin learning about what is going on inside their bodies, a common response to the question "Where do you feel tight or tense inside?" is "Everywhere." Unfamiliar with their own internal geography, it will be important for you to either ask questions about body parts, one at a time, and/or be firm in telling the child to choose one or two body parts that feel tighter or harder than any other parts.

Curricular Applications

- **Creating and Inventing (Articles 45–47)**
- **Content and Process (Articles 48–50)**

The first subsection of this unit is called *Creating and Inventing*. The three new articles chosen for this subsection are very appropriate, for they all focus on the value of play in the classroom. In some areas of the country, parents are beginning to register serious concern for play-based programs. It has become increasingly important for early childhood teachers and administrators to educate parents on the benefits of a play-based curriculum and the importance of children's developing a strong early foundation in exploration, self-initiated behavior, and skill in manipulating equipment and materials. When a curriculum is developed based on the children's interests and local conditions, and this is explained through visual, oral, and written formats, it can assist parents in understanding the value of play in the whole curriculum. But when parents receive little, if any, explanation and simply observe groups of children playing in various areas of the room with blocks or buttons, they fail to grasp the role of a play-based curriculum. Therefore, professionals in early childhood education have education as one of their major

tasks. Developing a philosophy and implementing an early childhood program that focuses on the developmental needs of young children requires, in addition to time and money, a thorough knowledge of how to select play materials and media for children of differing ages, abilities, and backgrounds. It also requires one to be skilled in conveying to others goals and objectives and how these will be attained.

The unit continues with three articles on the content and process of quality early childhood programs. The subsection starts with "The Many Faces of Child Planning," which details ways in which children indicate their plans for the day, and to what degree they outline how they will spend their time. Teachers often devote a great deal of thought and attention to planning activities, arranging the environment and selecting materials in which the children can participate and use during free choice, discovery, or work time, but never give a thought as to how to present the choices or how to assist the children in planning for and beginning their day.

Playing with materials and language is the way the young child conquers the world of objects and symbols and constructs knowledge about their properties. As children grow and begin to communicate through print, they are embarking upon one of the most challenging, yet rewarding, skills one can develop. The four-year-old who tells his mother to "Write this in a note to brother and put it on the counter. 'Dear Baba, do you want to sleep together tonight?' " is well on his way to understanding the use and power of the written word. The seven-year-old brother who replies in a note also left on the kitchen counter, "Mabe another night we can. I am going to see the harlm globtroters with Ryan tonight," should be encouraged to continue to put words on paper. Creative writing takes many forms, and just as learning to talk is a long process, so is learning to write. Teachers who are aware of steps children take in emergent literacy recognize the unique skills children bring to the reading process and capitalize upon their eagerness for learning and their insatiable appetite for encouragement while they are learning. In "Writing in Kindergarten: Helping Parents Understand the Process," answers to commonly asked questions are given, along with charts that show examples of children's writing at various stages of development.

The time that children spend in appropriate large muscle development is time well spent when one reads the numerous research studies detailing the inferior physical condition of children in the United States today. Teachers often are so focused on planning for the brief choice time each morning, which often centers on creative and cognitive activities, that gross motor development is left to the 30 minutes of free time spent running around on a poorly equipped and unsafe playground.

For the curriculum to be truly child-centered, teachers must get away from using pre-set themes that are recycled each year and have little if any interest to the children in a particular group. The knowledge and keenly aware professional will use his or her skills in observing and listening to young children at play, in conversations at snacks and meals, and during routines to develop a curriculum that is based on individual and local interests that appeal to the children. A program that presents to parents a neatly typed list of weekly themes for the year in September has little concern for planning to meet the individual needs and interests of the children in that center or specific class. The term child-centered can take on new meaning if teachers use their knowledge of child development while planning the curriculum.

Looking Ahead: Challenge Questions

What do young children actually learn by playing? How can play materials be evaluated for their contribution to children's development? What are the developmental characteristics of play?

What are the benefits of invented or temporary spelling in assisting the child to become literate?

What are the different types of planning one would be most likely to observe in preschool children?

How is the process of learning to read and write connected? What can facilitate this process in the classroom?

What guidelines should be established for block building?

How would a teacher go about planning movement experiences both inside and outside?

If children really learn best through play, what is the best way for a teacher to arrange the daily schedule to allow for the maximum amount of play time?

How Much Time Is Needed for Play?

James F. Christie and Francis Wardle

James F. Christie, Ph.D., is Associate Professor of Curriculum and Instruction at Arizona State University, where he teaches courses in reading and early childhood education. His research interests include children's play, early literacy development, and the integration of language arts activities. He has taught at the preschool, kindergarten, and early primary levels.

Francis Wardle, Ph.D., is Director of the Adams County, Colorado, Head Start. Currently on leave, he is teaching preschool and kindergarten children in the Hutterian Brethren community (makers of Community Playthings) of Farmington, Pennsylvania.

Early childhood educators have long believed that play makes important contributions to children's development and therefore must have a key role in preschool and kindergarten curriculums. These educators have also known that play is a rich, varied, and complex process that requires ample time, materials, and resources. These same teachers, however, face mounting pressure from parents and administrators to provide structured, formal instruction on the "basics." As a result, the amount of time allocated to play has been severely reduced in many early childhood programs. The question arises: Is the richness and maturity of children's play affected by this reduction in play period length?

The importance of time for play

Over the years, we have observed free play in many preschool and kindergarten classrooms. The amount and richness of the play we witnessed varied widely. In some classes, there was an abundance of elaborate group dramatizations and complex construction projects. The children in these classrooms were obviously enjoying the full advantages of these two important types of play. Surprisingly, in a number of other classrooms we saw little group-dramatic play

or extended constructive activity. Children either spent much of their time wandering around uninvolved, or engaged in low-level varieties of play. They would build and then tear down very simple block constructions, chase each other around the room until the teacher intervened, or engage in nonsocial forms of dramatic play, such as parallel-dramatic play in the housekeeping corner where each child would act out his drama with no social interaction.

In some instances the causes of low-level play were obvious—lack of appropriate materials, a large proportion of at-risk children, or negative teacher attitudes toward play. In many cases, however, these factors were not present. In such cases, the common factor we found was that the children did not have very much time for play. Indoor free play periods were brief, lasting only 10 to 15 minutes, or they were scheduled before school. Although before-school play periods tended to be moderately long (about 30 minutes), many children arrived and participated only toward the end of the period. The late-arriving children also tended to disrupt the play of those who had arrived earlier.

We suspected that insufficient play time was responsible for the low-quality play in these classrooms because it was inhibiting two of the most mature forms of play: group-dramatic play and constructive play.

Group-dramatic play

This type of play, in which several children adopt roles and act out a story, requires considerable time to plan and initiate. Prior to the start of group-dramatic play, children must recruit other players, negotiate the roles to be enacted, agree on the story line to be dramatized, designate the make-believe identities of objects, and determine the area of the room to be used. These preparations often take a considerable amount of time. Group-dramatic play can have several false starts as children jockey for

From *Young Children*, Vol. 47, No. 3, March 1992, pp. 28-32. Reprinted by permission of the publisher, the National Association for the Education of Young Children.

position or as a previously excluded child is later included in the play. Time is also needed as children sometimes start with a simpler form of play and then progress into dramatic play. For example, they may make a rectangle on the floor with large hollow blocks, then use the rectangle as a make-believe boat in a dramatization.

Short play periods may cause group dramatizations to stop just after they get started. When this happens a number of times, children tend to give up on group-dramatic play and settle for less advanced forms of play that can be completed in short periods of time.

Constructive play

Constructive play occurs when children build structures with blocks or other play materials. Like dramatic play, it requires lengthy play periods to reach its full potential. Time is needed for children to play and build elaborate structures and to use these structures in connection with dramatic play. For example, several children might build a replica of a city with unit blocks, pausing occasionally to enact scenes involving miniature figures and cars.

Short play periods tend to stifle constructive play. Children may just get involved in a construction when it is time to put the materials away. After a number of such experiences, children may abandon this type of play or resort to building very simple structures. As a result, many important benefits of extended constructive play—planning, persistence, cooperation, and problem solving—are lost. The opportunity for constructive play to evolve into dramatic play is also lost.

A case study

The issue of adequate play time led one of us to conduct a research study on the effects of play period length on children's play behavior (Christie, Johnsen, & Peckover, 1988). Because play is extremely sensitive to school setting variables (Christie & Johnsen, 1989), children in different classrooms were not compared. A repeated-measures design was used in which the play of each child was observed in both long and short play periods in identical settings.

The study involved 34 four- and five-year-olds in two classrooms of a preschool that primarily served lower-middle-class families. Each class had two indoor free play periods per day—a 30-minute session during midmorning and a 15-minute period in the afternoon. The classrooms were spacious and well-stocked with dramatic play props (small kitchen appliances, table, chairs, dishes, dolls, baby rocker, etc.) and constructive play materials (unit blocks,

Legos®, Tinkertoys®, etc.). The materials and adult caregivers present were the same during both the longer and shorter periods; thus, the only difference between the two periods was the amount of time available for play.

The children's free play was observed using a modification of the popular Parten/Piaget scale (Rubin, Watson, & Jambor, 1978), which simultaneously classifies play according to its social level (solitary, parallel, or group) and its cognitive characteristics (functional, constructive, dramatic, or games). Categories for unoccupied/onlooking/transition behavior and nonplay activities were also included. The observations, using a 15-second time sampling procedure, continued for approximately eight weeks until each child had been observed for 15 minutes during both the long and short play periods.

Research results

The results indicated that play time affected both the amount and the maturity of the children's play. During the long periods, children engaged in more

• total play activity,
• group play,
• constructive play, and
• group-dramatic play.

During the short periods, children spent more time engaging in

• unoccupied/onlooking/transition behavior,
• functional play, and
• parallel-dramatic play.

The findings confirmed our belief that longer play periods would encourage children to engage in higher social and cognitive forms of play. Longer play periods gave the children time to recruit fellow players and to engage in the negotiations necessary for cooperative play; this resulted in an increase in group play in general and in group-dramatic play in particular. Longer play periods allowed children to get involved in extended construction projects, making constructive play a more popular activity. Longer periods also enabled reluctant children to become involved in play and permitted play to evolve in different directions. Constructive play, for example, often turned into dramatic play.

Shorter periods, on the other hand, reduced both the amount and maturity of the children's play. During short periods, children tended to wander around more and not get involved in play at all. When they did play, children settled for simple play forms, such as functional (motor) play and parallel-dramatic play, which do not require much time to plan and execute.

Extra play time did not result in children getting bored and having nothing to do; rather, it prompted them to engage in more complex, productive play activities.

Guidelines for early childhood programs

The results of this study may not surprise early childhood educators, but they do indicate the need for teachers to insist on ample time for play in their programs. We suggest the following guidelines for structuring play time:

1. Ideally, provide daily free-play periods of at least 30 minutes in length. Experiment with even longer time periods and observe the results.

2. If brief play periods are scattered throughout the day, consider combining them into one longer period.

3. Re-evaluate the entire daily curriculum to create more play time. Perhaps naptime can be shortened, lunch time curtailed, or other schedules adjusted to free up time for play.

4. When curriculum pressures prohibit lengthy play periods, try to have several long play periods *per week* rather than shorter *daily* ones. This will at least enable children to experience the benefits of extended group-dramatic and constructive play on a regular basis. A better solution, of course, is to adjust the curriculum to allow more time for play.

5. Avoid scheduling play *solely* as a before-school transition. In addition to the problem of late-arriving children, play suffers because teachers tend to be heavily involved in academic preparations during such periods, making it difficult for them to enrich and extend children's play. Nothing is wrong with before-school play as long as it is accompanied by regularly scheduled play periods during the school day.

6. Work with parents so they understand that play is not "just play"—that children's play has educational value. Use workshops, newsletter articles, and orientation meetings to discuss with parents your program's position on play.

7. Establish program expectations that value children's play as a critical curriculum component. This will require staff training, dissemination of articles to staff and parents, and encouragement of a general climate that supports play.

8. Assist children who have difficulty entering into group play, and use subtle, nonintrusive techniques for enriching and extending ongoing play activities (see Griffing, 1983; Woodard, 1984; Johnson, Christie, & Yawkey, 1987).

9. Resist the temptation to structure play periods—

especially long ones—through use of unnecessary interventions or "play curriculums," and avoid imposing academic objectives, such as "counting the blocks as you build," on play activities. When adults take control of children's activities, play quickly changes to work (King, 1979). Always remind yourself of the basic nature of children's play (Wardle, 1987).

10. Make sure that support staff members (therapists, psychologists, and others) do not pull the same children out of play periods on a regular basis. All children—including those with disabilities—benefit from sustained, enriched play experiences (Saracho & Spodek, 1987). The removal of children also disrupts the play activities of other children.

11. Avoid using the elimination of play time as punishment. Disruptive children and children with other kinds of behavior problems need adequate play opportunities.

12. Remember that lengthy play periods on an outdoor playground are not a substitute for long indoor play periods. Children need *both*. Different types of play and, consequently, different types of learning and development occur in these two settings. Large-motor play—running, climbing, jumping—is more common outdoors than indoors (Roper & Hinde, 1978). Constructive play occurs more often in indoor settings because of the availability of constructive materials (Henniger, 1985). Other studies indicate that outdoor and indoor settings have different effects, depending on gender (Sanders & Harper, 1976) and socioeconomic status (Tizard et al., 1976). It seems clear that these distinctly different environments encourage different cognitive forms of play.

Conclusion

Play period length has a direct effect on the level and quality of young children's play. Our research suggests that at least 30 minutes is required for many children to progress through preparatory activities and arrive at group-dramatic play and elaborate constructive play. Young children do not automatically turn complex play activities *on* and *off*. Such activities need time to develop and evolve.

We suggest that programs serving preschool and kindergarten children not only recognize the critical importance of constructive and group-dramatic play, but also realize that these forms of play are more likely to occur in play periods of 30 minutes or more. We urge programs to adapt their curricula and daily schedules to include longer play periods.

For further reading

Dyson, A.H. (1990). Research in review. Symbol makers, symbol weavers: How children link play, pictures, and print. *Young Children, 45*(2), 50–57.

Engstrom, G. (Ed.). (1971). *Play: The child strives toward self-realization*. Washington, DC: NAEYC.

Fein, G., & Rivkin, M. (Eds.). (1986). *The young child at play: Reviews of research, Volume 4*. Washington, DC: NAEYC.

Nourot, P.M., & Van Hoorn, J.L. (1991). Research in review. Symbolic play in preschool and primary settings. *Young Children, 46*(6), 40–50.

Rogers, C.S., & Sawyers, J.K. (1988). *Play in the lives of children*. Washington, DC: NAEYC

Sawyers, J.K., & Rogers, C.S. (1988). *Helping young children develop through play: A practical guide for parents, caregivers, and teachers*. Washington, DC: NAEYC.

References

Christie, J. F., & Johnsen, E. P. (1989). The constraints of settings on children's play. *Play and Culture, 2,* 317–327.

Christie, J. F., Johnsen, E. P., & Peckover, R. B. (1988). The effects of play period duration on children's play patterns. *Journal of Research in Childhood Education, 3,* 123–131.

Griffing, P. (1983). Encouraging dramatic play in early childhood. *Young Children, 38*(4), 13–22.

Henniger, M. (1985). Preschool children's play behaviors in an indoor and outdoor environment. In J. Frost & S. Sunderlin (Eds.), *When children play* (pp. 145–155). Wheaton, MD: The Association of Childhood Education International.

Johnson, J. E., Christie, J. F., & Yawkey, T. D. (1987). *Play and early childhood development*. Glenview, IL: Scott, Foresman.

King, N. R. (1979). Play: The kindergartners' perspective. *The Elementary School Journal, 80*(2), 81–87.

Roper, L., & Hinde, R.A. (1978). Social behavior in play group: Consistency & complexity. *Child Development, 49,* 570–579.

Rubin, K. H., Watson, K. S., & Jambor, T. W. (1978). Free-play behaviors in preschool and kindergarten children. *Child Development, 49,* 534–536.

Sanders, K.M., & Harper, L.V. (1976). Free-play fantasy behavior in preschool children: Relations among gender, age, season, and location. *Child Development, 47,* 1,182–1,185.

Saracho, O. N., & Spodek, B. (1987). Play for handicapped children in an integrated setting, Part 1. *Day Care and Early Education, 15*(2), 32–35.

Tizard, B., Philps, J., & Plewis, I. (1976). Play in preschool centers—II. Effects on play of the child's social class and of the educational orientation of the center. *Journal of Child Psychology and Psychiatry, 17,* 265–274.

Wardle, F. (1987). Getting back to the basics of children's play. *Child Care Information Exchange,* 27–30.

Woodard, C. Y. (1984). Guidelines for facilitating sociodramatic play. *Childhood Education, 60,* 172–177.

Serious Play in the Classroom

How Messing Around Can Win You the Nobel Prize

Selma Wassermann

Selma Wassermann is Professor of Education, Simon Fraser University, Burnaby, British Columbia. This article is based on her keynote address at the ACEI Study Conference in San Diego, California, April 20, 1991.

The 3rd-graders sat quietly, politely, as the teacher went from table to table, giving each group of children a bundle of fabrics to examine. They were to talk with each other and make some observations of the fabric. The teacher had expected that their playful investigations would lead to further awareness of how fabric was made, particularly examinations of texture, thread, color, print and elasticity. Although this was the first time they had been involved in investigative play, and the experience of carrying on this self-directed examination to gather data was new, they went right to the task —examining the pieces of fabric, pulling, stretching, looking through the fabric at the light, scrutinizing texture, print, color. They played with the fabrics for a long time before the teacher asked them to give her their attention, since she wanted to hear about their observations. In the first few responses, the children talked about texture, thread and design. Then, Andre said, "My fabrics make different sounds."

When he was asked to tell more about what he meant, he demonstrated that when he put the fabric down on his desk and scratched along the woof or the warp, sounds of a certain pitch were produced. He also showed that when he scratched more quickly, the pitch was higher; when he scratched more slowly, the pitch was lower. Now clearly this has implications for music, pitch, sound and how music is made on stringed instruments; and this 8-year-old boy had come up with this discovery during his play with fabrics.

This is but one example of how play allows children to make discoveries that go far beyond the realm of what we adults think is important to know. But that is only one of the benefits of play. I believe that with play, we teachers can have it all: the development of knowledge, of a spirit of inquiry, of creativity, of conceptual understanding—all contributing to the true empowerment of children. Is it possible that serious play is, in fact, the primary vehicle through which serious learning occurs? If that is the case, might we consider introducing serious play at all stages of a student's learning, from kindergarten through graduate school? Given the present climate in education, such a proposal is tantamount to heresy. But what the heck? If you're sailing on the Titanic, you might as well go first class.

The Case for Play

Arguments to support serious play are found in many learned sources. Victor and Mildred Goertzel, whose seminal work investigating eminent adults resulted in *Cradles of Eminence* (1962), set out to see if they could find some common threads in the early childhood experiences of people who grew to eminence as adults. In their studies of the childhood of 400 eminent adults—writers, composers, inventors, statesmen and women, scientists, artists and others—they looked for keys to understand what factors contributed substantially to their later development as our "heroes." One of the common threads these researchers found was that, "by conventional standards, the attitude of the family toward normal schooling was negative. In many instances, some of the children were never sent to school at all" (p. 267).

To substantiate this point, the Goertzels use the example of the Wright brothers. As youths, these boys were tinkerers who enjoyed messing around. When they asked their mother for permission to stay out of school for several years, to "tinker around in the backyard," their mother agreed. What might have occurred if Mother Wright believed that school was the only place where serious learning could occur and what might that have meant for the later development of the airplane?

Another example of a tinkerer is Thomas Edison. He, too, was allowed to spend hours messing around and once again, it is interesting to speculate the future of

From *Childhood Education*, Spring 1992, pp. 133-139. Reprinted by permisson of Selma Wassermann and the Association for Childhood Education International, 11141 Georgia Avenue, Suite 200, Wheaton, MD. Copyright © 1992 by the Association.

his discoveries if he had been admonished to "get serious and get back to work and stop that messing around!"

Frank Lloyd Wright was another serious player. He was encouraged by his mother, from his very early years, to play with colored papers and cubes of wood. Mrs. Wright, in fact, actively cultivated Frank's play with these forms and believed that through such play, the boy's intellectual development would be advanced (Goertzel, pp. 85-86).

Another common thread found by the Goertzels in the families of the 400 eminent adults was that most mothers were quite permissive with their children, allowing them great degrees of freedom to make choices about what they wanted and did not want to do. Goertzels' data also reveal that for many of these adults, school was a place where creativity was stifled, rather than encouraged. It was to be avoided at all costs. These children liked best "those teachers who let them go ahead at their own pace and who gave them permission to work unimpeded in the area of their own special interests" (Goertzel, p. 267). Torrance, in his early research on giftedness, also observed that teachers considered highly creative elementary school children to be a source of great nuisance.

They seem to be playing around when they should be working at assigned tasks. They engage in manipulative and/or exploratory activities, many of which are discouraged or even forbidden. They enjoy learning, and this looks to teachers like play, rather than work. (Torrance, 1961)

Teachers preferred the high IQ student over the creative one. The creative children wanted to go off in new directions, producing new forms. Because they insisted on invention, rather than quietly submitting to what teachers asked of them, they were thought of as "obnoxious" and troublesome. The high IQ students were low risk-takers and teachers regarded them as "se-

rious, ambitious, and promising."
The Goertzels concluded that:

If a potential Edison or Einstein or Picasso or Churchill or Clemens had been in school in California in these days, he would surely not have been chosen to be screened for inclusion in the Stanford study of genius. (p. 279)

The creation of new ideas does not come from minds trained to follow doggedly what is already known. Creation comes from tinkering and playing around, from which new forms emerge. Composers play with sounds in their heads to make new music. Visual artists play with images, form and color to create art. Architects play with design and form. Poets and novelists play with words, literally and figuratively, in their literary creations. Although we may think of William Shakespeare's work as sacrosanct—the epitome of polished language usage—it helps to remember that he invented at least 1,700 words, which became part of our common language usage only after he introduced them into the language (Bryson, 1990). From all of this play, this messing around, serious and new creative forms are brought to life.

The freedom to create and invent appears to be closely connected with the development of creative, inventive, innovative adults. What about the benefits of play for cognitive development? Is play only for the gifted and talented potential artists, inventors, writers, architects—the creative geniuses? What can play do for all the other children for whom teachers wish to further conceptual development and extend knowledge?

Research of the renowned cognitive psychologist from Harvard, Jerome Bruner, supports the potential of play for cognitive development. Bruner's experiments on play reveal that not only does play promote concept development, but also that this occurs much more substantially through play than

through direct instruction. Bruner set up three learning groups and found that those children who had the opportunity to engage in previous free play with the creative materials were better prepared to solve the subsequent problems presented to them, than were the groups of children who were a) allowed to handle but not play with the materials and b) only shown the principles underlying the solutions by an adult (Bruner, 1985). Bruner has written that:

There is evidence that by getting children to play with materials that they must later use in a problem solving task, one gets superior performance from them in comparison with those children who spend time familiarizing themselves with the materials in other ways. Players generate more hypotheses and they reject wrong ones more quickly. Players seem to become frustrated less, and fixated less. They are more interested in finding out and learning from their explorations than they are in obtaining rewards. (p. 603)

Bruner further speculates that playful, flexible, mindful interaction early in a child's life may become a model later for what adults do when encountering problems. Having learned the habits of playing around, adults are more likely to feel encouraged to play around in their own heads.

There is another point worth making about the value of play in children's lives today. Authors like Elkind (1982), Postman (1982) and Winn (1981) have written powerfully about what they call "the disappearance of childhood." Children today have far fewer opportunities to live in the life of the mind, to be playful, to behave as children. In place of traditional childhood games that were still popular a generation ago, in place of fantasy and make-believe, in place of messing around, today's children have substituted television. Today, children play computer games in the amusement arcade and Nintendo at home, instead of messing around with colored paper and junk. They choose computer camps for holiday fun and ask for Apples for Christmas. If TV is contributing to the disappearance of childhood, how is the computer affecting the play of children? Such new "toys" may have very grave implications for the kinds of adults that today's children are likely to become and for the kinds of worlds they are likely to create. Perhaps we educators need to spend more time reflecting on these issues as we speculate about the future of this planet.

How Does Play Work To Produce These Results?

When we examine play more closely, we are able to see how it allows for the cognitive and creative development of children.

■ Play is generative. Anyone who is playing is creating something new, something that has not been created before. In play, we are not locked into conforming to a set standard of what is *right*. When children do worksheets or other pencil-and-paper exercises, they are expected to conform to an existing standard. What would have happened if, for example, little Billy Shakespeare had given his Grade 6 teacher a paper with the words *majestic* or *hurry* or *lonely* or *radiance*— all words that he had invented? The likelihood is great that his paper would have been returned slashed with red *X's* and an admonition to go to the dictionary and use proper vocabulary! It is play that sanctions what is different.

■ Play allows for risks to be taken, and the taking of risks is a normal part of play. This does not mean life-threatening risks. It means risks of invention, trying something that has not been tried before, thinking ideas that have never been thought before, conceptualizing something that has not been conceived before. In play, we risk and we do so within margins of safety, because we know it is not only all right to risk in play but that

The creation of new ideas does not come from minds trained to follow doggedly what is already known. Creation comes from tinkering and playing around, from which new forms emerge.

play demands we risk. Inventions of the new do not come from duplicating what is already there. They come from minds that are unafraid to take risks to try. Worksheets or pencil-and-paper exercises make risk a terrible threat. Nothing new or imaginative is dared to be written. Children must write what is acceptable, what has been written before, what has been decided as "correct."

■ In play, there is no fear of failure, because there is no failure. Failure occurs when children have not measured up to another's preconceived notion of what they should have done. No standards of right and wrong are articulated in play, and the absence of such standards is what allows for innovation. Play invites learning to value error as a means of learning more. In play, we really *do* learn from mistakes. On the other hand, in schoolwork, teachers may say to students that "we learn from our errors," but no child has ever been thus deceived. Children learn early in school that making errors or getting it wrong involves heavy penalties, of both the academic and psychological kind, carrying long-range and painful consequences. While in work we may be encouraged to try, we learn *not* to take chances, for fear of failure, for fear we may be wrong.

■ Play builds autonomy. Through play, self-initiating behaviors are developed. It encourages children to do their own creations, to build their own castles. In fact, children want the autonomy that play gives, and they enjoy the feel-ing of control that play gives them. Children who are serious players are the most autonomous. They don't need direction from others to tell them what to do now and what to do next. They enjoy making choices for themselves. In that way, play is ego-affirming as well.

■ Play gives the hands something to do. And when the hands are active, the mind engages. Ironically, this is the opposite of what most of us were taught when we went to teachers college. In those days, we were taught that children should not "fiddle." New data about fiddling around suggest that when hands are engaged, students pay closer attention to what is going on. Those of us who doodle during a meeting will immediately understand that doodling does not distract; it helps to keep attention riveted on the events of the meeting. Active involvement requires pumping adrenalin. Passive sitting and listening to talk that is largely boring do not lead to the pumping of adrenalin; therefore, there is very little mind engagement. When the hands are actively engaged in play, adrenalin is being pumped, and learning is more substantive.

These five principles are part of a larger theory of learning: experiential learning. Rooted in the work of Dewey, Lewin and Piaget, this theory—unlike other, more abstract learning theories— is teacher-friendly. It confirms and legitimizes what most teachers already know to be true: knowledge is not a fixed commodity. It is formed and reformed through experience. Each time we experience, we reshape and reform our ideas. Ideas are continually being sifted through the lens of new experiences.

This knowledge does not refer merely to names, dates and labels associated with the single, correct answers being sought on worksheets. Instead, it refers to the knowledge involved in being able to make meaning from information—the knowledge that means to *understand*. If students were studying the Civil Rights Movement in the United States, for example, all new student experiences—reading, looking at photographs, seeing films, listening to people who had played active roles in the movement—would cause a reshaping and reforming of their knowledge about the movement. The more powerful the experience, the more significant the reforming of the knowledge. This is part of the process of cognition, of thinking.

Active learning experience, or serious play, is the first step in advancing knowledge, in allowing learners to reach beyond names, dates and labels to deeper meanings. Active experience builds understanding. This is, of course, what schooling and education are really about. Not just to know the names, but to understand the meanings.

Learner experiences are enriched through a second stage of experience—the process of reflective observation. In this stage, learners are asked to think back on the experience; through certain questioning strategies, they are helped to see more, to look more deeply, to find important meanings.

Experiential learning, starting with active engagement with concrete materials and enriched by reflective observation, allows learners to build concepts and reach for theoretical understandings that lead, in turn, to students' ability to make more thoughtful decisions and solve more difficult problems.

Experiential learning, or serious play, builds habits of thinking.

Making Play Work in the Classroom

There are two kinds of play that I have observed in classrooms. One is more open and the other more focused. These are my definitions, and while others may see play differently, they at least serve to illuminate the paragraphs that follow.

In more open play, the teacher sets out materials so that children may mess around without any specific goal. The children use the materials to create their own inventions. These materials may include items that allow for creative opportunities, like blocks, paints, dress-up clothes, clay, wood and hardware, musical instruments, scraps of paper for collages. They may also include scraps of fabric, pine cones, seashells, buttons, mathematical counters, cuisenaire rods, attribute blocks, rulers and other measuring instruments that allow for creative investigations. Virtually any kind of material involving hands-on creations or investigations may be used for this more open type of play. The instruction to students is something like this: "Use these materials to make a design that you like." Or, "Here are some materials for you to play with." Or, sometimes, the materials are laid out with no instruction from the teacher about how they are to be used. With more open play, there is no predetermined idea or topic being investigated through these activities. In fact, the children themselves invent their own focus for the investigations.

In this more open play, children have lots of choices about what they are going to do with the materials. More open play has much greater potential for creation and invention, for risk-taking.

There's a down side to more open play. By later grades, some children have lost considerable autonomy as players; more open play,

where they have to create their own structures, defeats them. Consequently, they engage in what teachers call "behavior"—and their play may become, at worst, destructive or silly. More open play is for those children who are more autonomous, who can create structures to play from within themselves. For children who have lost the ability to play productively, teachers might prefer more focused play. In this type of play, teachers provide a specific focus to the play that sets some guidelines and gives children a structure for the activity. The structure may be quite open, but having a structure is security-giving for children who have lost the autonomy that very open play requires. Focused play results in far less "behavior."

In focused play, a teacher who wanted students to study clothing might gather about 100 photographs of different styles of men's and women's clothing over the last 100 years and focus the play by asking children to study the pictures and make some observations of how clothing has changed in the last 100 years. Even with that focus, much room remains for open investigation. It is important that a focus not be too narrow, lest the play be inhibited. In focusing the play, the teacher learns to be aware of the difference between guidelines that constrain and those that enable more productive plays.

The ideas behind serious play have taken root in primary and intermediate classrooms in British Columbia as part of the Ministry of Education's comprehensive education plan, *Year 2000* (Ministry of Education, 1990). In these classrooms, it is gratifying to see just how much curriculum content can be learned through investigative play. Far and beyond what is normally done in the arts and crafts, play is effectively and happily used as a vehicle to enable students to learn more about what is important in the "hard line" curriculum areas of math, science, social studies and language arts. Serious play is also emerging as a teaching strategy in "teaching with cases" in B.C. secondary schools as well (Wassermann, in press).

Building Curriculum Based on Serious Play

Developing curriculum experiences that are rooted in play is not difficult. A successful program, however, requires that certain conditions be met to ensure that students develop knowledge and conceptual understanding.

1. *The teacher must be able to design and orchestrate a curriculum rooted in play. This includes:*

- Visualizing how important curriculum concepts can be learned through play and being clear about the big ideas that are being studied in the curriculum
- Gathering the materials needed for the plays
- Organizing the class for cooperative group work on the plays and orienting students to this more student-centered, active learning format
- Allowing students time for play
- Trusting play to do the job of teaching the concepts
- Using classroom discussion skills that call for students' reflective observations on their play, or "debriefing" the play
- Providing for follow-up plays that enable students to develop their knowledge of principles as their learning is formed and reformed through added experience. (Wassermann, 1990)

The label *Play-Debrief-Replay* describes this curriculum design. It is a way of looking at how curriculum experiences may be organized. Recent classroom research carried out in Vancouver schools suggests that not only is such a way of organizing the curriculum productive

and exciting for teachers and students, but it is also enabling and empowering. When students are given the power to have control over their actions and their decisions, they are empowered (Wassermann & Ivany, 1988).

Virtually every important concept to be taught—whether it be at the primary, intermediate or graduate school level or whether it be in science, math, economics or business management—can be taught through the medium of serious play. Play may be either "minds on" or "hands on." Both experiences actively engage students in the examination of the concept or the big idea. Big ideas are the more important issues and concepts in the curriculum; for example: machines work for us, time and speed can be measured mathematically, living things grow and change, language is a means of communicating ideas, sound can be created and manipulated in a variety of ways, certain sounds in certain words provide clues to decoding those words.

Small ideas, on the other hand, reflect content that is considerably less substantive, that deals with acquisition of specific facts. Because small ideas are narrower in scope, they do not yield to productive, serious play. Some examples of small ideas are: buttons come in different shapes and sizes, bottles are used to hold liquid, mittens keep your hands warm, ducks quack and lions roar, some houses are made of wood, $3 + 4 = 7$.

A play that is rooted in the big ideas gives direction to what is being learned. When teachers are clear about the substantive issues they want students to study, they are in a better position to develop investigative play experiences that lead to more sophisticated understanding.

2. *The second, and equally critical dimension of effective play programs, is the teacher's belief that play can, in fact, deliver the learning goals considered important for that grade.* Without the teacher's belief in serious

play as the road to important learning, these ideas will never be realized in that teacher's classroom.

Obviously, this is not an approach for all teachers. Before considering such a program, teachers ought best consider the implications of children working as serious players and measure these in juxtaposition with their own beliefs about children's learning. In making such choices, teachers will be protecting their own right to decide how they will teach in their own classrooms. There are many ways to teach children and the way a teacher chooses must reflect that teacher's beliefs. If choice is taken away from teachers, and teachers are coerced into putting into practice an instructional plan that is abhorrent to them, teachers are disempowered. And disempowered teachers cannot empower children. Teachers who are thinking seriously about the implementation of a Play-Debrief-Replay program will want to consider, first, the "goodness of fit" between this methodology and their own educational goals for children. The "comfort zone" of teachers can be assessed by considering the following:

- Play activities involve learning that is open ended. They do not lead students to the right answers. *How comfortable are you with this?*
- Play experiences call for generation of ideas, rather than recall of specific pieces of information. *How comfortable are you with this?*
- Play experiences are messy. Children are, in fact, playing around. *How comfortable are you with this?*
- Play tasks focus on the big ideas, rather than on details and specifics. *How comfortable are you with this?*
- Children are actively involved in learning. They talk to each other, share ideas, speculate, laugh, get excited. In short, they are noisy. *How comfortable are you with this?*
- Children work together in co-

Virtually every important concept to be taught—whether it be at the primary, intermediate or graduate school level—can be taught through the medium of serious play.

operative learning groups. Cooperation rather than competitive individual work is stressed. *How comfortable are you with this?*

■ The content of the curriculum is not covered in a linear, sequential way. *How comfortable are you with this?*

■ Control over student learning is largely in the students' domain. *How comfortable are you with this?*

■ As children become more empowered, they become more independent, more assertive, more challenging themselves. *How comfortable are you with a class of assertive, independent thinkers?*

These questions are best examined before teachers climb aboard yet another educational scheme that promises much, but is likely to deliver little if teachers are discontent about the operating conditions in the play. If teachers do choose to work in these ways, however, the plan will deliver what it promises: the empowerment of children. Don't take my word for it. Try it and see for yourself. And look to the children for the answers. If you see your students growing in their autonomy, self-confidence, sense of *can do*, personal power, love for learning, then what you are doing in the classroom is clearly working to their benefit. If, on the other hand, you see the entrenchment of behaviors you find repugnant— passive, submissively obedient children who are afraid to take risks or rise to challenge, who shy away from new problems, content that once the answer has been found, there's no need to learn any further—that ought to signal that more, much more work needs to be done.

But the Nobel Prize?

But the Nobel Prize? Isn't that going a little far, in promising what serious play can deliver? Richard Feynman, Nobel Laureate in physics, is at least one eminent adult who makes the case for the relationship between childhood play and the Nobel Prize. In his wonderful book, *Surely You're Joking Mr. Feynman* (1985), Feynman writes about his childhood—messing around with stuff in the basement of his home and encouraged to do so by a wise and caring father. At age 10, Feynman started to play around in a lab he set up in the basement, playing with switches and wires, making his own fuses. With his own heater, so that he could cook French-fried potatoes, Feynman set up his own crystal set, invented a burglar alarm, experimented with electric motors, built an amplifier for a photo cell that could make a bell ring when he put his hand in front of the cell, repaired his own and the neighbor's radios.

As a child, Feynman developed habits of play, and he held onto these habits of play throughout his adult life. He also attributed his love for physics and his ability to be creative in theoretical physics to his ability to play:

Why did I enjoy doing it (physics)? I used to play with it. I used to do whatever I felt like doing. It didn't have to do with whether it was important for the development of nuclear physics, but instead whether it was interesting and amusing for me to play with. When I was in high school, I'd see water running out of a faucet growing narrower, and wonder if I could figure out what determines that curve. I found it was

rather easy to do. I didn't have to do it; it wasn't important for the future of science; somebody else had already done it. That didn't make any difference. I'd invent things and play with things for my own entertainment.

When Feynman felt he was growing bored with physics, he turned to play to revitalize his interest:

So I got this new attitude. Now that I'm burned out and I'll never accomplish anything, and I've got this nice position at the university teaching classes which I rather enjoy, and just like I read the *Arabian Nights* for pleasure, I'm going to PLAY with physics, whenever I want to, without worrying about any importance whatsoever.

He attributes his habits of play to the discovery that led to his Nobel Prize:

Within a week, I was in the cafeteria, and some guy, fooling around, throws me a plate in the air. As the plate went up in the air, I saw it wobble, and I noticed the red medallion of Cornell (University) on the plate going around. It was pretty obvious to me that the medallion went around faster than the wobbling.

I had nothing to do, so I started to figure out the motion of the rotating plate. I discover that when the angle is very slight, the medallion rotates twice as fast as the wobble rate: two to one. It came out as a complicated equation!

I don't remember how I did it, but I ultimately worked out what the motion of the mass particles is, and how all the accelerations balance to make it come out two to one. I still remember Hans Bethe saying to me, "Hey, Feynman. That's pretty interesting, but what's the importance of it? Why are you doing it?" Hah, I say. There's no importance whatsoever. I'm just doing it for the fun of it. His reaction didn't discourage me. I had made up my mind. I was going to enjoy physics and do whatever I liked.

I went on to work out equations of wobbles. And before I knew it, I was playing, and it was effortless. It was easy to play with these things. It was like uncorking a bottle. Everything flowed out effortlessly. I almost tried to resist it! There was no importance to what I was doing, but ultimately there was. The diagrams and the whole business that I got the Nobel Prize for came from that messing around with the wobbling plate.

If we teachers can free ourselves from the need to keep students quiet and "on task" with pencil-and-paper worksheets, filling in correct answers, following correct procedures, learning all the names and places, in all the subjects, and recalling them correctly so that they may pass examinations—the "safe and secure" road—we may open our classrooms to the more messy, the more generative, the more original, the more delightful world of play as a means of learning about the world. And in the process, who knows what future Nobel Prize winners we may be cultivating.

References

Bruner, J. (1985). On teaching thinking: An afterthought. In S. F. Chipman, J. W. Segan, & R. Glasser (Eds.), *Thinking and learning skills: Vol. 1* (pp. 603-605). Hillsdale, NJ: Lawrence Earlbaum Associates.

Bryson, B. (1990). *The mother tongue: English and how it got that way.* New York: Morrow.

Elkind, D. (1982). *The hurried child.* Boston: Allyn & Bacon.

Feynman, R. (1985). *Surely you're joking Mr. Feynman.* New York: Norton.

Goertzel, M., & Goertzel, R. (1962). *Cradles of eminence.* Boston: Little Brown.

Ministry of Education. (1990). *Year 2000: A framework for learning.* Victoria, British Columbia: Ministry of Education.

Postman, N. (1982). *The disappearance of childhood.* New York: Delacorte.

Torrance, P. (1961). *Status of knowledge concerning education and creative scientific talent.* Salt Lake City: University of Utah Press.

Wassermann, S. (1990). *Serious players in the primary classroom.* New York: Teachers College Press.

Wassermann, S. (in press). A case for social studies. *Phi Delta Kappan.*

Wassermann, S., & Ivany, J.W.G. (1988). *Teaching elementary science: Who's afraid of spiders?* New York: Harper & Row.

Winn, M. (1981). *Children without childhood.* New York: Pantheon.

Learning Through Block Play

Early childhood educators are greatly concerned about the value of classroom materials for young children's development. Blocks continue to be favored by many as a way of facilitating the developmental domains in children. In fact, blocks are considered the most useful and most used equipment in preschool and kindergarten programs. (Benish, 1978; Kinsmans & Berk, 1979). Variations in shapes, sizes, and weight foster learning experiences from infancy through early childhood.

Janis R. Bullock

Janis R. Bullock is Assistant Professor of Early Childhood Education, Department of Health and Human Development, Montana State University, Bozeman, MT.

Blocks provide many opportunities for children to develop in a variety of ways. The value of block building can be discussed in the four areas of physical, social, emotional, and cognitive growth (Cartwright, 1988):

Physical Growth

• Small and large-muscle development and coordination of muscles by lifting, carrying, bending, reaching, pushing, and pulling.
• Learning hand–eye coordination by reaching, grasping, and moving blocks.
• Learning a sense of balance and symmetry through building, stacking, and balancing blocks.
• Developing motor coordination by moving blocks.
• Understanding object–space relationships through placement of blocks.

Social Growth

• Promotion of social growth through experience in interpersonal relationships.
• Experience in taking turns, sharing, and respecting the rights of others.
• Learning to cooperate and play together.
• Opportunities to engage in several levels of play, from solitary and parallel to group.
• Increased confidence and self-esteem.

Emotional Growth

• Learning patience.
• Increasing independence.
• Contributing to a sense of accomplishment, which improves the child's self-image.
• Stimulation of imagination, creativity, and joy.
• Experimenting with a variety of roles and skills and feeling a sense of success.

Cognitive Growth

• Exploration of sizes, shapes, distances, proportions, and weight.
• Mathematical concepts such as "bigger than," "smaller than," or "need more or need less."
• Counting, one-to-one correspondence, classification, sorting, and matching.
• Experimentation, manipulation, and problem solving.
• Communicating with others (listening, speaking, and sharing).

Guidelines on Directing Block Building

The teachers's attitude toward block building will contribute to the quality of the child's experience. Teachers who understand and realize the benefits of block play convey important messages to children and arrange the environment appropriately. Children come to believe that the teacher really cares about what they are doing. The following are some guidelines for fostering positive attitudes through the direction of block play (Hirsch, 1984):

1. Block play requires plenty of room. Several children need room to build freely and to interact with one another. A small, cramped, cluttered area conveys to the child that the area is not valued. When not in use, the block area can be used for other purposes.

From *Day Care and Early Education*, Spring 1992, pp. 16-18. Copyright © 1992 by Human Science Press, Inc., 72 Fifth Avenue, New York, NY 10011. Reprinted by permission.

2. The rules of block area need to be clearly established. These often include building away from shelves, asking permission to use other children's blocks, building away from other children's structures, and not knocking down other children's structures, throwing, or walking on the blocks.

3. How high children can build with blocks will vary across classrooms. Children seem to enjoy the challenge of stacking blocks high; yet they need to know how high they may go and why. High buildings are not necessarily dangerous if children are taught respect and are supervised.

4. Some young or inexperienced children may attempt to hoard or take a majority of the blocks for themselves. Rules about this should be made in advance and conveyed to children. When deciding on your policy, the size of the group, the demand, and the quantity of the supply should be taken into account. Teachers should be sensitive to the variety of ways that children build. Some will retrieve one block at a time, while others will create a pile of blocks from which to build.

Supporting Children's Efforts

Children approach block building in a variety of ways. Some children are eager and enthusiastic about block building, while other children may need assistance. For children who may be unsure of what to do, teachers can sit with them and build together. Children can be requested to get blocks and place them somewhere on the structure. Teachers can stay with these children until they determine that the children feel comfortable building on their own.

The most important role a teacher can play is that of a genuine supporter of children's efforts. This is done by providing daily opportunities for block play, providing encouragement and guidance, offering suggestions, and asking open-ended questions to stimulate thinking. The teacher values the processes that children are involved in rather than the outcome or product.

Teachers should make sure that both boys and girls have equal opportunities to play with blocks. Observations in some classrooms suggest that boys will choose to play more often in the block area than girls (Beeson & Williams, 1979). In one classroom a young four-year-old girl told her mother she was not allowed in the block area because it was for boys only. Her perceptions were correct because it was the boys who dominated the area. Varma's (1980) study indicated that boys did play more frequently in the block area. Yet, when the block area was made more accessible by providing more blocks and space, girls spent more time with the blocks. In addition, when mixed-sexed groupings of children were given access to the block area, no sex differences were noted in the amount of play time spent in the area (Rogers, 1985).

There may be times when the teacher must take a more directive role in the block area and step in to intervene. Teachers may need to give reminders to children when safely rules are not followed, when other children's rights are infringed upon, or when children have difficulty settling their own arguments.

Using Accessories

Use of accessories can extend and add variety and creativity to block play. Accessories can range from simple salvaged props to commercial toys. Children seem to prefer to play with simple concrete objects, such as people and animal figures, and with transportation toys. Shelter materials (blankets, pillows, and flashlights) provide props that are familiar yet can contribute to much creativity. Wood accessories, decorations, and other odds and ends help to stimulate the imagination. The safety of the materials should be evaluated. To sustain interest over time, accessories should be rotated throughout the year.

Suggestions for Cleanup

When many blocks have been used, cleanup time may seem like an overwhelming task. Viewing this time as an important activity within itself, with many benefits to be gained, may help. Give ample warning to the children so they can anticipate the transition. Take time to acknowledge the children's buildings before they are disassembled. Ask the children if they would like to tell you about what they have done.

Assisting the cleanup helps to provide guidance and structure for the children. Cleanup can be organized in several ways. Clean up the accessories before picking up the blocks. Assign certain jobs to children based on the size, shape, and number of blocks; the shelf to be filled; or the area to be cleaned. Load and unload children with blocks. Consider different ways of moving blocks from the floor to the shelves, such as on chairs, on large trucks, or assembly-line style.

Rules about who cleans up need to be made clear. This may vary from only the children who were building, to everyone who is not cleaning up elsewhere, to all children cleaning up in all of the areas until the room is clean. Some children are eager to assist, while others resist. However, rules should be established that seem fair. Block cleanup should be viewed as an important fun time. Therefore, ample time should be allowed so that it is not perceived as a rushed and hectic chore.

Blocks should be stored on open low shelves. By marking block shapes on the shelves, children can figure out which blocks fit where. Teachers need to encourage children to return the blocks to their intended space. Haphazard and messy shelves of blocks do not invite participation.

Summary

How children approach blocks may depend on their experiences and developmental level. Less experienced and younger children may need more support and encouragement. Johnson

(1966) suggests that children go through a series of block-building stages. Stage 1 generally applies to the child under two years, who will carry blocks around and not engage in construction. Stage 2 children (approximately 2 to 3 years) produce repetitious horizontal and vertical structures. During Stage 3, simple bridging begins. In Stage 4, children begin to produce enclosures, considered the earliest technical building. Decorative patterns appear in Stage 5 (approximately 3 to 4 years). Naming of structures occurs in Stage 6 (4 to 6 years). During Stage 7 (five years), children's structures become more symbolic, with a greater emphasis on dramatic play. When teachers become aware of these stages, they are more likely to understand the child's block play and can provide appropriate support and guidance.

References

Beeson, B. S., & Williams, R. A. (1979). *A study of sex stereotyping in child-selected play activities of pre-school children.* Munice, IN: Ball State University. (ERIC Document Reproduction Service No. ED 186 201.)

Benish, J. (1978). *Blocks: Essential equipment for young children.* Charleston, WV: West Virginia State Department of Education. (ERIC Document Reproduction Service No. ED 165 901.)

Cartwright, S. (1988). Play can be the building blocks of learning. *Young Children, 43,* 44–47.

Hirsch, E. S. (1984). Block building: Practical considerations for the classroom teacher. IN E. S. Hirsch (Ed.), *The block book* (pp. 89–102).

Washington, DC: National Association for the Education of Young Children.

Johnson, H. M. (1966). *The art of block building.* New York: Bank Street College of Education Publications.

Kinsman, C., A., & Berk, J. (1979). Joining the block and housekeeping areas. Changes in play and social behavior. *Young Children, 35,* 66–75.

Rogers D. L. (1985). Relationships between block play and the social development of young children. *Early Child Development and Care, 20,* 245–261.

Varma, M. (1980). *Sex-stereotyping in block play of preschool children.* New Brunswick, NJ: Rutgers University. (ERIC Document Reproduction Service No. ED 197 832.)

The Many Faces of Child Planning

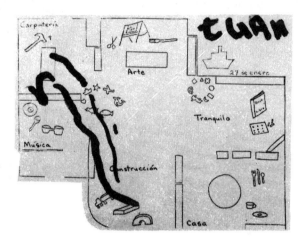

Mary Hohmann

High/Scope Educational Consultant

Child planning has a central role in the High/Scope Preschool Curriculum. (At "planning time," a regular part of the High/Scope daily routine, each child discusses what he or she wants to do that day. At "work time," which follows planning, children carry out their stated plans.)

Through these daily experiences with planning, children learn to articulate their ideas and intentions. They develop a sense of control over their own actions and learn to trust their inner resources. Child planning also enhances the "learning potential" of the play that grows out of it. Motivational research suggests that children's intrinsic motivation to learn is greater in activities that they select themselves. In addition, specific research on the High/Scope Curriculum suggests that the play resulting from planning is more complex and challenging than unplanned play.

Children's Plans: What to Expect

There are many good reasons, then, to encourage children to plan. As adults who wish to support child planning, we need to know **what to expect from young planners.** This article discusses some of the many possible forms that child plan-

ning can take and the implications for teachers and caregivers working to support child planning. Over the years, we've become increasingly aware of the range and variety of children's plans as we've observed planning time in many different High/Scope settings: in preschools, Head Start programs, day care settings, and home visit programs. From observational research conducted in High/Scope Curriculum programs, we've also learned about the planning process. Many of the insights about planning reported in this article come from a study conducted by C. Berry and K. Sylva of the plan-do-review process in British classrooms.

One dimension of child planning that most of these observers have noted is that **plans can be both verbal and nonverbal.** When asked what they would like to do, some young children respond by pointing, looking at a friend or toy, or simply going to one of the work areas and beginning to play. Other children respond in single words ("Cars," "Hammer"), phrases ("Over there by David"), brief sentences ("I want to make something for my mom"), or whole paragraphs ("First me and Lena are gonna' play dentist again. I'm being the dentist and she's the little girl. I'm gonna'

Reprinted from *High/Scope ReSource*, Spring/Summer 1991, pp. 4-6. Copyright © 1991 by High/Scope Press.

give her some special stuff so her mouth don't hurt"). Adults who value child planning are careful to acknowledge and support all plans that children make, whether or not they are expressed in words.

Children's plans also vary in focus and complexity. Based on their classroom observations, Berry and Sylva classified the plans children made into three different types: vague, routine, and elaborated plans.

Vague plans are minimal plans. In response to a question about what they are going to do, children just barely indicate a choice or beginning point, e.g., "Go over there," "House area," "Make something." Children who make such ambiguous plans seem to have an unclear picture in their minds of what they actually want to do. We have noticed that these children often end up doing one of three things: (1) going to a safe, unoccupied spot, picking up something like a doll or stuffed animal, and intently watching other busily engaged children; (2) wandering from place to place to explore the room and materials; or (3) seeking out an adult to join and follow them as they move about. Such children may be telling us: "I need to take in all the possibilities before I decide what to do or I want to do something really safe before I risk something new."

Routine plans are simple, specific plans in which children identify an activity, process, or material as their beginning intention, e.g., "Play with blocks," "Cutting-lots," "Computers." These children seem to have a clear picture in mind of themselves engaged in a particular experience or with a specific material. They know how they want to begin and generally get started right away, unless someone else is using the materials they had in mind.

Elaborated plans are more complex plans in which children mention an activity, process, or material as a beginning point, state a goal or outcome, and also mention one or more steps or materials needed to carry out their intentions. Here are some examples of elaborated plans:

- "Make a Robin Hood hat. With a feather, a real one like Michael's."

- "Use the Construx. Make a telephone truck with a very tall ladder. And I think I'll put a cab for the driver. And balancers on the sides so it won't tip over."

These children have a more extensive mental picture of what they want to accomplish and how they will go about doing it. They are generally quite persistent in pursuing their original intentions in spite of problems that arise along the way. Another dimension of child planning often noted by experienced caregivers is that **children's plans may be perfunctory or real.** Children are usually enthusiastic about planning. Adults can hear this enthusiasm in the tone of children's voices as they plan, and see it in their bodies as they lean forward eagerly to describe their ideas. There are times, however, when this enthusiasm is missing. Even though a child may clearly state an intention, he or she seems to be just "going through the motions" of planning.

A perfunctory plan is a signal that something is impeding or delaying planning. Perhaps the child cannot make a genuine plan until she shares an upsetting experience that happened on the way to school. Or a child may be waiting for someone: "Sometimes Noah just says something, anything, at planning, because I think what he really wants to do is play with John, who hasn't arrived yet." When adults are alert to the possible reasons behind a halfhearted plan, they can respond by discussing the child's concerns; suggesting to Noah, for example, that he wait until his friend comes and then make a plan.

Another variable that affects the kinds of plans children make is their experience with the planning process. Observant adults recognize that **children's plans change over time** as children become familiar with available materials and playmates and their own ability to make choices and follow through on them. Children's plans usually become increasingly verbal as time passes; they also become more focused and complex. In a 1984 study of the development of the planning process in young children, W. Fabricius reported, for example, that most 3-year-old children can keep a goal in mind, but generally work toward it one step at a time. They deal with problems as they encounter them, rather than anticipating and planning for them. Between the ages of $3^1/2$ and $5^1/2$, however, Fabricius reported that children gradu-

Setting the Stage for Child Planning

Wherever children plan in an early childhood program — in the living room, on the playground, in the art area, under the table — the setting has an impact on the quality of children's plans. Here are three key principles of arranging a setting for child planning.

Stability. Planning flourishes in a stable setting, so keep the adult, the other children in the planning group, and the physical setting fairly constant. When changes are to be made, alert children in advance: "Tomorrow, Becki's mom is spending the day with us, so there will be three planning groups instead of just two. Becki, Sandy, and Will from our table, and Devon and Mel from Bob's table will meet with Becki's mom. Everybody else will plan in their regular groups."

Visibility. Conduct planning in a space where children can see all the materials, places, and people available to them. This makes it easier for them to imagine what they will do. The younger the children, the more they need to be able to see the materials they are planning to use. In some early childhood settings — particularly in home day care, for example — children may not be able to see all the play spaces and materials as they make their plans. Adults can compensate for limited visibility in various ways: by touring the play spaces with children before planning, by bringing some of the available materials to the planning setting, or by planning in different parts of the center from time to time so that different materials are visible.

Intimacy. Planning is basically an intimate exchange between a child planner and a sup-portive adult in which the child indicates an intention and a way of acting on it, and the adult enters into a dialogue with the child about this plan. Since planning with a group of children involves a series of these one-to-one conversations, the smaller the group of children sharing their plans with an adult, the more intimate and unhurried is the planning exchange. In their study of the High/Scope plan-do-review process, Berry and Sylva found that children in smaller, more intimate, planning groups tended to make more detailed plans. They found that in planning groups of 1–4 children, 60 percent made detailed plans, while in planning groups of 8–10 children, only 15 percent made detailed plans. To explain these findings, they speculated that "staff become more concerned in larger groups with 'getting through' and not losing the attention of the group than in the quality of each child's plan."

Of course, in programs in which larger planning groups are a necessity, adults should be aware that encouraging children to make complex plans is *not impossible* in a larger group, only *more difficult.* Though the adults will need to engage the attention of the group (for example, by using role play, songs, games, tours, or chants), the focus should be on the individual child's plan. Adults can create an intimate atmosphere by listening attentively to the child's plan and using other one-to-one planning strategies. Another way to deal with the problem of too-large planning groups is to stagger the planning schedule: planning intensively with three or four children at a time, as they arrive in the morning. When adults are convinced of the importance of in-depth planning for each child, they usually find creative ways to make it happen.

Two Steps to Success

Planning involves a series of highly personal, individual conversations that occur in a group setting. The following steps take into account both the group and individual aspects of planning.

Step one: Engage the attention and interest of the planning group through a game-like activity, a special task, or challenge. For example, children might explore a collection of new materials; take a guided tour of the center in a make-believe vehicle; use special props or materials while making a plan; use pantomime, drawing, or writing to plan; participate in games or role play to decide whose turn it is to plan next (e.g., "Today we'll pass the planning pillow. When the music stops, whoever has the pillow will plan next").

Step two: Engage in one-on-one exchanges with each child. Talk about his or her plan. Talk to the child at his or her own level. Create an intimate, unhurried atmosphere by showing the child your genuine interest in his or her plan, and by listening and observing attentively as the child expresses an intention. Encourage the child to talk further about his or her plan by commenting or asking questions about materials, space, sequence, prior related work, and other details. Deal sensitively with any concerns that may be impeding planning.

---

ally gain the ability to plan a multistep course of action, foreseeing problems and ways of dealing with them before they launch into action. For example, a 5-year-old might incorporate anticipated problems in her plan: "I'll make a bird house. I'll use the big cardboard blocks for the walls, but I'll need a big enough board or something else for the roof. If there isn't a piece of wood big enough, maybe a piece of cardboard will work."

Adult Support for Planning

Children's plans, then, come in a wide variety of forms. The range of strategies adults use to support child planning is just as wide. Here we discuss just a few of the most important support strategies adults can use. We don't focus on **group** planning strategies — ways of engaging the interest of the entire planning group as each child takes a turn to plan — but on **individual** planning strategies — ways of enhancing the conversation with each child about his or her intentions.

One of the primary ways you can make these individual conversations more meaningful is to **listen attentively as the child states an initial plan.** Rushing through planning can cause children to feel hurried and anxious. After you question a child about his or her plan, it is important to pause and give each child ample time to respond. Whatever the child says or does tells you something important and suggests ways you might respond. Listen and observe for both nonverbal and verbal planning. If the child's communication is nonverbal, you may want to restate it in words or engage the child in a dialogue to clarify his or her intentions. Listen also for vague, routine, and elaborated plans to gain some idea of how well the child is able to picture the desired action sequence. Then think of ways you might help him or her foresee it more completely. Listen for perfunctory plans and deal sensitively with the issues behind them, reassuring children who are not ready to plan that it's okay to wait for a while.

Once children have indicated a plan in some way, the next step for adults is to **encourage children to develop their plans further.** At this point it makes some sense to distinguish between two groups of planners, nonverbal/vague planners and routine/elaborate planners. Interestingly enough, Berry and Sylva's research suggests that adults tend to question the first group extensively; the second, hardly at all. In their analysis, adults tend to keep after the vague or nonverbal planners until they arrive at a more complete picture of what they might do, but pass up the opportunity to converse with and question children who have the potential for thinking through and articulating quite elaborate plans. It's important to remember that *all* children need the opportunity to expand on and clarify their plans — even those who've stated an initial intention fairly clearly. There are many ways adults can encourage children to develop their ideas further. For example, they can talk with children about where they will work, the materials they will use, the sequence of their actions, and other details, and they can discuss the child's prior related work.

Is there time for a thoughtful planning conversation with each child? Yes, there is. First, even though such conversations take longer than a routine question-and-answer exchange (e.g., "What are you going to do?" "Play with blocks"), they don't take that much longer. In fact, thoughtful planning conversations often go rapidly, because they are intense and full of the unexpected. In addition, when adults converse attentively with children about their plans, children are generally able to get started with less adult help — because many potential problems and choices have already been dealt with. This leaves the adult free to focus on conversations with other children about *their* plans. In this sense, in-depth planning with each child is a group management tool, since well-conceived plans generally lead the planner to a focused and appropriate set of actions.

Note: For more information on the research cited here, see Berry, C. F., & Sylva, K. (1987, unpublished), The plan-do-review cycle in High/Scope: Its effect on children and staff *(write Carla Berry, Chicago AEYC, 410 S. Michigan Ave., Chicago, IL 60605); and Fabricius, W. V. (1984, doctoral dissertation),* The development of planning in young children *(available from UMI, 300 N. Zeeb Rd., Ann Arbor, MI 48106).*

Writing in Kindergarten

Helping Parents Understand the Process

Kathleen A. Dailey

Kathleen A. Dailey is Assistant Professor, Elementary Education Department, Edinboro University of Pennsylvania and Kindergarten Teacher, Miller Research Learning Center (campus laboratory school).

As a parent, how would you react to this work from a kindergarten child? Would you respond in the following manner?

"I can't believe Miss Davis let Tommy bring home a paper with so many mistakes."

"Doesn't she take time to spell the words for the children?"

"Shouldn't Tommy learn to make the letters correctly first?"

"How will he learn to spell correctly if she lets him spell like that?"

"He doesn't even know how to read yet and they expect him to write!"

Many parents may have this initial reaction, especially if the teacher has not prepared the parents for such work. Research in homes and schools suggests that the writing process of the child can be enriched by communication between teachers and parents. When parents first encounter the idea of writing programs for kindergartners, they need to be educated about the program. The following research-based answers to some of the most common questions are helpful in orienting kindergartners' parents to an early writing program.

Figure 1. *The flowers are coming out of the ground.*

How does my child learn to read and write?

Literacy, the process of learning to read and write, begins at home long before children enter school (Ferreiro & Teberosky, 1982; Hall, 1987; Schickedanz, 1986). This process does not officially begin at a particular age; rather, it develops as children gain experience with language and print. The two processes, reading and writing, develop simultaneously.

A variety of activities, which can be a part of daily living in many homes, enhance literacy development. Children learn purposes for reading and writing as the parent and child sing a lullaby, share a picture book, make a shopping list or write a telephone message. Many children *read* environmental print, such as the names on cereal boxes and restaurant signs. Likewise, children learn how a book *works* and realize that print conveys meaning as they partake in a variety of experiences with books. As 2-year-old Ryan sits propped on his mother's lap with a book, she points to the cat and says, "What's that?" "Ki-Ki," says Ryan. Young Ryan gathers meaning from the pictures and the dialogue with his mother. With increased book knowledge, he comes to understand that the black marks on the page tell a story as well as the pictures.

At the same time, children begin

From *Childhood Education*, Spring 1991, pp. 170-175. Reprinted by permission of Kathleen A. Dailey and the Association for Childhood Education International, 11141 Georgia Avenue, Suite 200, Wheaton, MD. Copyright © 1991 by the Association.

to experiment with different forms of writing that meet their needs and interests. Children may begin to copy letters and words from books, to write lines of squiggle or letters or to ask an adult to make models of letters for them. Children may write the names of family members and spellings of common objects. Writing interests may further develop as children choose to write letters, send postcards to friends, cast their superhero as the main character of their story or write a poem based on a favorite story, such as *In a Dark, Dark Wood* (Melser & Cowley, 1980) (see Figure 2).

The kindergarten reading program should be an extension of reading and writing that began in the home. It should help young children draw upon their past experiences to increase their understanding of how reading and writing function for specific and meaningful purposes (Dyson, 1984; Hall, 1987; Teale, 1982; Teale & Sulzby, 1989).

Do drawing and scribbling help my child learn how to write?

Children's first attempts at authorship are frequently accompanied by a drawing. Drawing is an integral part of the writing process because it is a way for children to plan and organize their written text (Dyson, 1988; Strickland & Morrow, 1989). A drawing can tell a story that written words cannot yet convey for the young child. Parents should accept their children's drawings and encourage them to talk about these drawings. Some researchers encourage parents and teachers to write down what children dictate so they can see their own speech put into words.

Young children will frequently scribble. Scribble drawing takes on a circular form. As children intend these marks to be writing, the scribbles take on a linear, controlled form. A page full of scribbles may be a letter to Grandma or a restaurant menu. When asked to *read* this message, the child may first glance at the picture then point

to the scribbles as he or she relays the content of the written work. As the child's print awareness increases, these scribbled marks become more refined and take on the characteristics of print (see Figures 3 & 4).

How can I encourage my child to write at home?

Research indicates that children engage in literacy events more in the home than in school (Schickedanz & Sullivan, 1984). This evidence supports the importance of parents as writing models. Observational studies of young children reveal that adults involved in writing behaviors such as writing a letter, making a grocery list or writing a check are often a stimulus for a child's early attempts to write (Lamme, 1984; Schickedanz & Sullivan, 1984; Taylor, 1983). When chil-

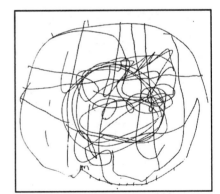

Figure 3. *Random scribbling*

Figure 2. *Poem based on the story, In a Dark, Dark Wood*
On a dark, dark path
In a dark, dark house
On a dark, dark stair
In a dark, dark room
Boo! Ha-ha-ha

Figure 4. *Controlled scribbling*

dren see adults writing for a variety of purposes, they discover ways in which writing is useful and meaningful.

Parents can create an environment that accepts and values writing by providing their children with many tools for writing. A variety of unlined paper and many different writing tools (markers, pencils, pens or chalk) are important materials for this craft. Children enjoy a variety of writing media. They may like the feel of writing letters or words in a tray of sand, pudding or jello. They may write using a computer or typewriter. Rich (1985) suggests using a "writing suitcase" as a portable writing station. The suitcase is filled with paper, markers, crayons, plastic letters and stencils. The child has access to the suitcase, is responsible for its contents and is free to add new items. The child is an active learner in the process. The writing that is produced is limited only by imagination.

Aren't paper-and-pencil activities, like workbook pages, the best way of learning to read and write? Children learn through direct participation in meaningful activities. When that learning is a complex process (like reading) rather than a skill (like tying shoes), it is even more important that the conditions of meaningful participation be met. Music is a good analogy. If we want young children to develop their musical abilities, we begin with enjoyment, not worksheets on musical notation. We accept their early efforts as well, realizing that the toddler who bounces in rhythm to a popular song may become a dancer or the child who pounds on a xylophone may play a musical instrument someday.

Reading programs that *teach* children to *read* and *write* through the use of dittos and workbook pages reflect practices that are developmentally inappropriate for young children (Elkind, 1986) for at least two reasons. First, the child's needs are not taken into consideration when the emphasis is on *every* child doing the same thing at the same time. Manuel has recognized the *M* at the beginning of his name and on the McDonald's sign since he was 3 years old. Manuel can write his own name and the word *MOM*. Manuel brings

Table 1
THE ASSOCIATION BETWEEN LANGUAGE DEVELOPMENT AND WRITING DEVELOPMENT

Language	Writing	Spelling
Babbling	Random scribbling	
Holophrase—one word utterance is used to express a complete thought: "Mama" means "Mommy I want to get up."		One letter spelling—one or two letters represent entire sentences or phrases: *H* = This is my house.
Repetition	Controlled scribbling—the same forms or the same letters are repeated as the child progresses toward mastery of that form.	Writing the same letters or words in order to attain mastery
Expanded vocabulary of frequently used words		Incorporation of conventional spellings with invented spellings
Grammatical rules are applied to speech. "I want up." replaces "Me up."		Transitional spelling—using simple rules to spell
Overgeneralization—internalization of grammar rules, but applied to more cases than those in which they work: "He runned after me."		Overgeneralization—reliance on rules applied in previous spellings, yielding errors due to inconsistencies of the language. "LETUS" (lettuce)
More precise speech		More precise spelling

Adapted from Lamme, 1984.

home a paper with neatly circled *Ms*. As he hands the paper to his father, Manuel replies, "It was boring!" Molly completed the same paper yet is unable to tell you the letter name. The way and manner in which children learn varies for each individual. Approaches that may be effective for one child may be ineffective for the next.

Second, workbook writing directs the focus away from the child. "When worksheets and phonics lessons are given to young children all the initiative comes from the teacher. When this happens, teachers unintentionally prevent children from developing their own natural initiative" (Willert & Kamii, 1985). On the other hand, activities such as drawing and writing about a trip to the zoo, reading alphabet books and enjoying songs and fingerplays about sounds and letters allow children to take an active role in learning to read and write.

I have difficulty figuring out what my child has written. How can I better understand what she writes?

The writing of children develops in overlapping stages that parallel language development (Table 1).

As children make the transition from scribbling to more conventional forms of writing, they may represent their written work with a random ordering of letters such as *mTEo* to represent house. This is followed by stages that reveal the child's understanding of letter-sound correspondence, which is a first step toward reading (Chomsky, 1971). These stages are referred to as "invented spelling" because children apply what they know about sounds and letters to their early writing. It is common, however, for children to be in several stages of spelling development at once and revert to earlier stages as they experiment with writing. The stages of invented spelling development are shown in Table 2.

These early attempts are systematic even though the spelling is unconventional (Richgels, 1987), as shown in the spelling of *monster*, *grass* and *class* (Table 2). This systematic process enables children to take control of their learning and become independent writers.

Should I correct my child's written work?

When a child says "ba" for bottle, parents understand what the child is trying to say and accept the pronunciation at the child's stage of development. Spelling development should be treated similarly. Early writing contains many words spelled unconventionally because children experiment with written form at particular stages of development. Children need models who are supportive and patient. When Jane asks, "Mommy, do you spell *tree*, T-R-E?" her mother responds, "That's the way it sounds, but that's not the way it is spelled. It's *T-R-E-E*." This response tells children that there are conventional spellings, but we also accept the way they spell. Criticism of misspelled words makes children fearful of making mistakes. Under these conditions, research shows that they write less and less well, sticking with *safe* known words. What is worse, they learn to dislike writing because they see it as a test rather than as a means of creative expression.

Parents may help children sound out words or spell words for them, but at the same time provide materials that foster independence in writing. Picture dictionaries provide children with an early reference tool. Parents need to show children how the dictionary is set up and how to locate words using the alphabet and picture cues. Parents can help children compile their own personal dictionary of frequently used words, such as objects in the home or names of family members. A set of words on cards serves the same purpose (Ashton-Warner, 1965). An accompanying illustration may help the child use the word cards independently. Understanding spelling development and fostering independence in writing through positive and nurturing practices are essential to a child's healthy attitude toward writing.

My child will write letters correctly one day and reverse them the next. Is that normal?

When parents of young children see a backwards *S* or *2*, they often

---

Table 2
THE DEVELOPMENT OF INVENTED SPELLINGS

Stage 1	Use of initial consonant to represent an entire word	M for monster G for grass C for class
Stage 2	Initial and final consonants serve as word boundaries	MR GS CS
Stage 3	Inclusion of medial consonant; awareness of blends; may divide blend	MSTR GRS CALS
Stage 4	Initial, final and medial consonants and vowel place-holder. Vowel is incorrect	MESTR GRES CLES
Stage 5	Conventional Spelling	MONSTER GRASS CLASS

Adapted from: Gentry, 1981; Graves, 1983; Lamme, 1984 & Strickland & Morrow, 1989.

worry that their child has a learning disability. Actually, such reversals are very prevalent in kindergarten, 1st and 2nd grade. It is common for children to experiment with reversed writing. Sometimes letters are reversed; sometimes they are placed upside down. These characteristics, including a tendency to write in any direction, are all related (Schickedanz, 1986). Children need practice with directionality and the orientation of printed symbols. Until children have attained consistency in left-to-right and top-to-bottom orientation and formed a mental image of what the letter *b* looks like, for example, they may continue to reverse written symbols. "All exploration is perfectly normal; it is a healthy sign that children are investigating print, getting used to it and figuring out how it works" (Marzollo & Sulzby, 1988, p. 83). If a child consistently reverses written symbols beyond 2nd grade, a parent may want to seek advice. Generally, however, reversals are not a cause for concern at an early age.

What should I look for in my child's writing program?

"Everywhere I look, I see children's written work," comments a visitor to the kindergarten classroom. This atmosphere reflects one in which young writers have been experimenting with different types of print since their first day of school. Each time children sit down to write, they increase their knowledge of written form just through the act itself. At the writing center, children are working in their journals or writing a story. Writing, however, is not limited to one area of the room. In the block area, Erin made a sign that says *CASO* (castle). In the kitchen area, Patrick posted the special food for the day, *APLS* (apples). Meanwhile, the post office clerk is busy delivering letters addressed to Santa Claus (see Figure 5).

Young children's writing, speaking and action are closely re-

Figure 5. *Letter to Santa Claus*
To Santa Claus
You are nice.
Get me a present.
I would like a Barbie.
I like you.

lated. Early writing is not only a paper-and-pencil activity, but also a social process. In her observation of children, Dyson (1981) comments, "I saw no quiet, solemn-faced scholars, struggling to break into print. Rather, I saw (and heard) writers using both pencil and voice to make meaning on the empty page" (p. 777). In a writing environment one may observe children engaged in the following activities:

- Asking each other for help
  How did you spell tyrannosaurus?

- Planning and creating
  I'm going to put brontosaurus in the water.

- Rehearsing ideas
  My brontosaurus will be eating plants.

- Questioning each other about their products
  What is your dinosaur doing?

- Sharing and reading their work to each other
  The Brotsrs is RunIng AWAW. (*The brontosaurus is running away.*)

- Evaluating their work
  That was a long sentence. I'll have to make more room on the paper next time.

  (Adapted from Lamme, 1984)

In a quality kindergarten writing program, the child's teacher serves as model and facilitator of the writing process, providing the children with an environment rich in opportunities to use and create written materials (Rich, 1985). The teacher observes children write, confers with them and accepts their work. "Teachers who grow writers in their classrooms also regard pieces of writing as growing things to be nurtured rather than as objects to be repaired and fixed" (Bissex, 1981).

What does the teacher do during the writing conference with my child?

The writing conference serves as a personal and meaningful interaction between the child and the teacher; both are learners in the process. Early in the school year, Ms. Hart established a routine for writing conferences. She chose the couch area as a comfortable place where the children can share their written work. Chris knows that his conference with Ms. Hart is every Tuesday. As the other children in the class continue to write, Chris takes his folder, journal, personal dictionary and a pencil and sits with Ms. Hart on the couch. This time together provides Ms. Hart with insights into Chris's writing abilities.

Throughout the writing conference, Ms. Hart asks questions that guide the process (Table 3). This format eventually allows the children to go through the same process independently as they reflect on their own writing. She focuses on the child throughout the conference, allowing the child to take the lead. Through careful observation of written work, the teacher assesses what the child already knows about written language. She may notice, for example, that a child uses letter-sound correspondence correctly for *D* when writing *dog* (*DG*) but confuses *B* and *P* when spelling *boat* (*PT*). She may have the child write for her during the conference to observe the process firsthand. Ms. Hart keeps detailed records of the child's progress and makes teaching recommendations based on specific needs.

5. CURRICULAR APPLICATIONS: Content and Process

Conclusion

Parents and teachers need to recognize that ". . . every child who can talk has the capacity to learn to write and also to seize upon its possibilities with enthusiasm" (Smith, 1981, p. 792). Parents and teachers have the responsibility to create an environment for children that develops confidence and success in writing. When parents and teachers understand the processes underlying writing development, they can help children participate in meaningful home and school activities that promote its growth. Thus, home and school partnerships built upon communication and understanding provide children with a firm foundation for successful writing experiences.

Acknowledgment: The author gratefully thanks Mary Renck Jalongo for her assistance in reviewing this article.

References

Ashton-Warner, S. (1965). *Teacher*. NY: Simon and Schuster.

Bissex, G. (1981). Growing writers in classrooms. *Language Arts, 58,* 785-791.

Chomsky, C. (1971). Write first, read later. *Childhood Education, 47,* 296-299.

Dyson, A. H. (1981). Oral language: The rooting system for learning to write. *Language Arts, 58,* 776-791.

Dyson, A. H. (1984). N spell my grandmama: Fostering early thinking about print. *The Reading Teacher, 38,* 262-270.

Dyson, A. H. (1988). Appreciate the drawing and dictating of young children. *Young Children, 43*(3), 25-32.

Elkind, D. (1986). Formal education and early childhood education: An essential difference. *Phi Delta Kappan, 67,* 631-636.

Ferreiro, E., & Teberosky, A. (1982). *Literacy before schooling.* London: Heinemann.

Gentry, J. R. (1981). Learning to spell developmentally. *The Reading Teacher, 34,* 378-381.

Graves, D. (1983). *Writing: Teachers and children at work.* Portsmouth, NH: Heinemann.

Hall, N. (1987). *The emergence of literacy.* Portsmouth, NH: Heinemann.

Lamme, L. L. (1984). *Growing up writing.* Washington, DC: Acropolis.

Marzollo, J., & Sulzby, E. (1988). See Jane read! See Jane write! *Parents, 63*(7), 80-84.

Melser, J., & Cowley, J. (1980). *In a dark, dark wood.* San Diego, CA: The Wright Group.

Rich, S. J. (1985). The writing suitcase. *Young Children, 40*(5), 42-44.

Richgels, D. J. (1987). Experimental reading with invented spelling (ERIS): A preschool and kindergarten method. *The Reading Teacher, 40,* 522-529.

Schickedanz, J. (1986). *More than the ABC's: The early stages of reading and writing.* Washington, DC: National Association for the Education of Young Children.

Schickedanz, J. A., & Sullivan, M. (1984). Mom, what does U-F-F spell? *Language Arts, 61,* 7-17.

Smith, F. (1981). Myths of writing. *Language Arts, 58,* 792-798.

Strickland, D., & Morrow, L. M. (1989). Young children's early writing development. *The Reading Teacher, 42,* 426-427.

Taylor, D. (1983). *Family literacy—Young children learning to read and write.* Exeter, NH: Heinemann.

Teale, W. H. (1982). Toward a theory of how children learn to read and write naturally. *Language Arts, 59,* 555-570.

Teale, W. H., & Sulzby, E. (1989). Emergent literacy: New perspectives. In D. S. Strickland & L. M. Morrow (Eds.), *Emerging literacy: Young children learn to read and write* (pp. 1-15). Newark, DE: International Reading Association.

Willert, M. K., & Kamii, C. (1985). Reading in kindergarten. Direct vs. indirect teaching. *Young Children, 40*(4), 3-9.

Table 3
INAPPROPRIATE AND APPROPRIATE RESPONSES
USED DURING WRITING CONFERENCES

Inappropriate Responses	Appropriate Responses
"Allison, will you read this? I can't figure out what it says."	"What are you writing about Allison?"
"What is it?"	"Tell me about your picture."
"Can't you write about something else besides the zoo?"	"Do you like writing about the zoo?"
"Tomorrow, I think you should write about our field trip."	"What do you think you will write about next?"
"The next time I want you to figure out how to spell these words by yourself."	"Allison, how did you go about writing this?"

Adapted from Graves, 1983.

The Values and Purposes of Human Movement

Recognizing the role that physical activity has in assisting young children attain desired objectives, early childhood educators should continually be investigating avenues for involving children in movement experiences. Caregivers should be aware that for the child, movement is one of the most utilized vehicles of nonverbal interaction and expression. All children enjoy physical activity. Playing makes a child happy.

Wayne Eastman

Wayne Eastman is on the faculty of the Fisher Institute of Applied Arts and Technology (Early Childhood Education), Corner Brook, Newfoundland, Canada.

For young children movement is at the very center of their life. It permeates all facets of their development, whether in the psychomotor, cognitive or affective domains of human behaviour. The unity of man makes it impossible to separate these three areas of human behaviour. (Eden, 1983, p.12)

Physical activity is one of the most important mediums through which young children form impressions about themselves as well as about their surroundings. Furthermore, physical activity is important to children because active learning provides opportunities through movement. A child climbs a hill to see how things look from this vantage point. An obstacle course challenges and is a means to manipulate his or her body through various settings. Children's motor initiatives are also an avenue for and an indicator of each individual's mental growth. "Physical activity enables children to progress along the developmental sequence from the sensorimotor intelligence of infancy to preoperational thought in the preschool years to the concrete operational thinking exhibited by primary children" (Bredekamp, 1987, p. 63).

Why are movement experiences worthwhile and, indeed, even necessary? Physical activity is accepted as having a positive relationship with good health, happiness, and vitality. As North Americans we have one of the highest standards of living in the world; however, studies have demonstrated that physical fitness levels in individuals begin to decrease at the age of five. Physical activity is a crucial component of an early childhood education environment. Research supports the fact that more than three-fourths of a child's basic motor movements are attained by twelve years of age. Consequently, a wide variety of carefully planned movement experiences at an early age is a necessary prerequisite for later motor development.

A precept of the implementation of a physical activity program in an early childhood setting is an understanding of the characteristics, interests, and needs important in curriculum planning. Early childhood educators need to be cognizant of the following domains: cognitive, psychomotor, and affective. For too long, movement for young children has been promoted along psychomotor lines, negating the contributions of physical activity to the cognitive and affective domains. Physical activity enhances psychomotor behaviors through developing such areas as motor-skill proficiency and physical fitness. Cognitive development, the thought process, is broadened when young children engage in physical activities which promote perceptual awareness, problem solving, and creativity. The preceding tenets should be addressed in a nonrestrictive environment with the early childhood educator acting as a facilitator of children's movement experiences. In recognition that physical activity is one of the child's most utilized means of nonverbal communication and expression, a preschool movement curriculum must contribute to the general affective results of pleasure, self-con-

From *Day Care and Early Education,* Summer 1992, pp. 21-24. Copyright © 1992 by Human Science Press, Inc., 72 Fifth Avenue, New York, NY 10011. Reprinted by permission.

cept, socialization, and self-discipline.

The strongest practical reason for a wide variety of movement experiences for young children is that it is at this age that basic motor skills are being established; by age five all the fundamental movement patterns have emerged. It becomes evident that young children require ample opportunities to pursue daily physical activities. The onus is on the early childhood educator to incorporate movement experiences into the preschool curriculum.

When discussing with parents why physical activity is a significant program component, the most vital explanation is that young children need to exercise their growing muscles. Preschoolers continually try out their range of bodily actions, whether in running, jumping, or playing a game. During these endeavors they learn about themselves as well as their surroundings. Furthermore, while physical activity affects their physiological maturation, movement experiences also teach cognitive concepts such as *small, large, around,* and *straight ahead.*

A human movement program also contributes immensely to social learning. Such social learning skills as sharing and cooperation are promoted when young children are engaged in movement experiences. Social values of physical activities have to be viewed in the context of the age of the child. For instance, one would not expect a two - to three-year-old to interact with other preschoolers for any length of time. At this stage young children prefer being on their own. Consequently, as in all other areas of an early childhood program, motor expectations have to be age-appropriate as well as individual-appropriate.

Educators have long been cognizant of the significance of movement experiences in the motor development of young children. Perhaps the best summary of the meaning of movement to children appears in *The Significance of the Young Child's Motor Development* (1988):

• To the young child, movement means life. Not only does he/she experi-

ence life in his/her own movements but also he/she attributes life to all moving things.
• Movement is, for the young child, an important factor in self-discovery. The emerging concept of self is ego-enhancing as he/she calls attention to his/her stunts and tricks.
• Movement means discovery of the environment. Movement assists the young child in achieving and maintaining his/her orientation in space. It is an important factor in his/her development of concepts of time, space and direction.
• What does movement mean to a young child? It means freedom – freedom from the restrictions of narrow physical confinements and freedom to expand oneself through creative body expressions.
• Movement means safety. In a basic sense it has survival value.
• To the young child, movement is a method of establishing contact and communication.
• Not the least among the meanings of movement for the young child is sheer enjoyment and sensuous pleasure. He/she runs and screams with excitement as an expression of joy in just being alive. (p. 53).

If movement has so much meaning to the young child, then just what activities should encompass a viable movement program and how would an educator carry out such a curriculum? Physical activity programs for an early childhood setting must be developmentally appropriate as well as stimulating and, most of all, fun, hence contributing to a comprehensive framework of motor development. Experiences which enhance motor development can be pursued through movement both with and without equipment themes. Early childhood educators need to expose young children to activities which include locomotor and nonlocomotor activities, manipulative rhythmics, and games.

There are several directions preschool teachers can take when promoting physical activities at their centers. The theme approach is one readily utilized by many educators. When using this method, early childhood educators would develop an activity-planning sheet comprising the following categories: theme, skill development, equipment, lesson, and evalua-

tion of the lesson (Curtis, 1982). If this method is to be successful, educators have to be cognizant of several factors: the activities should focus on large-muscle pursuits, the session must be active and challenging, and explanations must be kept to a minimum. Remember, the role of the early childhood educator is to facilitate childrens movement experience, but not to dominate it.

The theme chosen can be as broad as the imagination of the educator.

Such themes as special days — for example, Halloween or transportation — can be utilized to develop a lesson.

In today's society young children have few experiences with aerobic activities. This form of exercise has traditionally been reserved for adults. However, aerobic exercises can be used in a preschool environment. Aerobic activities can augment the theme approach and could even be a theme. When preschoolers are exposed to aerobic experiences, educators should modify the program so that it considers the physiological, affective, and socioemotional characteristics of a young child. One of the major indicators of acceptable work load when performing aerobic exercise is heart rate. The average adult's heart rate is 72 beats per minute while that of the four- to six-year-old is 100 beats per minute (Fish, Fish & Golding, 1989). Fish (et al.) explain aerobic activities to preschoolers as follows: "They are activities that make us huff and puff and breathe hard."

Aerobic exercises for young children can follow the same sequence as for adults: warm-up, workout, and cool-down. However, because of physiological factors, as well as attention span, the activities selected for these three categories have to be modified for preschoolers. The key to successfully involving young children in this form of movement is that the activities have to be relatively short and vigorous in nature and can be carried out with a minimum of directions (Fish, et el. 1989). The warm-up should include activities that involve every part of the body. Action songs can be used for one form of warming

> **SAMPLE LESSON**
>
> THEME: Space and direction
>
> SKILL DEVELOPMENT: Moving through space, high and low movements, and moving body parts toward, away from, in front of, behind, around, through, and between objects.
>
> EQUIPMENT: None
>
> LESSON: Always begin a lesson with an action song. Action songs are attention getters as well as a tool to lead young children into more vigorous and complicated movements. The "Hokey Pokey" would do nicely for this particular theme.
>
> The second component of this lesson entails vigorous activities which reinforce the theme. The selection of the activities should be predicated on problem-solving experiences. In this sample lesson, an obstacle course composed of hula hoops, a long bench, chairs, and a target game would accentuate the theme. Obstacle courses are so popular with young children and teachers because they bring many movement patterns together as well as enable children to engage in problem-solving experiences under the guise of fun.
>
> The third aspect of a movement lesson is the "game." The game selected should also reinforce the theme. Games should be simple in nature and scope and never competitive; the focus should be on personal challenge. There are a myriad of publications which can assist the early childhood educator to choose games that are age-and-stage appropriate. However, many teachers devise their own games, hence, developing a movement experience which is suitable to their specific setting.
>
> The final stage of the lesson is what can be best called the cooling down. Children play hard, therefore, a cooling-down period is necessary. The cooling-down activity is both beneficial from a physiological and a behavioral perspective. The activity or activities should be tranquil and designed to calm the child. Animal imitation, where children mimic slow-moving animals, is appropriate.

up. The workout segment should be premised on exploratory movements whereby the heart rate is elevated. Such activities as vigorous rhythmic parachute play will satisfy the preceding criteria. The early childhood educator could supplement the more "formal" workout with "informal" play, such as a brisk walk around the neighborhood.

Cool-down activities are necessary following the vigorous aerobic segment so that children can calm down emotionally as well as physiologically. The activities selected for the cooling-down process can be the same as those used for the warm-up except the tempo has to slow down considerably.

As early childhood educators we consider it our duty to make certain that the children under our care are cognitively, emotionally, and socially stimulated. However, educators often omit the fourth component in the developmental process: physical growth. Recognizing the role exercise has in helping children to attain desired goals, early childhood educators should be searching for ways to ensure involvement by young children in physical activity. The preceding thrust takes on increased significance in our North American society, where physical fitness levels begin to decrease at the age of five. Consequently, as teachers we need to provide preschoolers with opportunities to partake in physical activity so as to initiate a lifelong concern about having a healthy body. If we accept the reality of the preceding comment, then as early childhood educators what are our options? The answer is clear. As caregivers we should be sharing the movement experience with young children. Remember, habits are best formed when preschoolers see and hear. A movement program for young children should be diverse with the early childhood educator creating a supportive setting in which preschoolers can participate in a broad range of motor activities. This program should include activities for the fundamental motor patterns, such as running and walking; activities utilizing equipment, such as balls, hula hoops, bean bags, and ropes; activities without equipment, such as action songs, as well as other locomotor and nonlocomotor experiences; rhythmic parachute play; gymnastic-type activities; and outdoor play such as the use of wheel toys and climbing apparatus.

To ensure that the movement program is appropriate for a preschool setting, the following criteria should be addressed:

1.   Does it offer a variety of movement patterns?

2.   Is it creative?

3.   Is it fun?

4.   Does it enable the children to make decisions and solve problems?

5.   Does it emphasize safety and control?

6.   Is it age-appropriate?

"The early years represent a crucial time in laying foundations for children's physical competency. It may be suggested that physical play is not only a pre-requisite for physical and emotional development, it is also the most accessible and natural vehicle to use in the promotion of the development of children's intellect." (Jones, 1989, p. 167).

References

Bredekamp, S. (1987). *Developmentally appropriate practices in early childhood programs serving children from birth through age 8.* Washington: National Association for the Education of Young Children.

Curtis, S.R. (1982). *The joy of movement in early childhood.* New York: Teachers College, Columbia University.

Eden, S. (1983). *Early experiences.* Scarborough, Ontario: Nelson Canada.

Fish, H.T., Fish, R.B., & Golding, L.A. (1989). *Starting out well.* Campaign, Leisure Press.

Jones, C. (1989). Physical play and the early years curriculum. *The British Journal of Physical Education*, Winter, (1988).

The Significance of the Young Child's Motor Development (6th printing). The proceedings of a conference sponsored by the American Association for Health, Physical Education and Recreation and The National Association for the Education of Young children.

Reflections

Americans enter the mid-1990s in need of jobs and prosperity. Waves of recession and the weakness of the national economy brought about voting a new political party into office. President Bill Clinton's new cabinet faces major issues in education and jobs, technology, and trade.

On personal levels, Americans need restoration of their relationships. Racial animosities and disrespect are leading to increasing problems. While state-supported segregation may have ended, discrimination continues. Communities find themselves in conflict over racial issues.

As unemployment grows and community relations rupture, America's families are shaken. Some parents are without meaningful work or an income that pays for groceries. Communities become fearful places for children who want to play with friends. Increasing poverty puts more and more mothers and young children at risk for the basics of life. And crime is the only economy left in some places.

One unique organization has recognized the dire needs of America's families. For 60 years, Save the Children has gone about the business of helping families and communities to solve the problems facing children. Their operation is unique for several reasons. They work from a strong community base and believe that self-help is key to enabling families. They also work through local agencies to integrate services. This organization has left a legacy of changed communities across America.

State and local government cuts in education and public services affect all families with young children. Fortunately, new federal legislation will help offset some of these cuts. Money is expected to go to safe and affordable child care, Head Start, and increased health care for pregnant women and young children. Child immunization programs and shelters against homelessness may be given increased funding.

In the face of steadily rising poverty and violence, some national values are enduring, but in danger of being forgotten. These values need to be rediscovered and taught to children. At the heart of lessons learned from life is the premise that democracy is not a spectator sport. It is built from initiative and hard work. Families are the prime example of democracy for children. In the family, the child will learn fairness, decency, and initiative.

President Clinton's first year in office will be measured by how much of his strategy for rebuilding communities and revitalizing families is implemented. He has called for Home Instructional Programs for preschool children and full funding of Head Start. These programs are aimed at low-income families. He signed the Family and Medical Leave Act, enabling mothers and fathers to maintain their jobs while caring for newborns and sick children. During the political campaign, Clinton spoke repeatedly for better education, improved health care, and protection from violence for all of America's children. This will be the year to begin action on these reforms.

Looking Ahead: Challenge Questions

What are some of the most crucial problems facing families of children across the United States, whether in the hollows of Appalachia or the lower East side of New York City?

Why is it so difficult to put children's issues at the top of the U.S. agenda?

Can you identify one successful early childhood education program which helps low-income children and families in your community?

What do you know about President Clinton's strategies for assisting young children and their families? Where can you go for more information?

Unit 6

Ten Lessons To Help Us Through the 1990s

Anonymous

"Sometimes I would like to ask God why He allows poverty, famine and injustice when He could do something about it."

Speaker No. 1

"Well—why don't you ask Him?"

Speaker No. 2

"Because I'm afraid God might ask me the same question."

Speaker No. 1

I believe that we have lost our sense of what is important as a people. Too many young people of all races and classes are growing up unable to handle life in hard places, without hope, and without steady compasses to navigate a world that is reinventing itself at an unprecedented pace both technologically and politically. My generation learned that to accomplish anything, we had to get off the dime. Our children today must learn to get off the paradigm, over and over, and to be flexible, quick, and smart about it.

Children and young adults—all of us—face dazzling international changes and challenges and extraordinary social and economic upheavals. One decade's profligacy shifted our nation from a lender to debtor nation status. Our aging population and future work force depend on a shrinking pool of young workers, a majority of whom will be female, minority, or both. Our culturally diverse child and worker population confronts increasing racial and gender intolerance fueled by recession and greed. Our education system is drowning in the wake of the new skills required in a post-industrial economy. The nurturance of children is at risk as family nuclearization increases, both parents work, and more children rely on a single parent. Meanwhile, time and economic pressures mount and are unrelieved by extended family networks or family-friendly private sector and public policies.

Despite these social tidal waves, I believe there are some enduring spiritual and national values that we need

to rediscover on the eve of the five-hundredth anniversary of Columbus' arrival in America. I agree with Archibald Macleish that "there is only one thing more powerful than learning from experience and that is not learning from experience."

It is the responsibility of every adult—parent, teacher, preacher, and professional—to make sure that children and young people hear what we have learned from life, learn what we think matters, and know that they are never alone as they go to seize the future. So I have written my three wonderful sons a long letter sharing 25 of the lessons life has taught me, 10 of which I want to share here. Like so many parents, I worry that I may have been so busy making sure my children had all the "things" I didn't have, and would not face all the barriers I faced as a black child growing up, that I may not have shared as clearly with them the more important things I did have which got me through the tough days and troughs of life and which provide a steady anchor in troubled waters. While our children can take or leave these lessons, parents and other elders must make sure children can never say they were not told or reminded.

Lesson 1: There is no free lunch. Don't feel entitled to anything you don't sweat and struggle for. And help our nation understand that it's not entitled to world leadership based on the past or on what we say rather than how well we perform and meet changing world needs. Black, Latino, Asian American, and Native American youths should remember that they can never take anything for granted in America—especially now as racial intolerance resurges all over our land. Some of it, like David Duke's KKK brand of racism or the Bush campaign's cynical manipulation of Willie Horton, is blatant. But some of it is more subtle and very polite. Although it may be wrapped up in new euphemisms and better etiquette, as Frederick Douglass warned earlier, it's the same old snake.

White young people who have been raised to feel "entitled" to leadership by accident of birth need to be reminded that the world they face is already two-thirds nonwhite and poor and that our nation is becoming a mosaic of greater diversity. Of the total growth in the

Reprinted from *The State of America's Children, 1991*, Children's Defense Fund, 1991, pp. 13-15, 19, 20. From *The Measure of Our Success* by Marian Wright Edelman. Copyright © 1992 by Marian Wright Edelman. Reprinted by permission of Beacon Press.

American labor force between 1988 and 2000, only one in eight of these new additions will be white non-Latino males. As our fate becomes more and more intertwined with that of non-English-speaking people of color—in California, Texas, Iraq, Iran, South Africa, and Japan— economic and world survival will depend on awareness of and respect for other races and cultures.

Each American adult and child must struggle to achieve and not think for a moment that we've got it made. Frederick Douglass reminded all of us that "men may not get all they pay for in this world, but they must certainly pay for all they get."

While a high school diploma and a college degree today may get youths in the door, they will not get youths to the top of the career ladder or keep them there. Our young people have got to work their way up—hard and continuously. So we need to teach them—by example—not to be lazy, to do their homework, to pay attention to detail, to take care and pride in work, and to be reliable. Each of us must take the initiative in creating opportunity and not wait around for a favor. We must not assume a door is closed but must push on it. We must not assume if it was closed yesterday it's closed today. And none of us can ever stop learning and improving our minds. If we do, we and America are going to be left behind.

The rhetoric of the 1980s that told us we could have our cake and eat it, too, was a recipe for national disaster. A people unable or unwilling to share, to juggle difficult, competing demands, or to make hard choices and sacrifices may be incapable of taking courageous action to rebuild family and community and prepare for the future. Many whites favor racial justice as long as things remain the same. Many voters hate Congress, but love their own member of Congress as long as he or she takes care of their special interests. Many husbands are happier to share their wives' added income than the housework and child care. Many Americans decry the growing gap between the rich and the poor and middle class, and are outraged at escalating child suffering, as long as somebody else's taxes are raised and somebody else's program is cut.

Lesson 2: Set goals and work quietly and systematically toward them. We must all try to resist quick-fix, simplistic answers and easy gains, which often disappear just as quickly as they come. We must not feel compelled to talk if we don't have anything to say that matters. So many talk big and act small. So often we get bogged down in our ego needs and lose sight of deeper needs. It's alright to feel important if it is not at the expense of doing important deeds—even if we don't get the credit. You can get a lot achieved in life if you don't mind doing the work and giving others the credit. You know what you do and the Lord knows what you do and that's all that matters.

Lesson 3: Assign yourself. My daddy used to ask us whether the teacher gave us any homework. If we said no, he'd say, "Well, assign yourself." Don't wait around

for your boss or your friend or spouse to direct you to do what you are able to figure out and do for yourself to help others. Don't do just as little as you can to get by. Don't be a political bystander. Democracy is not a spectator sport. Run for political office, especially school boards. And don't think that you or your re-election or job are the only point once you do. If you see a need, don't ask, "Why doesn't somebody do something?" Ask, "Why don't I do something?" Don't wait around to be told what to do. There is nothing more wearing than people who have to be asked or reminded to do things repeatedly. Hard work, initiative, and persistence are still the nonmagic carpets to success.

Lesson 4: Never work just for money. Money alone won't save your soul or build a decent family or help you sleep at night. We are the richest nation on earth, but our incarceration, drug addiction, and child poverty rates are among the highest in the industrialized world. Don't confuse wealth or fame with character. And don't tolerate or condone moral corruption whether it's found in high or low places, whatever its color. It is not okay to push or use drugs even if every person in America is doing it. It is not okay to cheat or lie even if countless corporate or public officials do. Be honest. And demand that those who represent you be honest. Don't confuse morality with legality. Dr. King noted that everything Hitler did in Nazi Germany was legal. Don't give anyone the proxy for your conscience.

Lesson 5: Don't be afraid of taking risks or of being criticized. An anonymous sage said, "If you don't want to be criticized don't say anything, do anything, or be anything." Don't be afraid of failing. It's the way you learn to do things right. It doesn't matter how many times you fall down. What matters is how many times you get up. And don't wait for everybody to come along to get something done. It's always a few people who get things done and keep things going. This country needs more wise and courageous shepherds and fewer sheep.

Lesson 6: Take parenting and family life seriously. And insist that those you work for and who represent you do so. Our leaders mouth family values we do not practice. Seventy nations provide medical care and financial assistance to all pregnant women; we aren't one of them. Seventeen industrialized nations have paid maternity leave programs; we are not one of them and in 1990 our president vetoed and the business community opposed an unpaid parental leave bill to enable parents to stay home when a child is born, adopted, or sick. More than half of mothers of infants are in the labor force, and the men in Congress and the White House still are bickering about whether we can afford to fully fund Head Start and the newly enacted comprehensive child care bill designed to provide safe, affordable, quality child care for millions of parents who must work outside the home, or can afford to provide adequate child and income supports for working families. It is time for the mothers of this nation to tell the men of this nation to get with it and stop

Children Have Human Rights Too!

International and National Goals for Children: How Can We Make Our Nation Honor Them at Home and Abroad?

UNICEF's President James Grant detects a growing world ethos against preventable child suffering and death. Just as over time slavery and apartheid were rejected as moral offenses to civilized people, so now a new ethic is taking hold to give children first rather than last call on America's national resources, and to stem the 40,000 daily child deaths around the world that we have the technology and means but not yet the political will to prevent.

In 1989 the United Nations General Assembly approved an historic Convention on the Rights of the Child. The Convention spells out the economic, social, cultural, civil, and political rights of children. Among other things, it recognizes the right of all children to the highest attainable standard of health and requires ratifying nations to ensure prenatal care for pregnant women; prohibits discrimination against children based on their family's race, language, or religion; entitles all children to a free primary education and equal access to secondary and higher education; and establishes a right to an adequate standard of living and requires ratifying nations to assist parents who cannot meet this responsibility. So far, 58 nations have ratified the Convention. The United States is not among them. Our failure to commit to protecting children leaves us in the company of Iraq, Cambodia, and Libya.

In 1990 more than 70 world leaders met at the United Nations for a Summit on Children, adopting a declaration and plan of action to reach these and other goals for children. While President Bush spoke briefly at the Summit and the Agency for International Development handed out flyers describing our inadequate appropriations to help children in Third World nations, the president made no commitments to the millions of children living in the United States in Third-World conditions who are growing poorer every day.

The United States should be leading rather than lagging behind the world in ratifying and living up to the Convention on the Rights of the Child, the Summit goals, and the year 2000 goals for children—goals that right now remain more rhetoric than committed action and investment.

The U.S. Public Health Service, the Surgeon General, the president, and the National Governors' Association, among others, have established goals to improve the status of American children by the year 2000. Now it is time for concrete action to achieve them.

Goal	Status
Health	
Increase to 90% the proportion of women who receive prenatal care in the first 3 months of pregnancy.	In 1988, 76% of women received such care.
Reduce to no more than 5% the proportion of babies born at low birthweight.	In 1988, 7% of infants were born at low birthweight.
Reduce the infant mortality rate to no more than 7 per 1,000 live births overall, and no more than 11 per 1,000 births for black babies.	The infant mortality rate for 1988 was 10.0 deaths per 1,000; the black infant mortality rate was 17.6.
Eliminate polio, measles, and rubella; reduce the cases of mumps to 500 annually; and reduce whooping cough cases to 1,000 annually.	In 1990 more than 25,000 cases of measles, nearly 5,000 cases of mumps, and more than 4,000 cases of pertussis (whooping cough) were reported.
Eliminate exceedingly high blood lead levels in children younger than 5; ensure that no more than 500,000 have moderately high levels.	An estimated 1 in 6 children are at risk of lead poisoning; poor and minority children in the nation's cities face the greatest risks.

(continued on next page)

Goal	Status

Early Childhood Development

All American children will start school ready to learn. All disadvantaged and disabled children will have access to developmentally appropriate preschool.

Every parent will be a child's first teacher, and parents will receive the training and support they need.

Poor and minority children are less likely to be enrolled in preschool than middle-class white children; Head Start serves only 1 in 4 eligible children.

Many parents of young children are children themselves. In poor families, parents are often so overwhelmed by economic demands they can't focus on their children's broader needs. Few parent education programs available.

Academic Achievement

Increase the high school graduation rate to 90%; eliminate the graduation rate gap between minority and nonminority students.

Students will leave grades 4, 8, and 12 having demonstrated competency in challenging subject matter, including English, math, science, history, and geography.

By age 21, 83% of youths have a high school diploma or equivalency certificate. But this masks the dropout rates in some inner cities, which approach 50%, and higher grade retention rates for blacks.

The reading, science, and math levels of black 17-year-olds are about the same as those of white 13-year-olds.

Sexual Behavior and Teen Pregnancy

Reduce pregnancies among girls 17 and younger to no more than 50 per 1,000; reduce the pregnancy rate among black girls in that age group to no more than 120 per 1,000.

Reduce the proportion of adolescents who have had sexual intercourse to no more than 15% by age 15 and no more than 40% by age 17.

Increase to at least 90% the proportion of sexually active unmarried teens who use contraception.

The overall pregnancy rate for girls 17 and younger was 71.1 per 1,000 in 1985.

By age 15, 26% of girls and 38% of boys have had sexual intercourse; half of girls and two-thirds of boys have become sexually active by age 17.

In 1988, 78% of these teens used contraception the most recent time they had intercourse; 63% used contraception the first time they had intercourse.

Vulnerable Children

Reduce the rising incidence of maltreatment of children to less than the 1986 level of 25.2 per 1,000.

Reduce to less than 10% the prevalence of mental disorders among children and teens.

Families and communities should give special attention to children living under especially difficult circumstances, including homelessness.

In 1986, 2,954 children a day were abused or neglected. About 2.4 million children were reported abused or neglected in 1989, a 147% increase since 1979.

An estimated 7.5 million to 9.5 million children and teens have emotional problems; 70% to 80% of them are not getting help.

Homeless families with children make up about one-third of the nation's homeless population; every day 100,000 children are homeless.

Drugs and Alcohol

Reduce alcohol use by 12- to 17-year-olds to less than 13%; reduce marijuana use by 18- to 25-year-olds to less than 8%; reduce cocaine use by 18- to 25-year-olds to less than 3%; reduce the initiation of cigarette smoking to 15% by age 20.

More than one-quarter of 12- to 17-year-olds had used alcohol in 1988; more than 15% of 18- to 25-year-olds had used marijuana; 4.5% of 18- to 25-year-olds had used cocaine; and 30% had become regular cigarette smokers by ages 20 through 24.

the political hypocrisy so that parents can have a real choice about whether to remain at home or work outside the home without worrying about the safety of their children. Let's provide decent jobs and decent wages for those who seek to work and children's allowances and paid parental leave policies so that one parent may choose to stay at home and care for children without the stigma of welfare.

We must all stress family rituals and be moral examples for our children. If we cut corners, they will too. If we lie, they will too. If we spend all our money on ourselves and tithe no portion of it for our colleges, churches, synagogues, and civic causes, they won't either. And if we snicker at racial and gender jokes, another generation will pass on the poison my generation still has not had the courage to snuff out.

Lesson 7: Remember and help America remember that the fellowship of human beings is more important than the fellowship of race and class and gender in a democratic society. Be decent and fair and insist that others be so in your presence. Don't tell, laugh at, or acquiesce in racial, ethnic, religious, or gender jokes or any practices intended to demean rather than enhance another human being. Walk away from them. Stare them down. Make them unacceptable in your presence. Through daily moral consciousness counter the proliferating voices of racial and ethnic and religious division that are gaining respectability over the land, including college campuses. Let's face up to rather than ignore our growing racial problems, which are America's historic and future Achilles' heel.

How many potential Colin Powells, Condoleezi Rices, Sally Rides, Barbara McClintocks, Wilma Mankillers, Daniel Inouyes, and Cesar Chavezes is our nation going to waste before it wakes up and recognizes that its ability to compete and lead in the new century is as inextricably intertwined with its poor and nonwhite children as with its white and privileged ones, with its girls as well as its boys?

Let's not spend a lot of time pinning and denying blame rather than healing our divisions. Rabbi Abraham Heschel put it aptly: "We are not all equally guilty but we are all equally responsible" for building a decent and just America.

Lesson 8: Don't confuse style with substance or political charm with decency or sound policy. It's wonderful to go to the White House or Congress or State House for a chat, but words alone will not meet children's or the nation's needs. Political leadership and different budget priorities will. Speak truth to power. And put your own money and leadership behind rhetoric about concern for families and children in your own homes, law firms, medical practices, corporations, or wherever you pursue your career.

Lesson 9: Listen for the sound of the genuine within yourself. "Small," Einstein said, "is the number of them that see with their own eyes and feel with their own hearts." Try to be one of them. There is, Howard Thurman said, "something in every one of you that waits and listens for the sound of the genuine in yourself." It is "the only true guide you'll ever have. And if you cannot hear it, you will all of your life spend your days on the ends of strings that somebody else pulls." There are so many noises and competing demands in our lives that many of us never find out who we are. Learn to be quiet enough to hear the sound of the genuine within yourself so that you can hear it in other people.

Lesson 10: Never think life is not worth living or that you cannot make a difference. Never give up—I don't care how hard it gets. I know how discouraging it is to struggle to help the needy year after year with too few people and too little money and community support. An old proverb reminds, "When you get to your wit's end, remember that God lives there." Harriet Beecher Stowe wrote that when you get into a "tight place and everything goes against you, till it seems as though you could not hang on a minute longer, never give up then, for that is just the place and time that the tide will turn." Hang in with life. Hang in with your advocacy for children and the poor. The tide is going to turn.

And don't think you have to "win" immediately or even at all to make a difference. Sometimes it's important to lose for things that matter. Don't think you have to be a big dog to make a difference. You just need to be a persistent flea.

My role model, Sojourner Truth, an illiterate slave woman who hated slavery and the second class treatment of women, was heckled one day by an old white man. "Old woman, do you think that your talk about slavery does any good? Why, I don't care any more for your talk than I do for the bite of a flea." "Perhaps not," Sojourner rejoined, "but the Lord willing, I'll keep you scratching." Enough committed fleas biting strategically can make even the biggest dog uncomfortable and transform even the biggest nation, as we will transform America in the 1990s.

Shel Silverstein, the children's book writer, gets my last word.

> Listen to the mustn'ts, child,
> listen to the don'ts
> listen to the shouldn'ts,
> the impossibles, the won'ts
> listen to the never haves
> then listen close to me -
> anything can happen, child,
> ANYTHING can be.

If we dream it, have faith in it, and struggle for it. Let's together make it un-American for any child to be poor or to be left behind.

Marian Wright Edelman
President, Children's Defense Fund

Sixty Years of Save the Children Helping Families Help Themselves

How does a young woman in Minneapolis help a ten-year-old girl in Nepal learn to read and write? How can a seven-year-old Colombian girl, whose fatherless family lives in one room with a dirt floor, grow up to be a teacher? And what brought a Los Angeles bond broker to the Gambia last August to toil shoulder to shoulder with villagers to restore their community school? The answer in each case is Save the Children, *a unique assistance agency now celebrating its 60th year.*

Light at the End of the Tunnel

In the winter of 1932, millions of families struggled to survive the devastating effects of the Great Depression. As hopes for recovery grew dim, a small group of concerned citizens—with broad experience in social welfare, international affairs, and business—met in New York City. Too many children, they felt, were falling through the cracks of existing relief programs. Could they come up with a new kind of child-welfare organization—one that would help families and communities solve the problems that faced their own children? Out of this meeting Save the Children was born—an organization which has come to represent hope and self-sufficiency for many of the world's poorest people.

In its first year, Save the Children pursued one modest assistance program, in Harlan County, Kentucky. Today it sponsors hundreds of programs in 20 states and 37 nations. Despite its growth, the organization's approach to meeting children's needs remains the same. "Our programs are diverse," says president James J. Bausch, "but our mission is singular: to create lasting, positive change in the lives of disadvantaged children." All of Save the Children's work incorporates four characteristics: a strong community base, people helping themselves, an integrated approach to problems, and local people providing for their children over the long term.

The Harlan County Model

■ **A base in the community.** Among the most desperate of the poor in 1932 were the families of thousands of coal miners thrown out of work as mines shut down across Appalachia. Long-term unemployment, coupled with isolation and a century-long tradition of self-reliance, brought great hardship to these proud people, and especially to their infants and children. First, emergency relief in the form of food and warm clothing came in from Americans across the country. Then, believing that the lives of children cannot be significantly changed in isolation from their families and communities, Save the Children worked with local leaders to survey parents: What did they consider the most pressing needs of their children? After two months the answer came back: health care.

■ **Self-help is key.** No handouts were given. Instead, parents and neighbors chipped in to "pay" for the goods and services that Save the Children provided. A doctor and nurse held mobile clinics in rural schools and mining camps. Men and boys cut firewood in exchange for supplies and technical advice, and then delivered the firewood to schools and the families of disabled men and widows. Women formed sewing groups to repair the many tons of clothing donated by thousands of generous Americans, and men idled by the closing of the mines were tapped to build sanitary facilities for schools and private dwellings.

■ **Programs are integrated.** Once they had warm clothes and shoes, children could walk to school ready to learn. What needed to happen next? Balanced hot lunches. Nutrition, healthy living conditions, and parent education all needed to be in place before lasting health benefits could occur.

■ **Local leaders take over.** Whether in the hollows of Appalachia, a Navajo reservation in Arizona, or the Lower East Side of New York City, a key factor for success is involving local leaders. In Harlan County, a pattern was set that prevails to this day—working through a community group that is near the problem, both geographically and in understanding. In Bausch's words, a deliberate component of Save the Children's approach is "to work ourselves out of a job." Sometimes local leaders are developed and trained; other times new institutions, such as health post, food pantry, low-cost clothing store, or crafts cooperative, are created to generate income.

Exporting the Harlan County Model

The unique approach to relief and development that Save the Children pioneered in Appalachia has been replicated again and again. From Harlan County, Kentucky, in 1932, programs quickly spread to 119 counties in nine states. In 1940, the plight of children caught in the cross fire of World War II prompted Save the Children to bring its programs overseas. Emergency relief to six nations — including Germany and Italy — consisted of food, clothing, blankets, and medicine. At the same time, Save the Children provided materials to establish long-term solutions, such as shelters and nurseries for displaced children and their families.

Over the next fifty years, self-help community development programs were initiated in many of the war-torn and famine-afflicted areas of the world, always based on priorities set by local people. Here are just a few of the kinds of programs in place in other parts of the world today:

• *Cameroon* — instructing 173 health workers during eight workshops on "Training of Trainers for AIDS Education." These workers trained 648 other trainers.

From *Scholastic Pre-K Today*, April 1992, pp. 34-36, 66. Copyright © 1992 by Scholastic, Inc. Reprinted with permission.

Child Care Support Center
An Interview With Nancy Travis

Nancy Travis, whose child-care and education professional career spans fifty years, is presently the director of Save the Children's Child Care Support Center (CCSC) in Atlanta, Georgia. With child care for low-income single mothers a critical issue in America today, CCSC is one of Save the Children's most effective initiatives. Recently Travis spoke with Pre-K Today.

Pre-K Today: **Tell us a little bit about the primary objectives of CCSC.**

In very few words, our mission is to improve the lives of children in child care. More specifically, we work to improve quality, availability, and affordability in this area and beyond.

What are some of your specific programs?

We do a whole variety of things. Our child-care food program improves nutrition for children in 1,200 family day-care homes. We are a resource and referral service for 11 counties, and often get involved in finding funding for low-income families that otherwise couldn't afford it. Then we do lots of training to improve the quality of care in family day-care homes and in centers. Among our special programs are emergency care for families in crisis, and programs for refugee and homeless families.

You mention child care — but isn't CCSC associated primarily with family day care?

It's true that over the years we've become closely associated with family day care, although we do work with centers, too. But the fact is that home-based child care often is the best option for families on the edge — not just those on welfare, but also the working poor.

Is there a program that you're particularly proud of?

One thing we've done that I feel awfully good about is supporting our family day-care providers to the point where they now have a state association and about 28 local support groups. As an advocate for family day care, we've done a lot to help pro-

viders see themselves as part of the early childhood profession.

How does family day care tie in with Save the Children's philosophy?

You know, family day care really is economic development for many low-income women. It creates opportunities for mothers — and grandmothers! — to develop skills as child-care providers and to start their own registered day-care businesses. This has allowed thousands of women to break their family's cycle of poverty by modeling new standards of achievement for their children. This *is* the Save the Children model, and it's a win/win situation.

Family day care is growing up. We try to hire family day-care providers when they are ready to move on. The director of our referral service started out as a family day-care provider. We also have a family day-care provider on the newly appointed Governor's Commission on Child Care.

We know you've worked overseas with Save the Children, too. Would you share one of your memorable experiences?

We were in this little school building in a village in Nepal, training women to work with children. The whole time we were training, all the windows were filled with faces. We were talking about doing art with children, and one of the women had never held a crayon. She was so excited. Then we went out and collected items to make nature collages ... they were just so beautiful! And the children would come around by our little office at night and try to teach me to speak Nepalese.

This moved me particularly because half the children in this village die by their fifth birthday, mostly of diarrhea and intestinal diseases. Of those that survive until five, half will die by the time they're twelve. Save the Children is helping to pipe in clean water and educate the people about rehydration techniques to combat these terrible statistics.

What an experience it was. The mountains were breathtakingly beautiful and the people were all so nice, so gracious. One lady said to the translators that she thanked God that she lived long enough to meet me. How can you ever forget such an experience?

- *Philippines* — constructing a 600-foot well to provide clean drinking water for 300 squatter families.
- *Honduras* — vaccinating 94 percent of children in 54 communities, and maintaining 113 oral rehydration stations to improve child survival in cases of severe diarrhea.
- *Afghanistan* — training 96 Afghan refugee literacy teachers, who in turn taught 2,000 refugees.

Wherever Save the Children works, it applies the valuable lessons learned sixty years ago in the hills of Appalachia:

■ Emergency relief can, and often should, be used as a springboard for long-range, self-help community development.

■ When people organize themselves, define their own problems, and devise appropriate solutions, they increase their capacity for self-reliance.

■ The goal of improving the lives of children can motivate entire communities to act with purpose and energy, affecting positive change in their own lives and environment as they work together for their children.

Where Does the Money Come From?

From the start, Save the Children's programs have relied heavily on the generosity and compassion of the American people. In 1932, Americans sent tons of canned food and winter clothing to the coal mining families in Harlan County. Later, Save the Children introduced the concept of sponsorship, enabling donors to contribute $60 a year to particular one-room schoolhouses in Appalachia. These funds were used to provide food and supplies for the children and to improve the school buildings. When the overseas programs began in 1940, American "godparents" donated $30 a year to provide clothing and other basics to a particular child. By pooling sponsors' contributions, Save the Children was able to operate projects that benefitted all the children of a neighborhood or village. Today, Save the Children programs reach *more than 100,000 sponsored children and one million people at home and abroad.*

Another legacy of Harlan County is the revolving loan. In exchange for a basket of seeds to help start their gardens, farmers returned a bushel and a peck of potatoes. Or, to repay their

A 60th Anniversary Initiative: Coming Back Home

Save the Children's Action Network, an anniversary-year initiative to strengthen and expand the agency's presence in the United States, is a consortium of leading child advocates and experts. Honorary chair of the network, Senator John D. Rockefeller IV of West Virginia, headed the National Commission on Children and is one of the nation's most outspoken advocates for children's issues. Honorary members of the network's advisory committee include C. Everett Koop, M.D., Marion Wright Edelman, and T. Berry Brazelton, M.D.

The network is working to increase attention and create appropriate, lasting solutions to the growing problems facing America's children in crisis. Among its objectives:
• To put and keep children's issues at the top of the American agenda.
• To galvanize public and private agencies to work together to forge new and effective solutions to problems.
• To identify successful programs and create new ones that can be replicated in communities across the nation.

Areas of Concentration

The network is committed to helping low-income children and families in three basic areas: health and nutrition, early childhood education, and family support. Family support includes a range of programs that help families help themselves out of poverty, such as job-skills training, child-care referrals and training, teen parent counseling, and intergenerational support systems.

Plans for Action

Save the Children now operates in 20 states, and its programs cover every aspect of child development from pre-natal health care to afterschool tutoring. The Action Network will expand existing programs and innovate where needed, but will adhere to the same approach Save the Children has used since 1932: supporting children and families through locally controlled, community-based family support networks.

---

loan of canning materials, women returned one filled jar of beans for every twelve empties they received. Food collected through the revolving loan funds was used to make lunches for school children. This hot lunch program became the model for the federal program that still provides nutritious lunches for children across the country.

What Lies Ahead?

"Despite all our good work," says James J. Bausch, "I am sorry to say that children are still falling through the cracks. Twenty-three percent of American children under the age of six live in poverty. Worldwide, far too many desperately poor children still suffer. Their difficult lives are all the more tragic because we know what works."

Save the Children refuses to rest. It is determined to build upon the lessons of its past, and on its 60th anniversary, rededicate itself to its original mission, doing what it has always done — making lasting, positive change in the lives of disadvantaged children.

Editor's Note: Save the Children is a private, non-profit, non-sectarian, tax-exempt organization. In 1991 it ranked fifth on *Money* Magazine's honor roll of the 10 best-managed large U.S. charities, with 83.6 percent of donations going directly into good works. For information, or to sponsor your own individual child somewhere in the world, write Save the Children, 50 Wilton Road, Westport, CT 06880; or call (800) 243-5075.

You Can Make a Difference For
America's Children

Ways to get involved, even if you have only a few minutes a day.

Sheldon Himelfarb

Sheldon Himelfarb is a Washington, D.C.–based writer and commentator for National Public Radio.

Before the birth of her son, Travis, Clara Desantis-Stewart, an accounting supervisor, had missed only one day of work because of illness. After taking nine weeks of maternity leave, however, the first words she recalls hearing from her boss on her return were, "If you get pregnant again, you'll lose your job." When she took three hours off one morning because Travis had a 104-degree fever, she was asked, "Will you be out again?" She desperately wanted to quit but couldn't afford to until she found another job, which she eventually did—at one third her previous pay.

"The pressure put a strain on my marriage," she says. "On the last day at my old job, my husband, who's usually a laid-back guy, was so mad he almost went looking for my boss. He calmed down because Travis sure didn't need his dad in jail."

Samantha Buckby, a fifth-grader in Levittown, Pennsylvania, worries a lot about her dad but can't speak to him when she needs to. Her parents are divorced and he has been out of work since last year's massive layoffs by the Fairless Works steel mill. "I want to call him," she says, "but he doesn't have a phone." Samantha doesn't get to speak to her mom as much these days either because she is busy working seven days a week at a factory for $8.41 an hour to support the family.

Mathew Bartley, of Carmichael, California, has been on welfare since he was born five years ago. He and his mom, Bonnie, receive Aid to Families With Dependent Children (AFDC) totaling about $535 a month. Their rent is $435. Bonnie is studying to be a medical secretary in the hope of getting off public assistance, and is only one year away from receiving her diploma. Yet with AFDC slated for another round of cuts this year, she's afraid she won't make graduation if she and Mathew have to move to find cheaper housing.

Jeffrey Janek, of Frenchtown, New Jersey, was born in 1987 with two severely diseased kidneys—the same condition that claimed the life of his only sibling. Jeffrey's kidney transplant was repeatedly postponed as the hospital waited for the Janeks' insurance company to approve payment for the procedure. "There was no reason to delay, since I was going to be the donor," his mom, June, declares bitterly. "I'm convinced that the insurance company was hoping we'd miss a payment so that they could cut off our coverage. But what if Jeffrey died?" After about a year and a half, Jeffrey had his operation, which was a success—but only after his desperate mom contacted two U.S. senators on his behalf.

For over a year, three-year-old Tamika Davis has slept in the same bed with her mom, Shanika, and her two-year-old brother, Wayne. The family shares a single room in a friend's house as they wait for assistance from the public-housing authorities in Baltimore, who accepted Shanika's application in May, 1991. According to a case worker at The Family Place, in East Baltimore, where Shanika went for help, the delay could go on for years, given that there are over 30,000 people on the city's waiting list, "many of whom live eight or ten people to a room."

Unemployment, public-assistance cuts, inadequate health insurance, housing shortages, no parental-leave policy—meet the families behind these issues. Hardly a day has gone by this election year without a news story or candidate's speech reminding us of their desperation.

Are kids better off?

If you'd just come from the moon and heard all the campaign chatter, you'd think the country was poised for a revolution in dealing with the troubles of our children. The problem is, we've heard it all before.

In 1988, Democrats battling for the presidential nomination made day-care centers the photo-op of choice, most notably Democratic challenger Michael Dukakis's rousing performance of "Itsy-Bitsy Spider" at a Cincinnati center. Vice President Bush met the challenge with a Republican-party platform titled "An American Vision: For Our Children and Our Future." Through it all, professionals working with kids warned of election-year lip service and pandering. "When the election hoopla ends and the last balloon has burst, where will the children be?" was a question posed in the Child Welfare League of America brochure at the time.

The league was right to worry. Ask-

From *Parents*, November 1992, pp. 221-224, 227. Copyright © 1992 by Gruner & Jahr USA Publishing. Reprinted by permission.

ing whether children are better off today than they were four years ago elicits virtually the same response from every knowledgeable source: No way. "The child of 1992 leads a less safe, less healthy, and less privileged life than the child of 1980," said Doug Nelson, executive director of the Annie E. Casey Foundation, in Greenwich, Connecticut, as he announced the findings of a nationwide joint study called *Kids Count,* conducted by The Center for the Study of Social Policy and his foundation earlier this year.

Another report issued this year, from the Children's Defense Fund, in Washington, D.C., found that in 1990, 40 percent of the children in households headed by someone younger than 30 lived in poverty. In 1973, only 20 percent did. T. Berry Brazelton, M.D., the well-known pediatrician, describes the state of our children as "postdesperate."

"We are about twelve years too late in our commitment," says Brazelton, who cofounded Parent Action, a national organization dedicated to helping families. And who can argue when one in five of all American kids is poor, when our rate of vaccinations against preventable diseases is seventeenth in the world behind countries like Hungary, and when eighteen countries have a lower infant-mortality rate than we do. Our country's statistics on teenage pregnancy, homicides, suicides, child abuse, educational disability, and drug abuse are equally tragic.

It's tempting to blame this dire situation on the elected officials who make promises they don't keep, but before you do, consider this: Only one in two eligible voters went to the polls in 1988—*the lowest turnout in 64 years*—and the turnout has been even more dismal throughout this 1992 primary season. The Kids Count survey gave Washington, D.C., the lowest rating in the country for the health and well-being of its children, and yet voter turnout in the D.C. primary was only *15 percent*.

How can we expect government to work aggressively and effectively for our children when "We the People" make apathy an art? Sixty years ago, Judge Learned Hand, one of this country's finest legal minds, said, "The apathy of the modern voter is the confusion of the modern reformer." His words ring loud and clear today.

Getting involved.

How can we make sure that the voices of children are heard on election day and not forgotten afterward?

The first thing to do is to make the well-being of children a family issue—and that means family activism. When it comes to teaching kids to be responsible and influential citizens, "there's no substitute for parental example," insists Marian Wright Edelman, president and founder of the Children's Defense Fund, who attributes her own advocacy career to the values instilled in her as the daughter of a Baptist minister in South Carolina. "We are the ones who determine our children's values."

The implication of her remarks for the future of America's children is profound and powerful: First, parents who commit themselves to working on behalf of children today are likely to pass this commitment on to the parents of tomorrow—an absolute must if America is to escape this abyss of child neglect. Second, it is clear that the activist experience teaches children "I can make a difference" and communicates optimism, a vital part of an individual's emotional and physical well-being—not to mention the health of society in general.

"Perhaps the most significant shaper of who I am," reflects Rosalie Streett, executive director of Parent Action, "was my mother taking me with her when I was a child to the anti–Jim Crow meetings around New York. We were poor, on welfare, and yet I never felt powerless or ever thought of myself as a victim. We had a hand, we thought, in our own destiny, as opposed to feeling hopeless the way so many kids do today."

Whatever action one takes to make a difference—whether it be meeting with the neighbors to push for safer parks or working with disabled children—doing it as a family can enhance the experience.

Why activism feels good.

"In every family we interviewed," says Barbara Lohman of The Points of Light Foundation, which is studying family volunteerism, "both the parents and the kids said that the time they worked together was real quality time, and felt that the reward for their family was enormous."

Just ask the Johnson family of Washington, D.C. For years, parents Concha and Morris and their three children—Gemal, fourteen, Malik, six-teen, and Rashida, nineteen—have made a strong community spirit central to their family life, whether working in the youth programs of the Holy Communion Episcopal Church or registering voters. "Our family definitely thinks it strengthens us," says Rashida, who has joined her dynamic mom in passing out leaflets for more than one candidate. "But serving's no big deal," her dad's quick to add. "It's just something we do."

When the world in which we currently function already seems to make more demands on our time, our energy, and our pocketbooks than we can handle, taking that first step into the world of action is difficult for most of us.

But giving voice to children's needs doesn't mean you have to run for office, become a full-time lobbyist, or even try to duplicate what the Johnson family does. It can mean things that take just a little time, such as speaking up at the PTA, signing a neighborhood petition, or simply casting a vote.

In the case of this month's election, activism means casting an educated vote. Better still, "vote with your children in tow," says Marilyn Evans, president of Kids Voting USA, an innovative program that enlists kids in the battle against voter apathy by arranging for them to cast mock ballots alongside their parents at the polls. "The experience can influence whether or not they themselves will vote in the future."

There is never a good excuse for not voting, and now it's easier than ever to be an informed voter. The toll-free, nonpartisan hot line Project Vote Smart (1-800-786-6885), and online computer services such as Prodigy's new "Political Profile" (1-800-PRODIGY), offer general information on the positions of federal-level and gubernatorial candidates.

But how do you get information on where candidates stand on specific children's issues—say, funding for immunization programs, Head Start, and family and medical leave—if you don't see it mentioned in the papers or debates? Your key resource for this information is, conveniently, also your key resource for keeping the politicians' feet to the fire after the election is over: a nationwide network of advocacy organizations battling daily for our children's well-

"Hello, I'd Like to Help"

You're only a phone call away from connecting with a group that is working on behalf of kids.

Call **Association of Child Advocates,** 716-924-0300, to:
- Locate an advocacy group in your state or city that will help you become involved locally;
- Learn about annual conferences that cover a broad range of children's issues, from health care to child welfare;
- Join the association's vast advocacy network and receive its newsletter.

Call **Children's Defense Fund,** 1-800-CDF-1200, to:
- Have your name sent to advocacy groups in your area;
- Request an action packet, which includes *An Opinion Maker's Guide to Children in Election Year 1992*;
- Obtain a fact sheet about children in your state;
- Have your name added to the mailing list for *Legislative Alert*, a bulletin on pending federal legislation;
- Get information on individual legislators' voting records;
- Receive CDF's annual *State of America's Children* report.

Call **Parent Action,** 410-PARENTS, to:
- Become a member and receive its quarterly newsletter;
- Get advice on how to set up Parent Action networks in your state;
- Participate in consumer-discount programs;
- Learn which questions to ask a candidate for office and to get an incumbent's voting record;
- Be alerted to bills scheduled for immediate action and find out whom to lobby;
- Connect with other parents in your area for mutual support.

Call **Child Welfare League of America,** 1-800-8KIDS80, to:
- Become a member of its Children's Campaign and receive its publications;
- Work to bring greater visibility to the needs of abused, neglected, and vulnerable children and their families;
- Learn how to round up support for child-related efforts in your area;
- Know whom to lobby when a bill is scheduled for immediate action;
- Find out how to ask political candidates the right questions.

Call **Child Care Action Campaign,** 212-239-0138, to:
- Obtain a fact sheet about the nation's child-care crisis;
- Receive publications that contain information about child-care legislation;
- Get advice on how to advocate child care;
- Learn how to approach your employer about child care.

Note: Some items may require a fee.

being. And they're only a phone call away. (To link up with a national, state, or local agency, see "Hello, I'd Like to Help.")

Champions for children.

Today almost every civic organization—from PTAs and children's hospitals to Kiwanis Clubs, Junior Leagues, family-resource centers, and religious charities—has an oar in the vast waters of child advocacy. Hooking up with a group in your neighborhood is one way to get involved.

Also, every state now has at least one organization devoted exclusively to child advocacy. Such organizations track legislation and sometimes monitor the voting records of elected officials, thus playing a key role in state and local decisions on creating and funding programs for children. These groups lobby, do research, and organize public-education campaigns. Some welcome volunteers, while others can match you up with volunteer-hungry service agencies. And in most cases the group produces newsletters on local and national children's issues, available for a modest subscription fee. "Anyone can make a phone call or write a letter," says Bernice Weissbourd, president of Family Focus, in Chicago, and a cofounder of Parent Action. "It's a crisis. We must get involved!"

What issues concern you most?

The question now is not so much *how* to get involved but with whom. How do you decide which organization is for you?

"Easy," says Eve Brooks, president of the Association of Child Advocates. "You get involved with what's closest to your heart. Talk to the organizations; they do different things." And if they don't handle the specific issue that interests you, they can most certainly refer you to the right place.

Advocacy groups may have somewhat different priorities and programs, and yet they all seem to agree on this: Fighting for children's issues is not a substitute for time spent working and playing with your own kids and helping children in need. Voting regularly and intelligently, buttonholing your city-council member, writing the President and members of Congress—these are natural extensions of the time you spend with children.

In the Company of Kids—an organization in Akron, Ohio, devoted to both advocacy and child rearing—suggests, "It's one thing to be an outstanding parent and quite another to be an outstanding citizen. Today's children demand both."

Sometimes things happen as they should—parenthood meets activism—and then look out! As Barbara Gimperling, a mother of three in Crofton, Maryland, will tell you, the results can be as exciting as all the distress calls have been alarming.

About twelve years ago she began meeting with a handful of other parents to talk about the difficulties and isolation of child rearing and the lack of family support they experienced in their community. As their group expanded, they realized how many others felt the same way they did: frustrated and fed up. Taking matters into their own hands, they became partners in advocacy. The result: Their organization, Parents And Children Together (PACT), has now grown into three family-resource centers in Anne Arundel County, Maryland, serving 200 to 300 families a year.

In a similar vein, Andrea Berk, a California resident and mother of two children, successfully brought to her assemblyman's attention the importance of mandating changing tables in public restrooms.

And in Nashville, public-housing resident Brenda Morrow works with kids in the Edgehill Homes housing-development complex on community-service projects. "Just because the kids in public housing see a lot of negative things—like drugs and crime—doesn't mean that they have to go that route. The OK [Opportunities for Kids] program gives them an alternative."

Parents taking care of kids—now, there's an idea for the 1990's.

CHILDREN

Bill Clinton and Al Gore

For far too long we have failed to address the needs of America's children. We do not provide them with adequate health care, the best education, or protection from violence, and we do not address the special problems of the disadvantaged. We need bold reform to help all our children reach their potential.

Children are America's future. As parents, we have long fought to make that future bright—for better education, improved child health care, and real drug prevention. With renewed vigor, we will carry that fight into the future.

Our children and our country cannot afford another four years of neglect from Washington. The next generation of young people should not be America's first to grow up with less hope than their parents. It's time to act to help our children.

Here's how:

GUARANTEE AFFORDABLE QUALITY HEALTH CARE

• Control costs, improve quality, and cover everybody under a *national health-care* plan. Our plan will require insurers to offer a core package of benefits, including pre-natal care and other important preventive care benefits.

• Create a nationwide program like Arkansas's *Good Beginnings* to provide *health-care services to more low-income women* and their children.

• Develop a *comprehensive maternal and child health network* to reduce both the infant mortality rate and the number of low-birth-weight babies—because every child deserves a fighting chance to grow up healthy.

• *Fully fund the Women, Infants, and Children (WIC) program* and other critical initiatives recommended by the National Commission on Children that save us several dollars for every one we spend.

REVOLUTIONIZE LIFETIME LEARNING

• Make good on the Bush Administration's broken promises by *fully funding Head Start* and other pre-school programs.

• Through innovative parenting programs, like the Home Instructional Program for Pre-school Youngsters (HIPPY), *help disadvantaged parents work with their children* to build an ethic of learning at home that benefits both parent and child.

• *Dramatically improve K-12 education* by establishing tough standards and a national examination system in core subjects, leveling the playing field for disadvantaged students, and reducing class sizes.

• Give every parent the right to *choose the public school his or her child attends*, as is the case in Arkansas.

• *Create a Youth Opportunity Corps* to give teenagers who drop out of school a second chance. Community youth centers will match teenagers with adults who care about them, and will give kids a chance to develop self-discipline and skills.

• *Develop a national apprenticeship-style system* to give kids who don't want to go to college the skills they need to find high-wage jobs.

• *Give every American the opportunity to borrow money for college:* retain the Pell grant program but scrap the existing college loan program and establish a National Service Trust Fund. Those who borrow from the fund will be able to repay the balance either as a small percentage of their earnings over time, or through community service—as teachers, law enforcement officers, health-care workers, or peer counselors helping kids stay off drugs and in school.

MAKE OUR HOMES, SCHOOLS, AND STREETS SAFER FOR CHILDREN

• Crack down on violence against women and children. Sign the *Violence Against Women Act*, which would provide tougher enforcement and stiffer penalties to deter domestic violence.

• Launch a *Safe Schools Initiative* so kids can focus on learning again: make schools eligible for federal assistance to pay for metal detectors and security personnel if they need them; encourage states to grant school officials greater authority to conduct locker and automobile searches; and fund mentoring and

From *Putting People First* by Bill Clinton and Al Gore, Times Books, 1992, pp. 47-51.

239

outreach programs so kids in trouble with crime, drugs, or gangs will have someone to turn to.

• Establish *school-based clinics and drug education programs* to prevent drug abuse and to help kids who get hooked on drugs. Promote AIDS education in our schools.

• *Set standards for crime emergency areas* by making communities hit hardest by crime eligible for federal matching funds to assist in the war on crime when they adopt proven anti-crime measures.

• Fight crime by putting *100,000 new police officers* on the streets; create a National Police Corps and offer unemployed veterans and active military personnel a chance to become law enforcement officers · here at home.

• *Expand community policing,* fund more drug treatment, and establish community "boot camps" to discipline first-time nonviolent offenders.

• Sign the Brady Bill, which will *create a waiting period for the purchase of handguns* and allow authorities to conduct background checks before guns fall into the wrong hands.

• *Work to ban assault rifles,* which have no legitimate hunting purpose.

SUPPORT PRO-FAMILY AND PRO-CHILDREN POLICIES

• *Expand the Earned Income Tax Credit* to guarantee a "working wage," so that no American who works full-time is forced to raise children in poverty.

• Lower the tax burden on middle-class Americans by asking the very wealthy to pay their fair share; give middle-class taxpayers a *choice between a children's tax credit or a significant reduction in their income tax rate.* Virtually every industrialized nation recognizes the importance of strong families in its tax code; we should, too.

• *Sign into law the Family and Medical Leave Act,* which George Bush vetoed in 1990, so that no worker is forced to choose between maintaining his or her job and caring for a newborn child or sick family member.

• Create a *child-care network* as complete as the public school network, tailored to the needs of working families; establish more *rigorous standards for licensing child-care facilities* and implement improved methods for enforcing them.

• Promote *tough child support legislation* and develop stricter, more effective methods to enforce it: crack down on deadbeat parents by reporting them to credit agencies, so they can't borrow money for themselves when they're not taking care of their children; use the Internal Revenue Service to collect child support; start a national deadbeat data-bank; and make it a felony to cross state lines to avoid paying support.

Credits/ Acknowledgments

Cover design by Charles Vitelli

1. Perspectives
Facing overview—Elaine M. Ward.

2. Child Development and Families
Facing overview—United Nations photo by John Isaac.

3. Appropriate Educational Practices
Facing overview—Reed and Bergemann.

4. Guiding Behavior
Facing overview—EPA Documerica. 178—Photo by Elaine M. Ward.

5. Curricular Applications
Facing overview—The Shore Line Times photo by John Ferraro.

6. Reflections
Facing overview—United Nations photo by Y. Nagata.

PHOTOCOPY THIS PAGE!!!*

ANNUAL EDITIONS ARTICLE REVIEW FORM

■ NAME: _____ DATE: _____

■ TITLE AND NUMBER OF ARTICLE: _____

■ BRIEFLY STATE THE MAIN IDEA OF THIS ARTICLE: _____

_____

_____

_____

_____

■ LIST THREE IMPORTANT FACTS THAT THE AUTHOR USES TO SUPPORT THE MAIN IDEA:

_____

_____

_____

_____

_____

■ WHAT INFORMATION OR IDEAS DISCUSSED IN THIS ARTICLE ARE ALSO DISCUSSED IN YOUR TEXTBOOK OR OTHER READING YOU HAVE DONE? LIST THE TEXTBOOK CHAPTERS AND PAGE NUMBERS:

_____

_____

_____

_____

_____

_____

■ LIST ANY EXAMPLES OF BIAS OR FAULTY REASONING THAT YOU FOUND IN THE ARTICLE:

_____

_____

_____

_____

_____

■ LIST ANY NEW TERMS/CONCEPTS THAT WERE DISCUSSED IN THE ARTICLE AND WRITE A SHORT DEFINITION:

_____

_____

_____

_____

_____

*Your instructor may require you to use this Annual Editions Article Review Form in any number of ways: for articles that are assigned, for extra credit, as a tool to assist in developing assigned papers, or simply for your own reference. Even if it is not required, we encourage you to photocopy and use this page; you'll find that reflecting on the articles will greatly enhance the information from your text.

ANNUAL EDITIONS:
EARLY CHILDHOOD EDUCATION 93/94
Article Rating Form

Here is an opportunity for you to have direct input into the next revision of this volume. We would like you to rate each of the 54 articles listed below, using the following scale:

1. **Excellent: should definitely be retained**
2. **Above average: should probably be retained**
3. **Below average: should probably be deleted**
4. **Poor: should definitely be deleted**

Your ratings will play a vital part in the next revision. So please mail this prepaid form to us just as soon as you complete it.
Thanks for your help!

We Want Your Advice

Annual Editions revisions depend on two major opinion sources: one is our Advisory Board, listed in the front of this volume, which works with us in scanning the thousands of articles published in the public press each year; the other is you—the person actually using the book. Please help us and the users of the next edition by completing the prepaid article rating form on this page and returning it to us. Thank you.

Rating	Article	Rating	Article
	1. Where Did Our Diversity Come From? A Profile of Early Childhood Care and Education in the U.S.		30. The Assessment Portfolio as an Attitude
	2. Children in Peril		31. Tests, Independence, and Whole Language
	3. Homeless Children: A Special Challenge		32. Tracking Progress Toward the School Readiness Goal
	4. Prenatal Exposure to Cocaine and Other Drugs: Developmental and Educational Prognoses		33. Beating the Handicap Rap
	5. Good Things, Small Packages		34. Collaborative Training in the Education of Early Childhood Educators
	6. The Best Day Care There Ever Was		35. Preschool Classroom Environments That Promote Communication
	7. Who's Taking Care of the Children?		36. Implementing Individualized Family Service Planning in Urban, Culturally Diverse Early Intervention Settings
	8. When Parents Accept the Unacceptable		37. Parental Feelings: The Forgotten Component When Working With Parents of Handicapped Preschool Children
	9. Meeting the Challenge of Diversity		
	10. A Global Collage of Impressions: Preschools Abroad		38. Managing the Early Childhood Classroom
	11. Reggio Emilia: A Model in Creativity		39. A Positive Approach to Discipline in an Early Childhood Setting
	12. Public Preschool From the Age of Two: The *Ecole Maternelle* in France		40. Children's Self-Esteem: The Verbal Environment
	13. A Glimpse of Kindergarten—Chinese Style		41. Solving Problems Together
	14. Why Kids Are the Way They Are		42. The Role of the Child Care Professional in Caring for Infants, Toddlers, and Their Families
	15. How Boys and Girls Learn Differently		
	16. Holding Back to Get Ahead		43. The Tasks of Early Childhood: The Development of Self-Control—Part II
	17. Feeding Preschoolers: Balancing Nutritional and Developmental Needs		44. A Is for Apple, P Is for Pressure— Preschool Stress Management
	18. A Child's Cognitive Perception of Death		45. How Much Time Is Needed for Play?
	19. Beyond Parents: Family, Community, and School Involvement		46. Serious Play in the Classroom
	20. Easing Separation: A Talk With T. Berry Brazelton, M.D.		47. Learning Through Block Play
	21. How Schools Perpetuate Illiteracy		48. The Many Faces of Child Planning
	22. Children of Divorce		49. Writing in Kindergarten: Helping Parents Understand the Process
	23. Single-Parent Families: How Bad for the Children?		50. The Values and Purposes of Human Movement
	24. Readiness: Children and Their Schools		51. Ten Lessons to Help Us Through the 1990s
	25. Myths Associated With Developmentally Appropriate Programs		52. Sixty Years of Save the Children: Helping Families Help Themselves
	26. What Every Preschooler Needs to Know		
	27. What Good Prekindergarten Programs Look Like		53. You *Can* Make a Difference for America's Children
	28. Structure Time and Space to Promote Pursuit of Learning in the Primary Grades		54. Children
	29. School-Age Child Care: A Review of Five Common Arguments		

(Continued on next page)

ABOUT YOU

Name_____ Date_____

Are you a teacher? ☐ Or student? ☐

Your School Name _____

Department _____

Address _____

City _____ State _____ Zip _____

School Telephone #_____

YOUR COMMENTS ARE IMPORTANT TO US!

Please fill in the following information:

For which course did you use this book? _____

Did you use a text with this Annual Edition? ☐ yes ☐ no

The title of the text? _____

What are your general reactions to the Annual Editions concept?

Have you read any particular articles recently that you think should be included in the next edition?

Are there any articles you feel should be replaced in the next edition? Why?

Are there other areas that you feel would utilize an Annual Edition?

May we contact you for editorial input?

May we quote you from above?

ANNUAL EDITIONS: EARLY CHILDHOOD EDUCATION 93/94

No Postage
Necessary
if Mailed
in the
United States

BUSINESS REPLY MAIL

First Class   Permit No. 84   Guilford, CT

Postage will be paid by addressee

**The Dushkin Publishing Group, Inc.
Sluice Dock**
DPG **Guilford, Connecticut 06437**